Introduction to

e-Discovery

New Cases, Ideas, and Techniques

Ralph C. Losey

AMERICAN BAR ASSOCIATION
Defending Liberty
Pursuing Justice

Cover design by ABA Publishing

12 11 10 09 08   5 4 3 2 1

Library of Congress Cataloging-in-Publication Data

Losey, Ralph C.
Introduction to e-discovery : new cases, ideas, and techniques / Losey, Ralph C. — 1st ed.
     p. cm.
     1. Electronic discovery (Law)—United States. 2. Discovery (Law)—United States. I. Title.

10-Digit ISBN: 1-60442-380-3
13-Digit ISBN: 978-1-60442-380-8

KF8902.E42L68 2009   347.73'72—dc22
2009000373

Discounts are available for books ordered in bulk. Special consideration is given to state bars, CLE programs, and other bar-related organizations. Inquire at Book Publishing, ABA Publishing, American Bar Association, 321 North Clark Street, Chicago, Illinois 60610.

www.ababooks.org

Contents

Preface

Introduction to e-Discovery: New Cases, Ideas, and Techniques is derived from weekly Internet blogs I wrote on electronic discovery in 2008, with a few from late 2007, called the *e-Discovery Team Blog*. I am told by publishers that this new type of media, a paper book derived from an electronic blog, is called a "blook." My first book, *e-Discovery: Current Trends and Cases* (ABA 2008), was apparently the first legal "blook" ever published. It was derived from blogs I wrote in 2006 and 2007.

The essays you will find in this book are similar to those in the first and cover all areas of electronic discovery, but are on average longer, with more in-depth analysis. In that sense, this book is somewhat more advanced and provides a good sequel to the first book. Also, since it is more recent, it provides discussion and analysis of the latest cases and ideas. I have again tried to write about these complex and often very technical subjects in plain English, with as little jargon as possible. I have also tried to analyze and discuss the latest cases and ideas so that they can be understood on all levels, from the beginning student to the most senior specialists. Although this book is designed to be a plain English introduction, and thus its title, it is at the same time designed to provide substantial new information and opinions of interest to the most experienced experts.

Unlike my first book, this book includes two guest blogs written by two of my most esteemed colleagues, Jason R. Baron, the Director of Litigation, Office of General Counsel of the National Archives and Records Administration, and Michael Simon, my co-chair of Akerman Senterfitt's national e-discovery practice group. Jason Baron contributed the article in Chapter Four, *A Tale of Two London ESI Forums*. Jason is an internationally recognized leader in electronic discovery with deep insights into many areas of the field, but especially in the areas of search and project management. The day

Jason's article was published on the *e-Discovery Team blog,* readership and popularity spiked to an all-time high. Mike Simon wrote the article in Chapter Five, *Declaratory Judgment Approach to Burdensome Pre-Litigation Preservation Demand Tried and Rejected: Is This a Case of 'No Good Deed Goes Unpunished?* Mike Simon is located in Akerman Senterfitt's Los Angeles office and has assisted me throughout the year in law firm practice. Mike not only wrote this excellent article, but also provided me with help and advice concerning my blog in Chapter Five titled *California Proposes E-Discovery Laws that Governor Schwarzenegger Will Want to Terminate.*

The demands of writing a 3,000- to 5,000-word essay on electronic discovery every weekend for over two years now have been strenuous. Typically, each blog takes from eight to 20 hours to research and write, sometimes more. It takes this much time, as my guest bloggers quickly learn, because I am plagued with perfectionism and a desire to not only fully understand a new case, technique, or idea, but also to try to communicate the insights in a clear and coherent manner. Whenever possible, I also insist on adding some kind of humorous twist, with references to both popular culture and literary classics. For me, the ideal blog both educates and entertains on as many levels as possible. I may not always succeed, but that is my goal.

I have been encouraged in this effort by the popularity of the blog and encouragement from many of its readers, my law partners, clients, colleagues, friends, and family. My children, especially, have helped me to understand the growing importance of blogs, where Internet content is rapidly replacing newspapers, magazines, and other traditional print media. The *e-Discovery Team Blog* has grown in popularity since its inception in 2006 to the point where the essays are now read every week by at least 2,000 readers, with the numbers steadily growing. I have discovered with pleasure that my readers include most of the key experts in the field of e-discovery.

Those familiar with my first book will see that I have continued the same format, wherein I include comments received from readers. I think you will find that this time, many of the comments are of a very high quality and significantly add to the discourse of the book. A special thanks goes to my colleague Craig Ball, who provided many insightful and always technically correct comments. One of the good things about writing a book online, which is in effect what I am doing by publishing these weekly blogs later compiled into books, is that I have an opportunity for instant peer review from the best experts in the world. Since I am writing "in the clouds" with ephemeral digital information, when a peer finds a mistake (which from time to time happens), I go back and correct and edit the work. I therefore have many friends and peers in the industry to thank for helping me make this admittedly cutting-edge work as accurate as possible.

Like my first book, this book presents not only my own ideas, but those of many others in this growing field. Still, any personal opinions expressed here are mine alone, and not the opinions of my law firm, clients, or anyone else.

This second book would not have been possible without the support of my law firm, Akerman Senterfitt, which gave me the time and space needed to research and think deeply about these issues. I would also like to thank my clients and my readers, who have been very encouraging in the support of this weekly blog researching and writing effort. Appreciation also goes to my assistant, Joseph Volpe, who proofreads my blog every Monday and helps keep it as error-free and grammatically correct as possible. If you want to see the near-perfect version of my new weekly blogs, I suggest you take a look at them Monday afternoon, not when they are originally published by me from home on Sunday evenings. (See www.ralphlosey. wordpress.com.)

I would also like to express thanks to my colleagues in the field of e-discovery who are beginning to use my books and blog as part of their teaching activities not only at CLE seminars, but also at law schools around the country. A special thanks goes to William Hamilton, who is the first to use my book, *e-Discovery: Current Trends and Cases*, to teach a class on electronic discovery at the University of Florida, Levin College of Law. Several other professors and adjunct professors around the country are now following in Bill Hamilton's lead, and I am deeply honored by their choice. I strongly feel that electronic discovery needs to be taught in law schools so that the knowledge gap now hindering the profession can be filled by the bright young minds of the future. I hope that this book will also be of service to that end.

I would also like to thank my ABA editor, Timothy Brandhorst, and marketing director, Neil Cox. Their continued encouragement and assistance have made this second book possible.

I conclude my thanks with the people who are nearest and dearest to me, my family, especially my wife of 35 years, Molly Friedman Losey; my daughter, Eva Losey Grossman; and my son, Adam Colby Losey. A special thanks also goes to my son-in-law, Jeffery Grossman, who supplied much of the artwork in this book. Adam Losey is now finishing his third year in law school and often provided me with assistance in research, analysis, and writing. I commend all of my readers to check out Adam's interesting law review article, "Clicking Away Confidentiality: Workplace Waiver of the Attorney Client Privilege," 60 *Florida Law Review* 5 (December 2008) (www.floridalawreview.org/dec08/Losey_BOOK.pdf). My thanks also goes to Catherine Jackson, a summer associate at Akerman Senterfitt, for her help in researching case law.

I welcome any comments or questions that readers may care to make concerning this book or e-discovery in general. I can be reached through my personal e-mail account at: ralph.losey@gmail.com.

Ralph C. Losey

About the Author

Ralph C. Losey is a shareholder in the Orlando, Florida, office of Akerman Senterfitt, where he heads the firm's national electronic discovery practice group. He is the author of the ABA best-selling book on electronic discovery, e-*Discovery: Current Trends and Cases,* published in 2008. Ralph's work at Akerman includes supervision of the e-discovery aspects of major litigation handled by his firm and others; serving as national e-counsel to coordinate the discovery work of local counsel; and assisting large corporate and government clients to prepare for litigation by helping them to organize and operate their own internal e-discovery teams. His team-related services include advice on team organization and budgeting; records retention policies; litigation hold procedures; ESI identification, retrieval, search, and analysis; information management; software; hardware; and vendor selection.

He has practiced commercial and employment litigation since 1980 and has more than 70 published opinions. Ralph has also been an avid computer user and technologist since 1978 and is the author of the popular multimedia Internet blog *e-Discovery Team,* found at http://ralphlosey.wordpress.com, from which this book is derived. He has been involved with electronic discovery since the 1990s and is now an active member of The Sedona Conference and other e-discovery specialty groups. He regularly lectures on e-discovery subjects in continuing legal education courses and conferences around the country; he has also begun teaching e-discovery as an adjunct professor at the University of Florida Levin College of Law.

Ralph was one of the first attorneys in the country with an Internet Web site, which he still maintains at www.FloridaLawFirm.com. He has also written and contributed to several other books and articles on e-discovery and on the Internet. He wrote chapter 3, "Your Cyber Rights and Responsibilities: The Law of the Internet," for *Que's Special Edition Using the Internet* (McMillan Publishers, third edition,

1996) and the chapter on metadata for West-Thompson's book, *E-Discovery, a Report and Guide to the New Rules* (January 2008). Ralph has also written a law review article on the mathematics underlying e-discovery, "HASH: The New Bates Stamp," 12 *Journal of Technology Law & Policy* 1 (June 2007) and a law review article on the ethics underlying e-discovery, "Lawyers Behaving Badly: Understanding Unprofessional Conduct in e-Discovery," 60 *Mercer Law Review* __ (2009). He was certified by the Florida Bar as a mediator of computer law disputes in 1989. He received his B.A. from Vanderbilt University in 1973 and his J.D. in 1979 from the University of Florida College of Law.

Introduction to e-Discovery and e-Discovery Teams

1

WHAT GAME DOES AN E-DISCOVERY TEAM PLAY?

An e-Discovery Team is an interdisciplinary group of lawyers and IT professionals, usually joined by one or more representatives of business or records management. The team is dedicated to the tasks of electronic discovery. One of my fundamental premises, which you will see repeated throughout this book and my earlier book, *e-Discovery: Current Trends and Cases,* is that such teams are the most efficient and effective way to do e-discovery. In fact, in my view this kind of team solution lies at the heart of this new legal field. Such teams should be formed in law firms that do e-discovery and in most large organizations subject to routine e-discovery requests.

So, what exactly are the tasks of e-discovery? In other words, what games do e-Discovery Teams play?

"Hide the Ball" is certainly *not* the game for an e-Discovery Team to play. Some cynics think that is what litigation discovery is all about, and in the world of paper discovery, years ago, there was some truth to that. But not today, and certainly not in electronic discovery. It may be tempting to some, but if you play Hide the Ball in e-discovery and get caught, you may not only lose the case but your job as well, and maybe even your license. It is never worth it; just ask Qualcomm's

1

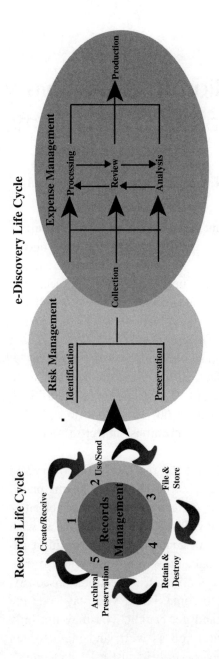

lawyers.[1] Instead, an e-Discovery Team plays a series of games that culminates in throwing the ball to the other side, not hiding it.

Before you can get to the final *throwing* step of production of electronically stored information (ESI), a series of preliminary games must be played. Here is how I summarize the e-Discovery Team playbook:

Find the Ball
Save the Ball
Pick Up the Ball
Shrink the Ball
Clean the Ball
Aim the Ball
Throw the Ball

The first game, Find the Ball, is called the Identification[2] step in the standard industry language of the Electronic Discovery Reference Model[3] (EDRM). By looking at the standard EDRM model below, you can quickly see how each game represents a basic step.

e-Discovery Team Play

---

1. http://ralphlosey.wordpress.com/2008/03/10/sanctions-have-been-lifted-against-the-qualcomm-six-and-a-new-trial-ordered-where-they-may-now-speak-freely-to-defend-themselves/.

2. http://www.edrm.net/wiki/index.php/Identification_N%20ode.

3. http://www.edrm.net/wiki/index.php/Main_Page.

The first step in the full nine-step model, Records Management, shown on page two as Records Life Cycle, is not really part of team play in the context of litigation, but rather is preparation to play the game. Still, it is a critical part of e-discovery teamwork and is discussed throughout this book.

Find the Ball

Finding the ball, or Identification, is far easier said then done. For most companies, the problem derives from storing terabytes of data. Imagine a string of warehouses storing a billion basketballs, and you have to search through and find the one ball among them autographed by Michael Jordan. Unless the team is well established, you probably do not have an accurate, detailed, up-to-date map of all of the warehouses. You probably have only a vague idea where this one basketball might be located. It might be somewhere in a centralized bin, or in any one of dozens of other locations, including closets in employee homes or off-site Internet storage lockers. It might even exist only in a shrunken-down version, hiding in the pocket of one of 1,000 employees—perhaps in their thumb-drive or iPhone. Moreover, every day 1,000 basketballs are destroyed (hopefully not the one with Jordan's autograph), and 1,200 new ones are added. Yes, it is a very challenging game indeed.

To make matters worse, you are never sure exactly what balls you are looking for, especially when the game first begins. You may have to guess, from a vague complaint, what balls are relevant. This is one of Anne Kershaw's[4] pet peeves, and rightfully so. Under federal notice pleading rules, very few details are required in a complaint to state a cause of action. So defense counsel is often left speculating what ESI will be discoverable and relevant in a new case. Still, you have to start making educated guesses to try to find the right batch of balls. From the large selection first identified, you will eventually throw a few to the other side.

---

4. A leading national consultant and attorney in the field of e-discovery. *See* http://www.akersaw.com.

The way most teams do this is to analyze the dispute to try to determine what the issues will be in the case. This gives you a general idea of the types of balls that may come into play. Then you start to determine a general time line; hopefully, the potentially relevant balls will be constrained by time. You may be able to know, with some certainty, that balls made before or after a certain time are not relevant and need not be searched. An e-Discovery Team will also try to limit the search to balls made or stored by certain *key players*. These are the people in your company who are likely to be involved as witnesses in the lawsuit. The team's search should be focused on the storage bins of these key players.

Finding the ball in my sports analogy is called Identification in the standard industry model and represents the first of three steps considered critical to risk management. The other two components are Preservation (saving the ball) and Collection (picking up the balls). If the team does these three steps correctly, it will protect the company or client from costly sanctions so common in e-discovery work, as the "Sanctions" chapter of this book illustrates.

Risk Management

Save the Ball

The next game is *Save the Ball*. Here the team devises ways to preserve most of the balls identified as potential evidence in the last game. Again, this can be a very challenging game, especially when your company has many different auto-destruct routines in place (and most companies do).

If you think it is easy to stop all of these programs, just ask Intel. They thought they had stopped deletion of excess e-mail for all the key players in the antitrust case brought against it by Advanced Micro Devices (AMD), but in fact the janitor programs remained in place for the most important players, including the top officers of the company. Their e-mail was deleted for years after the case was filed.[5] They tried to play a very complicated game of Save the Ball but failed. For a better idea of just how difficult this game can be, check out Intel's report to the supervising district court judge on their failed attempts to preserve evidence.[6] This mistake has supposedly already cost Intel millions of dollars to correct by forcing them to go to their backup tapes to find the deleted e-mails, and the meter is still running. AMD is, of course, claiming that the error was intentional.[7] They would like the court to enter sanctions for spoliation and turn this mistake into an outright win of the whole case.

So make no mistake about it, Save the Ball is one of the most important games an e-Discovery Team plays. As I have discussed before,[8] that is why most e-Discovery Teams focus on this game as soon as the team is formed and look for ways to improve their company's litigation hold procedures.

5. http://www.ciolaw.org/litigation-holds/amd-v-intel-part-one-a-look-at-the-%E2%80%98largest-electronic-production-in-history%E2%80%99/.
6. http://ralphlosey.files.wordpress.com/2008/02/intel-letter-to-court-explaining-email-loss.pdf.
7. http://www.theregister.co.uk/2007/03/06/amd_intel_missingemails/.
8. http://ralphlosey.wordpress.com/2008/02/17/e-discovery-teams-self-organization-and-development-of-evidence-preservation-protocols/,

Pick Up the Ball

Again, this game sounds easy enough—you just collect the relevant ESI from the data you have identified and preserved. Seems easy, but it is not. There are tricks and traps here aplenty. If you are not careful, you could collect too much or too little. Generally you do not want to simply pick up all of the balls you have saved. That will make the next games too expensive. You want to screen out the ones that are unlikely to be needed and probably are not relevant at all, but were preserved just in case. You want to *preserve* more broadly than collect, because you never want to play Save the Ball twice in the same case. Not only is that kind of do-over expensive, it also may be futile because in the meantime, routine processes may have deleted many balls not saved in the first pass.

You also do not want to pick up too few balls and leave behind many that are directly relevant and should later be thrown to the other side. That kind of careless collection can also be expensive. It can force you into an expensive do-over and open you to charges of hiding the ball. *See, e.g.,* "Court Disapproves Defendant's 'Hide the Ball' Discovery Gamesmanship."[9]

Careless collection often occurs if the team simply delegates this function to the key witnesses and does not properly supervise or follow up on their ball-picking efforts. The same comment holds true for the two prior games of ball identification and preservation. The team cannot delegate its responsibility to key players and then just hope for the best; the team must take responsibility to see they are played correctly. That is the whole purpose of an e-Discovery Team.

For that reason, in most cases it will not suffice to simply send out a preservation letter to the key players that describes the dispute, and then leaves it to them to find the relevant balls for themselves, save them, and pick them up. Without help and supervision from the team, the key players may not know which of their com-

---

9. http://ralphlosey.wordpress.com/2007/02/21/court-disapproves-defendant%E2%80%99s-%E2%80%9Chide-the-ball%E2%80%9D-discovery-gamesmanship/.

puter files are relevant, how to properly preserve this ESI, or how to collect it. They are sure to make mistakes. Thus, when the key players in a company are called upon to take part in the games—which in itself makes a lot of sense, since they should know their own information better than anyone else—they should be given expert help and advice from the e-Discovery Team. In other words, it is perfectly all right to delegate some of this work to the key players in the litigation, but the team must still supervise and follow up. Ultimately, the team should be responsible, since its members are trained and more experienced in collection than the key players. The team should have personal meetings with the key players and closely monitor their activities. In many cases, the team should also implement certain safeguarding mechanisms to supplement the key players' efforts, such as automated copying and keyword searches.

Another common mistake made in Pick Up the Ball is to carelessly change the ball in the very process of picking it up. You could, for instance, change the metadata of a file, such as information on when it was last viewed, saved, or revised. This is an especially high risk when the team attempts to rely upon key players to pick up the ball for them. Although this probably will not matter in most cases, in some cases, such as stock-backdating cases, this might be very important. As a general rule, the team tries not to change the ball too much by picking it up. The team may later strip a file of all or part of its metadata on purpose, if that facilitates later cleaning or throwing, especially if the metadata is not important in the case or not wanted, but they never want to do it accidentally.

A final common mistake, one of my pet peeves, is to neglect to hash the ball when you collect it, and properly preserve and tie the hash into each ball thereafter. I have described the process of using hash mathematics to authenticate ESI at length in my law review article, "HASH: The New Bates Stamp,"[10] in the June 2007 issue of *Journal of Technology Law & Policy*. I also discuss hash in several essays in the "Technology" chapter of this book.

---

10. http://ralphlosey.files.wordpress.com/2007/09/hasharticlelosey.pdf.

The team may already have hashed files as part of the preservation game; but if not, it is essential that they now be hashed at the collection stage. Hashing provides a unique identifying alphanumeric value for each computer file collected. This hash value can be checked later to prove that the file has not been altered since it was collected. This is a key step in ESI authentication to allow for admission into evidence at a hearing or trial. In most cases, hashing should be a normal part of ball pickup.

Collection is the last of the three steps that are critical to Risk Management (Identification-Preservation-Collection). It is also the first step of the final Expense Management section of the e-Discovery Team playbook as shown below. These last five steps are by far the most costly games the team must play to respond to e-discovery requests. For that reason, these are the tasks where excellent play by the team can save the company money, lots of money. Sucessful teams have found that they can pay for themselves many times over by playing these games, instead of attorneys or IT acting on their own. In fact, the first e-Discovery Team ever created in 2001 by CISCO claims to have reduced the company's overall litigation expenses by over 64%.[11] This, coupled with the risk management advantages of team play, are the main reasons many companies and law firms today are rushing to set up interdisciplinary e-Discovery Teams. The next essay in this

e-Discovery Team Play

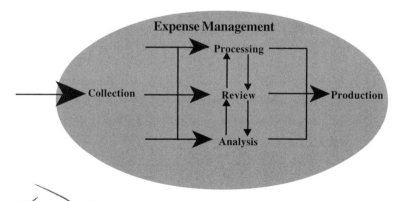

---

11. http://www.cisco.com/web/about/ciscoitatwork/downloads/ciscoitatwork/pdf/Cisco_IT_Case_Study_Legal_Storage_Summary.pdf..

chapter, *When and Why Should Inside Counsel Start an e-Discovery Team?*, will illustrate this case for e-Discovery Teams in detail.

Shrink the Ball

Shrink the Ball, or Processing, is the game where the team can save the company the most money. Thus, from a financial perspective, it is the most important game of all. In this culling step, you process the ESI to eliminate as much duplicate and irrelevant information as possible. Here good software and automated process are critical; so too is careful strategic thinking.

The goal is to significantly reduce the amount of ESI that must be reviewed and cleaned in the next steps. Thus, for instance, at the end of the last game you may have identified and preserved 1,000 gigabytes (1 terabyte) of ESI, and collected 500 gigabytes. To give you some idea of the amount of information we are speaking about, in some circumstances the 500 gigabytes may be equivalent to 500 truckloads of paper. It would cost a small fortune for teams of lawyers to read that much paper. We are talking about years of billable lawyer time to read that much data. It would also be a colossal waste of time because they would end up reading the same document dozens, if not hundreds, of times. So it is critical to aggressively eliminate the redundant and immaterial ESI in this processing stage. In many cases the 500 gigs can be cut down to 100 or 50 gigs, resulting in tremendous savings in the expensive review games to come.

From what I have seen, this is the game where most attorneys, acting alone and without strong knowledge of e-discovery law, tend to make the most mistakes. They are way too conservative in their play, and end up culling the ESI far less that they should. The result is that the team ends up having to review far too much useless information at great expense. You should play Shrink the Ball very aggressively, and be prepared to defend your actions in court if later challenged. The best way to do that is with careful documentation and expenses analysis. Be prepared to demonstrate the great expense you would otherwise have had to incur without such shrinkage.

Clean the Ball

Here is where some of the big money comes in—the cost to review the data for privileged, confidential, and irrelevant material. Still, most internal corporate e-Discovery Teams will not clean their own ball; they will hand it off to their caddy to do it for them, typically their outside legal counsel. That is why law firm e-Discovery Teams need to be especially adept and efficient at this game. A few of the more mature and well-organized corporate teams have started to review their own data and clean them the ESI themselves. They have teams of contract attorneys they employ to do this work at reduced rates; some even send the data to lawyers in India for review. But for most teams, this is advanced play that they do not have the time or skill to attempt.

This is a very important and risky step in the EDRM process, and companies want to be sure it is done right. You review the truckloads of e-mail and documents that have not already been culled out in the prior games so that you can remove the files that do not have to be produced. The last thing you want to do is produce privileged materials to your adversary. You need to clean your production of these secret files and produce a log of them instead. Even with a clawback agreement, an accidental disclosure can still result in waiver of your privilege to third parties. You also want to be sure the ESI review catches all confidential materials, and that they are produced with appropriate markings and confidentiality agreements. Trade secrets can be lost forever if they become a public record by filing with a court.

Aim the Ball

Now we come to the lawyerly game of Aim the Ball, where the ESI is analyzed to see how it fits into the case at hand. Here lawyers and paralegals tag each file to an issue, typically using review software. They also make final decisions as to whether and how information is responsive to discovery requests, or otherwise must be produced (or not). The files are categorized and rated for importance. Is this e-mail a smoking gun that could kill your case, or is it merely of marginal relevance to a secondary issue? You had better find this out, and fast, for each computer file you are about to disclose to the other side. If your analysis of the information to be produced shows you have a strong case, you will approach the case far differently than if your analysis shows you will surely lose when all of the cards are put on the table.

Obviously, this analysis stage requires the sure hand and steady aim of trusted outside counsel assigned to defend or prosecute the case. Still, the legal members of the team should assist and be involved in the analysis and evaluation of the merits of the case. This game concludes with final decisions by legal counsel on what should be produced and what should be withheld. These decisions must be rational and made in good faith.

If analysis shows you have a losing hand, you had better fold early before the other side realizes your position. You cannot do like Qualcomm and decide to withhold evidence just because you don't like it. You can see where hiding the ball got them[12]—they lost the patent they sued to enforce, they paid more than $8 million in fees to the other side, their general counsel resigned in disgrace, and their outside counsel are now fighting to retain their licenses. When you are a plaintiff and find yourself in this position, you do not file the suit to begin with or, if you discover it in midstream, you should dismiss and cut your losses. The same applies when you are in a defense position. It is not an option to try to hide the evidence that will hurt your defense. You must instead try to make the most of it and settle as best you can. That is how the American system of justice works, and all teams have to play by these same fundamental rules. Voluntary disclosure may not be the rule in the rest of the world, especially the civil law countries in Europe, but

---

12. http://ralphlosey.wordpress.com/2007/08/18/heavy-sanctions-loom-against-attorneys-for-e-discovery-and-other-aggrivated-litigation-abuses/.

that is how the game is played here. If you are defending or prosecuting a case in the United States, you are going to have to reveal your data to your adversary, even if that kills your case.

Throw the Ball

The last game is the culmination of all the rest. The analysis game resulted in final decisions on what files to be produced. Now you actually make the production. Throwing the ball is not really all that hard, as long as you enlist the aid of WORMs. No, not the creepy-crawly kind, but the "Write Once, Read Many" times kind, such as optical discs, CDs or DVDs. The ESI on these media cannot be altered after written, thus providing you, and the receiving party, with a certain amount of protection that the files will not be accidentally altered. WORMs help the parties maintain a permanent record of the ESI produced.

Another tricky aspect of production is deciding the form it will take. Do you produce in native format with full internal metadata retained, or do you produce in a TIFF or JPEG format with a load file ready for import into review software? This should have already been worked out with opposing counsel as part of the Rule 26(f) conference or the original production request; but if not, you have to make these decisions now.

Take the time to clearly mark and label the production media. One thing I hate is a CD production with no writing on it, or indecipherable handwriting. Write out a full description of the CD and the date of production and name of the case. Think of chain of custody issues, and do not forget to make multiple copies. Another thing I have noticed lately is the use of paper labels on CDs. That's ok, but beware of labels that peel off. As a safeguard, it is better to use ink-jet printers that print directly on the CD instead of glue-on labels. If you must use an adhesive label, put some kind of writing directly on the CD itself, just in case it peels off somewhere down the line.

Finally, if you use TIFF or other image-type files where you affix Bates stamp-type markings to identify individual ESI files, please consider adding a truncated hash value to the file ID. As discussed in *HASH: The New Bates Stamp*,[13] this will facilitate both identification and authentication, and allow for easier comparison with the native originals.

Concluding Thoughts

These games are difficult. Much like golf, it is not a game of "perfect." Mistakes are inevitable. Even Tiger Woods messes up from time to time and does not win them all, so why should you be any different? Document your efforts, play it safe, and use redundant systems whenever economically feasible. Thus, when a mistake is later discovered, you may be able to cover it with a backup system. Or, if that is not possible, you can at least show to the supervising judge that you made good-faith, reasonable efforts. The judge should understand and cut you a break, maybe even give you a mulligan. If the judge does not realize that mistakes are inevitable, he or she simply does not understand the game. Then it is up to you to explain it, or hire an expert who can.

Blog Reader Comment

Enjoy your blog. I am very experienced in complex litigation/e-discovery work and I must note that I have not yet seen a discussion of the best ways to properly prepare a client for all the tech support necessary to actually conduct the large-scale doc review (# 6) above. This process requires hiring from 30 to 100+ attorneys to work 60+ hours a week for months on end on large-scale projects. This is a very labor-intensive and expensive phase of e-discovery. It has been my experience that the software programs-vendors-consult-ants-servers-Internet pipelines, etc., etc., are poorly chosen (cost), causing serious delays and cost overruns on many projects. I also note that so-called service providers in this area often employ very junior and inexperienced people

---

13. http://ralphlosey.files.wordpress.com/2007/09/hasharticlelosey.pdf.

to serve as "techs" and "on-site trainers" who are not really up to the task of servicing the daily needs of complex project workflow. I understand that clients make cost-driven choices in these matters, but they wind up paying far more in the end in excessive attorney hours and overtime because they don't properly prepare for the review phase.

Ralph's Reply

You raise a good issue. Any thoughts on how to do that would be appreciated. Many people and companies seem to be penny wise and pound foolish. Most of the expense in large projects is review, and I have tried to make that point several times. In my view, the best way to reduce review costs is to be more aggressive in the precededing Processing step, what I call in my sports analogy "Shrinking the Ball." In other words, you need to drastically reduce the amount of ESI to review. Also, good search tools will significantly increase your speed of review.

WHEN AND WHY SHOULD INSIDE COUNSEL START AN E-DISCOVERY TEAM?

Should every company have an e-Discovery Team? If a company has only a few computers, say, less than 100, or rarely gets sued and has less than three lawsuits going at a time, then it does not need one. It is probably cheaper to just hire outside counsel and vendors to handle e-discovery cases when they occasionally arise. But for everyone else, especially in these times of cost-cutting budgets, it is a necessity. That is because, as my friend Ed Foster[14] likes to say, it can save your company *boatloads* of money! It saves on outside counsel fees and e-discovery vendor costs. It also saves on inflated settlements to avoid the expense, hassle and risks of e-discovery. Yes, a corporate e-Discovery Team does cost some money to set up, but as Benjamin Franklin said, "An ounce of prevention is worth a pound of cure."

---

14. http://www.akerman.com/public/attorneys/aBiography.asp?id=394.

Today millions of British pounds and U.S. dollars are being spent on e-discovery cures. This expense is a harsh reality of litigation. So too are the risks, mistakes and sanctions that frequently occur when a company puts its fate in the hands of ill-prepared legal counsel or profit-motivated vendors. Even in the best of circumstances, it is all too easy for a medium- or large-size company to burn through a few million dollars in e-discovery expenses in just a couple of months. *See Kentucky Speedway, LLC v. NASCAR*, 2006 U.S. Dist. LEXIS 92028 (E.D. Ky. Dec. 18, 2006). The solution is for a company to take control of its information and its e-discovery activities and not ignore the problem or delegate it to others. This means forming an internal e-Discovery Team.

But don't just take Ed Foster's word for it. Ask the people and companies who have already formed e-Discovery Teams. For instance, ask Jeff Ghielmetti of CISCO Systems,[15] who has more experience at this than anybody. Jeff often tells the story of how CISCO established the first internal corporate e-Discovery Team after the stock market crash of 2000-2001. At that time, CISCO was hit with a flood of litigation, often involving millions of pages of electronic documents. One of the first cases came with a $23,500,000 bill for e-discovery! CISCO could not continue at that kind of burn rate, so out of necessity they decided to try something new and go in-house. For help they turned to Jeff, a CISCO engineer and not a lawyer, but he had the full backing of CISCO's forward-looking (a/k/a "desperate") legal department.

Under Jeff Ghielmetti's direction, CISCO turned away from the traditional model of hiring law firms and e-discovery vendors to manage its data preservation, collection and analysis and set up the first internal, multidisciplinary corporate e-Discovery Team. It also developed its own proprietary software and computer systems to help the team perform its tasks. Jeff reports that CISCO's program has been a huge success, not only in cutting costs but also in better management of risks. According to CISCO's case study,[16] "Cisco

---

15. http://www.cisco.com/web/about/ciscoitatwork/data_center/san_for_data_management.html.

16. http://www.cisco.com/web/about/ciscoitatwork/downloads/ciscoitatwork/pdf/Cisco_IT_Case_Study_Legal_Storage_Summary.pdf..

has been able to reduce its discovery costs by approximately 97 percent—for an overall reduction in litigation expenses of 64 percent." Those are pretty impressive numbers. For detailed information on the CISCO Team and the centralized Storage Area Network (SAN) it developed for e-discovery, *see How Cisco IT Uses SAN to Automate the Legal Discovery Process.*[17]

If you don't want to take both Ed and Jeff's word for it, then you could also ask Laura Kibbe. She is the young attorney who helped Pfizer form its first e-Discovery Team in 2005. As a result of her work, Laura was named one of four of *Corporate Counsel* magazine's trailblazers in 2006.[18] The article on Laura[19] summed up the benefits of her work:

> Why pay millions for an in-house e-discovery system when, as most companies do, you can outsource the work? Simple—farming it out to law firms and consultants, all of whom really want the job, can cost even more. Especially when you are an oft-sued drug company like Pfizer. In just one year, Kibbe says, the new system saved "multiple millions of dollars," and served up several side benefits. She gave Pfizer a "repeatable process" that can find and extract information quickly.
>
> Pfizer General Counsel Allen Waxman is proud of what Kibbe has accomplished in just under two years. Her response team, Waxman says, has reaped "substantial efficiencies and added effectiveness." . . .
>
> Probably the best thing Kibbe brings to the tech table is the fact that she's a lawyer who has to use the system. That means that she doesn't need to rely on outside firms, who sometimes make promises to produce data that their client

---

17. http://www.cisco.com/web/about/ciscoitatwork/downloads/ciscoitatwork/pdf/Cisco_IT_Case_Study_Legal_Storage.pdf..

18. http://www.law.com/jsp/ihc/PubArticleIHC.jsp?id=1165244461565.

19. http://www.law.com/jsp/ihc/PubArticleIHC.jsp?id=1165244462425.

can't keep. This way, Kibbe can make sure that what Pfizer tells one court it can or can't do remains consistent in all courts.

You could also ask Kevin Esposito, the Pfizer attorney who is the current director of its e-Discovery Team. I have written about him before as one of the lead speakers at the ABA 1st Annual National Institute on E-Discovery.[20] He is adamant that the key to significant cost savings in the long run is to spend the time and money up front to develop an effective e-Discovery Team. He states that this requires careful mapping of all a company's data, and establishment of sound processes and procedures for preservation, identification and collection.

You could also ask Jonathan Eisenberg of Merrill Lynch. He co-heads its Global Litigation Department and supervises its e-Discovery Team. Jon realized that Merrill Lynch should begin to take e-discovery in-house when he saw how many of his experienced outside counsel were becoming ineffective in securities cases because of the complexities of e-discovery. The attorneys were experts in securities law and litigation, but not in e-discovery. Merrill Lynch responded and now has a well-developed team that performs most of the e-discovery work itself instead of relying on its outside counsel or vendors.

Jonathan describes an eight-step process that Merrill Lynch developed to manage e-discovery:

1. Established a full-time, in-house, interdisciplinary team of legal and IT professionals dedicated to electronic discovery—i.e., formed and funded an e-Discovery Team.
2. Established detailed litigation hold procedures that were later refined and improved over hundreds of cases. Jonathan describes this key process as having seven steps: a) ID the custodians; b) inventory and map the data sources, which takes many months the first time through; c) send written

20. http://ralphlosey.wordpress.com/2007/03/10/aba-1st-annual-national-instutute-on-e-discovery/.

notices and reminders to all impacted employees; d) monitor and enforce compliance with the litigation hold; e) interview the key players; f) collect the discoverable information; and g) export data for production to outside counsel. To that list, I would add the imposition of automated software holds and suspension of usual document retention procedures.

3. Wrote and implemented an aggressive document destruction policy. In my experience, this is a very challenging and time-consuming process, especially if a company does not already have an effective electronic document retention policy in place.

4. Purchased and refined custom search software to quickly locate electronically stored information across all of Merrill Lynch's systems that might be relevant to a particular case.

5. Developed a system and software tools to process all ESI and filter out all duplicates and other obviously non-responsive data before export to vendors for further processing and analysis.

6. Purchased and use what Jonathan calls "Encase-type" software tools to image and search for non-e-mail ESI.

7. Located and trained a pool of reliable contract lawyers to review pre-productions.

8. Trained several Merrill Lynch IT technicians to be forensic experts.

If Ed, Jeff, Laura and Jonathan's references were not enough, you could also ask James Wright. He is the project manager who leads Halliburton's Team. Jim has a power-point presentation online[21] that lists some of the key points on e-Discovery Teams. The presentation, which I have heard and previously written about,[22] begins by summarizing some of the benefits of taking e-discovery in-house.

---

21. http://www.pss-systems.com/resources/CGOC06_Wright.pdf..

22. http://ralphlosey.wordpress.com/2007/03/19/practice-under-the-new-rules-an-e-discovery-cle-by-bna/,

WHY SHOULD CORPORATIONS PARTICIPATE IN E-DISCOVERY?

1. Corporations own all the risk of litigation and pay all the costs.
2. It's just not a paper world anymore; data volumes changed everything.
3. Corporations know their e-data better.
4. E-discovery management is inconsistent among law firms.
5. Law firms' risks and incentives differ from corporations; law firms have a more conservative methodology toward discovery; a de facto disincentive exists for data reduction.

The fifth point made by Halliburton's team captain is twofold. First, law firms are naturally more cautious is making decisions and will always err on the side of including more data in the preservation, collection and review set. Second, there is a "disincentive," which Jim bluntly calls a conflict of interest, for law firms in which attorneys are paid by the hour to review documents they decide may be responsive. He implies it's like hiring the fox to guard the henhouse. Vendors are, of course, in the same position, since most charge by the megabyte of processed data.

And if all that were not enough, you could also ask Patrick Oot, the young but senior counsel at Verizon who leads its new e-Discovery Team. Patrick says that:[23]

> Managing electronic discovery is probably a number-one initiative at all legal departments. Depending on the volume of litigation an organization has, this can be one of the largest line items in your [legal] budget.

Patrick reports that his team approach is keeping vendor prices very competitive, and Verizon's overall e-discovery costs are now under control. Still, you need good vendors and outside counsel to represent you and handle much of the work. Patrick complains about

23. http://mike2.openmethodology.org/index.php.EDiscovery _Solution_Offering.

staffing[24] and observes that it is difficult to find experienced senior e-discovery counsel at many law firms. He urges law firms to invest in their own e-Discovery Teams so that they can better assist their clients' teams.

> The culture at many law firms dictates electronic discovery counsel and director positions as nonpartner-track positions. Although firm culture is shifting, many firms fail to place leadership emphasis with true decision-making power on this crucial position.
>
> It takes months to find a solid project management candidate. Firms need to re-educate their teams.

As an e-discovery attorney and partner in a law firm myself, I could not agree more.

All of the outside consultants with real expertise in the area agree with the need for e-Discovery Teams, at least the ones not employed by some of the smaller e-discovery vendors. In fact, Ben Hawksworth of Ernst & Young[25] calls the internal corporate team approach the new "holy grail" of e-discovery.

Still not convinced? Then it is unlikely that more references will persuade. To be honest, most companies are not moved by reason to form an e-Discovery Team, they are moved by experience—*bad* experience. Typically, a team is not formed until after a bad case. By that time, boatloads of money have already been spent for fees, costs, and a settlement with the plaintiff. The size of the loss in one case is typically far more than the total cost of team formation. Remember, CISCO was motivated to start the first e-Discovery Team by a $23.5 million bill. This tendency of large organizations to ignore the advice of Ben Franklin makes the plaintiff's bar quite happy, and more *Zubulake*-type judgments happen every day. I hope that does not happen to you, but without an effective team in place, it is very likely.

---

24. http://www.law.com/jsp/legaltechnology/pubArticleLT.jsp?id=1191967650493.

25. http://www.ey.com/global/Content.nsf/US/AABS_-_Specialty_Advisory_-_IDS_-_Overview.

Robert D. Owen,[26] the co-chair of Fulbright & Jaworski's e-discovery group, likes to say[27] that instead of taking the time to get prepared, many companies have decided to play "the e-discovery lottery. They have decided to take the chance that they won't be hit. It's a gamble." I agree completely. Many companies are gambling they won't be the next Morgan Stanley or Qualcomm. It's a bad bet. The only uncertainty is the size of the boatload of money and when it will sink.

Blog Reader Comment

Many aspects of proactive preparation for litigation can be implemented along with internal data management and retention practices, long before the onset of litigation. Doing so allows corporations to take control of their data, minimize risk and reduce costs, while assuring corporate compliance with federal rules. A strong e-Discovery solutions provider can help you implement the process internally.

E-DISCOVERY TEAMS: SELF-ORGANIZATION AND DEVELOPMENT OF EVIDENCE PRESERVATION PROTOCOLS

The preservation of discoverable ESI in litigation is a core activity of any e-Discovery Team. It is also a key component of risk management. Obviously, if you do not preserve electronically stored information and it is deleted, you will never be able to find it or collect it, much less review and produce it. Just ask the Bush White House[28] about that; they failed to preserve[29] over 5 million e-mails.

---

26. http://www.fulbright.com/index.cfm?fuseaction=attorneys.detail&site_id=311&emp_id=11700.

27. http://wolfs2cents.wordpress.com/2007/12/20/companies-still-struggling-to-find-way-on-e-discovery/.

28. http://en.wikipedia.org/wiki/Bush_White_House_e-mail_controversy.

29. http://www.computerworld.com/action/article.do?command=viewArticleBasic&taxonomyName=storage&articleId=9062642&taxonomyId=19&intsrc=kc_top.

The whole nine-step e-discovery process[30] depends upon proper preservation. So too does risk management. Unless you are the White House, your failure to preserve after notice is a sure road to sanctions. Risk control in e-discovery begins with the routine employment of effective litigation-hold procedures. This is the best way to minimize the chance of inadvertent or intentional destruction of relevant electronic records.

This is a difficult task in the best of circumstances. Intel's e-mail preservation losses[31] in the AMD antitrust case demonstrate that Intel was trying to implement a very complex litigation-hold procedure[32] to preserve relevant evidence, but despite strong efforts by its team, it lost thousands of e-mails. The loss was caused by a number of mistakes, including design flaws in the notice and collection procedures and the failure to suspend an automatic file deletion program for certain key witnesses. Spoliation was also caused by the simple human error[33] of forgetting to look at a second tab of an Excel spreadsheet listing more key custodians.

Even when no human errors are made and the system design is nearly perfect, spoliation can still occur for a variety of reasons. For one thing, even though a suit may already have been filed, you still may not be able to determine what ESI is relevant and should be preserved, and what isn't. Under today's liberal notice pleading rules in federal court, it can be difficult, some might say impossible, to know exactly what ESI should be preserved and who should be notified of the preservation obligation. Pleadings can be so vague that the scope of a litigation hold is frequently a guessing game, especially at the beginning of a case when the duty to preserve is triggered.

The typical analysis to determine preservation scope is three-fold: (1) what is the subject matter of the discoverable ESI that should

---

30. http://ralphlosey.wordpress.com/about/.

31. http://www.dailytech.com/article.aspx?newsid=6352.

32. http://ralphlosey.files.wordpress.com/2008/02/intel-letter-to-court-explaining-email-loss.pdf..

33. http://soundevidence.discoveryresources.org/-151-big-case-legal-holds-on-spreadsheetsdisaster.html.

be preserved; (2) who are the witnesses and custodians who may possess or control the discoverable ESI; and (3) what is the time frame of the discoverable ESI. In many lawsuits, it is not obvious from the pleadings what the dispute is really all about and what subjects could be relevant. In fact, most disputes usually morph a few times and develop new issues as the facts and law are better understood by the parties and the court.

This kind of subject matter and issue determination must be performed right after a suit has been filed. At this point, the defense lawyers may know little or nothing about the case beyond what is stated in a complaint. Even worse, the preservation duty may be triggered even before a complaint has been filed, when it is reasonably certain that litigation is likely. At that point, it frequently requires a crystal ball to try to guess all of the issues in a case. It is often just as speculative and risk filled to try to determine who the witnesses may be in the case, and what additional employees or third parties may be custodians of discoverable information, even though not direct witnesses. Even the time component may be vague, and you may not be sure how far back in time you should go, or how far forward.

You could say, why not just call opposing counsel and find out, but that presupposes a knowledgeable and cooperative adversary. In reality, it rarely works that way. If and when they do return your call, which may be days or weeks later, and you are in fact given "advice," it is often deliberately overly burdensome and oppressive, and you are sorry you asked. Gamesmanship is still very much alive and well in the adversary system.

In view of the importance of proper preservation to facilitate justice and avoid sanctions, and the inherent difficulties of "guesstimating" the scope of discoverability at the beginning of a case, the development of good preservation protocols is a prime directive of every e-Discovery Team. Internal corporate teams must try to set up systems that will mitigate against these inherent uncertainties and risks. But does this mean it is the *first* thing a new team should focus on? Should the team begin its work by developing final protocols in this area? Should the top priority be development of procedures for rapid response to litigation by preservation notices, suspension of automatic file deletion programs, and the like?

No! The development of formal hold systems is important, but the first task of a team must be to self-organize. You have to have a team before you can play the game, much less win it. This means finding the right team players. It also means having them come together and attain a certain level of training and cohesion. Only then can they take on a play as complicated and important as litigation holds. The team must also secure adequate funding and senior management support for the team mission. It has to be a team of winners with a promising future, not a dead end. Only after these preliminary organizational steps have been taken can the team function effectively. Recruiting the right team members is more difficult than most people think. So too is securing upper management buy-in and budget approvals.

Team staffing requires careful selection of compatible people from three different sectors: law, IT, and management. IBM consultants, like almost everyone else in the field, advocate for internal e-Discovery Teams. The IBM white paper[34] *The Impact of Electronically Stored Information on Corporate Legal and Compliance Management* advises companies to:

> Have a plan and a process for discovery of ESI that you can improve over time. Understand your end-to-end process from discovery to production and the implementation of "holds." This encompasses methods and practices that make sense for your organization, understanding where technology is needed to facilitate or improve process efficiencies or quality of results, and identifying which specific technology capabilities are required to make your end-to-end process effective. It is best accomplished through a cooperative effort among legal, IT, and the line of business (LOB) organizations.

---

34. http://www-03.ibm.com/industries/financialservices/doc/content/bin/ fss_the_impact_of_eletronically.pdf.

You can have a team with just lawyers and techs. The first e-Discovery Team by CISCO in 2001 started that way. But today, most agree you should also have a management/business component in the core Team. Members can come from several different departments, including records management, human resources, finance, risk management, compliance or operations. There are many different variations. It all depends on the particular organization, its structure and corporate culture. IBM explains that the line-of-business members are needed to assist legal and IT to "set and manage the business priorities; establish the policies and best practices; and enforce the organizational compliance."

The culture of business, law and IT are very different. That is why careful selection of candidates from each sector is important. Not all in-house lawyers are cut out to work with computer techs. He or she may be a good lawyer, but computer-phobic. They may have gone to law school precisely because they hated computers, math and science. The same applies to IT personnel. Many are not comfortable with "people" activities. They would rather work on code for hours than attend a meeting. That is, after all, why most of them went into that field. Management types drafted into this project may have similar prejudices and see this as a dead-end assignment. They hear that it has something to do with records management, lawyers and IT, and their eyes glaze over.

So, believe me, finding the right people for an e-Discovery Team is not easy. You should not simply pick the people who appear to have some time right now to work on this. Their aptitude and cultural readiness is more important. Most companies do not have interdepartmental teams, so there will be little precedent for this kind of cooperative endeavor, and high turnover at first is not uncommon. For all of these reasons, significant time must be spent on education at the beginning of the group's existence. That is why my involvement in a team is usually front-loaded, and my time lessens as the team self-organizes and becomes fully functional.

At the beginning, it is important to be sure everyone has a rudimentary understanding of the e-discovery process and the mission and future tasks of the team, including the need to design and implement good preservation protocols. These protocols and other projects will allow the team to better manage the high risks of litigation. They will also save the company a lot of money from reduced e-discovery costs.

The first members of a team typically consider whether additional members are needed. There should be at least two representatives from each of the three sectors, and frequently more than that, depending on the size of the organization, its history, and the complexity of the organization. A team needs enough members to accomplish its goals, but not so many as to become cumbersome and unworkable. If a team must have many members due to the complexity of the organization, then it usually breaks down into subgroups. When that happens, the initial education, communication, and cohesion process becomes much more challenging.

After a team is fully formed and operational, and members are fully briefed and understand its missions and upcoming activities, one of its first tasks is to address litigation-hold and collection procedures. Still, at this point you are not yet ready to design final preservation and collection procedures. For most teams, that is still a year or so away. Instead you create *interim* protocols.

Some companies have some kind of identification, preservation and collection system in place, even if it is not in writing. Typically, it involves preserving computer files by telling employees to look through their computers for relevant files, and when found, to save a copy onto a central location, usually a server. When there is already some kind of system like this in place, the team begins by studying the current procedures and looking for areas that need improvement. Usually existing systems fail to cover all ESI, fail to preserve metadata, fail to authenticate with hashing, and are otherwise of questionable legal validity. They are also usually not well documented, hard to follow, and fail to address many common contingencies.

More often than not, there are no protocols at all. Litigation holds have only been dealt with on an ad hoc basis by a number of different people, each with their own ideas on how to go about it, and what the law requires. There you basically start from scratch. But whether you already have written procedures in place, or are designing them for the first time, in either case you are only going to be able to create *interim* preservation procedures. Final procedures come much later in the work of the e-Discovery Team.

The procedures, even the interim procedures, must comply with the current laws. For instance, it is probably not legally sufficient to simply send employees an e-mail telling them not to alter or destroy relevant files, and then hope for the best. Much more follow-up is required. Otherwise, if a mistake is made, and ESI is destroyed or altered, the company could face severe sanctions. *See Cache La Poudre Feeds, LLC v. Land O'Lakes Farmland Feed, LLC,* 2007 WL 684001 (D. Colo. March 2, 2007) and my essay "Litigation Hold Is Not Enough," in Chapter Two of my first book, *e-Discovery: Current Trends and Cases.* For this reason, as a best practice, many companies are now moving to automated systems that supplement employee compliance. Also, as *Zubulake V* teaches, reasonable litigation-hold procedures should include direct interviews with the key players in litigation. *Zubulake v. UBS Warburg LLC,* 229 F.R.D. 422 (S.D. N.Y. 2004). *Also see "Zubulake* Duty," in Chapter Two of *e-Discovery: Current Trends and Cases.*

The hold procedures, even the interim procedures, must also be designed to cover *all* potentially discoverable information maintained by the organization, even the PST files that some "pack rat" employees may have all over the place. Sometimes the preservation obligation may include backup tapes, sometimes not. It depends on the computer systems and the particular case. Most of the time it will not be required. The hold and collection procedures must also be capable of preserving at least some of the ESI metadata. In some instances, it may not be acceptable to have employees copy files to a centralized repository, as that act in itself will change the file date metadata.

As this work begins, the team will become painfully aware of a number of deficiencies in existing systems, including problems with permitted computer use policies, retention policies, and computer systems. There is usually a lack of knowledge about exactly what information the organization has and where it is all located. It is, in effect, a lack of system *metadata,* or data about data. Most companies have only a vague idea of what they know, and who or what knows it. Few have complete, up-to-date knowledge of where all of their electronic information is stored. If you do not know what information you have or where it is all located, how can you possibly preserve it, much less produce it, as required by law?

This common deficiency must be addressed early on by the team. They must take a complete inventory of existing ESI and map it. Then they need to classify the ESI accessibility according to Rule 26(b)(2)(B). When the team looks, they always find that the organization has far more information stored in its systems than management realized, and that much of it is unneeded and should have been destroyed long ago. So then the team works on rehabilitating the organization's overall electronic records management and moves on to destruction of unneeded ESI according to Rule 37(f).

The many deficiencies in existing systems, coupled with the stringent requirements of the law, end up forcing the team to design hold procedures that are difficult to follow, time-consuming, expensive, and disruptive. That is because they must work with what they have and what they know. Frequently it is chaotic. For instance, employees may or may not have their own e-mail archives, or PST files. These files may be located on desktop PCs, laptops, thumb-drives, or CDs kept at home. Some employees may have multiple PST files, all of which now need to be searched and protected from alteration. Some may have none, but they may use their personal e-mail accounts for work from time to time. The process of studying current practices and computer storage systems, and trying to design standard hold procedures that will preserve all discoverable ESI, will inevitably highlight the need to change existing systems so that better, more efficient hold procedures can apply.

The team will not want the stop-gap procedures to be permanent. They are, after all, the people who must follow these protocols and implement the litigation holds. Most teams will recommend adjusting future IT purchases to include preservation criteria, typically adding or improving archiving and indexing software. It may also mean purchasing new software specifically designed to implement and manage litigation holds. The process usually requires a radical overhaul of existing document retention policies and practices and a tightening of permitted computer usage.

After the new policies and systems are in place, the team can then design a final protocol for preservation and collection. It will be far better than the patchwork program first developed, and far less likely to fail and expose the company to sanctions, as in the *Intel* case. It will also be far easier for the now-matured team to operate and to realize significant cost savings in the subsequent steps of ESI collection, analysis, review and production.

Blog Reader Comment

Very interesting blog; however, you are leaving out key member of your e-discovery team, and that would be the records management team. Most if not all IT personnel have no clue about records retention. They have avoided learning about records retention and how it applies to e-records. Records management, in conjunction with the legal department and the business owner of the records, designs, develops and implements the records retention schedule. The problem with e-records and discovery is that for years IT refused to accept the fact the records retention rules applied to what they were doing.

Another Blog Reader Comment

Ralph, love the long-term (as opposed to quick-fix) approach you're taking with thinking deeply about the e-discovery team and the process that's going to be required to drive this change in large enterprises. Here at Clearwell, many of our customers really are breaking new ground in their organizations with regard to putting more rigor and protocol in place around e-discovery (and figuring out how to do that in a collaborative way across the IT, legal, and business constituencies)! For our part, we're being pushed aggressively on the product and technology side to deliver solutions that can be used as a shared resource serving as the core/hub of the e-discovery team, but able to connect with the various "spokes" in a simple but integrated fashion . . . a tall order, to be sure, but one that's going to be critical for maturing the e-discovery process in leading organizations.

TWO NEW ARTICLES OF INTEREST ON E-DISCOVERY TEAMS

I discovered two new articles this week on my favorite subject, indeed the name of my blog, "e-Discovery Teams." The first is a cheerleader kind of easy read by Dave Buss of *Corporate Counsel*[35] magazine. He quotes many in-house counsel who are pleased with their team efforts. The second article is by attorney Eric Friedberg[36] of Stroz Friedberg.[37] It contains legal analysis and insights into the multidisciplinary team approach. Friedberg wrote this article in connection with an event for the Sedona Conference,[38] so you know it is a serious work.

David Buss's Article

Dave Buss's article on e-Discovery Teams is titled "Keeping Your Firm's E-Discovery In-House."[39] It is an informal report based on interviews with in-house attorneys and paralegals already involved with e-Discovery Teams. It highlights a truth already known by everyone in the e-discovery world—that the legal profession is entering a *Revenge of the Nerds*[40] phase of litigation. Buss reviews a few of the benefits of managing e-discovery in-house, as opposed to the more traditional solution of outsourcing everything to lawfirms and vendors.

Buss begins by noting that most corporations are just starting to realize the magnitude of the e-discovery problems they face from runaway electronic records mismanagement. This presents in-house counsel with a question of how to go about solving that problem:

---

35. http://www.law.com/jsp/cc/index.jsp.
36. http://www.strozllc.com/professionals/xprProfessionalDetails1.aspx?xpST=ProfessionalDetail&professional=4.
37. http://www.strozllc.com/.
38. http://www.thesedonaconference.org/.
39. http://www.law.com/jsp/legaltechnology/pubArticleLT.jsp?id=1208169988197.
40. http://en.wikipedia.org/wiki/Revenge_of_the_Nerds.

Corporate counsel first must decide whether to deal with these growing demands in-house, to outsource the function—or to use some combination of internal and external resources.

Many companies still outsource everything, but a few are now doing at least some of the work themselves. They refer out less and less to outside vendors by building a strong, internal e-discovery team to do the work.

The article quotes Thomas Avery, with the e-Discovery Team of Aon Corp., as recommending that "legal departments establish as much as possible of the ESI-management function in-house as swiftly as they can." The senior manager of legal operations for Raytheon Co., Woods Abbott, is said to strongly agree. So too does Patrick Oot, director of electronic discovery and senior litigation counsel for Verizon Communications. Patrick is quoted as saying, "It's difficult to trust a third party with your mission-critical case information." That is one reason Verizon is moving more of its e-discovery process in-house, even including many ESI review tasks. Another factor is the company's projected savings of several million dollars a year.

Another blogger, Jerry Bull, a young e-discovery specialist and consultant in Los Angeles with an IT background, has already written about Buss's article. See his tech-oriented blog, *E-Discovery in the Trenches*.[41] Bull notes the trend to taking it in-house, but also correctly points out a few of the dangers and difficulties in this path:

> IT departments aren't equipped to deal with the high-stakes nature of e-discovery work; and the personnel aren't suited at all to deal with attorneys and attorney requests. I used to be an IT guy, and I can tell you that we are bred with a troubleshooting mindset. Everything is up for experimentation and subject to trial and error (we deal primarily with Microsoft tools, after all). This approach simply doesn't work in litigation.

---

41. http://www.jerrybui.com/edd/.

Still, Bull appears to think it can be done with sufficient support, including full funding and staffing. As he puts it:

> Planning for an in-house staff of e-discovery professionals and a handful of reliable, independent consultants will go a long way in easing the transition.

I agree. An e-Discovery Team needs dedicated, trained players and plenty of time to practice. This is the only way to play competitively in the professional litigation leagues.

Eric Friedberg's Article

This nine-page article by Eric Friedberg, titled "New Electronic Discovery Teams, Roles, and Functions,"[42] is written in the style opposite to Buss's work. It is based on experience and analysis, rather than interviews. It is harder to read, but well worth the effort. Although I disagree with one minor legal statement in the article concerning preservation of "not reasonably accessible" ESI, I agree with everything else, including the meat of the article, his analysis, and insights into e-Discovery Teams.

The article starts with the observation that many of the mistakes made in e-discovery originate from problems in communication between IT and Legal. I call this the "Who's On First"[43] phenomenon of lawyer/tech miscommunication. Friedberg refers to Judge Shira Sheindlin's famous quote from the *Cool Hand Luke* movie: "What we've got here is a failure to communicate."[44] *Zubulake v. U.B.S.*, 229 F.R.D. 422, 424 (S.D. N.Y. 2004).

He sees the best solution to this problem, as do I, in the formation of interdisciplinary corporate e-Discovery Teams:

---

42. http://www.strozllc.com/publications/xprPubSearch.aspx?xpST =PubSearch.

43. http://ralphlosey.wordpress.com/2007/12/15/whos-on-first-new-case-repeats-the-classic-miscommunications-between-law-and-it/.

44. http://www.destgulch.com/movies/luke/luke18.wav.

Compliance with emerging electronic discovery obligations, and conducting electronic discovery in a consistent and efficient manner, requires new cross-disciplinary teams (hereinafter "New Teams"), with updated organizational roles (hereinafter "New Roles") and functions (hereinafter "New Functions"). These New Teams often draw representatives from an organization's in-house legal, IT, compliance, records management, and human resources departments at the corporate and business unit levels, as well as from the outside counsel and the forensic/electronic discovery vendor to whom the company looks for strategic advice.

The article points out a fundamental problem that sometimes dooms new teams to amateur status—insufficient buy-in and funding by upper management. The article points out that differing levels of support by team owners can have a dramatic impact on team effectiveness and morale:

At one end of the spectrum, senior management and the board back and fund a broad mandate to improve records management and electronic discovery processes, and support the requisite change management. In other cases, the New Team members do what they can to coordinate their respective functions but have little budget and less staffing, and struggle in tackling larger initiatives. In such cases, senior management seems to have little understanding of how records management and electronic discovery are increasingly interwoven with corporate governance, ethics, and compliance. While senior management is ultimately responsible for the increased risk inherent in failing robustly to support New Teams, the individual team members on the front lines often feel exposed in attempting to do more with less in an era of rising obligations and multimillion-dollar sanctions.

The above quote demonstrates one of the strong points of this article, which I recommend you read in full; it combines strong theoretical insights with good practical observations.

The article goes on to describe the work of the team, but without the sports analogies I employed in my article "What Game Does an e-Discovery Team Play?"[45] Friedberg focuses on the teamwork needed to create effective litigation hold procedures, new ESI archiving platforms, consistent positions in court, data mapping, and the collection and search of ESI. On these last key functions, which my article refers to as finding and picking up the ball, Friedberg points out a valid issue, or problem, that all teams must face—when and at what point to outsource:

> The key consideration in establishing these New Functions is to determine where the internal IT function leaves off and when outside vendors should be utilized. Even highly competent in-house forensic teams cannot handle spikes in collections required by large civil or regulatory matters, short deadlines, or a confluence of cases. In addition, it is much more difficult to search data effectively than to collect it. There is less external training available for electronic discovery search technologies and methodologies. As a result, in-house personnel typically rely on off-the-shelf software, which may fail to properly search data or to convert data to searchable form. . . .
>
> Many in-house IT personnel, for example, use the Outlook client to search Outlook mail. That client, however, does not search attachments or flag items that it cannot search. New Teams can address these risks by receiving outside consulting advice on acceptable protocols for searching electronic data. Determining where to draw the line between in-house and external resources is not only a technical issue. Cases that are high-profile or in which the prior role of IT has already been criticized may call for the use of independent resources.

True, true. For a good example of this, see *Louis Vuitton Malletier v. Dooney & Bourke, Inc.*, 2006 U.S. Dist. LEXIS 87096 (S.D. N.Y.

---

45. http://ralphlosey.wordpress.com/2008/04/13/what-game-does-an-e-discovery-team-play/.

Nov. 30, 2006). I previously wrote about this case showing incompetence by corporate IT in "Louis Vuitton Sanctioned for Sand-Bagging."[46]

Friedberg's article concludes with a discussion of outside electronic discovery counsel, whom he calls "one of the most important New Team members." Not surprisingly, I agree with that. I think all e-Discovery Teams, even experienced, well-established ones, should include an outside attorney. Since experienced outside counsel typically associate with and represent a number of different corporate teams, they can provide unique perspective and advice to each team they represent. Their independence can also serve an important function. It not only allows them to appear in court to represent the team, but also puts them in the best position to steer the team away from any *Qualcomm*-like disasters. Good outside counsel can make sure the team plays by the rules, even in the big-ticket, high-pressure games where employee players may come under a lot of pressure to win, no matter what the cost.

An outside attorney on the team can help keep the games clean and steer team members away from the kind of temptations that cost Qualcomm its patent, and its general counsel his job. Further, this kind of high-road team participation puts outside counsel in a strong position to protest any questionable calls made by the umpire.

The article also points out the many ways outside counsel can assist a team, including important training functions:

> The right counsel can facilitate the entire New Teams process, providing stewardship and key strategic advice to achieve compliance and help avoid sanctions. Indeed, New Teams are using outside counsel to train in-house Team members on emerging case law and the obligations under the New Rules. Not only does the substantive advice help the New Team, but in the event of an electronic discovery mishap, the training itself demonstrates the organization's good faith, which is a key to avoiding sanctions.

---

46. http://ralphlosey.wordpress.com/2007/01/22/louis-vuitton-sanctioned-for-sand-bagging/.

Friedberg also notes a danger in the use of outside counsel that are also trial counsel. Personally, I do not serve as trial counsel anymore. If I appear of record in a case, it is solely to handle electronic discovery-related issues. Apparently some attorneys still do both, and I admire their genius, but frankly I do not have enough time or talent for both roles. This limitation removes me from conflicts inherent in the dual role and allows me to provide independent advice in the area of my core competency. Friedberg correctly advises a company that uses the same attorney as trial counsel and e-discovery lawyer to beware of possible conflicts of interest inherent in such a dual role:

> First and foremost, a company's outside counsel must have deep expertise in electronic discovery law and strategy. When outside electronic discovery counsel is also trial counsel, the in-house team members should closely consider whether outside counsel's electronic discovery advice will be adversely affected by its role as trial counsel. Such an effect can take the form of over-preserving data so as to avoid any arguments that might, in trial counsel's view, "distract" from the merits of the case. This might be the right strategy in a particular case, but it can also cost the company substantial sums of money and create stockpiles of data that are difficult to manage thereafter.

The article also points out that the e-discovery lawyer may sometimes be called upon to testify in court, and explain to a judge what happened when the team's procedures are challenged. Here the credibility of your e-discovery lawyer becomes very important. Moreover, if a waiver of privilege is required to defend the team, it is easier to limit the scope of the waiver if the e-discovery lawyer played only a limited role in the case.

This is a balanced and well-thought-out article, and not simply a white paper pitch for services. Eric Friedberg also points out a problem with separate e-discovery counsel.

On the other hand, there are clearly inefficiencies in having multiple counsel, and separate electronic discovery counsel can struggle to become fully integrated in the matter so as to render their best advice.

This is very true, which is why it is important to have experienced counsel, capable of working closely with trial counsel to quickly understand the issues in the case.

Another problem, which the article does not point out, is the simple fact that using multiple counsel can be very costly, and may not be practical in smaller or even mid-size cases. The services of specialty e-discovery attorneys, especially ones with sufficient knowledge and skills to serve on an internal corporate e-Discovery Team, can be expensive. There are not that many attorneys with these specialty skills, and all the ones I know carry a high hourly rate. Some cases are simply not worth the expense. Unfortunately, these smaller-dollar-value cases can still have very complex ESI collection and e-discovery issues. The proportionality limits of Rule 26(b)(2)(C) can help, but even so, costly mistakes leading to sanctions can still be made.

Here a company could help itself with retainer agreements and other alternative billing arrangements. *See, e.g.,* the Law.com article[47] on Mark Chandler,[48] general counsel for CISCO, who champions alternative fee arrangements. That way a company could always get good "off the clock" advice on complex issues whenever it is needed, regardless of the size or economics of the case. Otherwise, it is all too easy for a stupid, nothing case to explode into a nightmare and, if your company is the defendant, force a settlement for far more money than it is worth. We have all seen it happen, even with *pro se* cases, where the courts tend to lean over backwards to allow a case to go forward. Having a technology attorney on call with some kind of creative retainer agreement, as Mark Chandler recommends, might be a good way to avoid that trap.

---

47. http://www.law.com/jsp/ihc/PubArticleIHC.jsp?id=1188291741577.
48. http://resources.cisco.com/servletwl3/FileDownloader/vamprod/427311/Mark_Chandler_bio-8-24-07.pdf..

LITIGATION SURVEY SUGGESTS FUTURE OF E-DISCOVERY

A recent survey of more than 300 corporate counsel on litigation issues suggests that the internal team approach to e-discovery is a fast-growing trend for mid- to large-size companies. In 2007, these companies turned primarily to e-discovery vendors, rather than outside counsel, to help form and support these teams. I predict the internal team approach will continue, but in coming years corporations will rely more on independent law firms and consultants to help them rather than e-discovery vendors. Vendors will still be core members of the team, but the lead will be assumed by impartial experts with nothing to sell but their time.

The study in question was sponsored by Fulbright & Jaworski.[49] It surveyed 253 U.S. corporate counsel and 50 U.K. corporate counsel. A copy of the Fulbright & Jaworski Fourth Annual Litigation Trends Survey Findings[50] can be downloaded after filling out a short questionnaire.

Although this is the fourth year Fulbright has commissioned this survey, it is difficult to extrapolate trends, because the demographics of the companies surveyed change each year. For instance, companies with over $1 billion in gross revenues made up 39% of the survey in 2007, but in 2006 they comprised 53%, and in 2005 only 29%. Also, the report does not provide details of the study. For these and other reasons, my suppositions of future trends based on this report could be wrong. On the other hand, this survey provides a unique glimpse of corporate boardroom attitude to litigation that cannot be found anywhere else and gives us some factual basis on current events upon which future trends can be predicted.

The 2007 survey included American and British companies ranging in revenue size from less than $100 million (25%) to between $100 million and $999 million (36%), to more than $1 billion (39%). Many different industrial sectors are included (although financials

---

49. http://www.fulbright.com/.
50. http://www.fulbright.com index.cfm?fuseaction=correspondence. LitTrends07.

are heavily weighted), and a little more than half of the companies are public.

The survey begins by confirming what most litigation attorneys already knew, that litigation overall is down. Still, the number of larger cases, those with $20 million or more at issue, remained about the same as last year. The types of lawsuits that are of most concern to corporate counsel are labor/employment, followed by contracts, regulatory and personal injury. This is the same as prior years. The most active jurisdictions are, once again, Texas, California, and East Coast/New England.

An entire chapter of the survey report is devoted to "E-Discovery/Document Production." The survey at page 22 first notes that e-discovery as an issue of concern is spreading from larger organizations to mid-size and smaller corporations.

The biggest change in e-discovery from 2006 to 2007 is in the percentage of companies using outside e-discovery vendors. For U.S. companies it jumped from 37% to 51%, and for U.K. companies it spiked from 8% to 71%. The percentage of companies retaining law firms with special expertise in e-discovery also increased, but much more modestly. For U.S. companies, it increased from 26% to 30%, and for U.K. companies, from 17% to 32%. Still, this means that almost one-third of the companies surveyed retain law firms, at least in part, for their e-discovery expertise, and demonstrates a consistent growth in this area.

The survey asked a related question as to whether a company has retained, or is now considering retaining, special national or regional e-discovery counsel "specifically for e-discovery issues that arise in matters." Here is the survey report on this key question:

> Taking the survey sample as a whole, those answering in the affirmative jumped from 17% in 2006 to 42% in 2007. It appears companies in the U.K., in particular, are embracing the concept. There were also equally significant increases across the three company size categories.

When you delve more deeply into these statistics, however, you discover a few very interesting surprises not apparent from this summary. First, although the overall increase was from 17% to 42%, the U.S.-based companies only increased from 18% to 39%, while the U.K.-based companies increased from 14% to 60%. Not too surprising when you consider the U.K. is still a few years behind the U.S. in e-discovery. But what *is* surprising is that most of the increase from 17% to 42% came from companies with under $100 million in revenues. They increased from 10% to 69%. That is a sevenfold increase!

Even more surprising, however, is that the larger companies supposedly reversed this trend altogether. Companies with revenues of $100 million to $999 million decreased retention of national e-counsel from 91% to 31%, and the companies with revenues of $1 billion and up decreased that retention from 77% to 48%.

I view these numbers with some skepticism, but assuming they are valid, I think they suggest a trend to internal corporate e-Discovery Teams. First of all, it is extremely unlikely that 91% of mid-sized companies and 77% of large companies employed national or regional e-counsel in 2006. No way! The question posed apparently stated "have or considered retaining" national or regional e-counsel. If these statistics are valid, this must mean that many of the larger companies *considered* going the national e-counsel route in 2006, and then rejected it. Apparently these companies opted instead to employ vendors, and that is one reason why vendors overall saw such a high growth rate in 2007.

To me, these facts suggest that mid- to large-size companies are starting to take their e-discovery work in-house instead of relying on outside counsel to do it for them. This supports what I am seeing, where many companies are starting to explore the option of creating internal e-Discovery Teams. These statistics suggest that most are now relying on outside vendors to help make it happen. Unlike many law firms, vendors have been quick to realize a need for these services. To date, very few law firms have moved into the new team-building approach I advocate. Instead, most firms active in e-discovery still follow the entrepreneurial model of legal services that I discuss in my "Star Trek" essay at the beginning of Chapter Two of this book. Under this model, the law firm does everything for the client, including acting as national or regional e-counsel. I doubt that this model will last much longer, and predict that in a few years only small companies will still support it.

Law firms may be slow to change, but they are smart. They will eventually respond to their clients' needs and embrace the new paradigm of e-discovery services promoted here. Under the e-Discovery Team model, outside counsel serve to empower their clients by helping them to form and operate their own e-Discovery Teams. As this change materializes, I expect the drastic growth rate in vendor usage to level off or even reverse somewhat as attorneys move into this field. Also, I would expect the use of national or regional e-counsel to increase again in the large and mid-size corporations, but this time based on a new client relationship and team functionality. The firms who help put the teams together will naturally stay and serve as national coordinating counsel, and speak for the internal teams that they helped organize and coach.

Admittedly, there is a lot of speculation in these predictions, because the question of internal e-Discovery Team formation was not asked in this survey. Hopefully it will be included in next year's survey.

I acknowledge that there is another explanation for these statistics that does not support the trend to team-based solutions. It could be that mid- to large-size companies are abandoning the national e-counsel idea in favor of hiring e-vendors to do everything, and doing little or none of the work themselves. This is probably true for some, but I doubt the majority are going this route. It is too expensive and too risky, as it abdicates control of key responsibilities of a corporation's legal and IT departments to a third party. Although some vendors would be happy to assume this responsibility, and charge plenty for it, most vendors I have talked to do not want that kind of responsibility. Instead, they seem to agree with the approach I advocate, and prefer to work with corporations to help them set up their own teams.

Smaller corporations with revenues of less than $100 million may not have the resources to establish and run their own team, and it makes sense that they would instead rely on outside counsel or outside vendors to do it all for them. That would explain the overall spike in reliance on outside national e-counsel by smaller corporations, and also help explain the overall growth in vendor usage.

Another very interesting set of facts in the survey pertains to companies' document retention and communication policies. This is the first year the survey has included these questions. The survey found that:

1. 54% of the companies allow instant messaging.
2. 24% allow the attachment of documents to instant messages.
3. 31% log or retain instant messages.
4. 40% retain voice mail.
5. 40% use technology to send voice mail to others via e-mail.
6. 72% allow access to the company network from home.
7. 48% allow use of outside e-mail accounts from company computers.
8. 40% have a chief privacy officer.

Further, although backup retention periods are said to vary widely, the median for all companies was approximately 60 days.

The survey also questioned companies about their attitude to the new rule changes. Twenty-seven percent said it made "handling these issues in federal court more difficult," and only 18% believed it "made the process at least somewhat easier." Sixty percent of both groups reported little change as a result of the new rules. That's got to make the Rules Committee members cringe.

Asked about litigation holds, almost all (98%) of the $1 billion-plus-size companies claim to have one, and almost all size companies are now at least working on it. Eighty-one percent of the U.S. companies and 90% of the U.K. companies have reviewed or revised their hold policies in the past 12 months.

Thanks go to Fulbright & Jaworski for this survey and helping all of us to get a better *hold* on e-discovery.

SURVEY OF RECORDS ADMINISTRATORS SHOWS NEGLIGENT E-RECORDS MANAGEMENT IS CREATING "STUNNING BUSINESS RISKS"

A new survey[51] of records managers by Cohasset[52] reveals continued neglect in the management of electronic records. The survey shows that 40% of organizations do not include electronic records in their retention schedules and 55% do not include e-mails; only 14% always follow their records retention policy; 44% do not include electronic records in their litigation hold procedures; and 46% do not think their electronic records are accurate, reliable or trustworthy. These statistics are amazing to me, especially when you consider this survey is limited to those organizations with full-time professional records managers. It is reasonable to assume that the statistics are far worse for companies that do not have a records management department. The bottom line of the study is:

> The majority of organizations are not prepared to meet many of their current or future compliance and legal responsibilities.
>
> The outstanding challenges associated with the management of electronic information assets have the potential to be devastating in terms of costs, professional careers, and even corporate reputations.
>
> The number and magnitude of organizational and operational problems reflected in the survey findings collectively represent stunning business risks.
>
> The integration of electronic records into the organization's records management program should be a priority, and electronic records control gaps should be the focus of immediate corrective action.

In a hopeful sign for the future, the survey shows that senior management of corporations and governmental entities are begin-

---

51. http://www.merresource.com/downloadWhitepaper.htm?fileId=1.
52. http://www.cohasset.com/.

ning to understand the consequences of this neglect and take steps to resolve it. Also, believe it or not, the survey shows improvement from prior years.

This work has a high degree of credibility and should be a wakeup call for corporate America. It was co-sponsored by the leading professional associations in this area, ARMA[53] (Association of Records Managers and Administrators) and AIIM[54] (Association of Information and Image Management, a/k/a Enterprise Content Management Association). A white paper titled Call for Collaboration,[55] by Robert F. Williams and Lori J. Ashley, reports on the survey. It was based on information from more than 1,600 respondents in 2007 and a total of more than 5,500 respondents in the survey's four prior years—1999, 2001, 2003, and 2005.

Although much of the report is written in polite and correct jargon, it does not mince words as to the significance of most organizations' failure to have a functioning litigation-hold procedure:

> The indisputable fact: an extraordinary number of organizations are negligent with regard to a formal system to ensure records hold orders are successfully administered. For any organization which is the likely target of litigation or regulatory inquiries, the absence of a formal plan to respond to discovery requests must be considered an unacceptable risk. Not having such a system is a legal land mine waiting for detonation. Where there is no formal system for records hold orders in their organizations, records management professionals need to work aggressively with their legal colleagues to correct this significant deficiency.

Another interesting finding is that most IT departments administer electronic documents, but they have no understanding of the basic premise of records management, that all records should have a "life cycle." That is, they are born, have a useful life of some duration

---

53. http://www.arma.org/.
54. http://www.aiim.org/.
55. http://www.merresource.com/downloadWhitepaper.htm?fileId=1.

appropriate for the type of record involved, and then die. In other words, records are only supposed to be retained for as long as they are needed to meet the organization's legal and business requirements. After that, they are supposed to be destroyed or, in some rare instances, as with historical documents, archived for preservation.

The survey shows IT has no clue about "records life cycle" (or at least that is what the records managers think). For this reason, IT tends to treat all electronic records like the original paper U.S. Constitution. They try to archive everything so that it will last forever, usually in multiple, ever-spreading copies. They tend to back-up and preserve electronic records forever, or at least for as long as the latest technology permits, and are lax in the destruction of records. IT fears that the day after they destroy a record, someone in senior management will have a rush demand to retrieve it. The mistaken desire for immortal records has had draconian consequences well described in this report:

- **Higher Storage Costs**—If electronic records are retained without a clearly defined disposition trigger (as determined by an organization's retention schedules), the volume of records will grow rapidly, and that growth will be mirrored in the cost for electronic records storage.
- **Greater Discovery Costs**—Since unnecessarily retained records can be the subject of legal discovery, the costs associated with producing records that should have been destroyed are totally unnecessary expenses.
- **Unwittingly Assisting Plaintiffs**—Unnecessarily retained records can be used against the organization in future litigation. This is potentially the most significant cost.

In line with the fundamental premise of this "e-Discovery Team" blog, the authors of this report recommend that senior management begin to address these problems by forming a "cross-functional Team (business, legal-compliance, IS/IT, records management) and collaborative approach to ensure an integrated and sustainable records management program."

The advice to in-house counsel is similar. They recommend that legal "establish an ongoing interactive relationship with IS/IT and records management regarding the organization's management of its valued information assets, especially electronic records."

I could not agree more. The "stunning business risks" created by the negligent management of electronic records is a high-priority problem. It is too big and too complicated a problem for any one branch of a large organization to solve on its own. It is time for the legal departments, IT, records management and operations management to stop working in isolation. They have to work together on this common task. Every study seems to reach this same conclusion. Only an interdepartmental approach will succeed in fixing this interdepartmental problem. Companies have to begin by forming, and empowering, a cross-functional team with members from each department, what I call an "e-Discovery Team." Only an e-Discovery Team can possibly clear the "legal land mine waiting for detonation" that was uncovered by this study, and many others like it.

Blog Reader Comment

For those of us who work in this arena, these statistics are, regrettably, not really that surprising. We consistently encounter organizations that are paying the price for inadequate records management processes. This price is paid in the form of often significant legal and businesses consequences that ensue from ill-conceived or negligent efforts. Too frequently, still, companies find themselves trying to sort out their electronic data after legal action has started, rather than proactively addressing it as part of a sound records management and retention program. And we heartily endorse the notion of a cross-functional approach to records management that spans the business owners of the data, the legal department, and IT staff. To this we would add the important role played by third party vendors like Cataphora that can provide advanced technologies and significant specialist expertise that reduce the risks and costs that poor or inadequate records management processes entail.

E-DISCOVERY AT THE HARVARD CLUB IN NEW YORK CITY

The stately 19th-century Harvard Club week hosted a cutting-edge 21st-century conference on e-Discovery. It was organized by American Lawyer Media (ALM),[56] which also puts on the Legal Tech[57] trade shows. I was curious to see this private club and happy to speak at this event for New York paralegals and attorneys. I was not disappointed by the wood-paneled Harvard atmosphere or the content of the CLE. The event, titled "Managing Today's Discovery Process,"[58] was well run, thanks to the organizer, Karen Abrams of ALM, and the program chair, Sherry Harris, the senior case management specialist for Hunton & Williams.[59]

David Shonka of the FTC

Before the event, I got a chance to speak with the head of the Federal Trade Commission's[60] e-Discovery Team, David Shonka. David is also the FTC assistant general counsel for litigation. David, like me, didn't go to Harvard and was delighted to see the inside of the Harvard Club for the first time. We started talking about *Qualcomm* and both agreed it was *The Big Case* of the year. He endured my righteous rant about Qualcomm[61] and attorneys who do not play by the rules, the ones who deliberately hide evidence they know should be produced. We also agreed that this kind of unethical conduct was nothing new or unique to e-discovery. It has always gone on, but in the olden days of paper discovery, it was far harder to expose. Today, with electronic discovery, Hide

---

56. http://www.almevents.com/.

57. http://www.legaltechshow.com/r5/cob_page.asp?category_code=ltech.

58. http://www.almevents.com/conf_page.cfm?pt=/CustomerFiles_sri/.agenda/detailed_agenda.cfm&web_page_id=9213&web_id=1089&instance_id= 24&pid=699&iteration_id=795.

59. http://www.hunton.com/home.aspx.

60. http://www.ftc.gov/.

61. http://ralphlosey.wordpress.com/2008/03/10/sanctions-have-been-lifted-against-the-qualcomm-six-and-a-new-trial-ordered-where-they-may-now-speak-freely-to-defend-themselves/.

the Ball is suddenly a high-risk undertaking. David picked up on my somewhat angry tone[63] (over the years I have suspected several opposing counsel of playing this game, but have never been able to prove it). He said that in view of my strong opinions on this topic, I would probably like his presentation.

He was right. The FTC e-Discovery Team leader began with an overview of the incredible facts of the *Qualcomm* case, which I also cover in detail in the Ethics chapter of this book. This was a prelude for the primary message, that there are only three fundamental principles to follow in e-discovery. They are, in his words:

> Don't lie.
> Don't hide things.
> Don't make promises you can't keep.

David pointed out that a law firm's reputation for truth and honesty are key. If David thinks he is dealing with a lawyer who does not follow these fundamental precepts, then the FTC will naturally be much more demanding in its requests for information and harsher in its treatment. Conversely, David is willing to negotiate and exercise leniency when an attorney is honest and forthcoming, and reveals the bad with the good. This attitude, in my experience, is also followed by most judges.

On the point of "don't hide things," he stated that anytime you have to have meetings to try to "figure out an argument why something is not responsive, it is responsive." You should produce it, not try to hide it. Otherwise, in David's words, you risk the principle that "you are known by your last lie." And that reputation will last for a long time. No doubt the boys in the 18th-century Harvard Philosophy and Advocacy Clubs (certificates shown above) would have agreed.

The FTC e-discovery chair stated that, in his view, parties have three general options for responding to discovery:

62. http://ralphlosey.wordpress.com/2008/01/11/qualcomms-monumental-discovery-violations-provokes-only-wimpy-sanctions/.

1. Hardball—prolongs investigation and is costly.
2. Let's-see-if-they-can-find-it—again, prolongs investigation and is costly.
3. Cooperation—fastest, surest results and is the least costly.

David said the third path of "negotiation" is only the way to go for all e-discovery situations, but especially if you are responding to the FTC.

Aside from general principles, David also had some practical advice on e-discovery and how to find the relevant information and not waste your time on non-responsive ESI. Here is his chart of the process he recommends:

Process of Narrowing ESI
1. Preliminarily Identify Issues and Sources of Information:
   a. Key players (12-36 max in any case)
   b. Occasional players (search only if you have to)
   c. Fringe players (rarely ever search)
2. Data
   a. Enterprise systems
   b. Local systems (particular office or groups)
   c. Individual systems
   d. Archives, e-Backups (and Legacy Data)

Most of the time, all of the relevant data needed for a case will be stored on the key players' Enterprise, Local and Individual systems. Sometimes you may also need to look at Archives too, depending on what you find in the more easily accessible stores and how difficult it is to get at the ESI on Archives. Backup tapes and Legacy Data are not usually needed. David explained that the FTC typically requires preservation of only two daily backup taapes, just in case they want to look at them later, which they usually don't. He noted with a chuckle that the FTC picks which two tapes to preserve, not the respondent, and they usually just pick two at random.

On the issue of litigation holds, the FTC team leader recommended that a senior, experienced attorney personally supervise the preservation process and deal with all of the key players directly. This is at odds with the practice of many companies and firms that tend to delegate this task to younger, less experienced attorneys or paralegals. It is probably not a good idea to do that when dealing with the FTC. If a second-year associate messes up, you are not likely to get much sympathy. If an older guy like me screws up (yes, it happens), maybe they will cut you some slack.

On a promising note for large companies, he said that parties and the courts should always remember that companies are not in the business of preserving and holding evidence to produce to adversaries who may someday sue them. If e-discovery becomes so burdensome that it impairs businesses' operations, then something is fundamentally wrong.

David's presentation also included the fundamental message of my blog and books, that building an interdisciplinary team is key to e-discovery compliance. He recommended, as do I, that the team include IT, in-house and outside counsel, and vendors. He also advised that you "get everybody in the same room." Otherwise, you will inevitably play the old child's game of telephone, where a simple message is whispered from one person to the next, and by the time it reaches the last person, it is totally screwed up. He said it may seem expensive to some companies to assemble such a multidisciplinary team and have them meet regularly and in-person, but he is convinced you save money in the long run.

Apparently the FTC has been using such a team approach to e-discovery for several years now, and they are pleased with the results. He told me that they now have two attorneys who only do e-discovery, and they have help from a number of techs and paralegals. Of course, the FTC cannot force companies under investigation to use a team approach and specialized attorneys, but David did say publicly that they will sometimes refuse to meet with a company's lawyers unless they bring the IT liaison with them to the meeting.

David also spoke of the serious risk of relying only on custodians for self-collection. They may print out, or transfer to a disk, but they are likely to do it in a way that messes up the metadata. He stated that metadata is only rarely needed for production, and depends on the case, but you should still try to preserve it as best you can. Still, the main reason you should not rely on custodians alone for collection is that they are "self-interested." They may, for instance, want to avoid embarrassment and not produce certain very relevant e-mails that they wished they had not written. In his opinion, you can do the collection in-house and do not have to hire an outside vendor, but you should use a qualified technician to go to the computers and collect the data. As to forensic imaging, where outside experts are typically used, that is needed only in special cases when there are indications of criminal conduct.

Sherry Harris

Sherry provided the opening keynote address. She has over 30 years' experience with Hunton & Williams[63] and is now the dynamo behind its e-discovery efforts. Although not an attorney, she knows far more about the subject than most experts. She commented on my sports analogy essay on e-discovery, *What Game Does an e-Discovery Team Play,* and said how important it was for paralegals to help make sure the attorneys they support never *drop the ball.* Like almost everyone else, she also talked about *Qualcomm,* and the outside counsel who now stand to be sanctioned. She emphasized that this is something you never want to have happen to your law firm. One way to avoid this is for lawyers and paralegals alike to, in her words, "stay aware of evolving case law." She also said that in her experience, "traditional discovery is gone forever; but right now people are resisting the changes." Her advice: "Make technology your friend."

Vendor Selection and Negotiation

Next, Jennifer Tomaino, attorney member of the Verizon[64] e-Discovery Team, and Oliver Gierke,[65] litigation case manager for White

---

63. http://www.hunton.com/home.aspx.
64. http://www.verison.com/.
65. http://www.whitecase.com/ogierke/.

& Case,[66] presented on Vendor Selection and Negotiation. It would be hard to imagine two people better qualified to speak on that topic. Jennifer is Patrick Oot's "right-hand man" (so to speak) for Verizon, and so has a good perspective on corporate e-Discovery Teams and their procurement of vendor services. Oliver is a key technical member of the White & Case e-Discovery Team, a law firm with 2,300 lawyers in 37 offices located in 25 countries.

Jennifer and Oliver both noted that paralegals play a key role in vendor selection, because they work closely with vendors to get the work done and are in the best position to evaluate performance. They also both commented on how big the e-discovery industry has become, now approaching $3 billion a year.

Jennifer Tomaino stated that Verizon does its own preservation and collection, and vendors do not usually get involved until the processing stage. Verizon is looking to take even more of the e-discovery process in-house in the next few years, and may move into review. In her experience, the review tools that vendors offer are all fairly similar. She cautioned that "technology can help, but is only as good as the people using it."

Jennifer suggested that you look for recommendations from others who have recently used a vendor. Also, you may want to employ a formal two-step procedure where you issue an RFI (request for information) and then an RFP—request for product proposal. She suggested you study the Sedona's sample RFP in their vendor selection paper, but do not simply use the form without thought and customization. Jennifer also noted, and Oliver agreed, that a vendors' project managers are key. They need to provide quality, accessibility and responsiveness. Since Verizon is, in Jennifer's words, a *serial litigant*, they can get the best rates because of the volume. Still, try to be creative in making deals with vendors, who usually charge by the amount of ESI, and/or time. For instance, she suggested trying to get a deal where you only pay for hits, not misses.

Oliver Gierke has found that vendors can offer both expertise and cost control. Their expertise includes: 1) data forensics, which he has never seen done in-house because you may need an inde-

---

66. http://www.whitecase.com/.

pendent expert to testify on authenticity and chain of custody; 2) collection; 3) processing; 4) hosting data for review because most companies and firms do not have the capacity to store large amounts of ESI; 5) production; and 6) consulting. Vendors can provide cost control by: 1) exclusive or long-term contracts at discounted rates; 2) retention of data only when needed; and 3) hiring contract lawyers for review. He thinks that a good vendor can save you a lot of money, although the expenses are front-loaded at the beginning of the case. Oliver also noted a few pitfalls of reliance on outside vendors. Their services are expensive, there is less control than when doing things in-house, and there is more opportunity for miscommunication.

Oliver recommends that you meet with vendors in person and know in advance who will be assigned to the project. You should make sure that the vendors can clearly explain what they will do in a way you can understand and explain to others. Beware of those who speak only in jargon. Also, and many who spoke at the CLE later emphasized this point, be sure to find out if the vendor is going to use subcontractors, and check them out as well. Look out for vendors who get the contract and then subcontract everything out to third parties. Finally, Oliver recommends that you renegotiate pricing with a vendor every 6-12 months. The industry is rapidly changing and prices are going down.

Tom O'Connor

Next up was Tom O'Connor,[67] who spoke on Cost Containment Strategies. Tom is an independent consultant from New Orleans and the director of the Legal Electronic Document Institute,[68] a nonprofit he organized. Tom noted that Gartner,[69] the technology consulting company, estimates that 20% of the e-discovery companies existing today will be out of business in a year. He suspects many of the rest will be lost through consolidation, with a few big companies buying all of the rest.

67. http://legal-edocs.org/TomOConnorBio.htm.
68. http://www.Gulfltc.org/.
69. http://www.gartner.com/.

Tom opined that process management is key to cost containment. You need to set up best practices that are repeatable, yet still flexible. Tom also pointed out the inherent tension between in-house counsel trying to preserve costs and outside counsel, who must answer to the judge and who have an ethical duty to the client and the court. Again he talked about *Qualcomm*, but pointed out that this is nothing new; there are many cases driven by this conflict.

The part of Tom's presentation I liked most was his discussion of the paradigm shift now in progress in e-discovery, as a mirror of the world. The old paradigm was based on single-page TIFF with Bates numbers, and review as single pages. It thought of documents in terms of paper pages. The new paradigm is native-file-based, where you produce, process and review in native format. Our idea of a "document" should completely change. It is all bits and bytes now. Stop treating it like paper, where you Bates stamp each page. Under what Tom calls the new "docucentric" paradigm, you set up a unified, enterprise-wide, relational database with data extraction as needed. Under the new system you automatically extract metadata fields and do de-duplicating, near de-duplicating, and other processing. He thinks that good content management systems are key to making this happen. The new native ESI paradigm is faster, more efficient, and far less expensive than old paper concept systems.

I agree with Tom wholeheartedly on these new native paradigm insights. Tom said that many object to "going native" because they think you need TIFF and Bates numbers in order to preserve authenticity and stay organized. Tom thinks that the Bates stamp has been replaced conceptually by hash[70] and cited to my law review article, "HASH: The New Bates Stamp."[71] He thought I was going to speak about that later (I wasn't). The bottom line for Tom is that there is a huge cost reduction possible by eliminating TIFF and working in native. Tom claims it is in the range of 30%–40%, but notes that some vendors claim the savings is more like 80%–90%.

---

70. http://ralphlosey.wordpress.com/computer-hash-5f0266c4c326b9 alef9e39cb78c352dc/.

71. http://ralphlosey.files.wordpress.com/2007/09/hasharticlelosey.pdf..

Afternoon Program

Next came lunch, followed by my presentation: "e-Discovery Teams: the New Gold Standard." I explained why corporations and law firms are moving to the multidisciplinary team approach, and corporations, especially, are taking it in-house. I covered the benefits of the team approach, and why so many companies are having trouble doing it. Everyone seems to agree it is the Holy Grail of e-discovery, but just like the mythical chalice, it is nearly impossible to find. I had a good time, because the attendees were very attentive and laughed at the right times. As a plus, I got to use my new Macbook Air[72] and Keynote 2008[73] presentation software.

After me came several good presentations, but they will be short-changed in this essay simply because I was too tired after my work to focus and take notes of what they said. Scott M. Cohen,[74] director of practice support for Proskauer Rose,[75] presented with Dottie Perillo, a paralegal from Dupont's[76] e-Discovery Team. They spoke on a subject close to mine, "Achieving a State of Litigation Readiness—Bringing About Effective Dialogue Between Inside and Outside Counsel and the IT Department." I do recall meeting Scott the night before and trading old computer stories. I do not run into that many people who remember my first computer, the TI-99/4A,[77] nor appreciate how amazing it was to be able to program both speech and animation on it back in 1981. Scott is also one of the few people I have met who actually used the whistle in the Captain Crunch cereal boxes as part of his telephony research[78] when he was a kid in high school.

Next came the unforgettable Monica Bay,[79] editor-in-chief of *Law Technology News*.[80] Her topic was "How EDD Is Changing the

---

72. www.youtube.com/watch?v=GBCfW9-hjKI.
73. http://www.apple.com/iwork/keynote/.
74. http://www.proskauer.com/lawyers_at_proskauer/atty_data/7438.
75. http://www.proskauer.com/index.html.
76. http://www2.dupont.com/DuPont_Home/en_US/index.html.
77. http://oldcomputers.net/ti994a.html.
78. http://en.wikipedia.org/wiki/John_Draper.
79. http://commonscold.typepad.com/about.html.
80. http://www.lawtechnews.com/r5/home.asp.

Job Market." I remember her strong presence and unbridled enthusiasm, but not enough of the content about the job market to try to summarize it. I think she said it was in fast transition, and right now no one is too sure where it is going. The only thing clear is that paralegals with good computer e-discovery skills are in very strong demand, and this demand is certain to increase. I also recall her scolding many blue chip law firms for not being inclusive enough of paralegals and IT. She also talked about Darwin and survival of the most agile, and that if the old-line big firms did not change fast and form bona fide interdisciplinary teams, that they will go the way of the dinosaur. They will not be able to compete, and their long-term clients will leave them for more agile specialists, ones not hung up on attorney old-boy networks. No, she does not mince words.

Kenton Hutcherson,[81] a sole practitioner from Dallas whom I had met before at Sedona, presented on using metadata to uncover Hide the Ball tactics by the other side. He told a story about a case he had just out of law school, a few years ago. He took a case all of the partners said was a loser and achieved a favorable settlement by analyzing the metadata in load files the defendant produced. He discovered what appeared to be intentional duplication of irrelevant files, coupled with attempts to bury the hot files. Kent then used a killer ESI spoliation motion to force a high settlement.

Kent says that he later heard both outside and in-house counsel were fired because of that case. One presumes it was because their fraud was exposed, but maybe it was just because they lost, not on the merits, but because of e-discovery blunders. In any event, I felt sorry for Kent because his PowerPoint did not work properly, probably because of the Microsoft version issues, and the fact that the laptop furnished by ALM was accidentally loaded with a trial version of Vista. Personally, I now always bring my own MacAir, but even then you can still face difficulties because it sometimes won't work with old projectors. The e-discovery presentation world is much like e-discovery itself: if something can go wrong, it usually does, and so it always pays to have a backup plan (or two).

---

81. http://www.hutchersonlaw.com/professionals-hutcherson.php.

Blog Reader Comment

Dave Shonka was right on the mark related to allowing clients to collect their own data, especially when both sides agree. It was refreshing to have him confirm what many believe. I can't tell you how many times I've heard from vendors the importance of allowing them to collect data in a forensically sound manner, rather than allowing the client's IT department to do so. There is so much FUD (fear, uncertainty and doubt) on this subject that it is mind-numbing.

TWO E-DISCOVERY GUIDES FOR JUDGES PROVIDE GOOD ADVICE FOR ALL

There are now two e-discovery guides for judges, one for state court judges and one for federal. Everyone involved in e-discovery, not just judges, should become familiar with these guidelines. After all, the judge who decides your case may consult one of these guides, or you may want to cite to them to support your argument.

The Federal Judges' Guidebook

The newest guide, *Managing Discovery of Electronic Information: A Pocket Guide for Judges*,[82] was released in late January 2008. It was written *for* federal judges *by* federal judges, namely Judge Barbara J. Rothstein and Judge Ronald J. Hedges, with the help of Elizabeth C. Wiggins, an educator of federal judges. The *Pocket Guide* was published by the Federal Judicial Center,[83] the education and research arm of the federal court system. The chairman of the board of the Federal Judicial Center is none other than the Chief Justice of the Supreme Court, currently Justice John Roberts.[84]

---

82. http://ralphlosey.files.wordpress.com/2008/02/pocketguidefor judges.pdf.
83. http://www.fjc.gov/.
84. http://www.supremecourtus.gov/about/biographiescurrent.pdf.

The lead author is Judge Barbara Rothstein. She has been the director of the Federal Judicial Center[85] since 2003 and has a strong interest in electronic discovery. Her co-author, Judge Hedges, is a former magistrate judge in New Jersey who is well known in e-discovery circles. Judges Hedges retired from the bench in 2007 to go into private practice as an e-discovery lawyer for Nixon Peabody.[86] The third co-author, Elizabeth Wiggins, J.D., Ph.D., is a project director and senior research associate at the Federal Judicial Center.

The *Pocket Guide* tries to persuade federal judges to be much more proactive in the management of e-discovery. As Judge Rothstein explains in her Preface, the *Pocket Guide* encourages judges to take the initiative in e-discovery issues:

> It [the *Pocket Guide*] encourages judges to actively manage those cases involving ESI, raising points for consideration by the parties rather than awaiting the parties' identification and argument of the matters.

With a few notable exceptions, this is currently *not* the practice in most district courts. In fact, very few federal judges have even modified their standard form Case Management Order to implement the new rules. Further, unless the parties raise ESI issues, they are rarely mentioned in Rule 16(b) conferences. Typically, judges wait until e-discovery disputes are raised by the parties. All too often, this still happens near the end of the discovery process and not the beginning, as the new rules contemplate. The bar has been slow to embrace the requirement that e-discovery issues be fully discussed at Rule 26(f) attorney conferences. This is primarily because most attorneys do not understand e-discovery, are not sure what to say, and may not even know for sure whether their case involves electronically stored information. (Hint: it almost certainly does.) They

---

85. http://www.fjc.gov/public/home.nsf/autoframe?openform&url_l=/public/home.nsf/inavgeneral?openpage&url_r=/public/home.nsf/pages/102.
86. http://www.nixonpeabody.com/attorneys_detail1.asp?ID=1324.

need "encouragement" from the bench, which is exactly what the authors of the *Pocket Guide* recommend at page 4:

> All too often, attorneys view their obligation to "meet and confer" under Federal Rule of Civil Procedure 26(f) as a perfunctory exercise. When ESI is involved, judges should insist that a meaningful Rule 26(f) conference take place and that a meaningful discovery plan be submitted.

The *Pocket Guide* includes a chart summarizing the topics that attorneys should discuss (remember, this is a 26-page pocket guide intended for quick reference, not a detailed text):

Discussion topics for a Rule 26(f) conference:

- What ESI is available and where it resides.
- Ease/difficulty and cost of producing information.
- Schedule and format of production.
- Preservation of information.
- Agreements about privilege or work-product protection.

The guide also identifies the reoccurring problems inherent in e-discovery so that judges will know what questions to ask and have a better appreciation of the issues. Here is the chart included in the Introduction at page 4 as a reminder to judges of how ESI differs from paper information:

How ESI differs from paper information:

- Volume.
- Variety of sources.
- Dynamic quality.
- Hidden information: metadata and embedded data.
- Dependent on system that created it.
- Deleting doesn't delete it.

The *Pocket Guide* explains how these differences make litigation holds imperative, often lead to disputes concerning the scope of discovery, make document reviews difficult, and make inadvertent production of privileged information much more likely. The important problem of proportionality is also discussed at page 5.

In addition, because deleted or backup information may be available, parties may request its production, even though restoring, retrieving, and producing it may require expensive and burdensome computer forensic work that is out of proportion to the reasonable discovery needs of the requesting party.

Rule 26(b)(2)(B)&(C) apply the proportionality principle for hard-to-access ESI and require a balancing test. The guide at page 8 properly suggests that judges first require the parties to search the available, easy-to-access ESI before even considering an expensive search of relatively inaccessible data.

When hard-to-access information is of potential interest, the court should encourage lawyers to negotiate a two-tiered approach in which they first sort through the information that can be provided from easily accessed sources and then determine whether it is necessary to search the less-accessible sources.

The *Pocket Guide* points out the seven factors judges should consider in a balancing test as to whether the benefits of production outweigh the burdens, as delineated in the Commentary to Rule 26(b)(2)(C).[87] It goes on to suggest a variety of available tools to assist in weighing these factors, including prior full review of the reasonably accessible sources, specific and tailored discovery requests, use of sampling techniques, discovery on these discovery issues, and cost shifting.

---

87. http://ralphlosey.wordpress.com/rule-26/.

The federal guide reviews all of the new rules on e-discovery in a similar manner. If you have not already studied the rules in depth, this would be a good place to start. To those already well versed in the rules, the *Pocket Guide* contains no surprises, just good common-sense advice on the meaning and application of the rules.

Pages 17 and 18 of the *Pocket Guide* address the issue of preservation orders. This important issue is addressed in the Comments to Federal Rule 26(f), and also in the state judges' guidebook. I will discuss these various approaches to preservation orders, including that of the Sedona Conference, together at the end of this essay.

The State Judges' Guidebook

An earlier state court judges' guide on e-discovery was completed in August 2006. It is called the *Conference of Chief Justices Guidelines for State Trial Courts Regarding Discovery of Electronically-Stored Information.*[88] The Conference of Chief Justices[89] is composed of the highest judicial officer of the 50 states and U.S. territories. It is designed to provide a forum for the top state court judges:

> . . . to meet and discuss matters of importance in improving the administration of justice, rules and methods of procedure, and the organization and operation of state courts and judicial systems, and to make recommendations and bring about improvements on such matters.

One such matter they considered important to the administration of justice was e-discovery. For that reason, they sponsored panels of experts to meet over a lengthy period to develop e-discovery guidelines for all state court judges. The public was also provided ample time for comments, and eventually the panels proposed 10 guidelines that were adopted by the Conference of Chief Justices. The *Chief Justice Guidelines*[90] are not binding law in any state but are

---

88. http://ralphlosey.files.wordpress.com/2008/02/chiefjusticesguide.pdf.
89. http://ccj.ncsc.dni.us/.
90. http://ralphlosey.files.wordpress.com/2008/02/chiefjusticesguide.pdf.

still important because they are endorsed by this prestigious body. They serve as an influential reference in state courts until such time as the states enact their own versions of the federal rules governing e-discovery. To date, very few have done so, although, as mentioned in the essay at the end of the "Rules" chapter of this book, California and many other states are now in the middle of this often politically charged process.

The Introduction to the *Chief Justice Guidelines* includes an explanation of its purpose:

> Until recently, electronic discovery disputes have not been a standard feature of state court litigation in most jurisdictions. However, because of the near universal reliance on electronic records both by businesses and individuals, the frequency with which electronic discovery–related questions arise in state courts is increasing rapidly, in all manner of cases. Uncertainty about how to address the differences between electronic and traditional discovery under current discovery rules and standards "exacerbates the problems. Case law is emerging, but it is not consistent and discovery disputes are rarely the subject of appellate review."
>
> These Guidelines are intended to help reduce this uncertainty in state court litigation by assisting trial judges faced with dispute over e-discovery in identifying the issues and determining the decision-making factors to be applied.

The guidelines begin with a definition of electronically stored information (ESI). Although I think the federal rules were right not to define ESI at all, since technology changes so rapidly, the chief justices did a better job with the definition than the Uniform Law commissioners later did in their proposed model state court rules. I discussed this in my essay on the Uniform Law Commission proposals in Chapter Three of my first book, and in this book at the end of the "Rules" chapter as part of my article on the proposed new California rules. The *Chief Justice Guidelines* define ESI as:

any information created, stored, or best utilized with computer technology of any type. It includes but is not limited to data; word-processing documents; spreadsheets; presentation documents; graphics; animations; images; e-mail and instant messages (including attachments); audio, video, and audiovisual recordings; voice-mail stored on databases; networks; computers and computer systems; servers; archives; back-up or disaster recovery systems; discs, CD's, diskettes, drives, tapes, cartridges and other storage media; printers; the Internet; personal digital assistants; handheld wireless devices; cellular telephones; pagers; fax machines; and voice-mail systems.

The *Chief Justice Guidelines* take the same "laundry list" approach to defining ESI that was earlier taken by the ABA in its 2004 Civil Discovery Standards.[91] The official Comment to the *Chief Justice Guidelines* states, however, that the list "should be considered as illustrative rather than limiting, given the rapid changes in formats, media, devices, and systems." How true!

The state guidelines then address the duty of lawyers to understand their clients' IT systems whenever ESI is involved in a case. This is often called the *Zubulake* duty, because it was so forcefully stated by Judge Scheindlin in *Zubulake V.* This is discussed in depth in Chapter Two of my first book, *e-Discovery: Current Trends and Cases.* The chief justices advise the state court judges at page 1 of the guidelines that:

In any case in which an issue regarding the discovery of electronically-stored information is raised or is likely to be raised, a judge should, when appropriate, encourage counsel to become familiar with the operation of the party's relevant information management systems, including how information is stored and retrieved.

---

91. http://www.abanet.org/litigation/discoverystandards/.

The guidelines go on to state that if a party intends to seek ESI in a case, then:

> that fact should be communicated to opposing counsel as soon as possible and the categories or types of information to be sought should be clearly identified.

When a party to a case does not follow this guidance, and instead waits until near the close of discovery to make ESI demands, judges should be skeptical. This could be a discovery tactic, a trap designed to try to win a case by charges of spoliation rather than on the merits. If a party wants ESI, they should ask for it early and clearly. They should not be allowed to lull the other side into a sense of complacency by their silence and wait until the end of a case to make ESI production demands, hoping that perhaps some ESI will be lost in the interim. Cases should be won or lost or settled based on the merits of the case, not discovery tactics or inadvertent spoliation. That is exactly what this guideline is trying to accomplish.

Many state court rules do not include mandatory discovery conferences between counsel at the start of a case or mandatory initial disclosure of information. For that reason, the state judge Guideline Three talks in terms of judges *encouraging* counsel to meet and confer about e-discovery and exchange information. But Guideline Three at pages 2-3 also includes a fairly exhaustive list of eight categories of information that judges may want to *order* the parties to provide to each other so as to facilitate agreement on e-discovery issues:

(1) A list of the person(s) most knowledgeable about the relevant computer system(s) or network(s), the storage and retrieval of electronically stored information, and the backup, archiving, retention, and routine destruction of electronically stored information, together with pertinent contact information and a brief description of each person's responsibilities;

(2) A list of the most likely custodian(s), other than the party, of relevant electronic data, together with pertinent contact information, a brief description of each custodian's responsi-

bilities, and a description of the electronically stored information in each custodian's possession, custody, or control;

(3) A list of each electronic system that may contain relevant electronically stored information and each potentially relevant electronic system that was operating during the time periods relevant to the matters in dispute, together with a general description of each system;

(4) An indication whether relevant electronically stored information may be of limited accessibility or duration of existence (e.g., because they are stored on media, systems, or formats no longer in use, because it is subject to destruction in the routine course of business, or because retrieval may be very costly);

(5) A list of relevant electronically stored information that has been stored offsite or off-system;

(6) A description of any efforts undertaken, to date, to preserve relevant electronically stored information, including any suspension of regular document destruction, removal of computer media with relevant information from its operational environment and placement in secure storage for access during litigation, or the making of forensic image backups of such computer media;

(7) The form of production preferred by the party; and

(8) Notice of any known problems reasonably anticipated to arise in connection with compliance with e-discovery requests, including any limitations on search efforts considered to be burdensome or oppressive or unreasonably expensive, the need for any shifting or allocation of costs, and the identification of potentially relevant data that is likely to be destroyed or altered in the normal course of operations or pursuant to the party's document retention policy.

Guideline Four then suggests that after this exchange of information, the judge hold a discovery hearing to address any disputes or remaining e-discovery issues. This seems like a very sensible approach.

Guideline Five address the scope of discovery and establishes a balancing test as to whether requested information should be produced. This is similar to the seven factors listed in the Comments to federal Rule 26(b)(2)(B)&(C), but much more exhaustive. The *Chief Justice Guidelines* list 13 factors based on the earlier ABA Civil Discovery Standards.

Guideline Six concerns form of production and tracks the language then under consideration for use in the federal rules, namely production in either the form "ordinarily maintained" or in a "reasonably usable" form. Like federal Rule 34(b), the state guidelines also limit ESI production to one format.

Guideline Seven covers the reallocation of discovery costs. It basically embodies the analysis conducted in *Zubulake III* (*Zubulake v. UBS Warburg LLC*, 216 F.R.D. 280 (S.D. N.Y. 2003)).

Guideline Eight governs the inadvertent disclosure of privileged information. It does not include clawback-type protections and presumptions against inadvertent waiver, as Rule 26(b)(5)(B) does, but does suggest that state court judges be careful in finding waiver of privilege and first consider:

A. The total volume of information produced by the responding party;

B. The amount of privileged information disclosed;

C. The reasonableness of the precautions taken to prevent inadvertent disclosure of privileged information;

D. The promptness of the actions taken to notify the receiving party and otherwise remedy the error; and

E. The reasonable expectations and agreements of counsel.

The Ninth Guideline is on preservation orders, which I will discuss at the end; but first the Tenth Guideline, on sanctions. This guideline closely tracks federal Rule 37(f) (which has since been renumbered 37(e)), the so-called "safe harbor" rule protecting routine, good-faith destruction of ESI before notice of a dispute.

Preservation Orders: State, Federal, and Sedona Guidelines

The issue of preservation orders, and when they should be issued by judges, is complex. For that reason, I think it helps to consider the exact language used on this subject by the federal *Pocket Guide*, the state *Chief Justices Guidelines*, and the Sedona Conference[92] commentary.

First, the Ninth Guideline for state court judges on preservation orders reads as follows:

A. When an order to preserve electronically stored information is sought, a judge should require a threshold showing that the continuing existence and integrity of the information is threatened. Following such a showing, the judge should consider the following factors in determining the nature and scope of any order:

(1) The nature of the threat to the continuing existence or integrity of the electronically stored information;

(2) The potential for irreparable harm to the requesting party absent a preservation order;

(3) The capability of the responding party to maintain the information sought in its original form, condition, and content; and

(4) The physical, technological, and financial burdens created by ordering preservation of the information.

B. When issuing an order to preserve electronically stored information, a judge should carefully tailor the order so that it is no broader than necessary to safeguard the information in question.

Contrast this with the advice provided to federal judges in the *Pocket Guide:*

In some cases, a preservation order that clearly defines the obligations of the producing party may minimize the risk

---

92. http://www.thesedonaconference.org/.

that relevant evidence will be deliberately or inadvertently destroyed, may help ensure information is retrieved when it is most accessible (i.e., before it has been deleted or removed from active online data), and may protect the producing party from sanctions. . . .

Because a blanket preservation order may unduly interfere in a party's day-to-day operations, may be prohibitively expensive, and may actually compound the information to be searched and produced, any order should be narrowly drawn to preserve relevant matter without imposing undue burdens. Early in the case, the court should discuss with the parties whether an order is needed and, if so, the scope, duration, method of data preservation, and other terms that will preserve relevant matter without imposing undue burdens.

A closing note about preservation orders: Courts are divided as to the standard for issuance of preservation orders. One line of cases holds that preservation orders are, in effect, case-management orders and are governed by Rule 16(b).[28] A few cases have handled preservation orders as injunctions.[29]

28. *See, e.g., Treppel*, 2006 WL 278170, *7; Capricorn Power Co. v. Siemens Westinghouse Power Corp., 220 F.R.D. 429, 433-34 (W.D. Pa. 2004); Pueblo of Laguna, 60 Fed. Cl. at 138 n.8.

29. *See, In re,* African-American Slave Descendants' Litig., 2003 U.S. Dist. LEXIS 12016, *7-8 (N.D. Ill. July 15, 2003).

Finally, consider the language of the Sedona Conference on this issue, contained in Comment 5.f. to *The Sedona Principles Addressing Electronic Document Production,*[93] Second Edition (June 2007):

In general, courts should not issue a preservation order over objection unless the party requesting such an order demon-

93. http://www.thesedonaconference.org/dltForm?did=TSC_PRINCP _2nd_ed_607.pdf..

strates its necessity, which may require an evidentiary hearing in some circumstances. Because all litigants are obligated to preserve relevant evidence in their possession, custody, or control, a party seeking a preservation order must first demonstrate a real danger of evidence destruction, the lack of any other available remedy, and that a preservation order is an appropriate exercise of the court's discretion.

That said, jointly stipulated preservation orders may aid the discovery process by defining the specific contours of the parties' preservation obligations. Before any preservation order is issued, the parties should meet and confer to discuss the scope and parameters of the preservation obligation. Whether agreed to or ordered over objection, preservation orders should be narrowly tailored to require preservation of documents and electronically stored information that are nonduplicative and relevant to the case, without unduly interfering with the normal functioning of the affected party's operations and activities, including the operation of electronic information systems.

Ex parte preservation orders should rarely be entered. Such orders violate the principle that responding parties are responsible for preserving and producing their own electronically stored information. More generally, preservation orders rarely should be issued over objection, and only after a full and fair opportunity to present evidence and argument. This is particularly important when dealing with electronically stored information that may be transitory, not reasonably accessible, or not susceptible to reasonable preservation measures.

Usually, neither the party seeking a preservation order nor the court will have a thorough understanding of the other parties' computer systems, the electronic data that is available, or the mechanisms in place to preserve that electronic data. For example, courts sometimes believe that backup tapes are inexpensive and that preservation of tapes is not burdensome. However, backup systems and technologies vary greatly. Without information about the specifics of the backup system in use, it is difficult to tell what steps are reasonable to meet the needs of the case.

The 2006 amendments to the Federal Rules carefully balance the need to discourage unnecessary, premature and/or overbroad preservation orders with the need to prevent the loss of information important to the litigation and to help parties who sought to memorialize agreements on the scope of their preservation obligations. As set forth in the Committee Note to Rule 26(f), "[T]he requirement that the parties discuss preservation does not imply that courts should routinely enter preservation orders. A preservation order entered over objections should be narrowly tailored. Ex parte preservation orders should issue only in exceptional circumstances." Rule 26(b)(2)(B) was also amended to make it clear that either party may seek immediate relief in connection with preservation obligations.

The *Sedona Principles* commentaries on this issue are well reasoned and more detailed than either the state or federal guides. I urge all judges, both state and federal, to supplement their guides with the *Sedona Principles*, not only on the preservation order issue, but on all issues.

All of the guides counsel against the imposition of preservation orders without a proper evidentiary showing of need. I think that the reasoning of *In re African-American Slave Descendants' Litig.* is correct, and preservation orders are injunctions. For this reason, all of the due process protections that apply to injunctions and protect enjoined parties should also apply to preservation orders, including bond requirements. The *Pocket Guide* recognizes a split in case law on this issue but does not decide it. Judges faced with this issue will be forced to decide. I urge the judiciary to err on the side of caution and treat preservation orders with the same care and caution afforded any injunctive relief.

TRIAL LAWYERS TURN A BLIND EYE TO THE TRUE CAUSE OF THE E-DISCOVERY MORASS

A distinguished group of trial lawyers recently completed a study on litigation that concluded that the main problem with the U.S. legal system today is e-discovery (see Interim Report & 2008 Litigation Survey[94]). Not too unexpectedly, they placed the blame squarely on poor rules, bad law, and judges. They overlook their own role in the problem. The report does not even acknowledge lawyer incompetence with technology as one of causes of the morass. Like the profession as a whole, including most law schools, they are blinded by their own shadow.[95] They have not yet realized the insights of Walt Kelly,[96] who said, in *Pogo*, "We have met the enemy and he is us."

I agree with the eminent trial lawyers and academics who conducted this study that our rules and law need reform, and our judges need to do a better job. But in my opinion, the fundamental cause of the e-discovery problem is the failure of the legal profession, especially the trial bar, to keep up with the rapid changes in technology. That is why new rules and legislation alone will never fix the problem. Such reforms must be coupled with an aggressive attorney education program that starts in law school. Some law firms today are starting to awaken to this problem and set up internal training programs. So too are a few law schools. But the vast majority of our profession still refuses to own up to the competency issue. They either ignore the problem of e-discovery altogether, like most academics, or they acknowledge the problem, like this report does, and then blame anyone other than themselves.

Interim Report & 2008 Litigation Survey

This interim report, aside from its competency shadow-blindness, is excellent and well written. It is a joint project of the American College of Trial Lawyers[97] task force on discovery and the Institute for

---

94. http://www.du.edu/legalinstitute/form-ACTL-survey.html.
95. http://en.wikipedia.org/wiki/Shadow_(psychology).
96. http://en.wikipedia.org/wiki/Walt_Kelly.
97. http://www.actl.com.

the Advancement of the American Legal System,[98] a group based out of the University of Denver. I applaud these groups for recognizing the problem and trying to do something about it. Their insights go well beyond e-discovery, and I recommend a full reading.

This is an interim draft report. Hopefully, they will take these criticisms as constructive and revise the final report to address the competency and education issues. Here is how they begin the report:

> The joint study grew out of a concern that discovery is increasingly expensive and that the expense and burden of discovery are having substantial adverse effects on the civil justice system. There is a serious concern that the costs and burdens of discovery are driving litigation away from the court system and forcing settlements based on the costs, as opposed to the merits, of cases. Recalling that one of the original purposes of the discovery rules was to avoid surprises and to streamline trials, many are now concerned that extensive and burdensome discovery jeopardizes the goal of Rule 1 of the Federal Rules of Civil Procedure and of the rules in those jurisdictions that have adopted similar procedures: a "just, speedy, and inexpensive determination of every action and proceeding." In fact, 81 percent of the respondents to the survey conducted by the Task Force said the civil justice system was too expensive and 69 percent said that it took too long to resolve cases.

I certainly agree with all of these points. The report then goes on to share the results of a survey conducted of the practicing attorney members of the American College of Trial Lawyers. This is a balanced group of plaintiff and defense-oriented trial lawyers who must be nominated for membership and are screened for competency. It is considered an honor to distinguish yourself enough to be invited to join. The College surveyed all of its 3,812 "Fellows," as they are called, and 1,494 responded—a pretty high rate. The report brags

---

97. http://www.du.edu/legalinstitute/.

that, on average, the respondents "had been practicing law for 38 years." Of course, what this means is that this is a very old group.

Correlation Between Age and Tech Savvyness

In my experience, as a general rule, the older you are, the more clueless you are about technology. Look at Senator John McCain, for instance, who candidly admits[99] he cannot use a computer and relies entirely on his wife. In fact, one of his young advisers insisted and even bragged, with a straight face, that McCain is indeed *aware* of the Internet.[100] This age/tech-ignorance correlation is especially true with trial lawyers, who tend to focus all of their technical attention upon the finer points of persuasion and the law, not on computers and algorithms. After all, if they had liked math and science, they would have gone to medical school.

I have been a trial lawyer myself for most of my career. To be honest, although I was pretty good at it, I was usually too distracted and interested in computers and technology to be one of the greats, not to mention the fact that my cases almost never actually went to trial. One side or another would almost always blink at the last minute and decide not to roll the dice on a judge or jury. I stopped doing general litigation work entirely more than two years ago so that I could devote myself full-time to what I really love, e-discovery.

In my work as a litigator, I have been fortunate enough to get to know many great, honest-to-God trial lawyers. They are a smart and gregarious group, but most are almost totally inept when it comes to computers. Some even secretly still use their secretaries to send e-mail. In fact, I recently heard about a senior litigation partner in a top national firm (not my own) who sent out a memo to his young associates asking if any of them knew how to use "the Google"[101] to try to find out something for him. Of course, they all found that hilarious. Well, at least the senior partner had heard of Google and knew it might be useful, even if he had never actually used it himself (way too complicated). I suspect that this same partner is prob-

99. http://www.youtube.com/watch?v=_R9wnMVZE_Q&feature=related.
100. http://www.youtube.com/watch?v=tYs8X0DZNI4.
101. http://www.youtube.com/watch?v=tYs8X0DZNI4.

ably a member of the College of Trial Lawyers and no doubt a big supporter of Senator McCain.

Don't get me wrong: these trial lawyers are probably all terrific in a courtroom, and could clean my clock in any jury trial. Just don't ever ask them to turn on a computer, much less process and review ESI in an economical manner. To them it is just a big nightmare, primarily, I propose, because they are on foreign ground and do not know what they are doing.

The Fellows Analyze Litigation

Here is how these College of Trial Lawyer Fellows analyze the problem with litigation in the 21st century:

> The discovery system is, in fact, broken. Discovery costs far too much and has become an end in itself. As one respondent noted: "The discovery rules in particular are impractical in that they promote full discovery as a value above almost everything else." Electronic discovery, in particular, clearly needs a serious overhaul. It is described time and time again as a "morass." Concerning electronic discovery, one respondent stated, "The new rules are a nightmare. The bigger the case, the more the abuse and the bigger the nightmare."
>
> In particular, 87 percent agree that electronic discovery, in particular, is too costly, and 76 percent agree that electronic discovery issues are not well understood by judges.

So the blame game begins, and the "new rules" and judges are the prime suspects. In fact, the new rules, if properly understood, are a powerful tool to help us all out of the morass. The other easy target is our underpaid judges. *They* should fix things *for us*. On that point the report states:

> Judges should take more active control of litigation from the beginning. Where abuses occur, judges are perceived to be less than effective in enforcing the rules. According to one respondent, "Judges need to actively manage each case from the outset to contain costs; nothing else will work."

I do agree with this point. Judges should be more active, especially to help manage costs, and, as I have often pointed out, they should not "wimp out" in the face of intentional abusive conduct by counsel. Still, judges need to be educated first, just like the rest of the profession, and given more time to work on each case; otherwise, their active control may well do more harm than good.

Here are some of the more interesting statistics from the survey:

Nearly 60% of Fellows reported having cases that raise electronic discovery issues. (My Comment: this means that 40% of these distinguished Fellows have never had a case with electronic discovery issues! And yet this same group, 87%, agree that electronic discovery is too costly.)

Nearly 77% of Fellows say that courts do not understand the difficulties in providing e-discovery;

Over 75% of Fellows agreed that discovery costs, as a share of total litigation costs, have increased disproportionately due to the advent of e-discovery;

71% of Fellows say that the costs of outside vendors have increased the cost of e-discovery without commensurate value to the client;

63% of Fellows say e-discovery is being abused by counsel; and

Less than 30% of Fellows believe that even when properly managed, discovery of electronic records can reduce the costs of discovery.

Candid Thoughts of Trial Lawyers about e-Discovery

Appendix B to the report consists of select quotations from the Fellows who responded to the survey. Many of these quotes pertained to e-discovery and you may find a few of them interesting, if not revealing:

"The new rules on discovery of e-mail will make litigation too expensive." (I disagree. The new rules do not even mention e-mail. In fact, e-mail discovery has long been too expensive, but it is not because of the rules—except maybe the old rule allowing discovery of irrelevant information, as long as it is reasonably calculated to lead to admissible evidence. It is too expensive because lawyers and judges do not know what they are doing, and do not know how to properly cull and review e-mail, and because clients are disorganized. Many of the e-discovery vendors are also misinformed, but often they do know better; they just have no pecuniary interest in aggressive culling. Some may even seek to line their own pockets in inflated discoveries.)

"We have sacrificed the prospect of attainable justice for the many in the interest of finding that one needle in the forest of haystacks." (I agree. In the field of ESI, this attitude arises out of misunderstanding and misapprehension of the staggering volumes of ESI now stored by most pack rat–dominated companies, and the impossibility of finding all the needles. Requesting parties and judges need to understand that only reasonable efforts are required, perfection is unattainable, and cost should be the primary factor in determining reasonable proportionality.)

"'E-discovery is a morass,' to quote Justice O'Connor."

"In many cases the cost of doing e-discovery may run into the millions of dollars (in some cases to each side). The cost of complying with e-discovery has become an impediment in the way to the doors of the Court House."

"My belief is that the greatest change that could be made is to reduce the scope and expense of discovery. The latest e-discovery adds incredible layers of work at the client's business and with its staff, as well as the lawyers, and has spawned a new layer of consultants all its own (a very bad sign), if one is looking to speedy and inexpensive, while being fair, justice."

"The courts need to get a better grip on e-discovery. The expense involved for all concerned in handling the massive amounts of data threatens to swamp the entire system by turning litigation into nothing but an e-discovery donnybrook." [For my younger readers "donnybrook" means a loud brawl or melee. To my really young readers, it's a mosh pit.]

"E-discovery is so expensive, it could ruin the system."

"The biggest issue facing litigants today is how to handle e-discovery. It can be incredibly expensive, and costs are not routinely passed on to the requesting party. The rules are trying to address this, but there has to be a better solution with more certainty."

"The rules on e-discovery are completely out of touch with the costs of such discovery."

"E-discovery rules are a disaster."

"E-discovery is crushing the system."

Trial Lawyers' Solution

So now you know what some of the country's most distinguished trial lawyers really think about e-discovery. As far as I can see from my study of this report, it has not dawned on any of them that they may be part of the problem, or that they need to better inform themselves on the technological issues underlying e-discovery.

The Press Release[102] announcing the interim report and survey explained what steps the American College of Trial Lawyers and the Institute for the Advancement of the American Legal System now plan to take to address these problems:

> Analysis of effective alternative civil procedure schemes in the United States and abroad; and
>
> Development of a set of proposed principles that might govern any major revision of the discovery or other provisions of the Federal Rules of Civil Procedure.

My Proposed Addendum to Their Plan

With all due respect to the distinguished Fellows, this plan will not work without including at least two more components.

First, we attorneys need to step out of our own long shadows

---

102. http://abajournal.com/files/Survey_Press_Release_Final.pdf..

and recognize that we are part of the problem. We need to admit that most of us are deficient in understanding the new technologies that drive today's world. As a consequence, we no longer understand the technological media in which our clients operate. We do not understand the evidence crucial to the outcome of most cases. We do not know where to find it, or how to gather it, or how to look at it properly when we do. We have delegated too much to e-discovery vendors, some of whom are driven by immediate profit motives, not the best interests of justice and efficient dispute resolution. Simply put, many of us are not competent to practice law in the 21st century where most evidence is digital, not paper. Until we recognize and acknowledge the competency problem, we will never be able to slog our way out of the morass with more committee meetings, rules, and principles.

Second and last, once we step out of our shadow, we need to address the problem with strong educational efforts in both the Bar and academic institutions. The work should begin in law schools. Most today do not even offer courses in discovery, much less electronic discovery. The professors do not find it theoretical or interesting enough to warrant their attention. That is irresponsible. The College of Trial Lawyers is correct to see e-discovery as a real problem, even if it does not yet understand the full dynamics of the problem. The academic colleges need to awaken, too, and start to train law students for the advanced technologies that await them in the real world.

The admissions departments of law schools should also take this pressing societal problem into account and recruit technologically sophisticated students. Computer science majors should be given a preference. It is a mistake to fill our law schools with only Political Science, Philosophy, and English majors. Moreover, law schools should start to consider offering dual degrees and collaborate with the Computer Science Departments. At the very least, there should be e-discovery certificate programs for law students. The employability of such graduates would increase dramatically.

Technology is rapidly changing, and if the law is to remain relevant, it must change and adapt just as fast. A lifetime of continuing education and study is needed to maintain competence in today's world. Lawyers must understand the world in which they live in order to serve their clients effectively. Lincoln learned the new, advanced technologies of his day: railroads. We must do the same to remain relevant.

Trial lawyers especially have to understand the digital information age in which we live. Their job is to investigate and prove the truth of what happened in the past in order to resolve the disputes of the present. The stories of what happened yesterday are all stored in computer networks around the world, waiting on clever lawyers to uncover and reveal the truth.

Conclusion

No one can operate effectively in the courtrooms of tomorrow without a good understanding of where the digital evidence is stored, how to retrieve and review it in a forensically sound yet cost-effective manner, and how to have it admitted into evidence at trial. These are tricky skills, even for those of us who do e-discovery, and only e-discovery, full time. Most of the Fellows who answered this survey are unlikely to have the time or inclination to study and master these new skills. A lot of the burden will necessarily fall on young lawyers and law students. They have the time, energy, and aptitude. They have grown up in a digital online world. They are the long-term solution to this problem. The sooner law schools recognize this, the better.

In the meantime, trial lawyers should accept that specialists in the field of e-discovery are a necessary evil. If an e-discovery specialist knows the field, he or she can save you money and take you out of the e-discovery morass faster and more reliably than a dozen new rules. The world today is too complex for one man or woman to do it all. In today's global, interdependent world, we all need to work together in teams. Trial counsel who do not love and understand technology should affiliate with those who do. When law schools get the message, there will be plenty of new associates available who are ready and able to fill the bill. In the meantime, deal with the consultants and other specialists.

Electronic discovery *can* be done in a cost-effective manner if you know how. The way out of this morass is learning, and the knowledge and wisdom that eventually come with it. Study is required by everyone: lawyers, judges, paralegals, technicians, professors, and law students alike. We all need to master technology, especially technologies related to electronic discovery. This, in turn, requires learning to work with information technology experts. The alternative is to turn back the clock to a paper world, turn off all of the computers, and stop sending e-mails. I know many lawyers out there who might like that. But since that is not likely to happen (your kids won't allow it), we need to start understanding all of these high-tech toys, at least well enough to find the evidence they generate and hold, and not break the bank in the process. It can and will be done as soon as we accept responsibility for this problem ourselves, stop blaming it all on the rules and judges, roll up our sleeves, and start learning how it all works.

Blog Reader Comment

I work in litigation support. Our company does e-discovery, scanning, printing for trial support, and various other digital litigation services. I can confirm that the majority of our clients have no idea what they need, and are forced to rely on our advice about what and how to produce—and we are not lawyers; we don't know what they need or want. We have a reasonable awareness of the legal requirements, but that doesn't tell us what they need for any particular case.

We regularly get scan jobs that say "scan to disc"—with no awareness that there's, at a minimum, file type and name choices involved. We've been asked to produce e-mail archives . . . and had the job cancelled, after a dozen hours of billing time, when the client realized that a 45mb e-mail archive could be 50,000 pages.

Many lawyers are apparently unaware that there is no correlation between "file size" and "number of pages." That many digital files can't be produced in any useful way. Since the iPod explosion, they're now aware of the existence of MP3s, so we can explain that sound files (and video files) can't be printed, but we have a harder time explaining that internal program code-files are gibberish when printed.

I've printed tens of thousands of pages for lawyers who can't figure out how to limit the print run, because they don't understand the digital filing system. Have delayed three days because the lawyer in charge was out of town, and we didn't know how they wanted digital files merged with the physical files we had to scan. (Which ones get numbered first?) Have tried to patiently explain that there is no such thing as an "exact printed copy" of an Excel spreadsheet, especially one with formulas and macros. Have converted hard drives to TIFs with thousands of place-holder pages saying "FILETYPE NOT SUPPORTED" because .dll files will not become useful images . . . and we didn't know if the lawyer needed evidence of the file being there (hey, at least the tif indicates a .dll with that name in that folder) or if they [sic] only needed the user-readable documents.

And that's before and outside of all the issues with metadata, file editing, duplicate files, and files with names like "PLAINTIFF'S RESPONSE TO DEFENDANT'S MOTION TO SUPPRESS PLAINTIFF'S MEMORANDUM IN SUPPORT OF MOTION TO VACATE SECOND ADMINISTRATIVE ACTION.PDF," which can crash programs if it's more than about two nested folders inside anything. (Which some scanner no doubt meticulously typed in, and charged for, because the lawyer who ordered the scans didn't explain what abbreviations are acceptable.)

More education about digital files is needed. For lawyers, for judges, for paralegals, for office clerks . . . everyone who handles these files, even at the level of "they left the disk for you; here it is," needs to have a basic understanding of what's going on with them.

Another Blog Reader Comment

Ralph: You say, "It is too expensive because . . . clients are disorganized pack rats." Are you saying enterprises should destroy more e-records more quickly? I argue the opposite.

Many recent cases show how tricky and dangerous a litigation hold is. I argue they motivate enterprises to give themselves a wide margin for error and therefore keep more records longer.

Ralph Replies

No, not after notice of the dispute. Obviously, they must implement a lit hold. My reference to pack rats is the near-universal tendency of both IT and management to save much more data than they need to before any notice of a dispute. They also tend to save it in a disorganized fashion that makes it hard to find things later when they need to, like after a lit-hold issues. This is a problem with records management. Most companies do a poor job with ESI records management and are reluctant to spend the time and money required to fix it. So they pay more to find stuff later when they need to, and they have to search through far too much junk.

Another Blog Reader Comment

by Stephen Mason[103]

Ralph is absolutely correct in pointing out the additional requirements. Many lawyers may not like or appreciate the decision reached by Klein, J. in *In re Vee Vinhnee, debtor, American Express Travel Related Services Co., Inc. v. Vee Vinhnee* 336 B.R. 437 (9th Cir. BAP 2005), but his refusal to admit the evidence because there were no proper evidential foundations must be right. This example clearly illustrates the point made by Ralph: 'Simply put, many of us are not competent to practice law in the 21st century where most evidence is digital, not paper.' It is becoming very difficult to argue that digital evidence does not have proper evidential foundations, especially with banking records. This is an issue that affects lawyers across the world, and many lawyers and judges fail to appreciate that digital records should be properly tested in legal proceedings. Banks often only wish to adduce evidence that, at best, is second- or third-

---

103. http://www.stephenmason.eu/.

hand (sometimes mere assertions), and rarely adduce evidence relating to the technical and organizational issues that should be introduced to demonstrate the integrity of the data and whether it can be considered to be trustworthy, which in turn can go to prove reliability (for which see the tests described by Professor Imwinkelried in his text *Evidentiary Foundations* (LexisNexis, 6th ed., 2005) and my comments in my text (chapter 4). Clients need to be informed clearly what digital evidence must be adduced to lay the proper evidential foundations (unless the evidence is not in dispute), yet it appears that lawyers often do not know what evidence is required to prove a point, and the opposing lawyer, because of their [sic] lack of knowledge, fails to challenge the inadequacy of the evidence.

This point leads on to Ralph's second requirement. I also concur with this condition. In the second editorial I wrote for the *Digital Evidence and Electronic Signature Law Review* in 2007, I made the position clear:

> The introduction of paper caused some lawyers consternation in Europe, mainly because lawyers did not know how to assess the veracity of the contents recorded on the paper carrier. As a result, elaborate rules were developed in some countries for the authentication of documents recorded on paper so as to prevent or counter attempts at fraud. At the time, the pace of change was probably slow enough to ensure that lawyers, judges and those that entered the profession were able to improve their knowledge and understanding of the evidential requirements relating to the introduction of paper relatively easily.

> However, some centuries later, a similar change has already taken place with respect to digital data, and, it seems, that a large majority of lawyers, legal academics and judges have failed to realize they are now living in a world dominated by digital evidence, and that digital evidence is now the dominant form of evidence. Although quantifiable figures are not available, it can be asserted with some confidence that the majority of lawyers, legal academics and

judges do not know they do not know; a smaller number know they do not know, and an even smaller elite know about digital evidence, but they are realistic enough to know they need to know more.

The law acts as a means to provide for social stability, yet if lawyers and judges fail to grasp that they need to begin to understand the attributes of evidence in digital format, individuals that are caught up in events such as those illustrated in the case of the *State of Connecticut v. Julie Amero* (January 2007, Docket no. CR-04-93292, Superior Court, New London Judicial District at Norwich, Ga.) will find themselves subject to the collective failure of the legal system: by the prosecution, defense and judge. This failure to become familiar with evidence in digital form by the participants in the legal system is further acerbated by the failure of the majority of universities and law schools across the world to incorporate any discussion of digital evidence into the curriculum. This means that the majority of students are taking degrees and participating in vocational training that ignores the new reality, that virtually all evidence brought before a court within the next three years will be from a digital source. . . . Yet the vast majority of students, lawyers and judges do not know how to assess such evidence, nor are they in a position to brief digital evidence specialists effectively, or to ask the right questions of such specialists during the legal proceedings.

This state of affairs will continue for some time, and it seems probable that many people brought before a criminal court may well face rough justice if the digital evidence is misunderstood by the lawyers and judge alike. In addition, parties in civil proceedings may also face serious obstacles if their lawyers and the judge fail to understand the importance of digital evidence: one European lawyer informed the editor this summer that they [sic] witnessed a judge refuse to receive photographic evidence taken on a mobile telephone of the damage caused to a motor car by another driver because, the judge asserted, the evidence could have been fabricated—there was not even a discussion as to the burden of proof or the procedure relating to which party could call into question the authenticity of the photographs—the judge blankly refused the admission of the evidence.

At the other end of the continuum, U.S. Magistrate Judge Paul W. Grimm in *Lorraine v. Markel and American Insurance Co.,* 2007 ILR Web (P&F) 1805, 207 WL 1300739 (D. Md. May 4, 2007), provided a useful academic paper on the authentication of digital evidence, yet failed to indicate why he decided to dismiss certain evidence because it was not authenticated.

Unless legal academics educate potential lawyers in digital evidence, and judges and lawyers concern themselves with the need to be educated in the topic, more rough justice can be expected across the globe. Not only rough justice. Lawyers in some jurisdictions can expect to face actions for negligence: this will then cause the professional indemnity insurers to take notice, and lawyers will then rush to become more educated. In the meantime, it is only to be guessed how many lay clients will be at the receiving end of poor legal advice in respect of digital evidence.

Ralph is absolutely correct. All aspects of digital evidence and electronic discovery (disclosure in England and Wales) ought to be part of the curriculum of universities and organizations that provide vocational courses (for instance, to be a barrister or solicitor in England and Wales, you are required to pass a one-year vocational course). At present, the educators are failing to educate. Lawyers are obtaining a qualification with no knowledge of digital evidence or electronic discovery. This is insane, and it is for the educators to understand that they have failed in their duty to the individual lawyer, to the clients that will seek advice and help from the newly qualified lawyer, and to society in general, for failing to include such important topics in the curriculum.

HOSPITAL DEFENDANTS MARTYRED IN THE CAUSE OF COOPERATIVE E-DISCOVERY

All of the experts in this field agree that, in addition to e-discovery teams, one of the best ways to control costs and risks in e-discovery is for the parties to cooperate with each other and make the process far less adversarial. Of course, cooperation is a two-way street, and it cannot be forced on the other side. This fundamental problem was raised by a recent ruling in a class action against six hospitals in Detroit. Unfortunately, the case produced a "gotcha"-type e-discovery ruling that unfairly punished the hospitals for trying to cooperate with opposing counsel. *Cason-Merenda v. Detroit Medical Center*, 2008 WL 2714239 (E.D. Mich. July 7, 2008).[104] Here is Magistrate Judge Donald A. Scheer's own words at the end of his opinion:

> Having elected to martyr itself rather than to seek relief in a timely fashion, DMC seeks an order imposing the cost of its choice upon its opponents. I find neither substantive merit nor equity in its request. IT IS THEREFORE ORDERED that Detroit Medical Center's Motion to Require Plaintiffs to Share Third Party Vendor Costs of Electronic Discovery is denied.

Judge Scheer held that the defendants had elected to *martyr* themselves by cooperating with plaintiffs and relying upon a stipulation that reserved the parties' rights to do e-discovery first and seek cost-sharing later. Judge Scheer's use of the inflammatory word "martyr" is ironic, and so is his reliance upon the Sedona Principles to try to justify his ruling. (To pile the irony on even higher, Judge Scheer misspells Sedona throughout the opinion and instead calls it the "Sadona" Conference.) It is ironic because the Sedona Conference's latest publication is *The Sedona Conference® Cooperation Proclamation*.[105] The Proclamation encourages parties to reach agreement

---

104. http://ralphlosey.files.wordpress.com/2008/09/cason-merenda-v-detroit-medical-2008-wl-2714239.doc.

105. http://www.thesedonaconference.org/content/miscFiles/Cooperation_Proclamation.pdf.

and specify plans. That is exactly what the defendant hospitals did here, but instead of rewards and accolades, they were punished.

The six hospitals are indeed martyrs, but not in the self-imposed manner that Judge Scheer's opinion suggests. They are martyrs to the cause of cooperative e-discovery that the Sedona Conference and many others promote. Their martyrdom was not voluntary, as the judge sarcastically suggests. It was caused by opposing counsel and the very judge who labeled them such. *Cason-Merenda* is bad law, but is nevertheless important. It is significant and deserves attention because it demonstrates that the cooperative approach will not work unless the judiciary understands and supports cooperation in both word and deed.

Defendants Cooperated as They Should

The defendants here met with plaintiffs at the beginning of the case and agreed to certain e-discovery. Instead of reaching an agreement on cost sharing at this early stage (which is nearly impossible, especially before anybody really knows what the costs will be), both sides agreed to defer the issue. They agreed to reserve their rights to later move for cost sharing. The court then approved the stipulation and made it into an order of the court. After that happened, defendants should have been able to rely on the order and make production first, without concern of waiver of rights. That is in fact what they did. Only later did they discover that reliance on this court's order put them on a path to martyrdom.

The six defendant hospitals acted in a cooperative manner to advance the process by doing the e-discovery work required and making the production. The opinion does not set forth any of the details, but in a class action like this, involving six major hospitals, the e-discovery work would almost certainly have been extensive and complicated. It is very hard to predict in advance the cost of this kind of work. That is the practical reason parties should be free to agree to defer this issue.

After defendants' first production, when they knew the actual costs as opposed to speculative predictions, they were then in a position to evaluate whether cost sharing was justified. Apparently they thought it was, and so contacted plaintiffs' counsel to try to reach an agreement. When plaintiffs' counsel would not agree to any cost sharing, defense counsel was forced to seek relief from the court by filing a motion.

These were not the crazed actions of a deluded martyr. Defense counsel was following the cooperative approach built into the rules and modern principles of e-discovery. They should not have been punished for trying to cooperate and work things out before filing motions. At the very least, the court should have provided them with their day in court and heard the issue of whether cost sharing was justified. But that is not what happened in *Cason-Merenda*.

Instead, the plaintiffs ceased their prior cooperative attitude and went into full adversarial mode. They not only opposed the motion on its merits, which is certainly fair, but they also challenged the defendants' right to bring the motion at all. Their procedural objection was unfair and excessive adversarial conduct, because it was contrary to their prior agreement. They had agreed that both sides preserved their rights to later seek cost sharing, but when defendants attempted to assert their right, they ignored their agreement. Instead, the plaintiffs pulled out all stops to try to prevent defendants from being heard. They confused the judge with arguments that the defendants must have waived their rights to seek cost shifting, and so the judge should not even address the more complicated merits of motion.

At this point, the judge should have put aside the plaintiffs' technical, forget-the-stipulation waiver arguments. He did not. Instead, the adversarial attack worked, and the procedural objections were sustained. What kind of message do you think this sent to the parties in this case?

Defendants Were Unwilling Martyrs

The court refused to hear the merits and instead denied the defendants motion on procedural grounds. Judge Scheer held that the defendants should have moved for cost sharing before they incurred the costs. Never mind the stipulation. He held that the defendants had waived any right for cost sharing. He called them martyrs who had voluntarily incurred the e-discovery costs, and now, after martyrdom, it was too late to seek any reimbursement or other relief.

Judge Scheer spent most of the decision explaining how the rules and law contemplate the filing of motions for cost sharing before costs are incurred. I think he is right on that point, as a general matter. But in this case, the parties entered into a contrary stipulation and order, and that should have changed everything. It did not, and thus fundamental principles of judicial estoppel were violated. Judge Scheer in effect vacated his prior order after the defendants had relied upon it. By this action, he avoided addressing the complex merits of the defendants' motion for cost sharing and punished them for taking a cooperative track.

At the hearing on the defendants' motion, they protested the plaintiffs' argument that they had waived their rights. Defense counsel pointed out that they had relied on the stipulation and order. Judge Scheer made short work of that argument in his written opinion by pointing to a provision in his scheduling order that required the parties to file discovery motions within 14 days after a discovery dispute arises. He held that this provision trumped the stipulated order. He determined, based on an affidavit filed by one of the plaintiffs' attorneys, that a discovery dispute existed between the parties on cost sharing no later than April 4, 2008. The defendants kept trying to resolve their dispute without judicial intervention after that date and did not file a motion until May 20, 2008. That was too late, according to Judge Scheer, who, at the urging of plaintiffs' counsel, determined that the deadline was April 28.

Fortunately, I rarely see this kind of hypertechnical "gotcha"-type ruling in U.S. district courts. They may make that kind of observation about questionable timeliness, but then they usually go on to address the merits of the motion. This was not done here. The judge refused to even consider or engage in any type of reasoned evaluation as to whether cost shifting was justified.

Martyrs to the Cause of Cooperation

Defendants here are true involuntary martyrs, worthy of admiration. They followed exactly the kind of collaborative process contemplated by the new rules, specifically Rule 26(f), *Federal Rules of Civil Procedure*. It is also the kind of cooperative arrangement contemplated by the Sedona Conference in its latest publication, *The Sedona Conference® Cooperation Proclamation*. The Proclamation encourages attorneys, parties, and judges to move away from traditional adversarial models of discovery into more cost-effective and balanced collaborative approaches. The cooperative model Sedona promotes follows the new rules and encourages parties to reach agreement and specify plans. Here is the introduction from the Cooperation Proclamation:

> The costs associated with adversarial conduct in pre-trial discovery have become a serious burden to the American judicial system. This burden rises significantly in discovery of electronically stored information (ESI). In addition to rising monetary costs, courts have seen escalating motion practice, overreaching, obstruction, and extensive, but unproductive discovery disputes—in some cases precluding adjudication on the merits altogether—when parties treat the discovery process in an adversarial manner.

The Sedona Proclamation goes on to explain how cooperative discovery is not only an economic imperative, but also an ethical one.

Cooperation in Discovery is Consistent with Zealous Advocacy

Lawyers have twin duties of loyalty: While they are retained to be zealous advocates for their clients, they bear a professional obligation to conduct discovery in a diligent and candid manner. Their combined duty is to strive in the best interests of their clients to achieve the best results at a reasonable cost, with integrity and candor as officers of the court. Cooperation does not conflict with the advancement of their clients' interests—it enhances it. Only when lawyers confuse advocacy with adversarial conduct are these twin duties in conflict.

Lawyers preparing cases for trial need to focus on the full cost of their efforts—temporal, monetary, and human. Indeed, all stakeholders in the system—judges, lawyers, clients, and the general public—have an interest in establishing a culture of cooperation in the discovery process. Over-contentious discovery is a cost that has outstripped any advantage in the face of ESI and the data deluge. It is not in anyone's interest to waste resources on unnecessary disputes, and the legal system is strained by "gamesmanship" or "hiding the ball," to no practical effect.

The effort to change the culture of discovery from adversarial conduct to cooperation is not utopian. It is, instead, an exercise in economy and logic. Establishing a culture of cooperation will channel valuable advocacy skills toward interpreting the facts and arguing the appropriate application of law.

But what happens when one side cooperates and the other does not? As this case shows, it can be dangerous. "Turn the other cheek" may be a noble thought, but it will not work in litigation. The Sedona Cooperation Proclamation notes this common problem at page 2:

And there remain obstreperous counsel with no interest in cooperation, leaving even the best-intentioned to wonder if "playing fair" is worth it.

They note the problem, but offer no solution, at least not in this short proclamation. The only solution I know of is to try to turn the aggression on the attacker, a kind of *aikido*-like maneuver that I discussed in *Adversarial Search, a "Perfect Barrier" to Cost-Effective e-Discovery, and One Litigant's "Aikido-like" Response* in the "Search" chapter. That is exactly what the eight hospitals did in *Cason-Merenda*, but instead of stepping in, the judge stepped out. The judge should have rewarded the good behavior; he should have at least considered the defendants' motion. Instead, he fell hook, line, and sinker for the plaintiffs' adversarial gamesmanship and joined in the attack. He even added insult to injury by calling defendants martyrs, all while invoking the ironic name of "Sadona." Sad indeed!

Cason-Merenda is important because it shows that the collaborative approach embodied by the Sedona Proclamation will not work without the active support and participation of the judiciary. Unless judges encourage and support the collaborative model, the presence of one obstreperous counsel in a case will act like a rotten apple in a barrel. I know that the Sedona Conference understands this well. In fact, at a "virtual press conference" on October 7, 2008, it released the first list of state and federal judges who have endorsed the Proclamation. You can find this updated list at the Sedona Web.[106] The courtrooms of these judges should be "martyr-free" zones.

The Cooperation Proclamation calls the move from adversarial to cooperative discovery a fundamental paradigm shift. Sedona thinks we can get there by a three-part process:

> **Part I: Awareness**—Promoting awareness of the need for and advantages of cooperation, coupled with a call to action. This process has been initiated by *The Sedona Conference® Cooperation Proclamation.*

> **Part II: Commitment**—Developing a detailed understanding and full articulation of the issues and changes needed to obtain cooperative fact-finding. This will take the form of a "Case for Cooperation," which will reflect viewpoints of all legal system stakeholders. It will incorporate disciplines outside the law, aiming to understand the separate and sometimes conflicting interests and motivations of judges, mediators and arbitrators, plaintiff and defense counsel, individual and corporate clients, technical consultants and litigation support providers, and the public at large.

> **Part III: Tools**—Developing and distributing practical "toolkits" to train and support lawyers, judges, other profes-

---

106. http://www.thesedonaconference.org.

sionals, and students in techniques of discovery cooperation, collaboration, and transparency. Components will include training programs tailored to each stakeholder; a clear-
inghouse of practical resources, including form agreements,
case management orders, discovery protocols, etc.; court-
annexed e-discovery ADR with qualified counselors and
mediators, available to assist parties of limited means; guides
for judges faced with motions for sanctions; law school programs to train students in the technical, legal, and cooperative aspects of e-discovery; and programs to assist individuals and businesses with basic e-records management, in an
effort to avoid discovery problems altogether.

Conclusion

The Proclamation came too late for the hospital defendants in *Cason-Merenda*. But hopefully their martyrdom will not be in vain. *Cason-Merenda* should drive home the point that judiciary buy-in and training is paramount to this movement's success.

Judges must not allow themselves to be duped into punishing parties who try to cooperate. They should not reward traditional gamesmanship. They should be trained to see through the clever smoke screens that experienced litigators can emit. If they are not sure, they should err on the side of ruling with the lawyers that cooperated. Hypertechnical "gotcha" litigation has no place in cooperative e-discovery. It should not be tolerated by the lawyers or the judges. If a district court judge sees a magistrate ruling like *Cason-Merenda,* he or she should not hesitate to reverse it.

Blog Reader Comment

I think this analysis ignores the simple reality that one form of "gotcha" tactics is to proceed with processing and production of ostensibly not reasonably accessible ESI without affording the requesting party the opportunity to examine the support for the not reasonably accessible assertion. There may be less expensive alternatives available, such as reading the header information without fully restoring the tapes, that could reduce the burden on both sides or even make clear to the requesting party that the likelihood of obtaining relevant, responsive information is less than the requesting party originally believed. Proceeding with production and attempting to shift costs without affording the requesting party the opportunity to reach an informed compromise is the antithesis of the cooperation the Sedona Conference works to encourage. As Judge Scheer noted:

> Rather than raising the issue of undue burden and cost before they were incurred, when there would have been an opportunity for the court to demand a showing of good cause by the requesting party, explore alternatives, impose conditions or otherwise encourage compromise, DMC elected to suffer the expense and only then seek contribution from the Plaintiffs.

Another Blog Reader Comment

I enjoyed the article very much but I do agree with my esteemed colleague['s] statement above. The plaintiff should certainly have a role in the costs being incurred and the data being searched if they [sic] are to be expected to share in the costs of such production. In addition, if the defendants are going to assert that certain ESI data is not readily accessible, under the definitions of FRCP Rule 34, they need to demonstrate a good-faith basis for such assertion. Although I do take issue with the improper reference to the Sedona Conference, as I am sure the people of Arizona do.

Ralph Replies

We do not know from the opinion whether the requesting party was afforded the opportunities mentioned or not. All we know is that the requesting party stipulated to considering shifting after the fact, and the court approved and adopted the stipulation. That is my real point here. Nothing forced the requesting party to stipulate, but once it did, and the other side relied on it, it should have been a "done deal."

New Technologies **2**

SHERLOCK HOLMES IN THE 21ST CENTURY: DEFINITIONS AND LIMITS OF COMPUTER FORENSICS, FORENSIC COPIES, AND FORENSIC EXAMINATIONS

If Sherlock Holmes were alive today, he would surely be a master of computer forensics. Just as he sometimes used his chemistry set in the 19th century to analyze clues, today he would use forensic software to examine digital devices. Holmes would know how to make forensic copies of computers, i-phones, thumb-drives, and other ESI storage devices, and also know when not to waste his time doing so. No doubt Dr. Watson would be amazed at the evidence Holmes would sometimes uncover. The forensic examination of computers is an important tool in 21st-century detective work, but it is no panacea. Sherlock Holmes certainly would know that it is not a substitute for clear thinking and rational deductions, and is not appropriate in every case.

Lots of trial lawyers do not really understand computer forensics and are prone to think that a full-scale forensic examination of all computers is needed in every case. They want their tech guys to make "forensic copies," work their mumbo-jumbo on each, and, like Sherlock Holmes, come up with an amazing and unexpected clue that solves the case. Sometimes this fantasy comes true, but only rarely. The attempt to search every bit and byte of every computer, including the deleted files and slack space, is expensive. Most experts agree that this kind of "deep dive" forensic examination work should be done sparingly and is not needed in most e-discovery cases. Even when a special case suggests it may be needed, such forensic exams rarely produce the killer e-mail that wins the day. The lawyer who uses this kind of full-scale forensics approach in every case is setting himself up for major disappointments and wasting his client's money.

What is "computer forensics" and the related terms, "forensic copy" and "forensic exam"? Let's begin by defining "forensic copy," which is fairly simple. A forensic copy is an exact bit-by-bit copy of the entire physical storage media, including all active and residual data and unallocated space on the media. This is also sometimes called an "image copy" or "mirror image." *See The Sedona Conference Glossary:*[1] *e-Discovery & Digital Information Management*, The Sedona Conference Working Group Series, May 2005.

A forensic copy allows for a "forensic exam" of the copy. You do not examine the original because the act of examination would, in itself, change the original. (This is called the Heisenberg Prin-

---

1. http://www.thesedonaconference.org/dltForm?did=tsglossary may05.pdf.

ciple[2] of computer forensics.) In a forensic exam, *all* of the information on a disk is carefully probed and searched, even the otherwise
hidden information: the deleted files, residual data, unallocated space,
corrupted files, encrypted files. In a forensic exam, everything that
is scientifically possible to restore and search is searched, including
ESI classified as not reasonably accessible under Rule 26(b)(2)(B).

The definition of the more general term "computer forensics" is
more challenging. It is not a specific procedure, like forensic copy
or exam; it is an entire field of study or scientific discipline. The
National Institute of Standards and Technology[3] special publication
(SP) 800-86, *Guide to Integrating Forensic Techniques into Incident
Responses,*[4] provides an authoritative definition of computer forensics:

> . . . the application of science to the identification, collec-
> tion, examination, and analysis of data while preserving the
> integrity of the information and maintaining a strict chain of
> custody for the data. Data refers to distinct pieces of digital
> information that have been formatted in a specific way. . . .

The NIST explains[5] how the process of computer forensics has
four basic phases:

- **Collection:** identifying, labeling, recording, and acquiring
  data from the possible sources of relevant data, while following procedures that preserve the integrity of the data.
- **Examination:** forensically processing collected data using a
  combination of automated and manual methods, and assessing and extracting data of particular interest, while preserving the integrity of the data.

2. http://www.porcupine.org/forensics/forensic-discovery/chapter1.html.
3. http://www.nist.gov/.
4. http://csrc.nist.gov/publications/nistpubs/800-86/SP800-86.pdf.
5. http://www.itl.nist.gov/lab/bulletns/bltnsep06.htm.

- **Analysis:** analyzing the results of the examination, using legally justifiable methods and techniques, to derive useful information that addresses the questions that were the impetus for performing the collection and examination.

- **Reporting:** reporting the results of the analysis, which may include describing the actions used, explaining how tools and procedures were selected, determining what other actions need to be performed (e.g., forensic examination of additional data sources, securing identified vulnerabilities, improving existing security controls), and providing recommendations for improvement to policies, procedures, tools, and other aspects of the forensic process.

A well known IT site, SearchSecurity.com,[6] provides another good definition[7] of computer forensics:

Computer forensics, also called cyberforensics, is the application of computer investigation and analysis techniques to gather evidence suitable for presentation in a court of law. The goal of computer forensics is to perform a structured investigation while maintaining a documented chain of evidence to find out exactly what happened on a computer and who was responsible for it.

Forensic investigators typically follow a standard set of procedures. After physically isolating the computer in question to make sure it cannot be accidentally contaminated, investigators make a digital copy of the hard drive. Once the original hard drive has been copied, it is locked in a safe or other secure storage facility to maintain its pristine condition. All investigation is done on the digital copy.

Investigators use a variety of techniques and proprietary forensic applications to examine the hard drive copy, searching hidden folders and unallocated disk space for copies of

---

6. http://searchsecurity.techtarget.com/.
7. http://searchsecurity.techtarget.com/sDefinition/0,,sid14_gci1007675,00.html.

deleted, encrypted, or damaged files. Any evidence found on the digital copy is carefully documented in a "finding report" and verified with the original in preparation for legal proceedings that involve discovery, depositions, or actual litigation.

The Sedona Conference Glossary[8] also defines computer forensics:

Computer Forensics (in the context of this document, "forensic analysis") is the use of specialized techniques for recovery, authentication and analysis of electronic data when an investigation or litigation involves issues relating to reconstruction of computer usage, examination of residual data, authentication of data by technical analysis or explanation of technical features of data and computer usage. Computer forensics requires specialized expertise that goes beyond normal data collection and preservation techniques available to end-users or system support personnel, and generally requires strict adherence to chain-of-custody protocols.

A recent commentary[9] by forensic expert Ken Zatyko in *Forensic Magazine*[10] focused on the difficulty of defining what he called "digital forensics," which, for purposes of this article, I consider equivalent to "computer forensics." Ken Zatyko is a recently retired Air Force lieutenant colonel who was the director of the Department of Defense Computer Forensics Laboratory for many years and is now an adjunct professor with John Hopkins University. Ken reviews several other definitions, as I have done, and then settles on his own definition that he urges others to adopt:

---

8. http://www.thesedonaconference.org/dltForm?did=tsglossarymay05.pdf.

9. http://www.forensicmag.com/articles.asp?pid=130.

10. http://www.forensicmag.com/.

The application of computer science and investigative procedures for a legal purpose involving the analysis of digital
evidence after proper search authority, chain of custody,
validation with mathematics, use of validated tools, repeatability, reporting, and possible expert presentation.

This is the best definition I have seen, and my personal favorite,
perhaps because it includes "validation with mathematics," a reference to my favorite subject in computer forensics, hash analysis
(*see* the "Technology" chapter of this book for several articles on
hash, and also my law review article on this subject: "HASH: The
New Bates Stamp").[11] Zatyko then goes on to delineate an eight-
step forensics process:

1. Search authority
2. Chain of custody
3. Imaging/hashing function
4. Validated tools
5. Analysis
6. Repeatability (quality assurance)
7. Reporting
8. Possible expert presentation

The various definitions make clear that computer forensics is a
disciplined, scientific approach to electronic discovery and evidence
validation. Computer forensics in this general sense should be followed whenever electronic evidence is involved in a legal proceeding, which in today's world means almost every case. In that sense,
the trial lawyer may need a person familiar with computer forensics
on every case to supervise e-discovery activities. Trial attorneys must
be able to verify that proper procedures, authenticity and chain of
custody were followed in order for the ESI discovered to be admiss-
able as evidence at trial. This is, however, a far cry from a full-scale
Sherlock Holmes forensic examination of all computers. It is important for attorneys to understand the difference between forensics as

11. http://ralphlosey.files.wordpress.com/2007/09/hasharticlelosey.pdf.

a general discipline to lay a proper predicate for evidence, and forensic copying and forensic examinations as particular applications of this discipline, which are not necessary in every case.

One person who has a good grasp of this difference is John Patzakis.[12] He is the general counsel of Guidance Software,[13] makers of EnCase,[14] the forensics software tool used by over 80 percent of computer forensics experts. Although it might be tempting for him to push the overuse of forensics, he does not do so. He and his company are a class act, which is one reason I am pleased that John agreed to do a West-Thompson Webinar with me later this year, "Computer Forensics and E-Discovery." We will be joined by another e-discovery attorney, a modern-day Sherlock Holmes of computers, Bill Speros,[15] who also understands this distinction very well, and by a well-known forensic accounting expert, Frank Wu, of Protiviti.[16]

John Patzakis was interviewed in 2007 by Forensic Focus,[17] a Web site for "computer forensics news, information and community." John's interview[18] provides some good advice on the prudent and restrained use of computer forensics in e-discovery.

> In general, eDiscovery tends to involve a "computer forensics-like" approach, if you will, where aspects of traditional forensics such as chain of custody, metadata recovery and preservation, documentation and reporting, and an overall defendable process are central requirements. Aspects of traditional forensics that are generally not as important include full disk imaging, deleted file and file fragment recovery, and deep-dive analysis involving various artifacts.

---

12. http://www.guidancesoftware.com/corporate/popup-bios.aspx# JohnPatzakis.

13. http://www.guidancesoftware.com/.

14. http://www.guidancesoftware.com/products/ef_index.aspx.

15. http://www.speros.net/.

16. http://www.protiviti.com/.

17. http://www.forensicfocus.com/.

18. http://www.forensicfocus.com/john-patzakis-interview-280607.

This reference to "traditional forensics" is what most people think of when they hear "computer forensics," the expensive "CSI"-type criminal investigations where computer disks are imaged and forensic exams are performed to restore and search deleted files,[19] fragments, Internet cache,[20] slack space, memory,[21] and the like. A diagram providing a simple overview of the forensic examination process using EnCase software[22] is shown below.

John Patzakis has written a comprehensive treatise on electronic discovery law related to his company's software tools and forensic related issues called the *EnCase Legal Journal*[23] (April 2007). At 143 pages and 446 legal citations, this is not your typical vendor white paper, and is well worth reading and using as a reference. Section 9.5 of the *Journal* is titled "Cost-Effective Searching of Data." It pertains to my original point that many trial lawyers tend to overuse computer forensics and seek full-disk imaging and other "deep-dive" analysis in every case.

Collection and preservation of ESI must incorporate a defensible process that accomplishes the objective of preserving relevant data, including metadata, and establishing a proper chain of custody. With the right technology, these results can be achieved without full-disk imaging. However, full-disk imaging and deleted file recovery are emphasized by many eDiscovery vendors and consultants as a routine eDiscovery practice. While such deep-dive analysis is required in some circumstances, full-disk imaging is unwarranted as a standard eDiscovery practice due to consider-

---

19. http://ralphlosey.wordpress.com/2007/06/02/when-should-you-search-for-deleted-files/.

20. http://ralphlosey.wordpress.com/2007/08/14/should-you-save-internet-cache/.

21. http://ralphlosey.wordpress.com/2007/09/02/judge-affirms-magistrates-decision-in-the-ram-memory-case-no-minimum-storage-time-for-electronic-information-before-it-is-discoverable/.

22. http://www.guidancesoftware.com/products/ef_works.aspx.

23. http://www.guidancesoftware.com/support/legalresources.aspx.

able costs and burden. Large-scale, full-disk imaging is burdensome because the process is very disruptive, requires much more time to complete, and, as eDiscovery processing and hosting fees are usually calculated on a per-gigabyte basis, costs are increased exponentially. . . .

Generally, courts will only require that full forensic copies of hard drives be made if there is a showing of good cause supported by specific, concrete evidence of the alteration or destruction of electronic information or for other reasons. *Balboa Threadworks, Inc. v. Stucky*, 2006 WL 763668, at *3 (D. Kan. 2006). However, "[c]ourts have been cautious in requiring the mirror imaging of computers where the request is extremely broad in nature and the connection between the computers and the claims in a lawsuit are unduly vague or unsubstantiated in nature." *Ameriwood Industries, Inc. v. Liberman*, 2006 WL 3825291, (E.D. Mo. Dec. 27, 2006).

I wrote about the *Ameriwood* case in Chapter Three of my first book. *Ameriwood* was one of the first decisions in the country to employ the new inaccessibility analysis under Rule 26(b)(2)(B). Although the court in *Ameriwood* was cautious, it decided to allow the employer to make a forensic copy of the employee's computer and search for otherwise inaccessible ESI, the deleted files and slack space. The court allowed this kind of forensic imaging only because the employer had made a special showing of good cause under Rule 26(b)(2)(B). The general rule is to be cautious and not allow such forensic exams absent a showing of good cause. Good cause can come in a variety of forms, but usually arises from suspicious circumstances that suggest spoliation, such as a story of a midnight hacker[24] erasing all of your files, or the loss of a laptop with all of your records just before a deposition *duces tecum.*

In another case, *Hedenburg v. Aramark American Food Services*, 2007 U.S. Dist. LEXIS 3443 (W.D. Wash. Jan. 17, 2007), the court

---

24. http://ralphlosey.wordpress.com/2006/11/11/recent-akerman-e-discovery-victory/.

applied the general rule and *denied* the application for a forensic exam. The employer requesting the forensic imaging did not provide good cause as required under Rule 26(b)(2)(B). I wrote about *Hedenburg* in the "New Technologies" chapter of my first book. This is an employment discrimination case where the employer wanted a forensic copy made of the employee's personal computers. The employer proposed that the copy then be examined by a computer forensic expert serving as a special master. The employer's attorneys had an expansive view of computer forensics not warranted by the facts or the law.

In a move reminiscent of Inspector Lestrade, employer's counsel provided no good reasons for the exam, and instead argued that such exams were common in these types of cases and might lead to important clues. The judge rejected the proposed forensics as a mere "fishing expedition." Blind hope may be a fisherman's credo, but it will not work in court, and is no substitute for the kind of cold logic and reasoned analysis made famous by Sherlock Holmes.

For more information on forensics, check out the audio CLE I did for West Legalworks titled "E-Discovery and Computer Forensic Investigations 101:[25] When Does Your Case Warrant the Full 'CSI' Treatment?" With me on the panel for this 1.5-hour webcast were J. William Speros, Consultant and Principal, Speros & Associates LLC; Michael Michalowicz, Associate Director, Protiviti; and John Patzakis, Vice Chairman and Chief Legal Officer, Guidance Software.

Blog Reader Comment

Rule 26(b)(2)(B) does not identify any particular class of data as inherently inaccessible, including deleted data or other data that is only available through forensic analysis as you defined it above. Rather, 26(b)(2)(B) refers to data that are "not reasonably accessible because of undue burden or cost." It easy to imagine that, in a case involving only a few computers but where claims reach into the millions, any

---

25. http://westlegaledcenter.com/program_guide/course_detail.jsf?courseId=11808398&sc_cid=1to1info.

court would find the relatively low cost of forensic analysis would be well worth it if the requesting party could show good cause and an analysis under 26(b)(2)(C) favored the discovery in question. The point is that while the term "inaccessible" is useful shorthand, it doesn't do justice to the letter of the rule, nor does it reflect the fact that 26(b)(2)(B) will be interpreted differently over time as technology changes. For example, the mere existence of such an excellent tool as EnCase means that deleted data are far more accessible (i.e., can be accessed with less burden and cost) than they would be otherwise.

Ralph's Reply

You make a good clarifying point. I agree. It requires case-by-case analysis, but, as a general rule of thumb, full forensic exams are for locating data that are otherwise not reasonably accessible, and thus require a showing of good cause. See my many other blogs on Rule 26(b)(2)(B) for a more complete picture on the application and meaning of the new rule.

STAR TREK LESSONS FOR E-DISCOVERY

All of the senior officers in *Star Trek* worked together on the bridge except for one, the chief engineer. Poor Scotty was always kept below, far away from the command center. Scotty was never really part of the core team. Sure, he had a high rank, but he was not a decision maker, and was only rarely allowed on the bridge. In fact, the rest of the team never even talked to him much unless there was a problem.

Still, there were problems aplenty, and the team needed Scotty to keep the Enterprise going. In just about every episode, he and the other techs would work around the clock to meet the Captain's unrealistic time demands to save the day. Indeed, the pleas of other members of the team for Scotty to beam them up out of trouble became the signature line of *Star Trek*. Yes, the senior officers needed Scotty, but he was never given the respect and equality he was due.

According to Dan Regard,[26] one of the keynote speakers at the Masters e-Discovery Conference[27] in Washington, D.C. last week, *Star Trek* has an important lesson to teach to e-discovery: bring the engineers onto the bridge and make IT an integral part of your core e-Discovery Team. Then, and only then, will the Enterprise succeed. As it turns out, many e-discovery aficionados are also Trekkies, and so this analogy received a strong positive response.

Dan is an attorney and one of the founders of LECG,[28] an expert services firm, where he is now a managing director in Washington, D.C. He has 20 years' experience as a consultant in the computer industry and in e-discovery. He is an obvious fan of the Vulcans on *Star Trek* because his other key message was to improve the e-discovery process by constantly asking *why*. In other words, subject your activities to reasoned analysis and logic. Do not impulsively do things because that is how you have always done them. Engage in extensive proactive analysis at the beginning of any project. Examine the assumptions behind your e-discovery activities. Do you really need to preserve your backup tapes for a particular case? Why collect, produce and review so much data? Dan claims that he has saved as much of 80% of projected costs in an e-discovery process by such an analytic approach.

Anne Kershaw[29] was another excellent keynote speaker at the Masters Conference. She is an attorney and consultant involved with high-tech litigation since 1993. Anne gave the first presentation I have heard concerning new proposals for amending Rule 8 of the *Federal Rules of Civil Procedure* concerning notice pleading. Rule 8(a)(2) merely requires a "short and plain statement of the claim showing that the pleader is entitled to relief" in order to state a cause of action. This notice pleading rule was enacted in 1938, and has been interpreted over the years to require only vague general plead-

26. http://www.lecg.com/website/LWBios.nsf/OpenPage/DanielRegard.
27. http://www.themastersconference.com/Main.html.
28. http://www.lecg.com/website/home.nsf/openpage/home.
29. http://www.akershaw.com/.

ing for a case to go forward. As Anne put it, in today's federal court, all you have to do is say "I'm hurt and you owe me."

The problem for e-discovery with this vague general approach is that defendants frequently have no good idea from such pleadings as to what evidence will be relevant. This forces defendants to guess what computer records may need to be preserved and collected. This drives up the cost of e-discovery and leads to mistakes when a defendant guesses wrong. Further, it allows frivolous lawsuits to proceed to expensive discovery that could have been weeded out by more stringent pleading requirements.

Anne and other members of the Rules Committee are proposing a series of possible amendments to the rules to require more particularized pleading of facts, especially in complex litigation. This would permit the earlier dismissal of cases without merit. This is a hot political issue that the plaintiff's bar has long opposed. You can help Anne out on this important project by sending her examples of frivolous lawsuits that ended up costing a small fortune to defend.

Another good event that I attended at the Masters Conference was the panel discussion on "Career Development & Hiring Trends in Legal Technology." The panelists were Jeff Scarpitti of The Kennett Group,[30] Clark Cordner of Orrick,[31] Ben Hawksworth of Ernst & Young,[32] and Jeff Ghielmetti of CISCO[33] and Legal on Ramp.[34] The group spoke about the entrepreneurial law firm model that has been always been dominant in e-discovery services. That is where law firms in effect create their own e-discovery vendor companies within their law firms. This captive billing center then provides e-discovery services to the firm's litigation clients. This entrepreneurial model has been quite profitable to law firms for many years and is appar-

---

30. http://www.kennettgroup.com/.
31. http://www.orrick.com/index.asp.
32. http://www.ey.com/global/Content.nsf/US/AABS_-_Specialty_Advisory_-_IDS_-_Overview.
33. http://www.cisco.com/web/about/ciscoitatwork/case_studies/storage_networking_dl4.html.
34. http://www.legalonramp.com/lor/.

ently still going strong. There are many employment opportunities in this area for both techie lawyers and IT personnel.

But one of the panelists, Jeff Ghielmetti, offered a new model, which in my view is the wave of the future. Jeff told the story of how CISCO established the first internal corporate e-Discovery Team after the stock market crash of 2000 and 2001. At that time, CISCO was hit with a flood of litigation, often involving millions of pages of electronic documents. One of the first cases came with a $23.5 million bill for e-discovery. CISCO could not continue at that kind of burn rate, so out of necessity it decided to try something new and go in-house. For help they turned to Jeff, a CISCO engineer, not a lawyer, but he had the full backing of CISCO's forward-looking (aka "desperate") legal department.

Under Jeff's direction, CISCO turned away from the traditional model of hiring law firms and e-discovery vendors to manage their data preservation, collection and analysis, and they started to do it themselves. CISCO set up the first internal, multidisciplinary corporate e-Discovery Team. Jeff reported that CISCO's program has been a huge success, not only in cutting costs, but also in better management of risks.

The CISCO model is basically the same internal team paradigm I promote on this blog, my books, and in my practice. Although I had heard rumors about Jeff and CISCO's team, I had never seen any writings about their program, and this is the first time I had heard Jeff speak. It was very encouraging. After explaining the background, Jeff went into some of the details of how the CISCO team operates. He explained that the teamwork begins by preparing a map showing where all of the company's ESI is located. At CISCO, they call that the "treasure map," and it is constantly updated.

Ben Hawksworth of Ernst & Young spoke of the consensus now forming that the internal corporate team approach is the "holy grail" of e-discovery. Under this new model corporations preserve and collect their own data, do initial processing and analysis, and then turn the data over to the outside law firm for review and production. Once again, this is exactly the model I have been promoting. It appears that the internal e-Discovery Team approach to e-discovery may finally be catching on, and will soon overtake the traditional law firm entrepreneurial model. In the language of *Star Trek*, Scotty's on the bridge and the Ferengi are on the run.

TECH V. LAW—A PLEA FOR MUTUAL RESPECT[35]

Ever wonder what the big tech companies moving into e-discovery really think of the field or the people in it, like you and me? Thanks to a recent article in *The Wall Street Journal* (WSJ), we now know. They think we're morons—or at least one CEO of a high-tech company does. There are so many mainline technology companies now muscling into e-discovery these days that the newspaper ran a feature article on the subject, "Tech Firms Pitch Tools for Sifting Legal Records," *Wall Street Journal* at B1 (Aug. 22, 2008). As part of this article, WSJ reporter Justin Scheck interviewed the CEO of a large British software company about its move into e-discovery. The CEO is quoted as saying that e-discovery ". . . is work that requires little brain-power or legal training." (Please see the CEO's comment below where he says he was misquoted, and that is not what he really thinks.) So it seems that e-discovery is the Rodney Dangerfield[36] of the tech world—"can't get no respect."

Conflict Between the Two Professions

You could say this is just one man's opinion, and the quote was probably taken out of context. Maybe, but I don't think so. This comment demonstrates a real antipathy between the Law and IT professions. It also illustrates a lack of understanding or appreciation as to what each side really does. For instance, the same CEO is also quoted by the *Journal* as describing what he thinks discovery lawyers do, and why they need help from super-tech gurus like him:

> The old-fashioned way of doing this was having a lot of lawyers doing a lot of simple things. You would literally have lawyers reading through things saying, "There was chicken for lunch." You don't need lawyers to know it's a lunch menu.

---

35. http://ralphlosey.wordpress.com/2008/08/24/tech-v-law-a-plea-for-mutual-respect/.

36. http://www.youtube.com/watch?v=9FPv2toi5og.

The article then goes on to describe how a host of technology companies, ones that have recently discovered the profit potential of e-discovery, are going to save the day with their advanced software. They are going to save law firm clients from being bilked by greedy, menu-reading lawyers. The fair and balanced *Journal* gives the so-called opposing view by stating:

> But big law firms, facing the loss of lucrative client fees, are crying foul. They question how much of the discovery process can be automated and how much money the tools will really save. They also claim companies could end up spending more to fix mistakes.

Obviously, both WSJ and the big-tech company executives they interviewed are clueless as to the real world of e-discovery.

This arrogance, misunderstanding, antipathy, and lack of respect is not a one-way street. For most of my career, the IT guy (and yes, it always used to be a guy) received about as much respect in a typical law firm as the copy machine repair man—not very much. Even when they were later hired as full-time law firm employees, techs were (and in some firms still are) considered rather dim-witted necessary evils, with lower status than secretaries and nowhere near the status of a paralegal. Law and lawyers were professionals. IT techs were—what? Did they even go to school? Why are we paying them so much?

The mutual lack of respect has, in my opinion, long characterized the relations between these two industries. I know this from firsthand experience going back to 1978, when I first became enthralled with computers in law school. When I started practice in 1980, computers were just beginning to be used by a few progressive law firms. I was the young associate who liked computers, and so I ended up handling all of the interface with the IBM technician. There was only one computer company in those early days: IBM. The "Big Blue" tech would come to your office to fix your mini-mainframe computer, then later your PCs, whenever there was a problem, which, after PCs came along in 1982, was pretty much all of the time. Eventually I ended up doing most of the tech work myself and would call IBM only on the rare occasion I could not figure it out on my own. After all, as every tech knows, just checking to see if everything is plugged in, or hard-booting, will fix most of the problems a typical idiot user has—you know, users like lawyers with "little brain-power" who read menus for a living.

This Problem Loses Cases

So we have a real respect problem, and since none of us is Rodney Dangerfield, it is not at all funny. This antipathy leads to widespread misunderstandings and miscommunication between lawyers and computer technicians. This is just mildly annoying for most lawyers and techs, but for specialists in e-discovery it is a disaster. That is because e-discovery is a blend of the two professions. It can only work properly when lawyers and techs work together and cooperate. (I have dedicated a whole Web site[37] to that proposition.) When this does not happen, the typical result is another disaster case. I will spend the rest of this article going over a good example of this: *Kevin Keithley v. The Home Store.com, Inc.*,[38] 2008 U.S. Dist. LEXIS 61741, 2008 WL 3833384 (Aug. 12, 2008). This is a case involving serious sanctions against defendants based in no small part upon techs' obvious lack of respect of the law and lawyers.

Kevin Keithley v. The Home Store.com, Inc.

Kevin Keithley[39] is a patent infringement case in San Francisco involving computer software and Internet Web sites. Defendants write code for and develop such well-known Web sites as Realtor.com, Homebuilder.com, Homestore.com, and Move.com. Most of the key ESI custodians on the defendants' side were software engineers and programmers of various types. Their disrespect of the law, lawyers, and the discovery process was obvious, so much so that the senior federal magistrate judge looking into their conduct, Elizabeth D. Laporte, said it was "among the most egregious this Court has seen." Judge Laporte begins her opinion with this observation:

---

37. http://www.floridalawfirm.com/.
38. http://ralphlosey.files.wordpress.com/2008/08/keithley.doc.
39. http://ralphlosey.files.wordpress.com/2008/08/keithley.doc.

While the Court does not impose sanctions of any type lightly, and would prefer to see the resources of the Court directed to addressing the substantive issues of the case on the merits, rather than the collateral issue of sanctions for discovery abuse, this is the unusual case in which Defendants' conduct warrants stiff monetary, as well as evidentiary, sanctions. See *United Medical Supply Co. v. United States,* 77 Fed. Cl. 257, 258-59 (Fed. Cl. 2007) ("Aside perhaps from perjury, no act serves to threaten the integrity of the judicial process more than the spoliation of evidence. Our adversarial process is designed to tolerate human failings—erring judges can be reversed, uncooperative counsel can be shepherded, and recalcitrant witnesses compelled to testify. But, when critical documents go missing, judges and litigants alike descend into a world of *ad hocery* and half measures—and our civil justice system suffers.").

Judge Laporte then imposed sanctions of $320,000, plus a devastating adverse inference instruction. She considered entering judgment against the defendants outright as the plaintiffs requested, but recognized that the case involved miscommunications, disrespect, and negligence, not outright fraud. These are harsh sanctions nevertheless, and in my view, Judge Laporte correctly implemented the First Circuit quote she likes and avoided the "cardboard sword" to fight this *ad hocery*:

As aptly stated by the First Circuit, "the judge should take pains neither to use an elephant gun to slay a mouse nor to wield a cardboard sword if a dragon looms." *Anderson v. Beatrice Foods Co.,* 900 F.2d 388, 395 (1st Cir.), *cert. denied,* 498 U.S. 891 (1990).

When Did the Duty to Preserve Begin?

The first interesting legal issue in this case is when the duty to preserve was triggered. The lawsuit was filed on October 1, 2003, so it definitely started at least by then. But the plaintiffs argued that it actually started on July 14, 1998, when they wrote the defendants requesting they license their patent. Judge Laporte did not buy that, because the letter did not threaten litigation or even mention infringement. But she did find the duty was triggered on August 3, 2001, more than two years before the suit was filed, by a letter from the plaintiffs to the defendants stating that "we assume that Homestore.com wishes to litigate this matter. Unless we hear otherwise by close of business Tuesday, August 7, 2001, we will advance this matter accordingly."

As Judge Laporte notes, this is all just an academic issue, "because Defendants did not satisfy their duty to preserve even after this lawsuit was filed and recklessly allowed the destruction of some relevant source code as late as 2004." For that reason, we probably should not tax our "little brains" about it, but still, it is slightly more interesting than whether "there was chicken for lunch."

Judge Laporte explains the triggering law by first citing to *A. Farber & Partners, Inc. v. Garber*, 234 F.R.D. 186, 193 (C.D. Cal. 2006), which held that "[t]here is no doubt that a litigant has a duty to preserve evidence it knows or should know is relevant to imminent litigation." She then clarifies the "imminence" requirement by referring to a quote from the holding *cf. In re* Napster Inc. Copyright Litigation, 462 F. Supp. 2d 1060, 1070 (N.D. Cal. 2006):

> The court in *A. Farber* thus held imminence to be sufficient, rather than necessary, to trigger the duty to preserve documents. Furthermore, the court in *A. Farber* did not reach the issue of when, exactly, the duty attached. The duty to preserve documents attaches "when a party should have known that the evidence may be relevant to future litigation." *Zubulake v. UBS Warburg LLC*, 220 F.R.D. 212, 216 (S.D. N.Y. 2003). *See also National Ass'n of Radiation Survivors*, 115 F.R.D. at 556-57. The future litigation must be "probable," which has been held to mean "more than a possibility." *Hynix Semiconductor Inc. v. Rambus, Inc.*, 2006 WL 565893 at *21 (N.D. Cal. 2006) (Whyte, J.).

Law Is Not a Science

So it looks like Judge Laporte considers "imminent" to mean "probable," which means something more than possible. A very vague standard indeed, exactly the kind of thing that drives computer engineers crazy. I predict the preservation trigger date issue will always be decided on a case-by-case basis and no bright lines will ever appear. That is why the practice of law is an art, not a science, and the human element can never be replaced by technology.

Unlike computer code, the rules of law are malleable and there are always exceptions. This, in turn, is one of the key reasons the two cultures of Law and IT have such a hard time understanding each other. It is also the reason a few inexperienced engineer types are delusionary and arrogant enough to think that e-discovery can be "fixed" with the right software algorithms. It cannot, because law is not a science; it is far too complex and chaotic for that. Or if it is a science, it is more like quantum physics,[40] where electrons are unpredictable and can be in two places at once, not the orderly world of Newtonian science that most engineers live in.

Yes, there are many computer programs that can be used as effective tools in the pursuit of justice. We lawyers need to wake up to that fact. But so too do the technologists who think the right software alone will fix everything. The human element is key in Law which is one reason that training is so important.

Where Are the Reports?

Getting back to the case, the defendants' chief information and technology officer testified that he was "instructed not to destroy any materials that might be relevant" to potential litigation. Unfortunately, none of the attorneys involved put those instructions in writing, or if they did, they could not find the hold notices five years later when the plaintiffs moved for sanctions. (Yes, law is slow, which is another thing IT cannot understand.)

---

40. http://www.youtube.com/watch?v=qzZDlXji0e0.

The failure to put hold notices in writing is a rookie mistake, especially when notifying engineers. Always put the litigation hold notices in writing (usually e-mail), confirm the receipt, send reminders, and keep a good record of everything. Then follow up, and ideally, collect what you need yourself instead of relying on self-collection. Also, a company should have litigation hold policies that specify how documents are to be preserved for litigation. It is dangerous to implement this in complex litigation on an ad hoc basis. The lawyers here did not do that, and so the door was left open for the IT personnel and other key custodians to completely ignore the requests from Legal. Here is Judge Laporte's reaction:

> The lack of a written document retention and litigation hold policy and procedures for its implementation, including timely reminders or even a single e-mail notice to relevant employees, exemplifies Defendants' lackadaisical attitude with respect to discovery of these important documents. *See, e.g., In re NTL Securities Litigation,* 244 F.R.D. 179, 198-99 (S.D. N.Y. 2007) (finding that the failure to have an adequate litigation hold in place and the failure to issue reminders to employees regarding the duty to preserve evidence was at least grossly negligent). The harm caused by the lack of a preservation policy was compounded by an egregious failure to diligently search for responsive documents in alternate locations until well after the eleventh hour, in the wake of the initial hearing on the motion for sanctions for spoliation.

The plaintiffs' motion to compel was based on many mistakes and failures to produce various categories of ESI requested. Judge Laporte's lengthy opinion considers many of them. One that sheds light on our disrespect and miscommunication theme here concerns plaintiffs' requests for production of "reports showing how the Web sites were used and the content of Defendants' databases." Defendants' attorneys first took the position "that it would be impossible to retain all reports because of space limitations." For that reason, the defendants said they could only produce report templates. Obviously, defense counsel were just repeating what IT told them.

The lawyers were told wrong. IT gave them this song and dance, I suppose, thinking that they could get away with it, that they could use a bit of double-talk about space limitations to avoid the time and trouble of actually searching for the reports. After all, lawyers are all computer-illiterate and they will never know the difference. As a result of this all-too-common tactic by IT, the lawyers were made to look like liars when the plaintiffs' attorneys did not take no for an answer. They kept pressing the issue, taking depositions, hiring IT experts of their own, filing motions to compel, all culminating in an evidentiary hearing on a motion for sanctions.

The next position the lawyers took on the requested reports, again at the urging of IT techs behind the scenes, was that the program "does not generate many types of reports." Then at the evidentiary hearing, where the engineers were obviously present and advising the lawyers on what to say, the poor defense counsel was questioned by an obviously frustrated Judge Laporte. Defense counsel does his best to respond to the judge but is obviously in deep water, way over his head. It does not turn out well. Here is Judge Laporte's description of what happened:

> Then, at the March 18, 2008 hearing on the motions for sanctions, in response to the Court's questioning, Defendants' counsel told the Court that Defendants do not store reports, but only permit users to make ephemeral queries and do not store the responses. In other words, Defendants did not keep any reports in the normal course of business, so nothing could have been lost or destroyed that should have been kept. Counsel concluded that:
>
>> Nothing's been destroyed. Move doesn't capture those reports that you are seeing; some other user does it. Just like you would, when you do a search on Google or Lexis. . . . We don't get a copy of when a—when a Realtor runs a query such as those, a copy goes into some files at Move. It's not been destroyed.

Mar. 18, 2008 Tr. at 26:10-20 (emphasis added). *This representation to the Court was false.*

Ethics 101—Thou Shalt Not Lie

Ouch, that hurts. That is not the kind of thing you ever want to read about yourself as a lawyer, that you made a false representation to the judge. This is not just a minor bad form error; it is a significant ethical violation.

> **Model Rules of Professional Conduct, Advocate—Rule 3.3—Candor Toward the Tribunal**
> (a) A lawyer shall not knowingly:
> (1) make a false statement of fact or law to a tribunal or fail to correct a false statement of material fact or law previously made to the tribunal by the lawyer; . . .
> (3) offer evidence that the lawyer knows to be false. . . .

If misrepresentations to the court do not lead to outright Bar discipline, it will certainly ruin your reputation with the Bench. Once that is lost, if you are a litigator, you might as well pack your bags and go home. In trial work, reputation and credibility are everything.

Looks like the defense lawyer here was set up and hung out to dry by his IT clients. The judge found his whole story to be false, a tale obviously fabricated by the IT witnesses who were "helping the lawyers" behind the scenes. Judge Laporte may have suspected as much during the hearing, but she found out for sure a few weeks later.

At the end of the hearing, Judge Laporte told the defendants that sanctions would be imposed against them, possibly including a final judgment. Then, just two weeks after this hearing and representation as to "no reports," the defendants in fact produced over 480,000 reports! No wonder Judge Laporte took the rare step of publicly chastising defense counsel in a written opinion.

Where Is the Source Code?

In a software patent case like this, the most important evidence is usually the source code. Naturally, this is exactly what the engineers here did not bother to properly preserve and produce. Again, the lawyers took the fall for it. Judge Laporte said they should have done a better job of notifying and reminding the software coders of their duty to keep old versions of the code. I disagree. In my view, sending more notices would have been about as effective as a cardboard sword against a dragon. Still, here is the way Judge Laporte saw it:

> Defendants had a duty to notify and periodically remind technical personnel of Defendants' preservation obligation and ensure that they took adequate steps to safeguard the data. At a minimum, Defendants were reckless in their conduct regarding the Development Computer. Had Defendants imposed a proper litigation hold in this case, the evidence on the Development Computer, in particular, the log of changes to the Web sites' source code, would have been preserved. Instead, evidence of prior versions of source code was destroyed.

The facts of source code spoliation came out at the sanctions hearing, the one that ended so poorly for the defendants. Then, after losing the hearing, when the whole case is on the line, another IT miracle happens. Old versions of the source code suddenly begin manifesting. Defendants started producing source code like crazy, thinking, I suppose, that this way they could avoid sanctions, or at least prevent an outright loss of the case. Here is how it all appeared to Judge Laporte:

> It appears that only after the Court held a hearing on the motion for sanctions and indicated that sanctions may be appropriate, and *fifteen months after the Court's express order to produce all versions of source code*, did Defendants

make any real effort to fulfill their discovery obligations to search for and gather source code.

Here is the story the defendants came up with to explain the sudden, unexpected production of millions of lines of source code. A few days after the hearing one of the senior engineers:

> [H]ad a resurgence of memory "some weeks ago" when he recalled that his work computer's hard drive, which likely contained copies of pre-pour-over source code, had crashed at some unspecified time and that he had stored the crashed hard drive at his home. *See* Declaration of Philip Dawley in Support of Defs.' Supp. Memo. re: Spoliation Remedy at ¶ 18-20. Engineers were able to reconstruct source code files from that hard drive.

Still more source code was found by simply asking one of the engineers in charge of the code project. What a brilliant idea! Funny they had never thought of that before. When the lawyers finally did talk to the engineer in charge of a key code-migration project, and she understood the company might be shut down for a patent violation, she remembered that she had made an archive copy on her own. She kept it on a DVD in a drawer in her cubicle at work. That is exactly the kind of thing techs do all the time (so do I), which is why these reclusive coders must be located and personally questioned when their ESI is first requested, not years later when a judge is ready to dismiss your case.

The court reacted to this by saying it was "frankly shocked" that the engineer had not been questioned earlier and the code produced long ago. There were even more productions and source code findings after that, but the story grows redundant at this point, and I yearn for a good lunch menu to read.

THE "BETTER LATE THAN NEVER" DEFENSE

Defendants responded somewhat apologetically, but basically said "no harm, no foul," we have now produced the code, so there is no need for sanctions. The "better late than never" defense did keep the case from the ultimate sanction of a default judgment, but they did not escape the adverse inference and the monetary sanctions. Here is Judge Laporte's response:

> The fact that Defendants have flagrantly disregarded their discovery obligations with respect to reports and source code calls out for sanctions. . . . Defendants engaged in reckless and egregious discovery misconduct as described above. . . .
>
> The facts—specifically that Defendants have no written document retention policy nor was there a specific litigation hold put in place, that at least some evidence was destroyed when the Development Computer failed, that Defendants made material misrepresentations to the Court and Plaintiffs regarding the existence of reports, and that Defendants have produced an avalanche of responsive documents and electronically stored information only after the Court informed the parties that sanctions were appropriate—show a level of reckless disregard for their discovery obligation and for candor and accuracy before the Court sufficient to warrant severe monetary and evidentiary sanctions.
>
> Defendants' reckless conduct not only warrants sanctions under Rule 37, which does not have a bad faith requirement, but also warrants sanctions under the Court's inherent power. Specifically, Defendants' pattern of deceptive conduct and malfeasance in connection with discovery and production of documents under this Court's order and reckless and frivolous misrepresentations to the Court amounts to bad faith for purposes of sanctions under the Court's inherent power. Defendants' conduct was not inadvertent or beyond their control or merely negligent; to the contrary, Defendants did not even come close to making reasonable efforts to carry out their preservation and other discovery obligations and to determine that their representations to the Court and to opposing counsel were accurate. As a whole, Defendants' discovery misconduct in this case was both reckless and frivolous. *See, e.g., Fink*, 239 F.3d at 994. . . .

However, because there is no evidence that Defendants engaged in deliberate spoliation, and dismissal is the most extreme sanction and would go beyond what is necessary to cure the prejudice to Plaintiffs, the Court does not recommend terminating sanctions.

A Call for Mutual Respect

In my opinion, all of the problems in this case derived from Law/IT miscommunications and disrespect, not from malicious intent. In fact, I suspect, and many I know agree with this, that such "Who's on First"[41] miscommunications are at the root of most e-discovery sanction cases. (There are some notable exceptions—can you spell *Qualcomm*?[42]) I have written about this before,[43] and often speak of the problem. The lack of respect can certainly cause a lot of trouble in e-discovery. Even Rodney Dangerfield[44] would have had a hard time making these sanctions funny.

Information Technology and Law are both honorable occupations. We must learn to work together to meet the challenges of e-discovery. This is a plea for mutual respect and cooperation. A little humor about the whole thing wouldn't hurt either.

Chicken sandwiches, anyone?

Blog Reader Comment

It is a great irony that you have to interpret my quote in the *Wall Street Journal* article in exactly the opposite way in which it was intended. The original quote given was "You would literally have lawyers reading through things saying 'there was chicken for lunch.' You don't need lawyers to know it's a lunch menu; by using the technology, it frees up the

---

41. http://www.youtube.com/watch?v=sShMA85pv8M.

42. http://ralphlosey.wordpress.com/2008/06/01/the-lessons-of-qualcomm-a-wake-up-call-for-the-whole-legal-profession/.

43. http://ralphlosey.wordpress.com/2007/12/15/whos-on-first-new-case-repeats-the-classic-miscommunications-between-law-and-it/.

44. http://www.youtube.com/watch?v=cMVvTl83gWg&feature=related.

highly trained e-discovery experts to turn their attention to the matters that need them."

Whilst it is a shame the original quote was edited down, it's also a leap to assume that the e-discovery technology world feels the e-discovery experts are 'morons.' It is a shame the article came out as some sort of confrontation rather than the collaboration interview I gave (although I cannot comment on what others may have briefed on).

So your comment " He says e-discovery work . . . is work that requires little brain-power or legal training" bears no relation to what I said, and, although less clear, the article itself.

Having read your blog, I suspect we are actually in agreement, but I guess this episode shows the importance of facts rather than assertion of views of actions to a person and also the ability to go back and check them . . . e-discovery in action?

Ralph's Reply

I am sorry to hear that *The Wall Street Journal* misquoted you. I am also relieved to hear that your words were twisted to make it look like you and others think that way. I am glad that you took the time to set the record straight, and in fact, out of fairness, I will revise the blog post immediately to point out your comment.

Still, with the quote the *Journal* provided, and the whole story they set up after your quote, you can appreciate how it looks. Your beef should be with the *Journal*, not me. My interpretation of the article itself stands. It was clearly an "us versus them" approach revealing condescending attitudes on both sides.

By the way, my article does not say the "e-discovery" technology world thinks e-discovery "experts" are "morons." It says the "big tech companies" think "people" in the field, like me and my readers, are "morons." The e-discovery companies think very highly of themselves and other workers in this area. The lack of respect I typically see comes from techs outside of e-discovery against other techs inside e-discovery, and against the legal workers in the field. Most do not appreciate the complexity and difficulty of the e-discovery technical tasks or legal issues.

Thanks for taking the time to comment. Perhaps we can have lunch together sometime? My treat, as long as it's chicken!

Blog Reader Comment

Two thoughts. First I take issue that in 1980 it was an IBM world, having cut my teeth on DEC equipment, as well as early Apple PCs. Who can forget the VT100? But such is picking nits. My real comment is the lack of broader IT respect for legal IT. Growing up near the Valley and making the conversion from tech to law in the mid '80s exposed me to the widely held attitude that legal IT was somehow second-rate. Many of my tech friends held the opinion that legal IT folks worked in legal because they couldn't get hired anywhere else. Put another way, why would you work for a bunch of lawyers when high-tech companies were making millionaires out of twentysomethings? This attitude prevailed right up to the bursting bubble. Having spoken with Mike Lynch, albeit too briefly, on the subject, I think he gets it. And I know there are lawyers at Autonomy Zantaz who get it. I think the biggest problem is that there are too many lawyers *and* IT folks who still don't get it. . . . The misinterpretation of the legal issues by lawyers as well as IT lead to many of the technical difficulties. Because after all, this is really just a collateral matter.

WHO'S ON FIRST? NEW CASE REPEATS THE CLASSIC MISCOMMUNICATIONS BETWEEN LAW AND IT

The "Who's on First?" wordplay by Bud Abbott and Lou Costello[45] captures the core problem of e-discovery today. In this famous co-

---

45. http://www.abbottandcostello.net/.

medic example[46] of miscommunication, the tall Abbott says one thing and the portly Costello hears another. (Abbot and Costello supposedly[47] rarely did this joke the same way twice, but here[48] is one good example of it.) No matter how they played the skit, the resulting confusion was always hilarious. Unfortunately, when this kind of miscommunication happens in the world of e-discovery, and I contend it happens every day in a thousand different ways, the results can be sanctionable. The recent case of *Great American Insurance Co. v. Lowry Development*,[49] 2007 WL 4268776 (Nov. 30, 2007, S.D. Miss.) provides us with the latest example.

You know, strange as it may seem, they give computer parts peculiar names nowadays. On a personal computer, we have memory, hard drives, files, and even a motherboard. All of these names were used frequently in *Great American*, although, based on the opinion, not always correctly. The plaintiff insurer moved for sanctions against one of the defendants, the insured's insurance broker, Danny Groves. Groves disposed of his personal computer after suit was filed when he had a duty to preserve all relevant information. He disposed of his PC after it was damaged by a lightning strike. Since I live in the lightning capital of the U.S., I happen to know a lot about what lightning can do to a computer, and none of it is good.

The parties all agreed that Groves' computer was hit by lightning, but aside from that, all of the other facts surrounding the destruction of his PC were disputed. So much so that the senior district court judge in Mississippi trying to sort this all out, L. T. Senter, Jr., required an evidentiary hearing.

After the hearing, where Groves and others testified, Judge Senter was persuaded that sanctions should be imposed against Groves because his disposal of the PC made it impossible for the insurer, Great American, to get documents from computer memory that could have been relevant. Groves argued there was nothing of

---

46. http://www.youtube.com/watch?v=sShMA85pv8M.
47. http://en.wikipedia.org/wiki/Who's_on_First%3F.
48. http://www.thejokester.net/ClassicFrame/Who's%20On%20First.htm.
49. http://ralphlosey.files.wordpress.com/2007/12/greatamericanins-co.doc.

value in his computer anyway, and so sanctions were not appropriate. To this, all the insurer could do was make speculative arguments that two documents might have been in Groves's computer, since they could not be found anywhere else, and admittedly might not even exist. But if these two documents did exist, the insurer was convinced they would probably support its position that the policy did not cover wind damage, and so they did not have to pay for damages caused by Hurricane Katrina. Here is how Judge Senter explains it:

> Other than these two documents, Great American has not specifically identified any relevant document that is missing from this record, but it is Groves's disposal of his computer, the very act at issue, that deprives Great American of the ability to specify the documents in the computer memory that may have been relevant to the issues in this case. Whatever information the computer contained is now permanently unavailable.

Of course, the documents in the computer memory, assuming there were any, were permanently unavailable the minute Groves turned his computer off for the night, not to mention when it was struck by lightning. Computer memory, which is generally understood to mean RAM memory unless otherwise specified, is inherently ephemeral, and only exists in the memory chips as long as they have power. The instant a computer is powered down, the data stored in memory is lost. This was explained in some detail in my article on the *Columbia Pictures* case in the "New Technologies" chapter of my first book, which concerned the discovery of the contents of memory before a computer is turned off or the data in computer memory is otherwise overwritten.

How did the judge in Mississippi get as mad as Costello at the end of the "Who's on First" routine? Well, perhaps not that mad, but upset enough to impose sanctions to support the insurer's "mutual mistake" argument. This argument is quite creative and bears some explanation. The insurer contends that it should not have to pay damages caused by Hurricane Katrina because when the policy was purchased, neither party thought that the policy covered wind damage, even if the courts in Mississippi now say it does. Since both parties were mistaken, the contract is voidable by the insurer. It is a novel defense, one I have made myself a few times, but I cannot recall that it has ever succeeded. Moreover, I would consider it a very long shot in these circumstances, where a jury in Mississippi must be convinced to side with an insurance company trying to avoid payment of a Hurricane Katrina claim.

But back to the circumstances in this case that agitated the judge enough to sanction Groves. It all started when Groves testified in his first deposition that his computer, the one he used in connection with the purchase of the insurance policy at issue, had been struck by lightning, and so he had no documents to produce. Groves testified that:

> Took it in, he couldn't fix it. He kept it. I don't know what he did with it. I bought a new one from Dell, and that's what I have.

The insurer followed up on this deposition testimony by requesting inspection of Groves's "electronic files." Groves's attorney, who presumably was sitting next to Groves when he testified at the deposition, wrote an objection to the request where he stated:

> . . . the only computer that contained such files and/or data was damaged by lightning in the summer of 2006. This computer was thereafter examined by Tech Advanced Computers and determined to be inoperable, and the files and data contained were not retrievable or capable of restoration. This motherboard of the computer was therefore replaced and the old motherboard discarded and is no longer in Groves's possession.

So, the motherboard was fried by the lightning strike—no surprise there. But was the hard drive also zapped? Cannot tell from this answer, but you can tell that the motherboard was replaced and the old motherboard was discarded. Didn't Groves just testify that the tech could not fix the computer, so he had to buy a new one from Dell? Did the lawyer think motherboard was the same thing as a computer?

Naturally, the insurance lawyer responded to that objection by talking to the Tech Advanced Computer technician who worked on Groves's computer, Shawn Cusolito, and persuaded Cusolito to sign an affidavit. The way these things usually work is that the lawyer interviews the witness, and then the lawyer prepares an affidavit for him or her to sign, using language as favorable as possible for his or her client, in this case the Great American Insurance Company. Not too surprisingly, the tech's affidavit contradicted both Groves's testimony and his attorney's reponse to the production request. For some reason, Shawn Cusolito was not called to testify at the hearing, and the judge instead relied only on the affidavit, thereby depriving Groves of any chance of cross-examination of this witness. Here is how the court summarized Cusolito's affidavit statements:

> . . . the technician reported that he was able to repair Groves's computer by replacing its motherboard and that he returned the computer to Groves in good working order. Cusolito's affidavit indicates that damage to the motherboard of this computer would not have caused a loss of any file or data stored in the computer.

I wonder how Cusolito knew that the lightning strike that fried the motherboard would not have caused any loss of data on the hard drive(s)? Did he run complete diagnostic tests on the hard drives to be sure no sectors were damaged? Did he even check that at all? Or did he just replace the motherboard, turn it on, and see that it booted okay? We'll never know, because all we have is his affidavit.

After the insurance company attorney got the Cusolito affidavit, he noticed Grove for a second deposition. This is unusual, but strangely there is no indication of any complaint by Grove or his attorney to a second deposition shortly after the first. At the second deposition, Grove was surprised by the affidavit and asked to explain the discrepancies with his prior testimony. Groves then admitted that his computer had been returned to him; in effect, the affidavit refreshed his memory about that. Still, Groves testified that the computer malfunctioned again a few days later, and this time he just threw it away, rather than waste his time with another repair trip. Once again, to anyone with any experience with computers damaged by a lightning strike, this has a certain ring of truth to it. If portions of a hard drive were damaged, or perhaps other components, then even after the motherboard was replaced, the computer could very well stop working again, or work only sporadically, until it needed to access damaged sectors of the drive.

Even though the judge never heard Cusolito testify and never heard any other expert testimony, he did hear Groves testify, and based on this evidence, he held that Groves's first deposition testimony was "untruthful" and Groves's attorney's response to the production request was "inaccurate and incomplete." The judge did not fault the attorney, however, stating that "the attorney could only have relied on Groves for the information set out as grounds for this objection." Not every judge would take such a forgiving attitude, especially in view of the ability to simply call Cusolito, like the insurer's counsel later did, to inquire of the facts before signing his name to the pleading in conformity with Rules 11 and 26(g)(1), *Federal Rules of Civil Procedure*. (Rule 26(g)(1) states: "By signing, an attorney or party certifies that to the best of the person's knowledge, information, and belief formed after a reasonable inquiry: (A) with respect to a disclosure, it is complete and correct as of the time it is made; . . .")

Judge Senter was inclined to go easy on Groves too, since Groves had suffered a terrible personal tragedy a few months before the deposition. For that reason, the judge was inclined to believe Groves's:

> . . . assertion that his misstatements were not the product of a deliberate intention to deceive but rather the product of his emotional distress and general inattention to his business affairs in the wake of his son's death.

Still, even though he was inclined to believe Groves's story of "inattention to business affairs," which is another way of saying "negligence," as a result of great personal distress, the judge held that Groves's deposition testimony, contradicted as it was by the Cusolito affidavit, was "sufficient to infer the necessary element of bad faith in connection with his actions."

For that reason, Judge Senter imposed spoliation sanctions against Groves for throwing away his old computer. He did so based on the assumption that the computer was in "good working order" as Cusolito's affidavit said, and that this meant there there was still retrievable data on the computer that might have supported the insurance company's mutual mistake argument against Groves. In explaining his decision, Judge Senter used the correct words this time, and did not refer to destruction of data in computer "memory," but instead correctly referred to "hard drive."

> I am of the opinion that Great American has established, by clear and convincing evidence, that the destruction of this computer has deprived the parties and the Court of the benefit of any records that may have been contained in the computer hard drive. I am also of the opinion that the data stored on this computer, whatever it may have been, was relevant evidence that Groves was under a duty to preserve during the pendency of this litigation. Great American has also established that the destruction of this computer was not a result of simple negligence or any cause beyond the control of Groves.

It is hard to understand how the insurer was able to prove, and to do so by "clear and convincing evidence," that the destruction was not the result of negligence, or of causes beyond Groves's control, such as a lightning strike of his computer.

Still, the sanctions imposed were really not too harsh. Mississippi law apparently imposes a strict "clear and convincing evidence" standard to prove that a contract should be rescinded based on mutual mistake. That is no doubt why the judge found the spoliation evidence met such a high standard, when the typical "preponderance of the evidence" standard (51% or more) is all that is required to prove spoliation.

The Mississippi mutual mistake recession law would require the Great American Insurance Company to prove by clear and convincing evidence that both it and the insured thought that the insurance policy did not cover wind damage at the time the policy was purchased. One wonders why they purchased it. There may be a good answer to that, but still, this defense seldom, if ever, succeeds. Certainly it would be a very hard sell to any jury in Mississippi considering a Hurricane Katrina claim. With a clear and convincing standard, instead of the typical "preponderance of the evidence" standard, it would be a proverbial wild goose chase.

The sanction imposed here for the alleged spoliation was merely to reduce the insurer's burden of proof from "clear and convincing" to "preponderance." The court will also allow the insurer to present evidence to the jury as to the alleged destruction of evidence. At such time Groves could also present his own evidence on the issue, including, I would hope, expert testimony as to the impact of a lightning strike on a computer. Moreover, Groves could, for the first time, cross-examine the key witness against him, the repair technician, Shawn Cusolito.

I am reminded of a well-known line[50] in the the Abbott and Costello movie *The Wistful Widow of Wagon Gap*:[51]

That wild goose chase of yours is going to lay an egg!

It remains to be seen whether it will be rotten or golden.

---

50. http://www.clown-ministry.com/Articles/funny-jokes/quotes-abbott-widow.html.

51. http://en.wikipedia.org/wiki/The_Wistful_Widow_of_Wagon_Gap.

Blog Reader Comment

(by the computer repair technician
described in the opinion)

Thought I would answer some of your questions.

"I wonder how Cusolito knew that the lightning strike that fried the motherboard would not have caused any loss of data on the hard drive(s)?" This is an alleged lightning strike as stated by the customer; I can neither prove nor disprove lightning damage, as there was no physical evidence of lightning damage

"Did he run complete diagnostic tests on the hard drives to be sure no sectors were damaged?" Thorough diagnostics were run on each and every component of the system prior to generating a quote for repair. Both the Dell diagnostics and a third-party diagnostic were run on the hard drive to check the sectors. Additionally, there was no evidence of corruption to the file indexes.

"Did he even check that at all? Or did he just replace the motherboard, turn it on, and see that it booted okay?" The faulty part was already identified, and the customer issued a quote for repair prior to a logic board ever being ordered based on the diagnostics of all of the components. I did not slap in a board and say "I reckon it was just the motherboard."

Additionally, it defies logic that one would spend money on a repair that carries both a labor and parts warranty, for them to simply discard the system.

Ralph's Reply

Thanks for commenting, Shawn. I am glad to hear from your comment that you did the right thing. Not all store techs are as careful, as I am sure you know. Moreover, from my reading, you never actually testified in court, so that is why I asked what I thought would be rhetorical questions. Who knew you would actually answer them on this blog! Also, your use of the term "logic board" instead of "motherboard" illustrates my fundamental point nicely.

As to why anyone would discard the system, the answer is not too hard to understand, but only if there was a lightning strike as Groves testified. Why waste more time on it? He trusted that you did your best and the logic board was functioning, but something else failed. Why return it to have another repair, and likely be told it is something else? If Groves was telling the truth and it was a lightning strike, then it's not too hard to believe the computer had more problems then an illogical board. He could be facing more charges to try and fix hopelessly damaged goods, and in any event, more wasted time and effort dealing with it. Lots of folks don't like coming in and talking to computer technicians and trying to enforce warranties. Good money after bad, he might think, might as well buy a new computer.

But you seem to question whether there was in fact lightning strike damage, and say you saw no evidence of that. That is troubling; there should be some evidence of it. I assume something was wrong with the mother board, since you replaced it, but you did not say what was wrong, or why it had to be replaced. What caused the damage? My analysis is based on the assumption that the computer was damaged by ligtning. The opinion indicates the insurer did not challenge this, so I assumed it. If there was no strike, then I agree, Groves's whole story falls apart, and it logical to assume that even his mother might not believe him.

Anyway, thanks for setting the record straight on your work, and giving us all better insights into this case!

Blog Reader Comment Again

Once I read your blog, I felt it was imperative that I responded to your questions, as my name was attached with a question of competence. It very often happens in a lightning-prone area, that people, unaware of the cause of an actual failure, will say it was lightning. I have even seen systems whose sole failure was viruses/adware/spyware checked in as a lightning strike. Because of this, we have to be very cautious to identify and isolate a system component failure. However, with a lack of physical evidence—scorched boards or components—it is considerably harder to indicate that a system has been damaged due to lightning.

Just noticed I didn't answer your underlying question. The board was not powering on at the time of diagnostic. While there were no physical signs of damage to the board, I cannot rule out a possible surge or EMP damage due to the lightning, it was never indicated by me that lightning caused the failure. On a daily basis I see multiple component failures, and have seen plenty of evidence of direct lightning strikes, often bearing some very nice indicators of arcing and burning—but these components are all created by man and can and do fail with or without lightning.

Ralph's Replies Again

Thanks again, Shawn. I'd be happy to take my computer to you for repair any day. I hear and agree with your comments.

MSG IS BAD FOR YOU! (EXPANSION OF AN EARLIER ESSAY ON METADATA)[52]

No, I'm not talking about Chinese food, I'm talking about an Outlook file format. Since Outlook e-mail is at the heart of many, if not most, electronic document productions today, it is essential to understand some of the different file formats this software uses, especially MSG and PST. Otherwise you can easily fall into an expensive and confusing MSG e-discovery trap. So, just as you want to avoid MSG in your food, you want to avoid it in your e-discovery production, too. On individual computers, Outlook can store e-mails in two different formats with two different file name extensions: MSG and PST. MSG stands for "Message." It is the file extension used to identify a single e-mail message. The PST extension is a Microsoft specialty that stands for "Personal Storage Table."[53] It is used to identify

---

52. This is an expanded revision of a prior article of the same name contained in the Metadata Chapter of my first book.
53. http://en.wikipedia.org/wiki/.pst.

all of the e-mails (with attachments) stored by one particular user. This is how almost everyone maintains and uses their personal Outlook e-mail program. They keep their e-mail in various folders, which all together make up one PST file. Indeed, this is the default procedure, although users can (assuming no administrative restrictions) separate their e-mails and scatter them all over their computer as separate and unrelated. In this event, the different extension of MSG is used to store the individual e-mails.

The situation is different in a corporate or enterprise server environment, something I did not mention when I first wrote about this. On Microsoft Outlook e-mail servers, the e-mails of individual users in the server group are all stored together in a single container file, an electronic database file with the file extension EDB.[54] (In Lotus e-mail systems, it's called NFS.) The individual users on the server do not have individual PST containers on the server, but the individual PST files can be easily created as a copy from the master EDB file on the server. This can be done at any time by the server administrator or even by the individual users, unless this feature has been disabled.

This function of Outlook is frequently disabled for individual users. Otherwise, users could create their own PST files on their hard drives, or even on their own portable storage devices, and the system administrator would never know about these backup files. This makes it very difficult to locate all e-mails in a large organization to find information, implement a legal hold, or collect responsive ESI. When there is a proliferation of unknown PST files, it is impossible to know if the EDB file is complete. This is because some e-mails in a user's section of a master EDB file may have been deleted from the EDB file, but still remain on the previously generated PST file.

In a corporate server environment, to respond to a native file production request or preservation notice, the e-mail of the individual users affected must be copied from the master container EDB file having everyone's e-mail into individual PST files of the users

---

54. http://technet.microsoft.com/en-us/library/bb124808.aspx.

whose e-mail might be relevant. The PST files created from the master EDB file must be searched for relevant e-mails, and non-responsive and privileged e-mails deleted, and then a new responsive PST file reconstituted for production. (Also, in an environment where users have the ability to create their own PST files at any time, you must ask about and preserve/search through these other PST files as well.)

Craig Ball,[55] an e-discovery expert with a deep understanding of forensics and technology, correctly points out that this is not a pure native production; that would require production of the original EDB container file. In his excellent article, "Re-Burn of the Native," found at page 73 of *Musings on Electronic Discovery*,[56] Craig calls it a "Quasi Native Production" and explains:

> Chockablock [yes, he talks like that] as it is with non-responsive material, there are compelling reasons not to produce "the" source PST. But there's no reason to refuse to produce responsive e-mails and attachments in the form of a PST file, so long as it's clearly identified as a reconstituted file containing selected messages and the contents fairly reflect the responsive content and relevant metadata of the original. Absent a need for computer forensic analysis or exceptional circumstances, a properly constructed quasi-native production of e-mail is an entirely sufficient substitute for the native container file.

Craig goes on to say that the production does not have to be made in a PST file to be "Quasi Native"; it could also be produced as an MSG file. Although that is certainly true, as MSG is also native to Outlook, in my opinion, the PST format is typically preferred. To understand why, it is helpful to use a paper file comparison.

Outlook, by default, keeps an individual user's e-mails all together in a filing cabinet–type structure. Received e-mails start in the Inbox folder. The user can then create various subfolders in which

---

55. http://www.craigball.com/.
56. http://www.craigball.com/BIYC.pdf.

to file the e-mails for later access. It is equivalent to providing a filing cabinet to store paper letters, but with a virtually unlimited number of blank folders and cabinet space. Just as in a paper filing system, with Outlook (and most other e-mail software, such as Lotus), you label the folders yourself, and file your e-mails in the folders you deem appropriate. This should result in some kind of rational record storage system that makes sense to users and allows them to retrieve old letters/e-mails more easily. The folders' names and ordering system often provide useful insights into the user's thinking, and sometimes help to explain the meaning of a particular document. For instance, if a user created a folder called "Important," her decision to place a particular document in that file tells you something about the document itself, or at least about the user's attitude toward that document. So when you take a single e-mail out of the Outlook folder, it is equivalent to removing it from a paper file folder and keeping it loose on your desk (or floor).

Parties today frequently specify the production of files in their native format so that all metadata will be preserved. Indeed, most commentators agree that native file production under the new rules, specifically Rule 34(b)(ii), is now the default mode of production absent agreement by the parties to the contrary. (There are, by the way, many good reasons to agree to non-native file production, as long as essential metadata is preserved, pertaining to the advantages of loaded TIFF files and trial preparation software.) Moreover, most believe that the primary purpose behind this rule specification is to preserve metadata. Rule 34(b)(ii) states:

> (ii) if a request for electronically stored information does not specify the form or forms of production, a responding party must produce the information in a form or forms in which it is ordinarily maintained or in a form or forms that are reasonably usable.

An argument can be made that both types of Microsoft e-mail files, individual MSG files, and collective PST files are "native" files, since they are both produced and used by Outlook. In that sense, they are both native to that software. But it is the PST form, not the

MSG form, in which almost everyone ordinarily maintains their individual Outlook e-mails, and so, in my opinion, that is the form contemplated by the rule. (I rule out production of the original native file in an enterprise server environment and production of the EDB or NSF files, because they include all e-mails of all users in the enterprise, and that would almost never be relevant and thus would be unwise, as Craig Ball explains well in his "Re-Burn of the Native" article.)

Rule 34(b)(ii) also provides an alternative to the native "ordinarily maintained" form by specifying that production can also be made in "forms that are reasonably usable." Under the alternate "reasonably usable" form, flatted image files, or Rich Text Format (RTF) file production, may arguably suffice. But in my opinion, and Craig agrees, they are only "reasonably usable" if fully searchable and if paired with attachments. Moreover, if other metadata is needed in a particular case that is not shown in the image file, then this metadata should be preserved in a load file for the image files to be considered reasonably usable.

When parties have agreed to native production and also to the preservation of metadata, then I suggest the situation is clear: Outlook files should be produced in PST format, not an MSG format. But before I complete the basis for this contention, further explanation of the terms might help. The *Sedona Conference Glossary*[57] (2005) defines "native format" as follows:

> Native Format: Electronic documents have an associated file structure defined by the original creating application. This file structure is referred to as the "native format" of the document.

Palgut v. City of Colorado Springs, 2006 WL 3483442 (D. Colo. Nov. 29, 2006) (discussed in Chapter Three of my first book) cites to the Judge's Guide and defines "Native format" as follows:

---

57. http://www.thesedonaconference.orgdltForm?did=tsglossarymay05.pdf.

"Native format" means all documents that are created in digital format (word processing files, spreadsheets, presentations, and E-mail) have a native file format—that is, a format designed specifically for the most efficient use of the information in which this kind of software specializes.

Outlook has designed the PST format for the most efficient use of the information it creates for individual users. That is why it is the default. True, it also has an alternative MSG format, but it is not the most efficient use of the information. The most efficient use is to keep all of the e-mails together, organized into different folders, the way the information was originally and ordinarily maintained. Further, when you take a single e-mail, remove it from the PST file, and put into into a stand-alone MSG format, you are stripping it of a key piece of metadata.

When Outlook e-mails are converted from their original PST format to MSG format, the metadata that shows where the e-mail was located in the custodian's folders is usually lost. It is equivalent to taking a filing cabinet full of letters that are filed and placed in appropriate drawers, files, folders and sub-folders, and dumping them all into one big box.

In short, you can see the original Outlook folder structure in a native format production of PST files, but you cannot and will not ever know this information in MSG format production. That makes review of the MSG production substantially more difficult and expensive than review of a PST production. Further, MSG production makes it impossible to determine what letters were originally filed together and hides the file names created by the custodian to identify these folders. Thus, for instance, if a user created folders labeled "hot," "unimportant," and "bogus," and then produced 100 e-mails from the unimportant folder, 20 from the bogus, and only one from the hot, this would no doubt lead to important deposition questioning.

So be wary of Outlook production in individual MSG files, which some parties may insist upon as less expensive than PST production. Instead, demand PST format. This is one of many items that savvy e-discovery lawyers will want to discuss in the initial meetings under new Rules 16 and 26.

Blog Reader (Craig Ball) Comments:

Dear Ralph:

Thanks for the kind comments. It's always heartening to know someone is reading what I write. It's even better when they see things the same way!

The points you make about the advantages of PST formatted production against production in MSG format are excellent. I couldn't agree more that preserving and producing the folder structure is unquestionably helpful and oftimes necessary. Like you, I'd rather get e-mail formatted as a PST.

But I don't think that necessarily mitigates against MSG when the folder structure is preserved—which can be done externally by something as simple as producing the MSGs within an identical folder tree or by furnishing the path data for each message in a load file.

Why am I stubbornly defending MSG when PST is superior?

It's because there are more off-the-shelf applications that can deal with the MSG format than the PST. By far the dominant standard for corporate e-mail, you'd think every tool would cut through a PST like a hot knife through butter. Instead, I find that the compressed and encrypted form of PSTs, along with their largely undocumented file internal structure, is something that trips up many tools. Moreover, until they are compacted, PSTs have a nasty propensity (or a wondrous propensity, depending on one's point of view) to carry double deleted files invisibly within their structure. That's probably not a big issue in the context of reconstituted production formats, but it's the sort of insidious risk that keeps us lawyers up at night.

One further comment. You indicate that a local PST isn't the default in an Exchange environment. Here, I mean on the user's PC hard drive. That's true, but it's almost universally supplanted by a file with the OST extension that holds synchronized Exchange e-mail in order to support offline access within Outlook. Accordingly, you almost always run into some sort of local e-mail storage file potentially at variance with what you'll find on the server. Additionally—as you well appreciate—the user may create any number of PST backup files at intervals and, to boot, there is often a need to look for auto-archive container files, locally on the machine or stored within the user's network storage areas or "shares."

Processing just the server-stored e-mail may be sufficient, but it's not often complete.

Looking forward to your book!

Craig Ball

Another Blog Reader Comments

I agree with your assessment that an MSG file is not ideally suited as a native file representation in Microsoft Outlook and Exchange environments. However, I do want to mention that the alternatives to produce native files are also beset with problems.

Technically, the most "native" of files in a Microsoft Exchange messaging environment is the EDB file that Exchange stores in its mail servers. This is because this is the file that contains all the mails for all the mailboxes on the Exchange Mailstore, and the place where all e-mails are actually maintained during the course of conducting business. However, the EDB files contain multiple users' mailboxes, and would contain confidential and privileged matter that should not be produced. To isolate an EDB to only the custodians that are relevant to a case would require their PSTs to be produced. Although the PSTs are a snapshot of a mailbox within an EDB file, it is technically not a native file that is used during normal course of business. Also, given that standard business processes and Microsoft's proven technologies are used for creating PST files from EDB files, there is a certain accepted belief that it is as close to native as we can get.

On the content of PST files themselves, I agree that it does preserve the complete meta-data of messages including the folder location and the chronological position within that folder. However, producing an entire PST as a responsive document is also not viable, since that would expose other e-mails that are potentially confidential and/or privileged. When [you] remove these messages from the original PST, that would alter the PST, thereby exposing [you] for spoliation. An alternative is to produce another PST designed for production and for delivering to the requesting party. The question then is whether this production step preserves the meta-data of the original message, including the original folder structure that is so vital to establishing certain aspects, such as user intent. Also, as one transfers an MSG from the original source PST to a target PST, the MSG's internal content changes. This is because an MSG's insertion into a new PST creates a new EntryID property. One could argue that the essential components of an MSG are preserved, but that is not provable by a hash of the MSG.

An alternative production approach could be to extract the responsive MSGs from the original PST, store each MSG in a separate file and compute its hash value. To preserve the meta-data, such as its original folder location, produce a second wrapper file in the form of XML that includes the file location of the MSG, its hash, the name of the original PST file it was extracted from, and the folder location within that PST. In this way, only the responsive MSG files need be produced, and as they are copied and transferred, the internal contents do not change, and the meta-data are preserved external to the MSG file in a corresponding XML file. The EDRM XML export mechanism provides a framework for producing multiple MSG files while preserving the original meta-data. This would seem to address the needs of native production while maintaining integrity of MSG as it existed in the original PST file.

BLOGGING AND PRESENTING AT LEGALTECH WEST 2008

I was at the LegalTech West[58] Convention in Los Angeles recently. There were several good presentations on e-discovery at this massive event, but the best by far was Craig Ball's *E-Discovery Jeopardy*. This was part of the *Game Show* theme that he dreamed up for three e-discovery CLEs.

If you think that is surprising, you might also be taken aback by the sign on the front row seats of each event: "Reserved for Bloggers." These seats were equipped with power strips to plug in blogger notebook computers. Looks like bloggers are finally getting some respect! Still, who wants to sit in the front row? The second and third rows were largely empty too, because no one likes to sit up front. I'll know blogging has truly arrived when we get the coveted back-row seats. Then I'll gladly plug in my MacAir and risk conspicuous over-the-shoulder snooping. In the meantime, for the most part, I prefer to remain just another suit in the crowd with a laptop. So too did almost everyone else, as the fron-row seats with the "Bloggers Only" signs were usually empty.

The Many Legal IT Vendors at the Convention (Most of Whom Were e-Discovery-Focused)

I spent a lot of time cruising the huge hall of vendors and checking out several new companies I had not seen before. This included a couple of new companies with a focus on Asia, such as Ji2, Inc.[59] It is a Japanese company, with offices in Tokyo and Los Angeles, that specializes in services to Japanese multinationals. UBIC[60] is another interesting Japanese company along the same lines as Ji2. They assist Asian companies with general computer forensics and e-discovery.

Attenex[61] was there as a major event sponsor, even though they

---

58. http://www.legaltechshow.com/r5/cob_page.asp?category_id=49304&initial_file=cob_page-ltech.asp.

59. http://www.ji2.com/.

60. http://www.ubic.co.jp/.

61. http://www.attenex.com/.

had just been purchased[62] by FTI Consulting.[63] They were the ultimate in low-key sales, since they did not know what they had to sell, and neither did the people at the nearby FTI booth. They did not know whether the Attenex software would still be available for purchase, like FTI's Ringtail,[64] or whether FTI would switch to pure service offerings like the Applied and Kroll software.

Like everyone else, I collected a bag full of freebies from the many vendors. I liked the Attenex glow-in-the-dark pens and the Kroll golf balls, but my award for the best giveaway goes to Exterro[65] (which I had never heard of before). They gave out a combination stress-release squeeze ball and magic 8-ball. Their corporate motto is "Empowering Legal Teams," and their software fits into the all important area of legal hold management. It is supposed to help you implement and track holds to try to "eliminate human errors in high-stakes litigation."

This kind of human error is exactly what happened to Intel in the big antitrust case it is defending, *Advanced Micro Devices, Inc., et al. v. Intel Corp., et al.*, C. A. No. 05-441-JJF. A tech forgot to look at page two of a spreadsheet and so did not suspend the auto-delete function on the e-mail accounts of several key executives. The mistake was not discovered until two years into the case. I have written about this unfortunate mistake several times before. No doubt the Intel error has been good for Exterro's business and several other software companies like it, who now specialize in legal hold management.

I had dinner with the good folks of Fios,[66] primarily for the opportunity to get to know Mary Mack better. She is the corporate technology counsel of Fios and has her own blog that I read regularly, Sound Evidence.[67] Fios gives out her newly updated

---

62. http://www.attenex.com/news_and_events/press_releases/june_10,_2008.aspx.

63. http://www.fticonsulting.com/web/.

64. http://www.ftiringtail.com/web/.

65. http://www.exterro.com/.

66. http://www.fiosinc.com/.

67. http://www.discoveryresources.org/technology-counsel/sound-evidence/.

book,[68] *A Process of Illumination: the practical guide to electronic discovery.* She was the gracious host at Roy's, a landmark Hawaiian restaurant in the historic section of downtown Los Angeles.

The event featured group discussions with many e-discovery luminaries and students alike, including, coincidentally, one of the senior partners in the firm representing Intel in the AMD antitrust case. He did not speak of that case, of course, but had many excellent insights. It's amazing how much agreement there is among experts in the field on all of the major e-discovery issues. This was a private event, so I will not get into the names and discussions, except to say they were lively and frank. If you get an invitation to a Fios dinner, be sure to accept it.

Presenting on Search and Cost Control

I was also occupied at Legal Tech by my participation in two CLEs: one on e-discovery search and another on cost control. They were LexisNexis[69]–sponsored panels and followed the game-show format set up by the master of ceremonies, Craig Ball.[70]

For the search panel, I followed Craig's suggestion and created a *Match Game* theme Keynote[71] presentation. The panel was led by Patrick Oot[72] of Verizon, with help from Phil Strauss of H5, Inc.[73] and Joe Utsler, a project manager of LexisNexis Litigation Services.[74] The best Match Game question I could dream up was a quote by Marcel Proust,[75] the French lawyer-turned-writer who lived from 1871 to 1922. "The voyage of discovery is not in seeking new landscapes, but in having _____."

---

68. http://www.fiosinc.com/news/pr/20080625_fios-updates-book.asp.

69. http://www.lexisnexis.com/.

70. http://www.craigball.com/.

71. http://www.apple.com/iwork/keynote/.

72. http://www.linkedin.com/in/patrickoot.

73. http://www.h5technologies.com/.

74. http://law.lexisnexis.com/full-service-law-firms/litigation-services-e-discovery.

75. http://www.kirjasto.sci.fi/proust.htm.

No one in the audience could fill in the blank, but unbeknownst to me, the father of one of the panelists, Phil Strauss from H5, was none other than Walter Strauss,[76] one of the country's leading Proust scholars. Phil, of course, knew the answer: "The voyage of discovery is not in seeking new landscapes, but in having new eyes." The idea here is that we need new eyes—namely, automated search technologies—to see the relevant evidence in ESI. Our human eyes are too slow, and weary too quickly, for discovery in the massive quantities of ESI that lawyers are faced with today. Since Phil's Dad had recently passed away, the unexpected Proust e-discovery connection was an especially nice touch for us all.

The main case we discussed was *Victor Stanley,* which I discuss in detail in the "Search" chapter of this book. There was some disagreement in the panel on the impact of *Victor Stanley* and whether and when attorneys should hire search experts to help them with a case. Phil Strauss, aside from being the son of a Proust scholar, is a practice director of H5, a linguistic/information retrieval and consultancy company. Naturally, he was the strongest proponent of bringing in experts to help on search issues, as Judge Grimm opined was necessary in *Victor Stanley.* But Patrick Oot, who heads up Verizon's e-Discovery Team, is far more reluctant to incur the added expense. I am somewhere in the middle, with the focus on scalability and proportionality, considering the size, dollar value of the case, and the cost of review. If hiring an expert or using special, albeit expensive, concept-type search software can reduce the volume of ESI enough to pay for itself, then by all means use it. The *new eyes* are then well worth it. The quality of retrieval will also improve as an added bonus to the cost savings.

For cost control, the game-show theme Craig suggested was "The Price Is Right." Here I was helped by Rick Hauser of Farmers Insurance.[77] He is an attorney on its e-Discovery Team and is in charge of litigation cost control overall. He was a good complement to my presentation focusing on e-Discovery Teams and how they are criti-

76. http://www.amazon.com/Proust-Literature-Novelist-as-Critic/dp/B000NUN0N6/ref=sr_1_8?ie=UTF8&s=books&qid=1214791629&sr=1-8.

77. http://www.farmers.com/.

cal to e-discovery cost control. As usual, the killer statistic in my presentation comes from CISCO, which brags that its e-Discovery Team saved it over $25 million in the first full year of operation.

It was a creative challenge to make slides on e-discovery issues with game-show themes, but one that I enjoyed. For instance, for "The Price Is Right," I came up with the question: "What is the price to review one terabyte of ESI?" The answer, upon the authority of Anne Kershaw, is approximately $18,750,000. (This assumes that one terabyte equals about 75,000,000 pages, a review time of 50 documents per hour, and thus 375,000 hours of review.) But by far the most imaginative e-discovery event in the whole show was Craig Ball's own "E-Discovery Jeopardy." There I was pleased to sit in the front row as the only confessed blogger for this entertaining CLE.

Craig Ball's e-Discovery *Jeopardy*

Craig created a terrific PowerPoint presentation that mimicked the "Jeopardy" game show perfectly, including effective use of video clips from the game itself. He has done this several times before with great success. Craig does an excellent Alex Trebek[78] impersonation and begins by selecting three volunteer contestants from the audience. At this show the contestants were Charles, Nancy, and Travis. Nancy was a paralegal specializing in e-discovery, and Charles and Travis were senior-level techs. Apparently no lawyers in attendance were brave enough to volunteer, myself included. Craig's PowerPoint slides mimicked the "Jeopardy" Answer Board perfectly, except that all of the categories, clues, and answers were related to e-discovery. In the first Jeopardy board, the six categories Craig came up with were: I Never Metadata I Didn't Like; EDD-ucation; Alphabet Soup; Down to Cases; E-Discovery Lingo; and By the Numbers.

The "I Never Metadata . . . " category had questions pertaining to metadata, the "Down to Cases" questions pertained to famous e-discovery cases, etc. For example, a clue on the Answer Board might be: "the fingerprint of all ESI," whereupon the correct answer would be, "What is hash?" Very clever stuff here, and the whole presentation had the look and feel of the game show. The contestants picked

---

78. http://en.wikipedia.org/wiki/Alex_Trebek.

a category and dollar amount that indicated degree of difficulty. If they thought they knew the answer, they would ring their bell. All of the "Jeopardy" rules applied, and there was even a panel of judges to decide who rang a bell first in close calls, and there were many. The contestants were all good sports, and tried very hard, especially since there was a real $100 gift certificate for the winner. They got the question right almost half of the time (ok, I'm being generous). After each answer, Craig would give the correct answer and explain why and how it is important to e-discovery. That is where the learning took place.

Craig has thus figured out a way to make the infusion of real knowledge, often very technical and dry information, a fun experience. It is especially enjoyable for the audience, which does not have to suffer the embarrassment of not knowing the answers. Still, when the contestants are all stumped, Craig gives the audience a chance to shout out the answers, which I enjoyed doing myself on a few occasions. So everyone gets to play along, including the judges, who were hand-picked in advance for having some sort of background and expertise in e-discovery.

Just like the real game show, E-Discovery Jeopardy also has a second round of Double Jeopardy, surprise Daily Doubles questions where you bet what you want, and even Final Jeopardy, where you can bet all of your winnings to try for a come-from-behind victory. The six categories in Double Jeopardy were again very clever: playing by the Rules; Geek Speak; Beginning with "E"; Search Me; More Alphabet Soup; and Computer Forensics.

By the time Double Jeopardy was over, one of the techs, Charles, who is a security expert, had amassed a huge lead. The Final Jeopardy question, which Craig was gracious enough to allow me to reveal in this blog, was:

> The jurors who convicted this domestic diva were disturbed by her reported efforts to tinker with ESI on her assistant's computer.

The correct answer of course was "Who is Martha Stewart?" and all of the contestants got it right. That meant Charles walked away with the gift certificate.

Congratulations to Craig Ball for coming up with the most creative e-discovery CLE yet. He covered 61 different e-discovery words/issues in an hour's time, and made it all fast-paced and entertaining. I have seen many, many e-discovery CLEs, and this was one of the best. Once again, Craig sets a high standard for the rest of us to follow. He has me thinking of how to make my own e-discovery contest. Perhaps some kind of reality show might work—"America's Got E-Discovery Talent," perhaps? If you get any ideas, please let me know.

Legal Tech Keynote Speeches

The keynote speaker on the first day was Charles James, Chevron's[79] general counsel and a former antitrust partner at Jones Day.[80] He admitted to technological illiteracy, and so explained his presence as the lead speaker of a high-tech event because, as he put it, "I am the target . . . my IT needs are astronomical." Seems somewhat odd to me, but who can say no to the general counsel of a big oil company. He explained that Chevron has more than 400 in-house lawyers, gets sued an average of 2.5 times a day, and spends $190 million a year on outside counsel, spread out among 500 law firms. Yes, Chevron is a big consumer of legal services, and it pays to know what the customers want.

Mr. James spoke of his successes since he became general counsel six years ago, none of which pertain to e-discovery, so I will skip them here. He did include e-discovery in his list of gripes, however, focusing his main wrath on the propaganda of vendors. He dislikes gross overselling of capability and functionality of products, and hates jargon like "complete enterprise solution" and "seamless integration." Certainly there were a few vendors in the hall nearby who could have profited from hearing this message. Most still puff and overpromise to an embarrassing extent. Of course, when everybody else is shouting, who can hear the plain talking whisperer?

---

79. http://www.chevron.com/.
80. http://www.jonesday.com/.

Mr. James says that compatibility between different software systems is a major issue for Chevron. So much for "seamless integration."

Finally, Mr. James, who was billed as a controversial speaker, delivered with statements such as: "Electronic discovery is a waste of society's resources." Instead, he imagines a world without plaintiffs' lawyers, litigation holds or prosecutors. Kind of like John Lennon's imagining a world without government, or me imagining cars that run on water. He wants a world where we all just get along, where no one would ever sue anyone else. Who doesn't? Still, back in the real world, his company is sued 2.5 times a day and counting; so, like it or not, e-discovery is here to stay.

The keynote of the second day was delivered by the decidedly uncontroversial Magistrate Judge Elizabeth D. Laporte, from San Francisco district court. She was well prepared and reviewed the holdings of many of the current e-discovery cases of the day. Her presentation included the major cases coming out of California, such as *Qualcomm* and *Columbia Pictures*. She read many of the key case quotes and, like a good judge, said nothing controversial or outside of the record. The audience seemed interested, and if you were new to e-discovery, and most in attendance seemed to fit that bill, you would have learned a great deal from her excellent speech.

Judge Laporte also agreed with Judge Scheindlin's *Zubulake* Duty.[81] She stated that legal counsel and their clients need to understand and learn about their ESI prior to attending Rule 26(f) "meet and confers" and other pretrial discovery conferences. She said the days of "drive-by conferences" were over. Lawyers today either have to learn the complex technologies themselves or bring in experts to assist them. This is now mainstream truth among the federal judiciary. Yet, it is too painful a truth for many attorneys to hear. In my experience, many attorneys, especially otherwise terrific trial lawyers, still live the lie that e-discovery is not important and can safely be ignored. In the words of the immortal Marcel Proust:

---

81. http://ralphlosey.wordpress.com/zubu-duty/.

Lies are essential to humanity. They are perhaps as important as the pursuit of pleasure and moreover are dictated by that pursuit.

THE DAYS OF THE BATES STAMP ARE NUMBERED

As a kind of strange lawyer midlife crisis, I wrote my first law review article last year: "HASH: The New Bates Stamp,"[82] 12 *Journal of Technology Law & Policy* 1 (June 2007). Following tradition, I tried to make the opening sentences as clever as possible:

> For over one hundred years, complex litigation has relied upon the ubiquitous Bates stamp to try and maintain order and clarity in paper evidence by placing sequential numbers on documents. In today's world of vast quantities of electronic documents, **the days of the Bates stamp are numbered**. Instead, the future belongs to a new technology, a computer-based mathematical process known as "hash." (emphasis added)

Ok, maybe not so clever, but still, I was delighted to see an article this week titled "Bates Stamps' Days May Be Numbered,"[83] by Tom O'Connor,[84] in Law.com's Legal Technology[85] section. No big surprise here, as I met Tom a few weeks ago and we talked about hash. (I tend to do that, a lot.) I liked how Tom saw the conversion from Bates stamping to hash as symbolic of a paradigm shift, not only in e-discovery, but in the world at large. Tom and a few others, such as Craig Ball,[86] see a significance in the move to hash beyond what I understood when I wrote the article. They also have a better grasp of how this fits with other e-discovery technologies and procedures to facilitate what Tom claims are huge savings in time and money. I gave Tom a copy of my article, as he had heard about it from Craig but not yet read it. (Yes, I usually keep an extra copy in my briefcase.)

---

82. http://ralphlosey.files.wordpress.com/2007/09/hasharticlelosey.pdf.
83. http://www.law.com/jsp/legaltechnology/pubArticleLT.jsp?id=900005634749.
84. http://legal-edocs.org/TomOConnorBio.htm.
85. http://www.law.com/jsp/legaltechnology/index.jsp.
86. http://www.craigball.com/about.html.

I mentioned Tom's ideas in e-discovery at the Harvard Club in New York City, based on his presentation at the CLE. The article Tom has since written provides more meat for the bones, which I will attempt to summarize here and place into proper hash context. For still more information, listen to Monica Bay's recent interview of Tom on Legal Talk Network.[87]

For those not totally clear on what hash is, I suggest you read my law review article.[88] But if the thought of reading a 44-page academic paper with 174 footnotes leaves you cold, I suggest you try the hash articles in the "Technologies" chapter of this or my earlier book instead. They will give you a pretty good idea of how hash is the mathematical foundation of e-discovery, not a corned beef dish, and why this math should render sequential numbering obsolete. These short articles do not go into law-review depth, but do lay a helpful predicate to understand what Tom is talking about.

Tom's article begins by noting that most people doing e-discovery today still rely on Bates stamping. They scan and sequentially number ESI as if it were a piece of paper. Then he observes, as I did in my introduction, that this system will not work "in today's world of vast quantities of electronic documents."

But that process is simply not effective when dealing with terabytes of data. To address the sheer volume, many vendors are advocating a new way of working with electronic documents that can reduce costs as much as 65 percent by eliminating the need for text extraction and imaging in the processing phase. Beyond immediate cost savings, this approach also provides cheaper native file production, reducing imaging costs for production sets and saving up to 90 percent of the time needed to process documents. How? By not using Bates numbers[89] on every page.

Later Tom explains that the alternative to Bates numbers is hash values. But first he details how and why this conversion can save so much time and money.

---

87. http://www.legaltalknetwork.com/modules.php?name=News&file=article&sid=272.

88. http://http://ralphlosey.files.wordpress.com/2007/09/hasharticlelosey.pdf.

89. http://en.wikipedia.org/wiki/Bates_numbering.

Currently, to provide Bates numbering, many vendors generate TIFF[90] images from native files and then Bates number those images. But this process complicates native file review and—at anywhere from eight to 20 cents per TIFF—adds considerable cost to the process. Typically, during processing, data is culled, de-duplicated; metadata and text are extracted; and then a TIFF file is created. An unavoidable consequence is that the relationship of the pages to other pages, or attachments, is broken—and then must be re-created for the review process. Page-oriented programs handle this by using a load file[91] to tie everything together from the key of a page number. But most new software uses a relational database that stores the data about a document in multiple tables. To load single-page TIFFs into a relational database[92] involves a substantial amount of additional and duplicative work in the data load process.

These steps are avoided by changing to an identification system based on hash values of entire ESI files (which Tom calls "documents") that eliminates the need for tracking of individual pages. Here is how Tom explains it, using a lot of e-discovery-oriented tech-talk, which, if he is speaking, is usually tempered by a few laughs and war stories:

A document-based data model, rather than a page-based approach, eliminates the text extraction and image creation steps from the processing stage and cuts the cost of that process in half. Documents become available in the review platform much faster, as imaging often accounts for as much as 90 percent of the time to process. This enables early case as-

---

90. http://en.wikipedia.org/wiki/TIFF.
91. http://en.wikipedia.org/wiki/Load_file.
92. http://en.wikipedia.org/wiki/Relational_database.

sessment without any processing, by simply dragging and dropping a native file or a PST straight into the application—which cannot be achieved with the page-based batch process. Relational databases allow for one-to-many and many-to-many relationships and support advanced features and functions—as well as compatibility with external engines for tasks such as de-duping and concept searching.[93] Applications that support these functions—such as software from Equivio,[94] Recommind[95] and Vivisimo Inc.[96]—are all document-based and will not perform in the old page environment. Programs that use the document model can eliminate batch transfer. This process increases data storage due to the need for data replication in the transfer process and is also prone to a high rate of human error. And elimination of the time that inventory (in this case, electronic data) is stationary will eliminate overall cost as well as reduce production time.

Tom also prepared a diagram to show the Bates stamp workflow model for traditional TIFF image e-discovery process and review. This procedure treats ESI as if it were paper and uses sequential numbering, instead of hash, to identify information. According to Tom, this traditional procedure requires a number of time-consuming and expensive batch transfer processes. He says these steps are unnecessary and can be eliminated in pure native review that relies on hash. The more simplified "Bates-free" process is, in his words, "an easier, faster and more cost-effective e-discovery process." Tom concludes that:

> A modern litigation support program must be able to review native documents that are not just paper equivalents, and

---

93. http://www.law.com/jsp/legaltechnology/pubArticleLT.jsp?id=1208861019151.
94. http://www.equivio.com/.
95. http://www.recommind.com/.
96. http://vivisimo.com/.

directly enable review of any file that is in common use in business today. The future belongs to these new technologies, where native files are processed without the need to convert to TIFF and are identified by their unique hash algorithm. Attorneys and clients who focus on a document-based system will save time and money and can conduct native file review. In today's world of vast quantities of electronic documents, the days of the Bates stamp are numbered.

I could not agree more, especially since, unlike the title, Tom now says the "days *are* numbered" and not "*may* be numbered." I have no doubt about it, even though it may still take many years to get there. Old habits die hard, especially in the legal profession. Still, someday Bates stamping will seem as quaint and antique as the original Bates numbering machine itself. The original was invented in 1893. The first section of my law review article explains the history of this invention, and how Thomas Edison[97] purchased the patent from Edwin G. Bates. Then I go into the theory of hash and native ESI. I explain that hash is the digital fingerprint that identifies every electronic file and reveals any change. I also explain how hash is used in various e-discovery processes, and examine just about every legal decision ever written that mentions hash algorithms.

In case you have never seen a hash value before, here is an example: 4C37FC6257556E954E90755DEE5DB8CDA8D76710. There are many different types of hash formulas, but all produce lengthy alphanumeric hash values such as this. The two most popular are the SHA-1 hash[98] algorithm, which creates a 40-place hash value (shown above), and MD5 hash,[99] which produces a 32-place value. Both are too long for a practical naming convention to replace a Bates stamp. So I propose that the value be truncated and only the first and last three places be used. Thus the above hash would be shortened to 4C3.710 . I also propose that the # symbol stand for hash. (The # symbol is already commonly known as the

---

97. http://www.thomasedison.com/.
98. http://en.wikipedia.org/wiki/SHA-1.
99. http://en.wikipedia.org/wiki/MD5.

hash mark in most of the world, but in many English-speaking cultures, including the U.S., it is also called the *number* sign[100] or the *pound* sign.[101]) So I propose to abbreviate the above SHA-1 hash with #4C3.710. Some of the technical details of this naming protocol are addressed in the law review article. Others will have to be worked out with time and experience, and the adoption of more standards in the e-discovery industry.

I conclude my article by imagining what a courtroom of the future might be like without the Bates stamp.

> In countless courtrooms today, a mantra something like this is heard often: "I am handing the witness a document pre-marked as 'Trial Exhibit 75' and Bates stamped as 'Dr. Smith 0573.'" In the future, the author expects something like this will be heard instead: "I am putting on screen for the witness to view an ESI file pre-marked as 'Trial Exhibit 75' and hash marked as 'Dr. Smith Hash 4F7.C3B (Dr. Smith#4F7.C3B).'" The ESI file may still sometimes be converted to paper, in which case it could be handed to a witness, instead of put on a screen, but the same naming protocol would apply and it would bear a "hash mark" somewhere on the bottom: "Dr. Smith#4F7.C3B."

> Sorry, Mr. Bates, your 100-plus-year reign is over.

Blog Reader Comment

Several years ago I worked out a simple way to Bates number electronic files for eDiscovery (which I set out in my chapter on litigation support in *The Handbook of Computer Crime Investigation*). Dan Mares, one of the greats of digital forensics, wrote the first Bates-numbering tool based on my idea. Later, Christopher Brown, of Technology Pathways, implemented my Bates-numbering technique into his

---

100. http://en.wikipedia.org/wiki/Number_sign.
101. http://en.wikipedia.org/wiki/Pound_%28mass%29.

ProDiscovery forensics tool. So, Bates numbering doesn't have to die in the digital age, but you are quite correct that the old paper-based thinking does. Thanks.

Another Blog Reader Comment

Why are they so trusting of MD5/SHA1? Both are circumventable. There are now ways to make the hashes match even if there are totally different files.[102] There are also several tools now to modify MD5/SHA1.[103]

Ralph's Reply

Thanks for the comment. The articles you reference are interesting, but the false collisions engineered by experts that are discussed at these sites and elsewhere are not a cause for any real concern in the e-discovery arena. Here we primarily use hash to verify that ESI has not been altered, and to determine if two files stored on systems are identical. e-Discovery is not using hash for encryption purposes. These studies do, however, explain why the spy agencies are moving to new hash formulas.

TRADE SECRETS CASE USES MD5 HASH AND KEYWORD SEARCH TO PROTECT DEFENDANTS' RIGHTS—MAGISTRATE'S PRIVILEGE WAIVER ORDER IS REVERSED

A district court judge in Philadelphia recently reversed a magistrate's order requiring a defendant in a trade secret case to produce a forensic image of two of its computers. *Bro-Tech Corp. v. Thermax, Inc.*,[104] 2008 WL 724627 (E.D. Pa. March 17, 2008). The computers in question were servers located in Michigan and India. The order required production of full images to plaintiff's counsel.

---

102. http://www.schneier.com/blog/archives/2005/06/more_md5_collis.html.

103. http://www.stachliu.com/collisions.html.

104. http://ralphlosey.files.wordpress.com/2008/03/brotech-v.doc.

The defendant was willing to produce forensic images to the plaintiff's computer forensic expert, but not to its legal counsel. The defendant wanted to protect its confidential information on these servers by limiting the expert's search to the trade secret documents, or files that might contain information about these secrets. Accordingly, the defendant would only agree to allow the expert to search for files with matching MD5 hash values,[105] matching file names, or files containing the plaintiff's keywords. Hash value searches are often used in trade secret cases. *See, e.g., Creative Science Systems, Inc. v. Forex Capital Markets, LLC,* 2006 WL 870970, at *4 (N.D. Cal. 2006). As I explained on pages 17-20 of my article, "HASH: The New Bates Stamp,"[106] 12 *Journal of Technology Law & Policy* 1 (June 2007), "the irreversibility quality of hashing makes it possible to perform a hash search of a computer for specific hash values without revealing the actual contents of the computer searched."

Further, the defendant was willing to allow these searches of its servers only if it could protect its attorney-client communications and work product. To do this, the defendant proposed the standard procedure typically used for productions of this kind. *See Playboy Enterprises v. Welles,* 60 F. Supp. 2d 1050 (S.D. Cal. 1999). After plaintiff's expert performed the search of the forensic images, the files found would first be produced to the defendant for a privilege review. The defendant would have a right to remove any privileged files, prepare a log of the files removed, and produce the rest to the plaintiff.

Judge Cynthia M. Rufe agreed with the defendant. She held that it was clear legal error for the magistrate to require production of the forensic images "without any limitation as to the scope of the disclosure or prior filtering for privileged or work-product materials that the images might hold." In other words, she reversed because the order was too broad and did not protect the defendant's secrecy rights. Instead, the magistrate erroneously assumed that the defendant had waived all of its confidentiality rights to all of the informa-

---

105. http://ralphlosey.wordpress.com/computer-hash-5f0266c4c326b9a1ef9e39cb78c352dc/.

106. http://ralphlosey.files.wordpress.com/2007/09/hasharticlelosey.pdf.

tion on the servers by the mere act of having these servers examined by its forensic expert.

Case Background

Before I go into the intricacies of the waiver argument, it is helpful to review the case background. It is a trade secret action brought by Bro-Tech against one of its competitors, Thermax, and seven former employees who went to work for Thermax USA, Ltd.[107] The plaintiff, Bro-Tech Corporation, a/k/a The Purolite Company,[108] designs and manufactures chemical solutions—namely, ion exchange resins—used to remove impurities from water and air. The 28-page amended complaint alleges 12 causes of action:

> Purolite asserts the following causes of action: (1) misappropriation of trade secrets; (2) misappropriation of trade secrets through inevitable disclosure; (3) common law unfair competition; (4) breach of contract; (5) breach of the duty of loyalty; (6) tortious interference with existing and prospective business relationships; (7) conversion; (8) violation of the Computer Fraud and Abuse Act, 18 U.S.C. § 1030; (9) commercial disparagement; (10) unjust enrichment; (11) violation of the Racketeer Influenced and Corrupt Organizations Act, 18 U.S.C. § 1962(c) and (d); and (12) civil conspiracy.

Defendants responded by denying all allegations, and the competitor corporation, Thermax, countersued. Thermax alleged that Bro-Tech was intentionally interfering with its relationships with its customers by making false accusations that Thermax stole Bro-Tech's trade secrets. It also claimed that Bro-Tech itself stole trade secrets, in a kind of two wrongs cancel each other out defense, known as a "clean hands" affirmative defense (it seldom works). In other words, this is a typical trade secret case with competent counsel on both

---

107. http://www.thermax-usa.com/.
108. http://www.purolite.com/.

sides. In fact, dozens of lawyers from Philadelphia and New York have appeared of record in this case, including Baker & McKenzie[109] for the defendants.

The amended complaint seeks, among other things, temporary and permanent injunctive relief requiring the return of any trade secrets that the individual defendants took with them or disclosed to their new employer, Thermax. Apparently to avoid a temporary injunction hearing early in the case, the defendants, in 2005, agreed to a Stipulation and Order (the "May 23 Order") that "imposed an ongoing obligation on Defendants to return to Plaintiffs any Purolite files in their possession, and then to purge said files from their possession, custody and/or control." *Bro-Tech Corp. v. Thermax, Inc., supra* at *1.

In late 2007, the plaintiff deposed the defendants' computer forensic expert, Stephen Wolfe, of the Huron Consulting Group. Wolfe testified that he had searched forensic images of defendant Thermax's Michigan and India servers to see if they contained the hash values, file names, or keywords used by the plaintiff's expert, Lawrence Golden, to identify the plaintiff's trade secret files. Here is how the court described it:

> Wolfe searched India and Michigan servers for (1) the unique electronic "fingerprints" (or MD5 hash values) of all Purolite documents identified as such in this litigation; (2) the file names of the identified Purolite documents; and (3) certain search terms drawn from the Golden Exhibits.

Id. at note 8.

Wolfe admitted in his deposition that his search uncovered a number of matching files. Wolfe then filtered out files that were obviously false hits, such as standard application files that happened to contain the keywords. He then submitted the rest of the files with hits to Thermax's legal counsel for review. Wolfe did not actually review the contents of the India and Michigan files himself, but he

---

109. http://www.bakernet.com/BakerNet/default.htm.

did review the contents of files on other Thermax computers. The court explains that:

> hits in the India or Michigan servers apparently were not substantively evaluated by Wolfe, but were categorized and identified according to more superficial file characteristics, filtered for "false hits" by reference to external attributes, and submitted to Thermax's counsel for review of the actual content of the files.

Id.

The plaintiff responded to this testimony by arguing that the hits Wolfe admitted finding on Thermax's servers in India and Michigan showed that the May 23 Order had not been followed. The order required Thermax to return and purge any trade secrets on all of its computers. The plaintiff argued that it was therefore entitled to production of the full images of these servers and moved to compel. Magistrate Judge Carol Wells agreed, after an evidentiary hearing, that production was required to permit a determination of whether the defendants had violated the May 23 Order. Judge Wells ordered the production of the full images to "designated counsel only." *Bro-Tech v. Thermax*,[110] 2008 U.S. Dist. LEXIS 8970 (Feb. 7, 2008).

Defendant appealed the magistrate judge's ruling to the district court judge, arguing clear legal error on two grounds. First, they argued:

> that before any disclosure of the contents of the India and Michigan servers to counsel for Purolite occurs, Thermax has the legal right to filter the information to be disclosed in order to remove any attorney-client communications or work product material therein.

Id. at *2.

Second, defendants argued that:

---

110. http://www.electronicdiscoveryblog.com/cases/bro_tech.pdf.

they should be required to disclose to Purolite (after a review for privileged materials) only files which yield hits during a targeted search of the India and Michigan servers for evidence of Purolite files, and not, as the February 7 Order requires, to disclose the entire content of the India and Michigan servers for Plaintiffs' counsel's review.

Id.

Plaintiff argued that the magistrate's order should be upheld because only inspection of the entire India and Michigan servers by the plaintiff's counsel could ensure that no violation of the order had occurred. The plaintiff also argued that the defendant had waived privilege to any confidential content on these servers "by disclosing the servers to Stephen Wolfe, who authored an expert report for Defendants, albeit one which did not, in any way, concern the content of the India or Michigan servers." *Id.*

Waiver Argument

The magistrate erroneously found waiver on the basis of Rule 26(a)(2)(B), Fed. R. Civ. P.[111] This is the expert witness rule that requires a party to disclose all material considered by its expert in formulating an expert report to an opposing party. Plaintiff argued that this disclosure applied to all otherwise privileged materials, regardless of whether the expert actually examined the materials or relied upon them in a report. For authority, the plaintiff relied upon *Synthes Spine Co., L.P. v. Walden*, 232 F.R.D. 460, 463-64 (E.D. Pa. 2005) (disclosure requirements of Rule 26(a)(2)(B) override all claims of attorney-client privilege), and *Vitalo v. Cabot Corp.*, 212 F.R.D. 478, 479 (E.D. Pa. 2002) (overrides work product privilege).

Defendant countered that Wolfe had not examined these two servers as a testifying expert, but rather as a consultative expert, and so Rule 26(a)(2)(B) did not apply. Wolfe had examined and prepared reports on other computers owned by the defendants, and thus was a testifying expert for these other computers. But he had

---

111. http://www.law.cornell.edu/rules/frcp/Rule26.htm.

not prepared a report to be used as evidence on the Michigan and India servers. Instead, he had only examined these computers to help the corporate defendant, Thermax, evaluate its case. Thus, he was only a consultative expert, and not a testifying expert, as to these two servers.

Although not discussed in this opinion, Thermax probably also argued that even if Wolfe had been a testifying witness as to these servers, and thus Rule 26(a)(2)(B) did apply, its privilege could only be waived as to specific attorney-client communications actually disclosed to Wolfe and relied upon by him to form the expert opinion stated in the report. Since Wolfe testified that he never examined the contents of any files on these servers, there was no disclosure and, of course, no reliance.

Judge Rufe rejected the magistrate's overbroad construction of privilege waiver and allowed the defendant to protect its privileged communications. Here is the judge's discussion and analysis of the law.

> When privileged communications or work product materials are voluntarily disclosed to a third party, the privilege is waived. [FN18] An exception to this rule exists for disclosures to third parties which are necessary for the client to obtain adequately informed legal advice. [FN19] Under this exception, Thermax has not waived its privilege or work product protections in the India and Michigan server files disclosed to Wolfe. When searching these files, Wolfe was functioning in his capacity as "a non-testifying expert, retained by the lawyer to assist the lawyer in preparing the clients's case." [FN20] Thermax did not waive any protections it might have in the India and Michigan servers by disclosing them to Wolfe for consultative expert assistance in this litigation. Accordingly, this Order must provide for a privilege and work product filter.

This was obviously the correct decision, not only for the reasons stated, but also because Wolfe had only looked at information about the files (names, hash, and whether they contained keywords chosen by plaintiff), and had not actually examined the contents of the files themselves. Further, only a small percentage of the files on these servers had these matching characteristics.

Holding

Here is Judge Rufe's actual holding reversing the magistrate's order:

> *3 In this instance, the Court must overrule as contrary to law that portion of the February 7 Order which compels Thermax to produce to Plaintiffs the entire India and Michigan servers for Plaintiffs' review, without regard for privilege, on Rule 26(a)(2)(B) grounds. Wolfe repeatedly stated under oath that the India and Michigan servers were outside the scope of his expert report, and that he did not consider them in his testifying expert role. [FN15] Instead, his expert report exclusively concerned the contents of other devices. Because the information on the India and Michigan servers was not disclosed to or considered by Wolfe for purposes of his expert report, Rule 26(a)(2)(B) does not apply to the materials on those servers, and does not provide a legal basis for requiring their disclosure to Purolite.

Although Judge Rufe agreed with the defendants that they had a right to protect their privileges, she did want a search of these servers performed to determine whether the defendants had retained any of the plaintiff's trade secret information in violation of the prior stipulated order.

> Notwithstanding the foregoing ruling, the Court wholly agrees with the Magistrate Judge that, in present circumstances, a significant measure of disclosure of the contents of the India and Michigan servers is necessary to ensure that Thermax has not retained Purolite information in violation

of the May 23 Order. The fact that Wolfe's electronic search of the India and Michigan servers using search terms designed to find Purolite information yielded numerous hits suggests the strong possibility (if not providing conclusive proof) that Purolite information is improperly contained in those servers. Furthermore, the parties agree that some disclosure is now necessary, although they disagree on the proper scope of the disclosure. [FN16] Thus, disclosure of the images, to some extent, shall be required.

Id. at *3.

Judge Rufe suggests that if the limited disclosure does reveal any intentional violation of the prior court order to return and purge any trade secrets, then a full search of the imaged server hard drives might be permitted. Such an inspection would include deleted files and slack space, and this might provide further evidence of intentional violation of the order or spoliation.

*4 The Court finds that there is not, at present, evidence of an intentional violation of the May 23 Order by Defendants, as would warrant full disclosure. We know too little about the contents of the files that yielded hits during Wolfe's search of the India and Michigan servers to reach such a conclusion at this time. Wolfe's search may have yielded false hits, or may otherwise have signaled files that were properly in Thermax's possession; conversely, the hits may indicate a Thermax violation. Lacking clear evidence of an intentional violation, the Court will not impose the type of disclosure ordered previously in materially different circumstances involving Defendant Sachdev. Instead, a more measured, yet still significant, disclosure will be required.

Based on these findings, the court followed the defendant's suggested protocol for limited production and required the following:

*5 (1) Within three (3) days of the date of this Order, Defendants' counsel shall produce to Plaintiffs' computer forensic expert forensically sound copies of the images of all electronic data storage devices in Michigan and India of which Huron Consulting Group ("Huron") made copies in May and June 2007. These forensically sound copies are to be marked "CONFIDENTIAL—DESIGNATED COUNSEL ONLY";

(2) Review of these forensically sound copies shall be limited to: (a) MD5 hash value searches for Purolite documents identified as such in this litigation; (b) File name searches for the Purolite documents; and (c) Searches for documents containing any term identified by Stephen C. Wolfe in his November 28, 2007 expert report;

(3) All documents identified in these searches by Plaintiffs' computer forensic expert will be provided to Defendants' counsel in electronic format, who will review these documents for privilege;

(4) Within seven (7) days of receiving these documents from Plaintiffs' computer forensic expert, Defendants' counsel will provide all such documents which are not privileged, and a privilege log for any withheld or redacted documents, to Plaintiffs' counsel. Plaintiffs' counsel shall not have access to any other documents on these images.

Conclusion

Judge Rufe has, I think, done the right thing under these circumstances. A waiver of attorney-client privilege should never be implied from a forensic expert's mere review of a party's computer. Otherwise, parties would hesitate to employ experts and other skillful persons to help them evaluate a case. Would justice really be served by uneducated guesses or blind ignorance? Do we really want to discourage clients from telling their lawyer the full story for fear that their secrets will not be safe?

It was obviously not the defendant's intent to waive its privileges in this case. The magistrate judge's finding of waiver appears to have been a kind of improper punishment of the defendant for its assumed violation of the prior court order. But, as Judge Rufe implies, that is putting the cart before the horse. The violation of the order has not yet been proven. The hits Wolfe testified to may all be false positives resulting from overly broad keywords by the plaintiff's expert.

In any event, even if a violation is later proven by, for instance, multiple hash value matches (which is a common way to prove trade secret theft), this would still not justify stripping the defendants of their attorney-client privilege. It might justify sanctions and further search of the computers. It might even result in the defendant's loss of the case on all 12 counts. But even losing defendants have a right to communicate with their lawyer in private. It is unfair to deprive a litigant of this fundamental right as a punishment for perceived misconduct.

The United States Supreme Court has repeatedly recognized, since at least 1826, that the attorney-client privilege is a fundamental right. Public interest demands maintenance of the privilege so that a client may communicate freely and confidentially with his attorney. In *Chirac v. Reinicker*, 11 Wheat. (24 U.S.) 280, 294 (1826), the Supreme Court, through Justice Joseph Story,[112] declared that "it is indispensable for the purposes of private justice" that our legal system preserve the confidentiality of facts "communicated by client to counsel" in confidence. Later, in *Blackburn v. Crawfords*, 3 Wall. (70 U.S.) 175, 192-93 (1865), the Supreme Court quoted with approval the following statement from an earlier English case: "If the [attorney-client] privilege did not exist at all, everyone would be thrown upon his own legal resources. Deprived of all professional assistance, a man would not venture to consult any skilful person, or would only dare to tell his counsel half his case."

The judiciary should be wary of unwarranted intrusions upon this essential right. Judge Cynthia Rufe, like Justice Story before her, was correct to reverse the magistrate judge and uphold the attorney-client privilege.

---

112. http://en.wikipedia.org/wiki/Joseph_Story.

NEW CASE WHERE POLICE USE HASH TO CATCH A "PERP," AND MY FAVORED TRUNCATED HASH-LABELING SYSTEM TO IDENTIFY THE EVIDENCE

Part of my discipline as an e-discovery specialist is to try to read (or at least skim) every published opinion on the subject. Lots of attorneys specializing in this area do that. But there is one other type of case I also read, every opinion that uses the word "hash." No, I do not need help from Narcotics or Overeaters Anonymous. The kind of hash I am addicted to is purely algorithmic. This hash comes in many flavors, but the best known, and the ones usually employed in e-discovery, are called MD5 hash,[113] SHA-1 hash,[114] or the latest and greatest, SHA-2 hash.[115]

Hash is the mathematical foundation of e-discovery and the most powerful tool of any forensic investigator. It reveals the unique mathematical fingerprint of every computer file and allows for perfect identification and authentication of electronic evidence. I became fascinated with the powers of hash a few years ago, and ended up writing a lengthy law review article on the subject: "HASH: The New Bates Stamp,"[116] 12 *Journal of Technology Law & Policy* 1 (June 2007). A few months ago I wrote a blog on the article called *The Days of the Bates Stamp Are Numbered*, found in the "Technology" chapter of this book. There I talk about some of the more recent developments in this area of the law, especially the shift from TIFFing and linear flat-file Bates stamping to native file hash marking.

In the process of researching the original law review article, I am pretty sure I read every legal opinion and legal article ever written that mentions hash. I also read a few scientific and cryptological articles as well, most of which I did not really understand. Having put that much time and effort into the subject, I try to keep up by reading every new legal opinion or article mentioning hash. That is

---

113. http://en.wikipedia.org/wiki/MD5.
114. http://en.wikipedia.org/wiki/SHA_hash_functions.
115. http://csrc.nist.gov/groups/ST/hash/statement.html.
116. http://ralphlosey.files.wordpress.com/2008/07/hasharticleloseycorrec ted.pdf.

why I have a standing search for all cases using the term and automatically receive a copy of them by e-mail as soon as they are published. I can be in the middle of dinner and my BlackBerry will buzz alerting me of a new hash case. Lest you think that's a tad weird, I am willing to bet that there are a few other hash enthusiasts out there (Craig Ball comes to mind) who do the same thing. (*See* Craig Ball's excellent article[117] "In Praise of Hash" at pg. 52.)

Hash and Child Pornography

Most of the new hash cases I see have nothing to do with e-discovery per se. Instead, they are usually criminal law cases typically involving one of the most disgusting of crimes, child pornography. Police have been using hash to catch perpetrators in this area for years. Police can determine if certain child pornography files are on a computer (usually videos or still photos) by looking to see if the hash values for these files are present. That is a bit of an oversimplification, but suffice it to say that there are lists of hash values that are known to be associated with computer files that are unquestionably child pornography. New York Attorney General Andrew Cuomo explained the process in a press release[118] in June 2008 announcing a deal with major Internet providers to block major sources of child pornography:

> As part of the undercover investigation, the Attorney General's office developed a new system for identifying online content that contains child pornography. Every online picture has a unique hash value that, once identified and collected, can be used to digitally match the same image anywhere else it is distributed. By building a library of the hash values for images identified as child pornography, the Attorney General's investigators were able to filter through tens of thousands of online files at a time, speedily identifying which Internet Service Providers were furnishing access to those images.

---

117. http://www.craigball.com/.
118. http://www.oag.state.ny.us/press/2008/june/june10a_08.html.

United States v. Warren

I recently received a new hash case alert from a district court in Missouri—*United States v. Warren*,[119] 2008 WL 3010156 (E.D. Mo. July 24, 2008). A quick review showed it was yet another child porn case, so I did not think much about it. I just added it to my reading list for more careful study later, just in case there might be something special about it. When I got around to reading *Warren* yesterday, I was very pleasantly surprised, as this was indeed a special case.

Warren is a case considering and rejecting a motion to suppress evidence, namely computer video files of underage teens having sex. The motion to suppress was based on a series of hypertechnical challenges to the affidavit that the St. Louis police submitted to the judge to receive a search warrant of the defendant's computer. The affidavit explained how the police had searched the Internet for files "whose digital SHA-1 value was identical to that of a file known to contain child pornography." They found a computer with an Internet Protocol address[120] of 70 . . . 167 offering to share one such known file, and then subpoenaed AT&T to get the physical address of the subscriber with that IP address. The computer was located in Affton, Missouri.

The police detective's affidavit explained how the hash values and offer to upload established "that a computer in Missouri was 'offering to participate in the distribution of known child pornography.'" Based on this affidavit, the judge found probable cause to issue the search warrant of the computers located in Warren's home. The police then went to his home, found no one there, forced entry, and seized his computer. Warren himself later came along and, foolishly enough, voluntarily went to the police station, waived his right to counsel several times, and spoke at length to the police. The opinion includes extensive excerpts of the taped interview, which Warren later argued was made in violation of his right to legal counsel.

---

119. http://ralphlosey.files.wordpress.com/2008/08/us-v-warren-highlightedversion.doc.

120. http://en.wikipedia.org/wiki/IP_address.

The defendant's technical search warrant objections forced the court to delve into many of the characteristics and evidentiary properties of hash. For that reason alone, the case is useful to any practitioner trying to better understand the subject. But what is really special about the case, at least for me, is the system of hash file identification used by the court to identify the offending videotape at issue in this case. That video computer file was the key piece of evidence, the "smoking gun."

Six-Place Hash Truncation Naming Protocol

The opinion by Magistrate Judge David D. Noce in *Warren* is unusual and special because it is the first case to use the truncated hash-value labeling system I proposed in "HASH: The New Bates Stamp."[121] My article was not mentioned, and apparently Judge Noce was not aware of it. He used the six-place hash truncation system I proposed in my article because it was, in his words, "convenient" to do so, and because the detectives had used that system in their affidavits and testimony. I doubt the police detectives had read my law review article either, which makes their use of the abbreviation system all the more important. It shows that it is a natural and reasonable thing to do, although this is the first time it has been utilized or mentioned in a legal opinion.

So what is the six-place hash truncation system I proposed that these Missouri officials are now using? Before I can answer that, I have to go into a little more depth about hash and Bates stamps. "HASH: The New Bates Stamp"[122] not only explains hash and its importance to e-discovery, it also argues for the legal profession and e-discovery industry to adopt a new type of electronic document–naming protocol that uses hash values, instead of sequential numbering, to identify electronic evidence. I argue that the time has come for the legal profession to abandon 19th-century Bates stamp paper mentality and adopt 21st-century ESI hash mentality. I propose that

---

121. http://ralphlosey.files.wordpress.com/2008/07/hasharticleloseycorrected.pdf.

122. http://ralphlosey.files.wordpress.com/2008/07/hasharticleloseycorrected.pdf.

sequential Bates stamps be replaced by non-linear, intrinsic hash values.

The hash values would not only identify ESI, they would authenticate it, too, something the lowly Bates stamp could never do. But the problem with using hash values instead of Bates stamps to identify ESI is that hash values are too long and awkward for the human mind. Here is what a typical 40-place hexadecimal SHA-1 hash[123] value looks like:

2B37BC6257556E954F90755DDE5DB8CDA8D76619

Police detectives, lawyers, and judges cannot go around describing computer files used as evidence with such long alphanumerics. They are too cumbersome to replace the Bates stamp. So my common-sense proposal, which Judge Noce in *Warren* calls "convenient," is to only use the first three and last three places of the hash value, instead of all 40. So the hash value above becomes the much more manageable 2B3 . . . 619. That truncated hash value becomes a pretty good document name and, in my opinion and that of many others, should replace the arbitrary Bates stamp.

It turns out that the detectives in Missouri were already following this six-place truncation protocol at the time my article was published in June 2007. Perhaps they and other law enforcement agencies have been using this system for years. I don't know for sure, although I doubt it has been a widespread practice. I have talked to many e-discovery forensic experts about the hash-naming proposal over the past two years. Many of these experts did police work before going into e-discovery, and none ever mentioned having done this before. Also, it certainly does not appear in the legal literature on the subject—that is, until *United States v. Warren*.

Hexadecimal Values v. Base32 Number System

At first, I was disappointed to see that Judge Noce's introduction of the truncated hash-value naming protocol was flawed with two obvious technical errors. See if you can catch them.

---

123. http://en.wikipedia.org/wiki/SHA-1.

The search turned up a list of files, including one with a 32-character alpha-numeric SHA1 designation of "**H4V . . . UTI.**" Fn4

FN4—For convenience, in this opinion the SHA1 value set out in full in the search warrant affidavit will be referred to as "H4V . . . UTI." The affidavit defined the term "SHA1" (also known as "SHA-1") as being a mathematical algorithm that uses the Secure Hash Algorithm (SHA), developed by the National Institute of Standards and Technology (NIST), along with the National Security Agency (NSA) . . . Basically the SHA1 is an algorithm for computing a condensed representation of a message or data file like a fingerprint.

Warren, at *1.

First of all, the SHA-1 hash generates a 40-character hexadecimal string, not 32-character. The other kind of hash, MD5 hash, is the one that uses a 32 character string, not SHA-1. For this reason, my first reaction was that the judge, or police, mixed up the two different types of hash and meant to say 40 characters, not 32.

But then there seemed to be yet another, even bigger mistake. The letters *H V U T* and *I* should not have been in the hash value name. The values generated in e-discovery work to represent SHA-1 and MD5 hash are always hexadecimal. That is a numerical system with a base of 16. This is typically represented by the numbers 0–9 for the first 10 values, and A, B, C, D, E, and F to represent the last six, for a total of 16. In other words, a hexadecimal value does not employ any letters after F. Yet, the so called SHA-1 alphanumeric stated in the *Warren* opinion uses the letters H, U, T and I: "H4V . . . UTI."

I thought the police or Judge Noce must have messed things up, but I also seemed to remember reading somewhere that were other ways to express hash values, and anyway, I am always very careful before I tell a judge that he or she is wrong. So doing a little online research, I learned that there are indeed other ways to display hash values using different binary-based number systems, typically the

32-base or 64-base number systems. Base32 is defined in IETF RFC 3548[124] as using the characters A-Z and 2-7, while Base64 is defined in IETF PEM RFC 1421[125] as using the characters A-Z, a-z, 0-9, / and +.

My Online Investigation of Base32 Hash Math Led to a Shocking Discovery

Coming back to the *Warren* opinion, the hash values "H4V . . . UTI" are not hexadecimal, but they could be either Base32 or Base64. At this point, I did a little more online research about Base32 hash, and quickly found that there are many Web sites where you can locate music and videos to download based on their hash values. Almost right away, by simply using Google, I located a site where you can find media to download based upon their SHA1 Base32 value. It then took less than a minute to find the Web page where the Base32 SHA-1 hash values were listed that began with "H4V." That is how all of the media on the site was listed, in numerical order based on the first three numbers of their Base32 hash values.

There were 83 entries on the Web page whose hash values began with H4V. The site included listings of music and videos ranging from Beethoven's *Symphony No. 9* to a video of Lee Trevino's Golf Instruction. One video listing that was 11.1 MB in size had a disturbing title that suggested it could contain the kind of porn referenced in *Warren*. It was dated May 29, 2003. I clicked on its hash value button and saw that the full SHA-1 hash value for this video was H4VIBLSKAZ477WRTKH7IURE6NXEDCUTI.

When I saw that hash value, it shook me up. The first and last three values exactly matched the hash described in *Warren*: H4V . . . UTI. My academic investigation of the mathematical properties of hash had led me right to the smoking gun in *Warren*! I knew from my article, and the research of Bill Speros described in note 168, that this match of the first and last three values meant there was a 98.6% probability that this was the exact same file referenced in *Warren*. Mr. War-

124. http://tools.ietf.org/html/rfc3548.
125. http://tools.ietf.org/html/rfc1421.

ren was charged with a felony for distributing this same video. I think it is a crime to even have it on your computer.

I do not know for sure if it is the same file, since the *Warren* opinion nowhere states the full hash value, but in view of the description of this video, it is just too much of a coincidence for it not to be. It was astonishing on many levels to see just how quickly you can find a file like this on the Internet, simply by knowing the first three hash numbers.

It is probably not possible to actually download or view the file from this Web site. I do not really know for sure, since that would involve clicking on this file, which I was not about to do. But when I clicked on the link for Beethoven's *Symphony No. 9*, a piece of media that I do not find morally reprehensible, it took me to another Web page. This page had links to other computers where you may in fact have been able to download Beethoven's music. (I did not try, recognizing that might be a copyright violation.) At that point, the referring Web site included a statement that it "ONLY HAS INFO *ABOUT* FILES, AND DOES NOT OFFER ANY FILES FOR DOWN-LOAD." Still, if any law enforcement agency wants to contact me for the full Web site address, including Cuomo's group, I would be happy to provide it. It is really very easy to find, and so I assume the proper authorities are already well aware of this site and its hash values, or lack thereof. I am certainly no police officer, and even if I was, I would not have the stomach for this kind of investigative work. Reading the e-mail of parties in civil suits is about as much as I can handle.

Judge Noce Was Right

This little investigation proved to me that Judge Noce and the St. Louis police were correct. There is a SHA-1 hash that has 32 places, not 40, and it can use the whole alphabet, not just A-F.

The hash value H4V . . . UTI is indeed a correct first- and last-place truncation of a full SHA-1 hash value. But it is a SHA-1 hash that is expressed in Base32, not hexadecimal. Although the hash values used in e-discovery are almost always hexadecimal, the hash values used in Peer-to-Peer Web sites include a variety of different numerical systems, frequently including the Base32 system.

In addition, in my brief investigation of the P2P Webs, I learned that countless P2P-type Web sites now commonly use the first three places of hash values as a convenient shorthand naming system. For all I know, the "perps" may also. As Judge Noce says, it is the convenient thing to do. So when will the e-discovery vendors start doing so as well?

Blog Reader Comment

I have been thinking about using abbreviated hash for some time, to make the process of identifying due diligence documents easier, and was just getting to the stage of thinking "mmh, wonder could we patent this?" when I found your articles. We're implementing a truncated hash system on our virtual dataroom. For due diligence, it's just great when the index document has an automatic, easy-to-reference number, to ensure you're talking about the same file—even if it gets moved around in the dataroom.

VENUE ANALYSIS TRANSFORMED BY E-DISCOVERY AND THE DIGITIZATION OF SOCIETY

The location and availability of documents have always been important considerations in determining whether venue should be transferred for "the convenience of parties and witnesses, in the interest of justice." 28 U.S.C. § 1404(a). Not any more. Two new cases have shown that the digitization of records and electronic discovery are quickly rendering these criteria obsolete: *Victory Int'l (USA) Inc. v. Perry Ellis Int'l, Inc.,*[126] 2008 WL 65177 (D. N.J., Jan. 2, 2008), and *ICU Medical, Inc. v. RyMed Technologies, Inc.,*[127] 2008 WL 205307 (D. Del., Jan. 23, 2008).

When parties argue about venue, and what court is better situated to hear a case, they argue about convenience. These arguments

---

126. http://ralphlosey.files.wordpress.com/2008/03/victory-v-perry-ellis.doc.

127. http://ralphlosey.files.wordpress.com/2008/03/icu-medical-v-rymed.doc.

include not only the location of witnesses but, traditionally, also the location of records. If a court is located closer to where the original paper records are stored, that is supposed to be a factor favoring selection of that court.

This law developed in the last century when almost all documents were paper. At that time it made sense. If a case involved a warehouse full of paper records, then the proximity of a court to that warehouse was an important consideration. It made document productions, depositions, hearings, and trial easier and less expensive. The proximity to original records was one of several factors of convenience and justice that a court would consider in determining whether to transfer venue.

In this new century, well over 90 percent of business and other records are now in digital form. The electronically stored information can be fairly easily, and sometimes almost instantly, transferred from one computer to another, regardless of where the computers are located. With hash verification[128] in place, the electronic document in the second computer is just as much an original as the electronic document in the first. It is exactly the same computer file. Paper printouts of these multiple original electronic records can then be made anywhere on demand. For instance, they can be made if and when needed for depositions, hearings and trial. The proximity of the courthouse to the location of the computers used to create and store the information is irrelevant.

Victory Int'l v. Perry Ellis Int'l

The *Victory* case involves a fight over perfume and the right of Victory International to distribute Perry Ellis fragrances. *Victory Int'l (USA) Inc. v. Perry Ellis Int'l, Inc.*[129] was brought by a single plaintiff in New Jersey against a host of companies and individuals. As is common in antitrust type cases like this, the plaintiff, Victory, alleged a long list of complaints:

---

128. http://ralphlosey.wordpress.com/computer-hash-5f0266c4c326b9a1ef9e39cb78c352dc/.

129. http://ralphlosey.files.wordpress.com/2008/03/victory-v-perry-ellis.doc.

Victory seeks relief against the defendants for violation of Section 1 of the Sherman Act (15 U.S.C. § 1), violation of the Donnelly Act (N.Y. Gen. Bus. Law §§ 340-347), interference with contract, interference with prospective business advantage, breach of contract, fraud, deceit, unjust enrichment, violations of the Florida RICO statute, deceptive trade practices, restraints of trade, and unfair competition under the common law of the State of New Jersey and the other states of the Union.

The plaintiff and a couple of the defendants were located in New Jersey where the suit was filed, but 13 of the defendants were located in South Florida. The defendants moved the district court in New Jersey to transfer the case to the district court in Miami. The parties all agreed that both courts had jurisdiction, so it was strictly a venue issue.

Senior New Jersey District Court Judge Walls begins his analysis with the federal statute governing venue transfer: 28 U.S.C. § 1404(a). It states that if two district courts have jurisdiction, then for "the convenience of parties and witnesses, in the interest of justice, a district court may transfer any civil action to any other district or division where it might have been brought." Judge Walls goes on to explain:

A determination of whether to transfer must incorporate "all relevant factors to determine whether on balance the litigation would more conveniently proceed and the interests of justice be better served by transfer to a different forum." *Jumara v. State Farm Ins. Co.*, 55 F.3d 873, 879 (3d Cir. 1995) "Transfer analysis under Section 1404 is flexible and must be made on the unique facts presented in each case." *McGee & Co., Inc. v. United Arab Shipping Co.*, 6 F. Supp. 2d 283, 288 (D. N.J. 1997). "While there is no definitive formula or list of the factors to consider, courts have considered many variants of the private and public interests protected by the language of § 1404(a)." *Jumara,* 55 F.3d at 880.

One of the factors so considered in almost every venue argument in the past was the location and availability of documents and other evidence. Here the plaintiff, Victory, argued that most of the documents underlying this antitrust case were located in New Jersey and New York. That was one of the reasons advanced for opposing the defendants' motion to have the case dismissed in New Jersey and transferred to Miami. Judge Walls understands the realities of the electronic age. He rejected plaintiff's argument on the basis of the inherent portability of electronic information and the tools of e-discovery:

> This Court gives little weight to the location of documents because of the ease in which documents may be produced through electronic discovery. The location of documents only plays a role "where the documents 'may not be produced in the [ ] forum.'" *Cadapult Graphic Sys., Inc. v. Tektronix, Inc.*, 98 F. Supp. 2d 560, 568 (D. N.J. 2000) (quoting *Jumara*, 55 F.3d at 879). "[W]hen documents can be transported and/or easily photocopied, their location is entitled to little weight." *Clark v. Burger King Corp.*, 255 F. Supp. 2d 334, 339 (D. N.J. 2003).

Accordingly, Judge Walls granted the defendants' motion and transferred the suit to Miami.

ICU Medical v. RyMed Technologies

In the other recent venue case, *ICU Medical, Inc. v. RyMed Technologies, Inc.*,[130] the roles were reversed. Here the defendant moving to have the case transferred alleged that the new court would be better because it was located near the records.

This is a patent suit filed by ICU Medical (ICU), whose principal place of business is in San Clemente, California. The defendant, RyMed Technologies (RyMed), is headquartered in Tennessee, but also does substantial business in California. Still, ICU sued RyMed

---

130. http://ralphlosey.files.wordpress.com/2008/03/icu-medical-v-rymed.doc.

in Delaware, not California, because, like many U.S. businesses, both ICU and RyMed are incorporated there. In fact, the only connection both of these defendants had with Delaware was incorporation. That gave the Delaware court proper jurisdiction.

Of course, ICU conceded that the California district court also had jurisdiction. For this reason, and preferring California to Delaware, RyMed had filed its own lawsuit against ICU in California shortly after it was sued in Delaware. RyMed thought it would have a better chance defending the patent claims in California because ICU had recently lost other cases in that court trying to enforce the same patent. RyMed thus moved the Delaware court to transfer the patent suit to California, where it could be consolidated and tried with RyMed's later-filed suit over similar claims.

Delaware District Court Judge Joseph J. Farnan, Jr., found no evidence that ICU had filed the patent case in Delaware for the improper purpose of avoiding precedent in California. He considered the other cases ICU had lost there to be easily distinguishable. Moreover, Judge Farnan did not think the technology issues involved in the patent dispute were very complicated, and so the California court's prior experience was given little weight:

> The Court acknowledges that the Central District of California's familiarity with the patents at issue is a factor to consider, but the Court does not find that factor to be dispositive, particularly where, as here, the technology at issue is not complex, and the balance of the factors weighs in favor of ICU's choice of forums.

Still, RyMed argued for transfer due to convenience, noting that the inventor and other witnesses resided in California, and so did all of ICU's records pertaining to the patent. Judge Farnan began his venue analysis with a recitation of the law, again relying on *Jumara*.

> The Third Circuit has set forth a list of factors for district courts to consider when deciding whether or not to transfer. *Jumara, Id.* 55 F.3d at 879-80. These factors include six pri-

vate interests: (1) the plaintiff's forum preference as evidenced by his or her original choice, (2) the defendant's preference, (3) whether the claim arose elsewhere, (4) the convenience of the parties due to their relative physical and financial condition, (5) the convenience of the expected witnesses, but only so far as the witnesses might be unavailable for trial if the trial is conducted in a certain forum, and (6) the location of books and records, to the extent that the books and records could not be produced in a certain forum. *Id.* at 879.

Judge Farnan then considered RyMed's record proximity argument, but rejected it. He did so on the basis of the easy transferability of electronic records and the powers of e-discovery to locate and use these records. Judge Farnan begins by setting out the opposing arguments:

> RyMed contends: . . . . (5) access to relevant documents and design prototypes will be easier logistically and less expensive if this action is litigated in the Central District of California.
>
> ICU further contends that: . . . . (3) because RyMed's technical and damages-related documents will primarily come from Tennessee, not California, documents will need to be transferred some distance regardless of where the case is tried, and electronic discovery "eliminates any claim of burden based on location." (D.I. 16 at 9.)

Judge Farnan then agrees with ICU's arguments, and denies RyMed's motion to transfer venue:

> With respect to the location of records and other documents, and access to design prototypes, the "technological advances of recent years have significantly reduced the weight of this factor" in the Court's analysis, because they have "substantially reduc[ed] the burden of litigating in a distant forum." *Affymetrix, Inc. v. Synteni, Inc.*, 28 F. Supp. 2d 192, 205 (D.

Del. 1998). Thus, even if the Court credits RyMed's contention that many of its documents regarding "manufacturing and distribution activities are located in the Central District of California," rather than in Tennessee at RyMed's headquarters (D.I. 21 at 6), this factor weighs only minimally in favor of transfer. *Affymetrix*, 28 F. Supp. at 205.

Conclusion

I agree with these judges. The physical location of documents is now of no importance in most cases in determining appropriate venue. The old cases that include document location on the list of common factors to be considered are, to that extent, no longer valid. The reference has, in effect, been overturned by advances in technology. Unless you have a rare case of voluminous dead-tree-only documents, it should not even be argued. It is better to focus on other factors that still have relevance, such as witness location and witness availability. But in today's world of commonplace air travel and video connections, even these criteria are lessening in importance.

The parochial view is becoming less relevant on all levels. The world is flat,[131] as Thomas Friedman likes to say. Technology is pushing us into a new kind of global society. Our laws and legal analyses must also change to adapt to the times. These two venue cases provide a small example of this larger flattening trend.

---

131. http://www.thomaslfriedman.com/worldisflat3.htm.

Spoliation and Sanctions | 3

"BOOK 'EM, DANNO": HAWAIIAN JUDGE SANCTIONS COMPANY FOR TRUSTING ITS TOP OFFICERS AFTER ONE WIPES HIS LAPTOPS, ALLEGEDLY TO HIDE PORN

A federal court in Hawaii recently imposed severe sanctions against a company for facilitating spoliation by trusting its top officers not to intentionally destroy evidence. *In re Hawaiian Airlines, Inc., Debtor; Hawaiian Airlines, Inc. v. Mesa Air Group, Inc.,*[1] 2007 WL 3172642 (Bankr.

---

1. http://ralphlosey.files.wordpress.com/2007/11/in-re-hawaiian-airlines.doc.

D. Haw., Oct. 30, 2007). The defendant's chief financial officer (CFO) panicked after he received a litigation-hold notice and wiped files from his laptops. The plaintiff later claimed these files would have proved its case. The CFO said no, he was just trying to hide porn, but the judge didn't believe him and threw the book at them instead.

The defendant, a regional airline company, Mesa Air Group, Inc., was sued by a bankrupt competitor for an alleged breach of a confidentiality agreement. Mesa responded by sending out a written legal-hold notice. The notice instructed key players to preserve all electronically stored information (ESI) on their computers that might be relevant. Mesa timely sent out the first hold notice to its top three officers the day after the suit was filed. It trusted that they would comply with the notice and the law. It trusted that they would not act in bad faith and intentionally destroy relevant evidence.

Big mistake, according to U.S. Bankruptcy Judge Robert F. Faris. The defendant should not have trusted its employees, even its top officers. It should have assumed they might disobey the hold notice and the law. Mesa should have assumed its people would respond to a hold notice by destroying evidence, not preserving it. It should not only have sent out a hold notice, it should have made backup copies of the hard drives of all of its employees who might have discoverable ESI on their computers. That way, if they responded to the hold notice by deleting incriminating evidence, the company would still have a backup copy of everything to produce to the other side. (For this strategy to work, the company would have to have made these copies before the hold notice was sent.)

To do any less than that was, according to Judge Faris, to "facilitate" the spoliation of evidence, subjecting the company to severe sanctions—in this case, multiple adverse inferences and a fee award. The sanctions were imposed in this case even though the CFO acted alone, and there was no evidence that Mesa or its attorneys "knew of or condoned" the destruction of evidence.

According to Judge Faris, Mesa should have distrusted its chief fiinancial officer and assumed that he would destroy all relevant evidence on his three company computers (two laptops and a virtual drive on a server) as soon as he found out about this lawsuit. On the off chance their CFO had something incriminating to hide and was willing to break the law to hide it, Mesa should have made copies of his various computer hard drives and not simply relied upon a written notice. In Judge Faris's words:

> 13. Mesa could have taken reasonable steps that would have prevented, or mitigated the consequences of, Mr. Murnane's destruction of evidence. For example, Mesa could have made a backup of Mr. Murnane's H drive and the hard drives of Laptop 1 and Laptop 2 promptly after HA filed suit. Doing so would not have been costly, burdensome, or unduly disruptive of Mesa's business. Instead, Mesa simply told Mr. Murnane to preserve all evidence and trusted him to comply. Even though Mr. Murnane was a valued, trusted, high-level employee of the company, Mesa could and should have taken reasonable steps to prevent all of its employees from doing wrongful and foolish things, like destroying evidence, under the pressure of litigation. Because Mesa failed to take such steps, Mesa facilitated Mr. Murnane's misconduct.

It is true that the imaging of two laptops and a virtual drive would not, in and of itself, have been terribly burdensome or expensive. But does that justify the mandatory stealth imaging of all impacted employees? Mesa[2] is an airline of over 5,000 employees, generating revenues of over $1.4 billion per year. The opinion states that only the three top officers of Mesa were sent the original preservation hold notice: the CFO, the CEO, and the president. If in fact only three custodians were involved throughout, which to me seems unusual, then the court's low cost and burden argument has some merit, even if it is still questionable on policy and practical grounds. But if other hold notices were later sent out to dozens of additional ESI custodians, which to me seems more likely, then the court's economic analysis is flawed.

The policy of mistrust is also, in my view, not well considered. Although hindsight is 20/20, how was Mesa to have known when suit was filed that its chief financial officer might destroy evidence?

---

2. http://www.mesa-air.com/.

There is nothing in the opinion to suggest he was anything other than a trusted and reliable senior management employee. If Mesa could not trust its chief financial officer, then it could not trust anybody. By this logic, in every lawsuit Mesa would have to image the computers of all key witnesses and ESI custodians who might have discoverable ESI in them. Any of them might do "wrongful and foolish things" under the pressure of litigation. Where would this lead? I am reminded of the quote by Ralph Waldo Emerson: "Our distrust is very expensive." The copying of dozens, if not hundreds, of computers can become very expensive. Is it really reasonable to expect large organizations to always act out of mistrust and fear that it might have a renegade employee, one who is willing to break the law and destroy evidence? Is it really fair to hold that an employer facilitated its employees' bad-faith destruction of evidence simply because it did not copy all potentially impacted computers as soon as a suit was filed?

Also, as a practical matter, how was Mesa supposed to have copied its top officers' computers before they had notice of the lawsuit, and thus an opportunity to delete files from these computers? They are the first ones to learn of a suit like this, and are necessarily involved in discussions with the lawyers on what to do, who should be provided with a hold notice, and the like. Is it realistic to require legal counsel to copy everything on the computers of the top officers of a company anytime a suit is filed where they might be involved as a witness? Should in-house counsel be required to do so surreptitiously, even before the officers are told about the lawsuit? I doubt they would last very long if they did! Such extreme measures should, in my opinion, be employed only in very rare circumstances where there is strong evidence that the action is required, otherwise there is a substantial likelihood evidence will be destroyed. Even then, it should be used with caution. The extreme process of imaging all computers should never be used in a case such as this, where there is no advance warning of possible spoliation, much less a strong showing of likely destruction of evidence.

Beyond the questionable holding, the facts underlying this case are interesting on a number of levels, including the technical "geek" perspective. Mesa's CFO was said to be "an experienced and knowledgeable computer user." He installed a program called System Mechanic Professional 6[3] on both of his company-owned laptops, and used it to superdelete[4] files from them. He attempted to disguise the timing of these deletions by changing the dates on the computers before he ran the software. He did not know that forensic analysis can easily detect such system clock changes. The CFO also stored files on a company server, called his "H drive," but he did not use special software to superdelete any files there. Some files on his H drive were deleted, and apparently could not be later restored due to normal usage, but were recovered from backup tapes of the server. These and other technical details are explained by the court:

> System Mechanic has a subprogram called DriveScrubber2[5] that permanently deletes files from a computer.
>
> 7. When an active file (a file that a user can view) is deleted on a computer using the Windows operating system, the data comprising the file is not erased; instead, the file is removed from the "index" of all active files on the disk, and the disk space that contains the deleted file is gradually written over as new files are written to the disk. A person with the appropriate skill and software can analyze the bits of data left on the "unallocated space" of the drive (the portions of the disk that, according to the "index," do not contain active files) and reassemble some or all of the deleted files. "Disk wiping" programs like DriveScrubber2 render deleted files unrecoverable by writing meaningless data (usually repeated strings of hexadecimal characters) to the unallocated space of the disk, permanently eliminating the residue of previously deleted files.

Later forensic exams of the CFO's laptop computers could not recover the superdeleted files, but they did prove that Drive Scrub-

---

3. http://www.iolo.com/.
4. http://ralphlosey.wordpress.com/2007/07/07/ghostsurfer-wipe-out-leads-to-jail-order-sanction-in-bankruptcy-court/.
5. http://www.soft32.com/download_188306.html.

ber was used *after* the hold notice was received. The exams also revealed a clumsy attempt to conceal the disk wipes by changing the system clock to a time before the hold notice. As to the files ordinarily deleted from the network server H drive, Mesa was able to recover "many, if not all" of them by restoring the backup tapes of that drive. Some of the restored files were relevant, but none were "smoking guns."

The CFO did come up with a creative defense to his actions. He claimed he was trying to hide the fact that he had been viewing "adult materials." Judge Faris did not believe this testimony. For one thing, Mesa's CEO, who was a good friend of the CFO and thus obviously trusted him, testified that his friend had "told him he had wiped the hard drives in order to conceal adult content on his computers." Still, according to Judge Faris:

> It was absolutely clear from Mr. Ornstein's words and demeanor on the witness stand that he did not believe Mr. Murnane's "adult content" explanation.

I do not know what the CEO's demeanor was like when he testified about his friend's excuse—no doubt he was embarrassed—but obviously the CEO believed him or he would not have offered the story. Also, the opinion admits that evidence was offered that the CFO's laptop was previously found to have adult content in two prior incidents in 2003 and 2004. But Judge Faris was more impressed by the facts that no adult materials were found on the laptops or on the H drive now, and the IT tech who "regularly worked" on the laptops testified that he had never seen adult content on the computers.

Also, Judge Faris commented that the CFO never took the stand to testify, and he found that:

> It is not credible to suggest that a high-level officer and busy person such as Mr. Murnane would have done a mundane task like this himself rather than leaving it to Mesa's IT department.

That does not have the ring of truth to me. If a person, no matter what his rank, has the time and indiscretion to view porn on his company laptop, then it seems he would also have time to wipe it clean, and would not want talkative IT employees to do it for him. No one, especially a "high-level officer," would want to entrust such a sensitive and potentially embarrassing task to the company's IT department. The superdeletion process is not really too hard or time-consuming, as the judge here seems to recognize by calling it a "mundane task." So it is not at all surprising, much less "not credible," that someone would want to do it himself.

The timing of the CFO's deletions of alleged "adult materials" was too suspicious. There were also several indications that the CFO had taken and used confidential information of the bankrupt Hawaiian Airlines, and thus Mesa had breached the confidentiality agreement as alleged. These other facts seemed to color the court's analysis of the spoliation motion and conclusions that:

> b. The confidentiality agreement provides that "Mesa shall be responsible for any breach of this agreement by Mesa's employees, officers and Representatives . . . ." Mesa should also be responsible for the intentional destruction by one of its highest-ranking officers of evidence that could have shown whether Mesa complied with that agreement.

> c. Mesa could have prevented Mr. Murnane from destroying evidence, or at least limited his ability to destroy evidence, by taking reasonable, inexpensive, and non-burdensome steps. Mesa failed to do so and is responsible for the consequences of that failure.

For these and other reasons, Judge Faris granted the plaintiff's motion for sanctions, imposed multiple adverse inferences and taxed fees, but stopped short of entry of a default judgment as the plaintiff had requested.

WELLS FARGO IS ROBBED OF STAGED DOCUMENTS AND SEEKS THE DEATH PENALTY FOR THE LAWSUIT, BUT GETS AN ADVERSE INFERENCE INSTRUCTION INSTEAD

In Reno, Nevada, Wells Fargo used e-discovery as a weapon to help defend against a disgruntled mortgagee in *Johnson v. Wells Fargo Home Mortgage, Inc.*, 2008 WL 2142219 (D. Nev. May 16, 2008).[6] Wells Fargo moved for dismissal as a sanction for intentional spoliation of computer evidence. Magistrate Judge Robert A. McQuaid, Jr. did not dismiss the case, but did order an adverse inference jury instruction that will probably be outcome-determinative. The instruction requires the jury to assume that all of the information the plaintiff deleted from his hard drives would have supported Wells Fargo's defense.

I have never seen a defendant lose a case after being granted a key jury instruction like that, but still, the expense of going forward with trial can be considerable, and you never know what might happen. No doubt Wells Fargo was disappointed with the result, and, as I will explain here, they have every right to be.

Facts of the Case

The plaintiff sued Wells Fargo alleging violation of the Fair Credit Reporting Act. Wells Fargo supposedly reported to credit agencies that two of the plaintiff's loans from Wells Fargo were in default when they were not. The plaintiff also claims that Wells Fargo foreclosed on one of the loans, even though he was current in payment. The plaintiff claims that he "spent nine months making multiple phone calls and sending correspondence, including cancelled checks and loan documents, verifying the loans were current." *Id.* at *1. The plaintiff attached some of the correspondence and other documents as exhibits to his complaint. Wells Fargo not only denied the complaint, it alleged that the plaintiff manufactured the evidence and

---

6. http://ralphlosey.files.wordpress.com/2008/06/johnson_v_wellsfargo2.doc.

that the whole thing was staged. According to Wells Fargo, the alleged communications never happened, and the documents were backdated frauds.

To prove its electronic document forgery defense, Wells Fargo, on July 28, 2007, asked the plaintiff to produce for inspection the two laptop computers he used to write these documents. Wells Fargo hoped that a forensic exam would prove that the plaintiff's case was fabricated. It expected the forensic examination to show that the key documents supporting the plaintiff's case were prepared just before suit was filed and backdated to support his story of prior communications. The plaintiff objected to the request on September 14, 2007, stating that he would only produce specified files. Wells Fargo made several attempts to resolve the dispute, but ultimately was forced to file a motion to compel production of the hard drives on October 10, 2007. *Id.* at *3.

The motion was granted, and the plaintiff was ordered to produce the hard drives of his two laptop computers. When the drives were produced and examined by the computer forensic expert retained by Wells Fargo, he discovered that both drives had been "reformatted and/or reinstalled." *Id.* at *1. The forensic exam showed that "Plaintiff deleted files and reformatted both hard drives on September 25, 2007 and October 5, 2007." *Id.* at *3. That is two months after the request to produce. In other words, plaintiff secretly had his hard drives reformatted and reloaded while the parties were in negotiation over the production.

The expert said that the reformatting prevented him from retrieving useful information about the files that were on the disk before it was reloaded with new files. (This does not, however, mean that more information could not be gleaned by further study.) Still, among the new reloaded files the expert was able to find two of the letters that were key to the plaintiff's claim. The expert also found evidence to prove that these documents were created more than one year after the plaintiff claims to have written them. In fact, consistent with Well Fargo's suspicions, he found that they were created just a few weeks before suit was filed. It was not explained exactly what evidence the expert had to prove the backdating, but I suspect it was in the word documents' internal metadata.

Wells Fargo also stated that it would be able to recover still more information from the hard drives, even though they had been formatted, if additional, more expensive forensic recovery work were performed. This would be possible because when a disk is reformatted, all of the original data remains on the disk and is not fully destroyed. Instead, the areas on the disk containing the data are merely marked as available. The old data stays there until overwritten with new files. Wells Fargo confidently predicted that additional forensic study would uncover more forged documents. However, they did not want to incur that additional expense. They wanted the case dismissed.

Naturally, Wells Fargo was upset by the inability to get at all but two of the documents that it claimed the plaintiff had forged and backdated. It had hoped the forensic evidence would be conclusive and the case would promptly end with a summary judgment. Wells Fargo responded to this discovery of spoliation with a motion for sanctions, seeking the ultimate remedy of dismissal of the plaintiff's case. Here is Judge McQuaid's summary of Well Fargo's motion:

> Defendant asserts that "Plaintiff has altered numbers on correspondence and checks, fabricated evidence to bolster his position, and most recently, erased his hard drives knowing the information on them was relevant to this action." (*Id.*). Defendant goes on to assert that Plaintiff's "despicable behavior was intended to hamper the fact-gathering process by preventing Wells Fargo from obtaining highly relevant information that may have defeated his only remaining claim under the Fair Credit Reporting Act and his damage claims." (*Id.*). Defendant contends an adverse jury instruction and monetary sanctions are not enough because the relevant documents no longer exist and that, instead, Plaintiff's calculated and willful misconduct warrants dismissal of this action (*Id.*).

The plaintiff tried to justify his secret reformatting of the hard drives with a convenient story about his computers becoming infected with a virus. In these circumstances, that is about as convincing as "the dog ate my homework." Here is the court's summary of his excuse:

> Plaintiff argues that his laptops were infected with computer viruses and spy-ware and that a computer technician diagnosed the problem and recommended wiping clean and reformatting each hard drive and then reinstall the operating systems (Doc. # 133 at 4). Plaintiff claims that before this procedure is performed, data on the hard drive is backed up and saved and then downloaded back onto the hard drive after the operating system is reinstalled (Doc. # 133 at 4). Thus, Plaintiff argues Defendant's motion should be denied because no data has been destroyed (*Id.*).

One problem with the plaintiff's story, aside from the fact that he did it in secret months after the request to produce, was that the plaintiff refused or was unable to produce any of the backup files of these computers. Further, there are the aggravating circumstances of the testimony of the plaintiff's wife and the affidavit that Well Fargo obtained from the technician the plaintiff hired to reformat the laptop. (Apparently the plaintiff himself has not yet been deposed.)

The deposition of plaintiff's wife occurred just two weeks after the hard drives were formatted, yet in response to questions she denied that any work had been done to their computers. To make matters worse, the plaintiff's technician who formatted his laptop stated that he only formatted one laptop. He said the other laptop was formatted by the plaintiff's wife two weeks later, with his help and instructions over the phone. Further, the plaintiff's tech said that he never backed up the files on the laptop before the formatting and did not instruct the wife on how to do so. *Id.* at *8. This certainly impeaches the deposition testimony of the plaintiff's wife, and shows that the plaintiff was trying to hide his reformatting actions, apparently in the naive hope they would never be discovered. It also contradicts the plaintiff's claim that he backed up both computers before having them reformatted.

The fact that the plaintiff had to hire an expert to format his laptops, and the expert had to talk the wife through the process, tells me that they are both computer novices. Formatting a disk is very easy to do, and is not something you normally need to take to a technician. You might retain a tech to try to get rid of viruses, but there is little evidence the plaintiff's technician was ever even asked to try to fix the virus problem. Normally a tech could find several less drastic methods than reformatting to rid a disk of viruses and spyware.

Also, when you think about the plaintiff's virus story, you realize it makes little sense. Plaintiff said he copied all of the files onto backup discs, had the hard drive formatted, and then reloaded the files back onto the computer. How would that get rid of the viruses? The backup discs would include the infected files. When you restore the files onto the freshly formatted hard drive, the virus files would be restored, too. You need to delete or quarantine viruses to get rid of them, not copy them back and forth. Alternatively, if you reformat, you do not reload the same files that were on the original infected disc, at least not until inspecting and cleaning all of these files to remove all of the malware.[7]

The plaintiff here also showed his lack of expertise with computers when he tried to hide ESI by simply formatting the disk. More experienced users typically try to hide evidence by wiping a disc, not formatting it. This is easy to do with several off-the-shelf software programs. I have written about this in prior articles, including "IT Tech's Fast-Talk Had Zero Persuasive Value with Judge,"[8] and "GhostSurfer Wipe Out Leads to Jail Order Sanction in Bankruptcy Court."[9] These other attempts to hide ESI by unscrupulous litigants, although more sophisticated, also ultimately failed. Even when better software does clear a disk of all incriminating ESI, there are still records left on the computer that these "Evidence Eliminator"[10]–

---

7. http://en.wikipedia.org/wiki/Malware.

8. http://ralphlosey.wordpress.com/2007/07/26/it-techs-fast-talk-had-zero-persuasive-value-with-judge/.

9. http://ralphlosey.wordpress.com/2007/07/07/ghostsurfer-wipe-out-leads-to-jail-order-sanction-in-bankruptcy-court/.

10. http://www.evidence-eliminator.com/.

type programs were run. Either way, there is almost always a way to catch a fraudster.

As to the two documents that Well Fargo's expert found and claimed were backdated, the plaintiff argued that this was pure speculation and "completely meaningless unless it is known whether the date and time set on the computer were correct when the documents were created." *Id.* at *7. Again, that is a lame argument of a computer novice, to claim that the dating evidence is meaningless simply because a computer's clock could have been changed. Why would it have been changed? Moreover, there are ways to detect computer clock resetting, as the CFO in *Hawaiian Airline*[11] found out. I wrote about this and forensic recovery in my article "Book 'em Danno: Hawaiian Judge Sanctions Company for Trusting Its Top Officers after One Wipes His Laptops, Allegedly to Hide Porn." An employee who changed the date on his resume by changing the computer clock learned the same lesson in *Plasse v. Tyco Elec. Corp.*,[12] 2006 WL 2623441 (D. Mass. Sept. 7, 2006). In *Plasse,* the plaintiff's case was dismissed for this attempted fraud on the court.

Motion for Sanctions

Wells Fargo's motion for sanctions was based on both Rule 37 and the court's inherent power. Judge McQuaid made short work of Rule 37 and held that it did not apply simply because plaintiff's "conduct was not in violation of any discovery order governed by Rule 37." That is a very narrow construction of the rule, and he did not try to explain or justify it, instead focusing on Well Fargo's other grounds of the court's inherent authority to impose sanctions. Judge McQuaid's legal analysis was based on Ninth Circuit law in this area, primarily *Anheuser-Busch, Inc. v. Natural Beverage Distributors*, 69 F.3d 337, 348 (9th Cir. 1995). *Anheuser-Busch* requires courts to consider several factors "before imposing the harsh sanction of dismissal," including whether the misconduct was intentional or in bad faith,

---

11. http://ralphlosey.files.wordpress.com/2007/11/in-re-hawaiian-airlines.doc.

12. http://ralphlosey.files.wordpress.com/2008/05/plasse.pdf.

whether there was a "relationship between the sanctioned party's misconduct and the matters in controversy, such that the transgression threaten[s] to interfere with the rightful decision of the case," and the effectiveness of "less severe alternatives than outright dismissal." *Id.*

The plaintiff here conceded that the reformatting was intentional, but he denied this caused any evidence to be lost. Further, he claimed his actions were all done in good faith, so his case should not be dismissed.

Court's Holding Denied Dismissal, but Imposed an Adverse Inference Instruction

The court disagreed with the plaintiff's stories and pleas of good faith, and instead held:

> The timing of Plaintiff's reformatting of his hard drives is also very suspect. Plaintiff reformatted both hard drives within a few days of each other, not only during the period of time he knew Defendant sought production of the hard drives, but also after Defendant informed Plaintiff, on September 20, 2007, that it intended to file a motion to compel production of the hard drives (*Id.,* Exh. 6). Within five (5) days of being notified that Defendant intended to file a motion to compel, Plaintiff reformatted his first hard drive (*Id.,* Exh. 1). Then within ten (10) days of reformatting his first hard drive, Plaintiff reformatted his second hard drive (*Id.*). During this entire period of time, Defendant sent numerous e-mails to Plaintiff attempting to settle the dispute over production of the hard drives (*Id.*).

Plaintiff's explanation that he reformatted his hard drives because they were infected with viruses and spy-ware and then he downloaded all the files back onto the hard drives is of little help to the court in finding an absence of willfulness or bad faith. At no time did the Plaintiff inform Defendant that his hard drives were infected with viruses or spy-ware, despite having knowledge Defendant requested production of said hard drives. And, as previously stated, Plaintiff has produced no evidence of any backup files, nor has he indicated that he will produce any backup files to show that he did, in fact, download all the files back onto the hard drives.

> ***5** Under these facts, the evidence weighs heavily against Plaintiff and tends to show Plaintiff did, in fact, willfully reformat his hard drives knowing Defendant was vehemently requesting production of those hard drives. Thus, this factor also weighs against Plaintiff.

So far, so good, for Well Fargo's request to have the case dismissed because of spoliation. All of the factors the court considered as required by *Anheuser-Busch* weighed in defendant's favor, except for the last one: whether alternatives less severe than dismissal might be appropriate. Here the court was inclined to give the plaintiff a break and just order an adverse inference instruction instead of outright dismissal. As I stated before, although this means Well Fargo is almost certain to win, it will still be put to the great expense and burden of trial, and it is always possible a jury will rule for the plaintiff. Judge McQuaid must have had some unexpressed doubts about this case to let it go to trial like that. It is also possible he just wanted to play it safe and not risk reversal. It is hard to say without knowing more about this case and the personalities involved. In any event, here is Judge McQuaid's explanation for his ruling:

> Under these facts, it appears the evidence that Defendant's forensic computer expert retrieved, together with the timing of Plaintiff's conduct, actually lend support to Defendant's theory of the case—that Plaintiff manufactured this action and the evidence he planned to use to support the action— rather than prevents Defendant from fully developing its theory as Defendant suggests. Accordingly, for the foregoing reasons, the court finds a jury instruction creating a presumption in favor of Defendant that the spoliated evidence

was unfavorable to Plaintiff is a more appropriate, less drastic sanction.

Basically, Judge McQuaid is saying that since the plaintiff's fraudulent destruction of evidence confirms the defense position that the whole case is a fraud, that makes it more appropriate to allow the case to continue to trial than to be dismissed. I am not sure I understand that kind of "two wrongs make a right" logic. A plaintiff who manufactures a case out of whole cloth should not for that reason have *carte blanche* to commit more fraud. The court should have granted Wells Fargo's motion and dismissed this case.

SANCTIONS IN THE SAN DIEGO *HOBIE CAT* CASE NOT THE TIGER WE NEED TO KEEP OUR COURTS FAIR

San Diego has long been famous in golf circles for having one of the best public golf courses in the country, Torrey Pines.[13] This is where the U.S. Open was held in 2008, and where Tiger Woods won one of the most dramatic golf tournaments of all times. Last year San Diego became famous in legal circles for the *Qualcomm* case, which I examine in detail in the "Ethics" chapter. In *Qualcomm,* a plaintiff and many of its attorneys were, in a courtroom drama, caught playing "Hide the Ball" with 46,000 e-mails. The San Diego district court spoke harshly about Qualcomm's attempted deception. The judges condemned the actions as unethical and imposed some sanctions against Qualcomm. The court is now engaged in an extended process of imposing some type of sanctions against six of Qualcomm's outside counsel.

Most commentators described the *Qualcomm* sanctions, like the high rough at Torrey Pines, as either suitably tough or too severe. Apparently, I am the only commentator to criticize the sanctions as too lenient. I do not think the punishment was proportionate to the enormity of the discovery misconduct, and for this reason I previously called the sanctions "wimpy" ("Qualcomm's 'Monumental Discovery Violations' Provokes Only Wimpy Sanctions"). A new

---

13. http://www.sandiego.gov/park-and-recreation/golf/torreypines/.

opinion from the same federal court in San Diego seems to follow in the footsteps of *Qualcomm* and provides only a paper tiger[14] response to e-discovery abuses. *R & R Sails, Inc., d/b/a Hobie Cat Co. v. Insurance Company of the State of Pennsylvania,*[15] 2008 WL 2232640 (S.D. Cal., April 18, 2008).

The opinions in *Qualcomm* show that the presiding judges considered Qualcomm's conduct to have been intentional and in bad faith. *Qualcomm* was not a case involving accidental omissions, miscommunications, or simple lawyer/IT mistakes. If it had been, my opinion would be completely different. As I have noted before, e-discovery is like golf. Perfection in both is impossible to achieve. Even Tiger Woods sometimes makes mistakes. He did at Torrey Pines many times, including a double bogey on the first hole. He roared back from these mistakes, overcoming great pain in his left knee, and pulled off miracle shots when needed. He did so primarily because of his fierce warrior determination and uncompromising intensity.

If *Qualcomm* had just involved mistakes and errors in judgment, a lenient response would have been appropriate. But according to the San Diego judges, Qualcomm intentionally "hid the ball" on a grand scale. They crashed well past the line between zealous representation and unethical practice. In a situation like that, involving a strong showing of bad faith, the sanctions should match the misconduct. The intensity of Tiger Woods is called for. Proportionate and just consequences are the only way to send a credible message that fraud will not be tolerated in our courts. Harsh rhetoric alone will not suffice. That is why I thought the sanctions in *Qualcomm* were too weak.

The *Hobie Cat* case is, again, no tiger. Moreover, it seems to confirm my hypothesis that *Qualcomm's* sanctions were not severe enough to deter Hide-the-Ball play, even in the same court. But see what you think. Consider the findings that Magistrate Judge Louisa S. Porter made in the *Hobie Cat* opinion. Then decide whether you think this defendant took the *Qualcomm* message seriously—or even heard it at all.

---

14. http://en.wikipedia.org/wiki/Paper_tiger.
15. http://ralphlosey.files.wordpress.com/2008/06/rrsails.doc.

The Facts of *R&R Sails, d/b/a Hobie Cat Co. v. Insurance Company of the State of Pennsylvania*

The defendant in this case is an insurance company, and is thus a serial litigant. Insurance companies are routinely embroiled in litigation, and I know from long experience that they are frequently forced to defend frivolous claims and to respond to outrageous demands. This can sometimes lead to jaundiced behavior by claims examiners and attorneys. I make this observation not to excuse the actions in this case, but to explain how it can sometimes happen, even to the best of companies.

The plaintiff here, Hobie Cat Co., makes recreational and racing sailboats. A wildfire in Australia destroyed one of its manufacturing plants. This made it impossible for Hobie Cat to fulfill a contract to provide 60 catamarans for use in a racing event in April 2002. The insurer paid Hobie Cat for the loss of property but would not pay for loss of income, business interruption, and other expenses. Suit was filed in San Diego state court in May 2007 and removed to federal court in June 2007. The suit alleged bad-faith claims handling and also alleged that the laws of Australia should apply. (This choice of law argument was denied by the court in an earlier ruling.)

The insurer responded to the first request for production in August 2007 by producing paper documents, but did not include the adjuster's computer notes. This information is key to most insurance disputes, especially ones that involve allegations of bad-faith claim denial. The file usually documents all of the claims adjuster's notes and analysis. It also logs all conversations concerning the claim, both in person and by phone. The key computer file is often called the claim activity log, and many insurers, including the defendant here, use an AEGIS[16]–type database software system for that purpose.

All insurers today keep such records, using some kind of software or another, and so the failure to include these notes was an obvious oversight. Here is how Judge Porter describes plaintiff's counsel's response to this non-production:

---

16. http://en.wikipedia.org/wiki/Aegis_%28management_software%29.

On September 7, 2007, Plaintiff sent a letter to Defendant noting that "[c]onspicuously absent from [Defendant's production of documents] are electronic or handwritten daily activity records/logs which are generally kept with an adjuster's notes and telephone call records." This letter was followed by another letter on September 10, 2007, in which Plaintiff's counsel listed topics to be discussed at a requested meet-and-confer regarding discovery. This letter states: "we have not been provided with any electronic or handwritten daily activity records/logs which are generally kept with an adjuster's notes and telephone call records."

Hobie Cat at *1 (record citations omitted in this and subsequent quotes).

At this point, the activity log should have been produced, and this little game of Hide the Ball would only have drawn a smile and comment from the plaintiff's counsel of "Nice try, but I was not born yesterday." However, defense counsel continued to insist that they had no activity logs to produce. Plaintiff's counsel then did what they had to do. They asked the court for a hearing to resolve the dispute. Here again, defense counsel had another opportunity to "find" the file and produce it prior to a hearing before the judge. Most of the time, that is how this sort of situation plays out. Most counsel will not want to chance a referee's review of a hide-the-ball play.

However, this defendant was apparently willing to take a chance. Counsel for the defendant showed up at the hearing and continued to assert that the insurer did not keep activity logs, either in paper or electronic format. Judge Porter, an experienced magistrate who has no doubt heard thousands of insurance company disputes, did not believe the story. No modern insurance company investigates a claim without keeping a computer log of events. Here is how Judge Porter describes what happened at this hearing at *2:

At that time, Defendant's counsel represented that a complete copy of Plaintiff's claim file had been produced on

August 30, 2007. Defendant's counsel asserted at the conference that Defendant had responded to Plaintiff's request for discovery and explained that no daily logs or telephone records had been produced to Plaintiff because no daily logs or telephone records were maintained by Defendant's insurance adjusters. The Court expressed skepticism about counsel's claim and ordered on November 29, 2007 that "Defendant shall either produce all daily activity logs or a verified declaration that Defendant is not in possession of daily activity logs."

Here was yet another chance for the defendant to come clean and find the "missing" logs before filing a sworn affidavit with the court. Instead, on December 14, 2007, the defendant filed an affidavit by its senior adjuster swearing that "[t]here were no daily activity logs or telephone record logs that were created or maintained in connection with plaintiff's claim."

The defendant insurer should have anticipated that the plaintiff's next move would be to take the deposition of the affiant, the senior adjuster. That is exactly what happened. At this point, the insurer claimed that it had suddenly found the missing logs. This supposedly happened while defense counsel was interviewing the witness to prepare him for his deposition. Counsel provided no explanation as to why this revelation did not occur earlier, especially as this same witness must have been (or at least should have been) previously interviewed for his affidavit. The defendant printed out the computer notes, and then faxed 11 pages of log files to plaintiff's counsel. However, due to unfortunate timing, no doubt completely accidental, the fax was not received by plaintiff's counsel until after he was on a plane to New York en route to take the senior adjuster's deposition.

Still, plaintiff's counsel got the fax the night before the deposition and asked the senior examiner some questions about it the next day, January 9, 2008. Now under oath and before a court reporter, the senior claims examiner, Blaise Lombardo:

[C]onceded on the record that his declaration dated December 14, 2007 was incorrect and that a claim log was maintained electronically by Defendant, separately from the paper-form claim file that had been produced to Plaintiff. Lombardo also represented that all documents responsive to Plaintiff's discovery requests had since been produced.

Id. at *2. So apparently the Hide the Ball game was over; or was it?

After this admission, plaintiff's counsel refused to conclude this deposition and instead demanded more time to study the production and readjourn the deposition another day to ask Lombardo more questions. Defense counsel refused, and plaintiff's counsel was able to get an emergency hearing with Judge Porter by phone at the deposition in New York. Judge Porter, of course, agreed with plaintiff's counsel:

Defendant opposes Plaintiff's request to suspend the deposition on the ground that the deposition ought to be completed as scheduled because Plaintiff is now in possession of all the records necessary to depose Lombardo. . . . the deposition shall be adjourned and the remainder of [Lombardo's] deposition shall be taken at a later date. Plaintiff's counsel reserves a request for sanctions.

Here is where, in my view, things become really bizarre. Lombardo's deposition was scheduled to continue on February 13, 2008. In addition, Lombardo's supervisor, Joseph Chianese, who initially handled the plaintiff's coverage claim before Lombardo took over, was scheduled to be deposed on February 12, 2008. Here is how Judge Porter describes the defendant's version of what happened next:

On February 11, 2008, while preparing for Chianese's deposition, Defendant's counsel "realized for the first time that [he] had failed to produce six pages of the computer notes that Mr. Lombardo had provided to [him] in January." According to counsel, "[u]nfortunately, in my rush to provide plaintiff's counsel with the notes, I mistakenly faxed only eleven of the seventeen pages . . . I did not realize my error until I was back in New York for the deposition of Mr. Chianese in early February."

Defendant's counsel produced the remaining pages of claim log entries to plaintiff's counsel on February 12, 2008, the morning that the plaintiff was scheduled to depose Chianese. The additional six pages of log entries were all from the period of time when Chianese managed the plaintiff's claim. The parties agreed immediately to continue Chianese's deposition to a later date.

The following day, plaintiff's counsel took Lombardo's deposition for a second time. Lombardo testified that he had given counsel all of the information that he printed out from the defendant's electronic database in January. After questioning by plaintiff's counsel regarding the defendant's database, whether data stored in the database could be altered, and whether all relevant data had in fact been produced, Lombardo's deposition ended prematurely and was subsequently scheduled to be taken yet a third time.

Every time there is a deposition, more documents are discovered and produced at the last minute. I could understand this if we were talking about a database of thousands of documents, but here there were only 18 pages. (One page was withheld for privilege, although the privilege log was apparently never served.) Not only that, but the deposition is adjourned for unexplained reasons when questions are asked as to whether any of the electronic files were modified before production, and whether still more files might exist. These questions are left unanswered by the opinion.

So what do you think? Were the sanctions in *Qualcomm* tough and scary enough to send a convincing message to would-be "hide the ball" litigants? I point out that all of the facts in *Hobie Cat* occurred *after* the *Qualcomm* revelations in August 2007. *Qualcomm Inc. v. Broadcom Corp.*, No. 05-CV-1958-B(BLM) Doc. 593 (S.D. Cal. Aug. 6, 2007);[17] *Qualcomm Inc. v. Broadcom Corp.*, No. 05-CV-1958-B(BLM) Doc. 599 (S.D. Cal. Aug. 13, 2007).[18]

---

17. http://ralphlosey.files.wordpress.com/2007/08/case-qualcomm _8_6_07_order_on_remedy.pdf.

18. http://ralphlosey.files.wordpress.com/2007/08/case-qualcomm _8_13_07_show_cause_order.pdf.

The Parties Sanction Arguments in *Hobie Cat*

Of course, the plaintiff responded to these overzealous defense games by moving for sanctions. Here is how the court summarized the plaintiff's position at *3:

> Plaintiff argues that sanctions are warranted in this case under Federal Rule of Civil Procedure 37, for violations of the Court's order that Defendant produce claim logs if they existed, and for violations of Federal Rules of Civil Procedure 26(e) and 26(g). Plaintiff contends that production of the claim log was an especially important part of the discovery process because of the significance of the log to Plaintiff's claim that Defendant exhibited bad faith in handling Plaintiff's insurance claim. Plaintiff quotes the Advisory Committee Notes to the 1983 Amendment to Federal Rule of Civil Procedure 26(g), which state: "[i]f primary responsibility for conducting discovery is to continue to rest with the litigants, they must be obliged to act responsibly and avoid abuse." Plaintiff argues that Defendant's representations to Plaintiff and to the Court that a claim log responsive to Plaintiff's discovery request did not exist violated Rule 26(g) and represent at least a negligent failure by Defendant to locate, review and produce discovery.

The defendant responded that these were all just "honest mistakes" that were promptly remedied as soon as discovered. Here is the court's summary of the defendant's explanation of the false affidavit at *4:

> Though Defendant concedes that Lombardo's signed declaration was incorrect in stating that the claim log did not exist, Defendant explains that Lombardo did not associate Plaintiff's document request with the electronically-stored records which are maintained on his computer rather than in hard-copy, paper form. Defendant seeks to explain the incomplete production of the claim log, once identified, as another "inadvertent mistake" unworthy of sanctions.

Apparently this is the best explanation they could come up with, that they did not think key records had to be produced because they were only stored on a computer and had not been printed out. This kind of argument might have had some credibility 10 years ago; but today? Also, the affidavit filed with the court said: "[t]here were no daily activity logs or telephone record logs that were created or maintained in connection with plaintiff's claim." Remember that this affidavit was filed at the judge's request after the judge found it hard to believe that there were no computer logs. If you were the judge, how would you respond to all this? How should a judge respond to deter that kind of conduct by other litigants in the future?

Court's Ruling in *Hobie Cat*

Here is what Judge Porter did. She starts off by chiding both sides for not solving their e-discovery problems at the initial 26(f) conference.

> In 2006, Federal Rule of Civil Procedure 26(f) was amended "to direct the parties to discuss discovery of electronically stored information during their discovery-planning conference." Advisory Committee Notes to 2006 Amendments. In this case, the parties' discovery plan made no mention of possible sources of discovery and gives no indication that the parties discussed the discovery of electronically-stored information at their 26(f) conference.

Personally, given these facts, I do not see how a more complete 26(f) conference would have made any difference. The spirit of cooperation necessary to make these conferences effective was clearly never present in this case.

Next, the magistrate chided the plaintiff for not making a specific request for the electronic activity log files, and instead just asking for all "documents" related to the claim. I do not understand the point of those remarks. Judge Porter then recognizes that this error by the plaintiff, if you can call it that, was corrected in the subsequent communications and conferences. After that, the defendant clearly knew that the plaintiff wanted to see the electronic log files, and not just the portions of the claim file that happen to be in paper.

Judge Porter then lays out the facts of defendant's disingenuous denials and piecemeal, last-minute productions, and moves on to the governing law at *5:

> Federal Rule of Civil Procedure 26(g) requires that every discovery response be signed by an attorney and the signature "certifies that to the best of the person's knowledge, information, and belief formed after a reasonable inquiry" that the response is complete and correct. This rule is enforced by a mandatory sanction under Rule 26(g)(3), which reads:
>
> If a certification violates this rule without substantial justification, the court, on motion or on its own, must impose an appropriate sanction on the signer, the party on whose behalf the signer was acting, or both. The sanction may include an order to pay the reasonable expenses, including attorney's fees, caused by the violation.
>
> Defendant's production of electronically stored claim log entries on January 8, 2008 demonstrates that Defendant had made incorrect certifications to Plaintiff as well as representations to the Court that Defendant's production of discovery was complete.

Judge Porter then makes short work of the defendant's attempt to dress up its actions as "honest mistakes." Her writing on this is excellent, although it is of course written in a typical restrained judicial fashion:

> Sanctions under Rule 26(g) must be issued unless violation of the rule was "substantially justified." Defendant claims substantial justification for maintaining the position that no claim log was in Defendant's possession, based on Lombardo's misunderstanding of the discovery being requested of Defendant. According to Defendant, Lombardo failed to recognize that the AEGIS database that he entered

notes into contained the "daily activity logs or telephone records" that Plaintiff had been requesting.

Lombardo has been an insurance adjuster for 26 years and explains that he did not associate the AEGIS database with the claim file that he maintains because "[t]he AEGIS computer system records are kept on a computer system that is separate from my file materials and I do not have a practice of printing them out to put in my file."

Defendant argues that this "honest mistake" substantially justifies the incorrect certifications made to Plaintiff, as well as the false declaration provided to Plaintiff in response to this Court's Order of November 29, 2007. However, to give meaning to the certifications provided on discovery responses, Rule 26(g) requires attorneys or parties to sign their responses "after a reasonable inquiry." Evidence of such an inquiry prior to January 2007 may provide this Court with justification for the incorrect certifications provided to Plaintiff. Instead, this Court is presented with evidence that Lombardo was maintaining a claim log on his own computer using the AEGIS system while failing to recognize that this log was the same "record/log" being requested by Plaintiff. Lombardo entered notes of a communication with counsel into the AEGIS system on November 16, 2007, immediately prior to counsel's representation to this Court that such a system was not possessed by Defendant and close in time to his signing a declaration that no such notes are maintained. The Court cannot find that a reasonable inquiry was made into whether Defendant possessed discovery responsive to Plaintiff's requests, and therefore the Court does not find Defendant's incorrect certifications to be substantially justified.

*6 Defendant is liable for sanctions, pursuant to Federal Rule of Civil Procedure 26(g), for making incorrect certifications to Plaintiff regarding discovery responses. Those certifications caused Plaintiff unwarranted attorney fees and costs.

The incorrect certifications were not only made to the plaintiff, but also to the court. A false affidavit was filed with the court. Yet Judge Porter does not include this as a basis for sanctions. What kind of message does this send?

Next, the opinion explains that sanctions are also appropriate under Rule 37(c) for failure to timely supplement initial disclosures. Here is how the defendant violated this rule:

> Once Plaintiff established, at Lombardo's January 9, 2008 deposition, that Defendant's earlier certifications and Lombardo's declaration regarding Defendant's discovery responses were incorrect, the parties jointly contacted the Court. At that time, Defendant represented that Plaintiff was in possession of the entire claim log which Plaintiff had earlier requested. However, one month later, when Plaintiff's counsel traveled again to continue the deposition of Lombardo and also to depose former insurance adjuster Joseph Chianese, Defendant produced additional portions of the claim log. Lombardo declares that he printed all pages of the claim log maintained in the AEGIS system prior to his deposition scheduled for January 9, 2008. Defendant's production of additional claim log entries on February 12, 2008 demonstrate that Defendant did not complete the disclosure of the claim log in a timely manner.

Then the court concludes by determining what sanctions are appropriate for this type of conduct. As every lawyer who has ever moved for sanctions knows, this is the part of the order that you really care about. The statement of facts and law are interesting, but the sanctions are what count. If an order is filled with tough talk but not tough sanctions, like *Qualcomm*, it is just a barking dog with no bite. You can ignore it and carry on.

The plaintiff sought sanctions of $67,154.72 to fully compensate it for the fees and costs it incurred because of the defendant's hide-the-ball tactics. They did not get it. Instead, the judge cut the award down to $39,914.68, and made the sanction payable by both defendant and its legal counsel:

IT IS HEREBY ORDERED that Defendant and Defendant's counsel are jointly and severally liable for attorneys' fees and costs caused by the failure to search for and timely produce electronically-stored information. Defendant and Defendant's counsel shall pay Plaintiff, in care of Plaintiff's counsel, the amount of $39,914.68, **within thirty (30) days of the date of this order.** These monetary sanctions are SO ORDERED by this Court and are not made on a report and recommendation basis.

The plaintiff also sought non-monetary sanctions, primarily preclusion of the defendant's use of any evidence that it had not already produced. This seems like a pretty mild request to me. I cannot understand why the plaintiff did not ask for much more, such as striking defenses or total preclusion of the claims files. Of course, this slap on the wrist was granted:

*9 Based on Defendant's past failure to timely produce electronically-stored information, and Plaintiff's concern that additional responsive electronically-stored information may be in Defendant's possession, the Court finds it necessary to recommend non-monetary sanctions "aimed at resolving the compliance issue and restoring some confidence in the discovery process." *Board of Regents of the University of Nebraska v. BASF Corp.,* 2007 U.S. Dist. LEXIS 82492 (D. Neb., Nov. 5, 2007) (ordering sanctions where responsive documents were produced one day before the deposition of a key witness but without evidence of a willful failure to produce).

The Judiciary Must Act Forcefully to Restore Confidence in the Discovery Process

In my view, *Hobie Cat,* like *Qualcomm,* is more bark than bite. This kind of mild judicial response will not restrain future hide-the-ball tactics. For many litigants, it is business as usual. Words alone are not enough for an effective wakeup call. This is one reason I predict we will see more cases like this in San Diego, and other courts, in the coming months.

Litigants and attorneys are to blame for this, but so is the judiciary. The bench underestimates the temptation of parties to hide the ball, and overestimates the chilling effect of harsh rhetoric. Many litigants and lawyers are by no means boy scouts. It is naive to treat them as such. We need stronger responses by the judiciary to resolve compliance issues and restore confidence in the discovery process. Only strong sanctions will stop this cycle of abuse. We need more tigers on the bench—tigers that are willing to roar *and bite* in the face of bad faith.

"WATER PIPE BURST" EXCUSE FAILS TO PREVENT COSTLY ORDER TO RESTORE BACKUP TAPES AFTER COUNTY FAILS TO IMPLEMENT A LITIGATION HOLD AND SAVE E-MAILS

A story of a burst water pipe in a room where backup tapes were kept was one excuse provided for not producing e-mails in a recent case in New York, *Toussie v. County of Suffolk*,[19] 2007 WL 4565160 (E.D. N.Y. Dec. 21, 2007). The defendant county offered the "pipe burst" excuse to try to avoid the expense of backup tape restoration and sidestep charges of spoliation. Sanctions were sought based on gross negligence by the county and its attorneys for failing to implement a litigation hold and preserve evidence. The county compounded its errors by making wildly exaggerated claims of the cost and time to restore and search the backup tapes.

The case started when the plaintiffs filed suit in 2001 claiming that their rights had been violated by the county's refusal to allow them to participate in an auction of several parcels of real estate. A second action was commenced in 2005 with more plaintiffs, and the cases were consolidated. Apparently the plaintiffs in the 2001 case were under a federal criminal investigation at the time the county

---

19. http://ralphlosey.files.wordpress.com/2008/01/toussie-v-county-of-suffolk.doc.

would not let them participate in the auction. My guess is the county considered their case frivolous, and that is why it never implemented a litigation hold. That turned out to be a very expensive mistake for everyone except Kroll Ontrack.

After five years of litigation, a discovery dispute arose between the parties in 2006 as to the adequacy of the county's production of only two e-mails! The plaintiffs moved to compel.

U.S. Magistrate Judge Arlene Rosario Lindsay responded by ordering the county to have its Information Technology Department search the County's servers for responsive e-mails and supplement its prior meager production. The county did not comply, and so on Halloween 2006, the plaintiffs moved for sanctions. The county responded by claiming it "lacked the resources to perform the court-ordered search for additional e-mails." *Id.* The county chief information officer further explained in an affidavit that they had no archive system. He claimed that in order to look for e-mails in that time period, they would have to restore and search backup tapes at a cost of $32,000, plus 1,700 man-hours of search time.

This affidavit caused the magistrate to schedule a hearing where she expressed her admitted "exasperation" with the county's position by stating:

> You can't just throw up your hands and say we don't store [e-mails] in an accessible form and then expect everybody to walk away.

Id. at *2. The court then helped the county out somewhat by narrowing the search to "35 search terms on the servers of five key County departments for the period May, 2001 thru January, 2006." The county was ordered to prepare a plan to comply and, despite Judge Lindsay's exasperation, no sanctions were imposed.

Two weeks later, the county wrote Judge Lindsay a letter claiming that the narrowed search ordered would require the restoration and search of 470 backup tapes. The letter claimed that the cost for this search was estimated to be $934,000, plus 960 man-hours. That is quite a dramatic increase in cost, from $32,000 to $934,000, especially when you consider the scope of discovery was supposedly tightened.

Naturally, the court responded by scheduling another hearing. There Judge Lindsay again expressed her concerns that:

> notwithstanding the County's clear obligation to preserve relevant e-mails, the County had taken no steps to preserve its e-mails or to store them in a manner which would permit ready access and review.

The court still did not impose sanctions, but instead directed the parties to meet with their respective e-discovery consultants "to discuss how to implement a better, and perhaps less costly plan, for this production" and prepare and submit a joint discovery plan.

The parties and their IT experts met only by phone. In my opinion, they should have met in person on multiple occasions. That, along with a substantial shift to a non-adversarial attitude[20] by both sides, was the only way the judge's plan could have possibly worked. Predictably, the phone call approach failed, and no agreements were reached. Instead of filing a joint plan, the plaintiffs again filed a motion to impose sanctions against the county. The motion outlines a list of IT incompetency by the county, including the county's failure to explain how the cost estimate went from $32,000 to $934,000, and failure to preserve e-mails after the suit was filed.

The county responded by submitting a search plan, which it again said required exorbitant costs and burden beyond its ability to pay. This time the number of backup tapes they said they would have to search was 412, and not 470. (Judge Lindsay points out that the number of backup tapes changes without explanation in all of the county's filings with the court.) The county still claimed it would cost $934,000, plus the full-time efforts of two of its employees over 450 days, just to restore the tapes. Then, to really pile it on, the county claims that after the restoration work, a computer forensic detective from the police department would have to spend another 70 weeks to search through the restored tapes.

---

20. http://floridalawfirm.com/peace.html.

This is one of those cases where you need a calculator to understand a party's truly incredible position. By my calculation, the county now claimed that it would take 10,000 hours to restore and search the tapes! It would take 7,200 hours to restore the tapes, and 2,800 of police detective time to search them. The 7,200 hours to restore assumes an 8-hour day, and two employees (16 x 450 = 7,200). The 2,800-hour search calculation assumes a 40-hour week (70 x 40). So, once again the county makes an astronomical increase in its cost estimate, increasing its projected time from 960 hours to 10,000 hours. As the court points out, this represents an estimate of over two and a half years to complete the discovery request. *Id.* at *3.

Once again, the court responded by scheduling another hearing for February 2, 2007. This time both sides were ordered to bring their IT witnesses with them to answer the court's questions. At this hearing the county came up with a new excuse for the great expense, claiming that a water pipe had burst in 2004 where the backup tapes were stored. This accident supposedly made three out of four of the tapes unrecoverable. Apparently, the county's IT department waited quite some time to tell the lawyers about their little accident, and then, as we will see, greatly exaggerated the consequences of the water damage. *Id.* at *4 and note 3. This is a good example of the *failure of IT and Law to communicate*.[21] It is also a good example of the common false assumption by IT professionals that they can bluff their way in court with wild, unsubstantiated claims as long as they dress them up in technical jargon. This may work back in the office, but it will not fly in most federal courts. *See: IT Tech's Fast Talk Had Zero Persuasive Value With Judge.*[22]

Magistrate Lindsay responded to the testimony at the hearing by the county's IT department by telling the county's lawyers that she was considering the entry of spoliation sanctions. Specifically, she was considering the imposition of an adverse jury instruction, which is usually a fatal blow to a defense. Suddenly the frivolous case looked like it was going to be lost because of e-discovery

---

21. http://floridalawfirm.com/index.html.

22. http://ralphlosey.wordpress.com/2007/07/26/it-techs-fast-talk-had-zero-persuasive-value-with-judge/.

blunders and IT hubris. This warning from the bench produced what the court called a "sea change" in the county's attitude. The county then agreed to "solicit bids and hire an outside vendor to recover the e-mails." The court ended the hearing by making this agreement into an Order.

Next, the county reported to the court that it had received a bid from Kroll Ontrack to do the work at a price range of between $418,000 to $963,500. The county did not say whether Kroll had actually been retained, and so the court scheduled another hearing on March 22, 2007, and again ordered the IT technicians to appear and answer questions.

At this hearing the county reported it had not yet retained Kroll, but somehow had managed to recover a number of e-mails from key players on its own. Moreover, the county reported that the water pipe break had only destroyed a few of the backup tapes, and not three-quarters as they had previously thought. I certainly would not have wanted to be the lawyer bearing that news to the judge. The county's CIO also testified at the hearing, testimony that Judge Lindsay called contradictory. *Id.*

After this hearing, the county then notified the court that the county legislature had passed a special bill to pay for Kroll's services. *Id.* at *5. The county advised that it would hire Kroll soon. The plaintiffs responded by calling this a delay tactic and renewed their motion for sanctions. The court then ordered the county to provide a specific timetable. The county complied with Kroll's estimate that it could complete the work in 74 days. Based on that, the court ordered the county to complete production by August 10, 2007.

In spite of the county's earlier estimate that it would take two and a half years to restore and search its waterlogged tapes, Kroll met its deadline. In fact, Kroll is the only one in this case who came out looking good. Here is the court's description of what Kroll accomplished in 74 days (we are never told the final bill):

> Kroll has restored 417 backup tapes and searched for e-mails responsive to the criteria set by the court. 18 of the 417 tapes were damaged and Kroll was required to implement disaster recovery procedures on those tapes. Data from 2 of the 18

damaged tapes was ultimately recovered. Kroll also determined that 20 additional tapes were in "brick format," meaning they could not be converted into a readable format. Thus, Kroll was unable to recover e-mails from approximately 36 tapes or 9% of the tapes.

In the end, the Kroll process yielded 2,403 pages of e-mails and attachments to those e-mails, of which approximately 200 were withheld on the basis of privilege, a far cry from the two e-mails originally produced by the County.

After receiving this production, the plaintiffs complained again that this was inadequate and renewed their motion for sanctions. This motion is the subject of the December 21 order.[23]

The plaintiffs complained that most of the e-mail produced was not useful, and most of the 2,403 pages consisted of "inane" attachments to e-mails. They refused to believe that all relevant e-mails had in fact been produced, arguing that in view of the number of people involved, there had to be more. They argued that e-mail had been destroyed and asked for a default judgment, or at least an adverse inference. With these long and convoluted facts as background, the court for the first time ruled on the plaintiffs' motion for sanctions.

The court began its legal analysis by holding that the county's duty to preserve began when suit was filed, and not before, as plaintiffs had argued, when a few of its employees should have reasonably anticipated litigation:

> In this case, it is likely that a handful of County employees anticipated that the plaintiffs would sue after they were denied the right to purchase real estate at the 2001 auction, but there is no evidence to suggest that a substantial number of key personnel anticipated litigation prior to October 11, 2001. Accordingly, the duty to preserve arose in October 2001, when the complaint was first filed.

---

23. http://ralphlosey.files.wordpress.com/2008/01/toussie-v-county-of-suffolk.doc.

The court held that the county was *not* under a duty to back-up and save every e-mail it generated, but should have saved e-mail in four key departments that concerned the real estate transactions at issue. The county should have implemented a litigation hold to suspend its normal document retention/destruction policies. The county did not do that in this case. In fact, it appears that a litigation hold notice was never provided. For that reason, e-mails were made inaccessible or destroyed according to the county's usual practices. The court concluded that this was a violation of the county's obligation to preserve this limited set of highly relevant e-mails. *Id.* at *7.

Having found a breach of duty, the court then considered the second prong of the spoliation test, whether there was a culpable state of mind. Unlike some circuits which require proof of actual malice, or at least gross negligence, to prove culpability, the Second Circuit only requires a showing of negligence. *Residential Funding Corp. v. DeGeorge Fin. Corp.,* 306 F.3d 99, 108 (2d Cir. 2002).

The plaintiffs in this case argued that the county had been grossly negligent because the county's *attorneys* had never informed key employees of the need to maintain relevant e-mails. Due to this failure, key employees were free to delete e-mails from hard drives, backup procedures were not modified, and highly relevant e-mail exchanges were lost. Notice how the attack at this point is getting personal, and plaintiffs are now pointing their fingers at both the county and their attorneys.

The court agreed with the plaintiffs in part, rejecting their argument on the backup tapes, but still holding that the second culpable state prong of the spoliation test had been met:

> Thus, while the County's failure to implement a litigation hold amounts to gross negligence, its failure to preserve all potentially relevant backup tapes was "merely negligent." *Id.* In either case, the second requirement for the imposition of spoliation sanctions is met.

Id. at *8.

The third and final prong of the spoliation claim required the plaintiffs to prove that the missing e-mails were relevant and that they would have been favorable to them. That can be tricky to prove, as many courts have noted, since you "don't know what you don't know." This final prong of the test is usually presumed to be met, absent evidence to the contrary, when the culpability is shown by malice, but requires evidence when culpability is established by gross or simple negligence.

In this case, in spite of the strong facts against the county, the court concluded that plaintiffs failed to prove that the e-mails destroyed were relevant or helpful. This result was clearly influenced by the great cost and expenses that the county finally incurred with Kroll. Equally important is the fact that the e-mails recovered at such great expense proved to be a waste of time. The plaintiffs could not point to a single relevant e-mail that helped their case from the 2,403 pages produced. The plaintiffs attached six e-mails to their final sanctions motion, but the court pointed out that these e-mails helped the defense, not the plaintiffs. The e-mails showed that one reason the county opposed the plaintiffs' proposed purchase is that the county learned the plaintiffs were under criminal investigation by federal authorities. Here is Judge Lindsay's ruling on this issue:

> While the evidence is clear that at least 9% of the backup tapes were destroyed and the plaintiffs may be correct that e-mails have been deleted by users, there is no reason to believe that any of those e-mails would have provided any additional support of plaintiffs' claims. Accordingly, the plaintiffs have not sufficiently demonstrated that the destroyed/ lost e-mails were favorable or relevant and the motion for a default judgment or an adverse inference instruction is denied.

Still, even though there was insufficient evidence of relevance to justify an adverse inference instruction, the court had witnessed for itself a long series of e-discovery failures. The burst water pipe story and the widely varying estimates of cost to restore tapes, to name just a few. All this had forced five hearings on the subject and clearly aggravated the judge. Since the county's e-discovery negligence and IT hubris caused significant unnecessary expenses, the plaintiffs were awarded fees. But for the last-minute heroics and sanity of Kroll, the results for the county could have been much worse.

GIVE PEACE A CHANCE: FEDERAL JUDGE TRIES EXPERIMENTAL METHOD TO RESOLVE A MAJOR E-DISCOVERY DISPUTE IN NON-ADVERSIAL MANNER

District Court Judge William Haynes, Jr., in Nashville recently tried to move litigants out of a traditional adversarial approach to e-discovery and into a more cooperative *kumbaya* mode. How did he do it? He scheduled a hearing and requested all of the attorneys and their IT experts to be present. When they arrived, he asked all of the lawyers to leave so that the experts could work things out in peace. I kid you not!

Judge Haynes faced a frustrating maze of technical disagreements on e-discovery issues when he took over a politically charged class action from another judge. He hoped that if the parties' computer experts could just talk amongst themselves about the complex technical issues, without the "help" of all of the lawyers, they could solve the problems and reach an agreement. *John B. v. Goetz*,[24] 2007 WL 3012808 (M.D. Tenn. Oct. 10, 2007), and the 187-page Memorandum Opinion (Memo) filed with it (which can be downloaded here in four parts: pages 1-47;[25] pages 48-94;[26] pages 95-144;[27] and pages 145-187[28]) (not yet published).

At first, Judge Haynes's surprise tactic worked beautifully. The lawyers went away quietly, the technical experts remained in the courtroom, and by day's end they had reached an agreement on a

---

24. http://ralphlosey.files.wordpress.com/2007/11/goetz.doc.
25. http://www.floridalawfirm.com/Goetz.part1.pdf.
26. http://www.floridalawfirm.com/Goetz.part2.pdf.
27. http://www.floridalawfirm.com/Goetz.part3.pdf.
28. http://www.floridalawfirm.com/Goetz.part4.pdf.

number of issues, including a list of 50 keywords to search the defendants' computers. In Judge Haynes's words:

> In reliance upon precedents in this district involving com-
> plex matters, the Court directed the parties' computer ex-
> perts to confer, without the presence of their counsel, to de-
> velop a protocol and/or memorandum of understanding to
> address the cited problems with electronic discovery. The
> "experts only conference" was held without objection by
> any counsel and yielded positive results that were appreci-
> ated by the parties' counsel.

Memo pgs. 39-40. The experts' agreement was made on the
record and later converted to a stipulated Order.

Judge Haynes seemed to be onto something here. By simply
requiring experts to hash out agreements on technical e-discovery
issues by themselves, these disputes could be resolved quickly and
relatively inexpensively. Judge Haynes's idea to transcend the
adversarial process, at least for purposes of e-discovery, is in line
with that of most experts. They all agree that complex e-discovery
issues do not lend themselves to effective solution in the adversarial
model. Complex technical issues are best solved with a degree of
cooperation and transparency previously unheard of in our adversarial
system. The Bench and Bar are being pushed in this new and, some
would say, "radical" peaceful-collaborative direction out of necessity. The traditional "hide the ball" model simply does not work in
complex ESI discovery. It frequently costs the parties far more than
the case is worth and can produce huge, time-consuming, and sometimes outcome-dispositive mistakes.

The judge had the right idea, but clearly the method he employed (ordering the attorneys to leave) was doomed to failure, especially in a very political case like this. Since the parties and their
counsel did not initiate the departure, their return with a vengeance
was inevitable. Still, kudos to the judge for trying. Perhaps in another case the "expert only" courtroom dialogue technique might
work, especially if it is not imposed upon the parties by the judge.

But in this Tennessee case, after a promising start, the experiment quickly failed. When the defendants later conducted the keyword search, they decided not to follow the agreement/order. Instead, "Defendants unilaterally selected two search terms and insisted upon a date-limited search." The defendants' lawyers later argued that they had no choice but to depart from the agreement of their experts and use only two search terms instead of 50 because they were rushed for time due to a pending evidentiary hearing on another issue. Later, the defense attorneys added a new argument, that the 50-term search would be too costly, that it would have produced far more ESI than the state could ever afford to review. (Odd their experts never thought of that.)

When the court heard these reports, it scheduled another "experts only" conference for April 11, 2007, "to define the parties' technical disputes and to implement the Court's Orders requiring the production of responsive ESI." Memo pgs. 41-42. At the commencement of this second "no lawyers allowed" conference, two lawyers appeared and objected to their exclusion. These objections were overruled, and the conference proceeded without attorneys, but with a court reporter. The transcript was later filed under seal. The judge only appeared and participated in the "expert only conference" to announce protocol for the conference and to hear the experts' reports on their progress. Memo pg. 42.

Once again, the "no lawyers allowed" courtroom conference purportedly went very well, and the experts reached a number of new agreements. At the conclusion of this hearing the judge directed the defendants' lead expert "to prepare a written summary of the experts' agreements and to circulate that document among all experts for comment and to file that report with the Court."

After the conference, the lawyers got involved again, and, as the court puts it, "disputes resurfaced." The plaintiffs then renewed their earlier motion to compel. The court gave up on the "experts only" approach and instead scheduled a full evidentiary hearing, a mini-trial on e-discovery issues with everyone invited, experts and lawyers alike.

Before I go into e-discovery findings and holdings that came out of this trial, a little background into the case itself is needed. This is a class action to require the State of Tennessee, and the health care providers under contract with the State, to provide the children of Tennessee with the minimum health care required by federal law. The case started in 1998, at which time Tennessee and other defendants almost immediately consented to a judgment. Six years later, the judge assigned to the case, Judge Nixon, held that the State defendants had consistently violated the terms of the Consent Decree and disobeyed a series of his orders. Judge Nixon was clearly upset with Tennessee's willful noncompliance and hard-ball discovery tactics. The situation deteriorated to such an extent that in late 2005, Judge Nixon felt he had to recuse himself from the case.

In February 2006, the new judge assigned to the case, Judge Haynes, scheduled his first hearing to discuss the case status. At that conference, one of the defendants' many attorneys "announced that the Defendants had achieved compliance with the Consent Decree." Memo pg. 34. This announcement thereafter triggered a new round of discovery from the plaintiffs seeking evidence of the claimed compliance, including extensive ESI production. This led to a series of motions and arguments on e-discovery that prompted Judge Haynes to try his "expert only" conference tactic.

As discussed, these "no lawyers allowed" conferences succeeded at first, but ultimately failed when the lawyers took over again. Most of the 187-page October 10, 2007, Memorandum consists of a complete listing of the parties' evidence and the court's findings and holdings. The two-page Order accompanying the Memorandum provides instructions on what the parties are to do thereafter. *John B. v. Goetz*, 2007 WL 3012808 (M.D. Tenn. Oct. 10, 2007).

The Memorandum begins by agreeing with the plaintiffs that the 1998 Consent Decree required production of the State's "electronic data files" as needed to verify compliance. In spite of this, the defendants never sent out a legal-hold notice until 2004. Even then, there was no follow-up to the notice; no attempts were made to implement the hold or to verify compliance. In the words of the court:

the proof is that Defendants left their employees to decide on their own what to retain without evidence of any written instruction or guidance from counsel on what is significant or material information in this complex action.

Memo pg. 126. The State could not even show who it sent the notice to, much less verify that there was adequate compliance.

Some of the key custodians testified that they were not sure they ever received a notice, and never made any special efforts to preserve the relevant ESI on their computers or in their departments. There was also evidence of computers wiped after employees left and other evidence that computer files were destroyed. Moreover, the State's standard six-month ESI retention policy was not suspended. This resulted in an automatic deletion of ESI on almost a daily basis.

Fifty of the key custodians produced no e-mails at all, including the governor and several of the named defendants in the case. Further, a privilege review had never been conducted for most of the ESI that was collected. The defendants said that such a privilege review was too burdensome, and they would not produce ESI without first reviewing for privilege. So virtually no ESI production was ever made, just reams of paper documents, including printouts of e-mail.

The paper production was obviously incomplete and deprived the plaintiffs of all metadata. The plaintiffs wanted native files with metadata intact. The defendants argued that they had to produce in paper so that they could Bates stamp everything to ensure authenticity, and that you cannot Bates stamp a native file. The judge saw through that and pointed out that "'Hash coding' can be attached to metadata to ensure its integrity." Memo pg. 137. See my law review article, "HASH: The New Bates Stamp,"[29] 12 *Journal of Technology Law & Policy* 1 (June 2007), for much more on that topic.

This Memorandum Opinion is very long. So you could go on and on describing the nearly never-ending parade of horribles, including exaggerated estimates by the defendants' experts of the costs

---

29. http://ralphlosey.files.wordpress.com/2007/09/hasharticlelosey.pdf.

of compliance, but you get the point. The Memo also includes 83 pages of legal conclusions discussing a wide variety of e-discovery legal issues, including the new rules, and relying heavily on *Zubulake*. Memo pgs. 102-185. (So much for the "heartlands are unlikely to follow Manhattan" argument.)

The court's handling of the defendants' undue burden argument is interesting. Memo pgs. 139-142. The court found that the defendants "unduly exaggerated" the projected costs of their ESI collection and privilege reviews. Further, the court was convinced that the defendants could reduce their projected costs by the use of keyword searches for privilege review and by sampling. Nevertheless, the court accepted the defendants' numbers for purposes of the undue burden analysis. The defendants argued that the 50-keyword search performed on 50 key custodians would produce 493 gigabytes of ESI, equivalent to 15 million pages of documents. They claimed it would cost them $10 million to collect and review these documents.

The court did not find these costs unreasonable in view of the number of plaintiffs in the class. Since the class comprised more than 550,000 children, "the unit cost for this ESI discovery is approximately 25 pages per class member at a cost of $16.66 per Plaintiff class member." The court acknowledged that this analysis might not be reasonable in a typical discovery situation, but pointed out that this motion to compel discovery was made in the context of enforcement of a judgment, and there had already been "repeated judicial findings of the Defendants' violations of childrens' rights." Memo. pg. 141.

Even assuming the ESI discovery imposed an undue burden on the defendants, the court said it would still compel discovery in view of the total equities of the case, that the plaintiffs had established good cause under Rule 26(b)(2)(C)(i)(ii) and (iii). Memo pg. 143, 148–52. In short, the benefits that are likely to accrue to the 550,00 children from the discovery far outweigh the monetary burden to the State, especially since the court has already determined that the rights of these children to medical care under federal law has been violated by the State. The "think of the children" argument is indeed very powerful and colors this whole opinion.

The defendants also argued that the plaintiffs should pay for at least part of the discovery expenses. The judge found this argument "outrageous," pointing out that the class was composed of "550,000 children whose economic resources are non-existent." Memo pg. 150. All of the factors in the rule, and in *Zubulake I,* were addressed, and all were found to favor the ESI production demanded by the plaintiffs. Memo 148–52.

The court also addresses many types of privilege issues: attorney-client, work product, joint defense, deliberative process, and state statutory privileges. Memo pgs. 53-176. The defense arguments were all rejected.

The court concluded by reserving ruling on the issue of sanctions until completion of the ESI discovery ordered.

As mentioned, a two-page Order was issued at the same time as the Memorandum Opinion. *John B. v. Goetz*, 2007 WL 3012808 (M.D. Tenn. Oct. 10, 2007). Here the court granted the plaintiffs' renewed motion to compel and ordered a series of specific actions in connection with the mandated ESI production, including the following:

> It is ORDERED that the Defendants shall provide complete responses to the Plaintiffs' discovery requests for ESI with the agreed search terms, the designated key custodians and for the time period of June 1, 2004 to the present within one hundred (100) days from the date of entry of this Order. The ESI required under this Order and responsive to Plaintiffs' discovery requests shall include all metadata as well as all deleted information on any computer of any of the Defendants' designated key custodians.

The next paragraph of the order gets very specific in its dictates, and raises my favorite subject.

> Given the need for hash coding of the ESI, Brent Antony's limited formal computer training and the Defendants' position about possible alteration of ESI, the Plaintiff's expert,

Thomas Tigh, or his designee shall be present for the Defendants' ESI production and shall provide such other services to the Defendants as are necessary to produce the metadata, as ordered by the Court. Mr. Tigh or his designee shall inspect the Defendants' computer system to assess whether any changes have been made to hinder the ESI production required by the Consent Decree or previous Order by the Court.

This reference to hash[30] is puzzling. Hash coding is a standard procedure for all competent e-discovery vendors, and this process should be well known to computer experts, regardless of their level of formal training. I am not sure, but the comment appears to be a dig at one of the defense experts. The court goes on in the next paragraph to say:

Given the intensity and sensitivity of these discovery disputes, the Court is considering the appointment of a monitor who has the Court's confidence and is likely to be acceptable to all parties to serve as monitor to oversee the Defendants' and MCC's ESI production.

The appointment of a "monitor" or a special master in contested e-discovery cases appears to be a coming trend, especially when the technical issues are complicated and counsel and the court's IT proficiency is limited. I expect to see more appointments like this in the future, at least until such time as counsel are able to transition from the adversarial model for e-discovery issues. In my experience, outside of Sedona, that is not likely to happen any time soon, so the role for special e-discovery masters is likely to grow quickly and last a long time.

Postscript: The court in fact later appointed a monitor, former U.S. Magistrate Judge Ronald J. Hedges[31] from New Jersey. He was

---

30. http://ralphlosey.wordpress.com/2007/09/07/law-review-article-published-on-the-mathematics-underlying-e-discovery-hash-the-new-bates-stamp/.

31. http://www.nixonpeabody.com/attorneys_detail1.asp?ID=1324.

assigned the difficult task of overseeing the State of Tennessee's court-ordered ESI production. He is one of the best possible people to be assigned this task, and it will be interesting to see how he does.

So far there has not been much for him to do aside from read briefs. In later motions, the court clarified that the plaintiff's expert, along with the monitor, could inspect the ESI storage devices of the 50 key custodians and enter the state's premises to do so. The plaintiff's expert was also allowed to make full forensic copies of the computers involved, including the governor's computers. The U.S. Marshall was ordered to accompany the inspection so that these orders could be peacefully effectuated.

Not too surprisingly, the State then filed emergency appeals to the Sixth Circuit to try to prevent these inspections, including a petition for a writ of mandamus. On November 26, 2007, the appeals court stayed the district court's Order pending further briefing and ruling by the Sixth Circuit.

So far, at least, the attempt in this case to force a truce by ordering the attorneys away has done nothing but add fuel to the fire. It will be very interesting to see what the Sixth Circuit now has to say about all of this.

Second Postscript: The Sixth Circuit said no, you've gone too far, and reversed. *John B. v. Goetz*, __ F.3d __, 2008 WL 2520487 (6th Cir. June 26, 2008). The Sixth cited concerns about comity and excessive intrusion into state government and the privacy rights of non-parties, namely the many government employees whose computers, including home computers, were subject to seizure by federal officials. The Sixth Circuit found a "demonstrable abuse of discretion" by the district court that justified the extraordinary remedy of a writ of mandamus. The mandamus set aside all of the forced forensic imaging orders, but expressed no opinion on any of the other provisions of the district court's orders.

Judge Rogers delivered the opinion of the court, which was joined in by Judge Gibbons. Judge Cole wrote his own, separate concurring opinion. Here is Judge Rogers's explanation of the reversal.

The orders at issue here compel the imaging and production of various state-owned and privately owned computers and electronic devices, and that media will almost certainly contain confidential state or private personal information that is wholly unrelated to the TennCare litigation. Plaintiffs are correct that the discovery orders merely call for the imaging of the relevant media and that the district court has yet to determine how to proceed with respect to the information contained on that media. Nevertheless, the mere imaging of the media, in and of itself, raises privacy and confidentiality concerns. Duplication, by its very nature, increases the risk of improper exposure, whether purposeful or inadvertent. Further, counsel for plaintiffs conceded at oral argument that the information contained on the hard drives, including information not related to this litigation, must eventually be accessed to determine relevance.

Judge Rogers was then careful to point out that the district court's discovery orders not only covered computers and devices of the defendants, but also computers and devices in the custody of individuals who were not party to the litigation. The language suggests that the court may have reached a different result if the order had been limited to the litigants.

Although the overintrusive imaging order was reversed as clearly erroneous, the basic premise behind the discovery order was affirmed: namely, the defendants' duty to preserve computer evidence. I am pleased to say that the appeals court relied heavily upon the Sedona Conference writings to affirm this fundamental law.

*9 As a general matter, it is beyond question that a party to civil litigation has a duty to preserve relevant information, including ESI, when that party "has notice that the evidence is relevant to litigation or ... should have known that the evidence may be relevant to future litigation." *See Fujitsu Ltd. v. Fed. Express Corp.*, 247 F.3d 423, 436 (2d Cir. 2001); *see also Zubulake v. UBS Warburg LLC*, 220 F.R.D. 212, 216-18 (S.D. N.Y. 2003); *The Sedona Principles: Best Practices, Recommendations & Principles for Addressing Electronic Document Production*, Second Edition 11, 28 (The

Sedona Conference Working Group Series, 2007), *available* at http:// www.thesedonaconference.org/content/miscFiles/ TSC_PRINCP_2nd_ed_607.pdf. It is the responsibility of the parties to ensure that relevant ESI is preserved, and when that duty is breached, a district court may exercise its authority to impose appropriate discovery sanctions. *See* Fed. R. Civ. P. 37(b), (e); *The Sedona Principles, supra,* at 70 (noting that sanctions should be considered only if the court finds a clear duty to preserve, a culpable failure to preserve and produce relevant ESI, and a reasonable probability of material prejudice to the adverse party).

Although the duty to preserve ESI is now "beyond question," the power of courts to compel preservation by court-ordered forensic examinations is less clear. Here is the explanation of the Sixth Circuit, which once again relies heavily upon the Sedona Conference.

There is less clarity, however, surrounding the question of a district court's authority to compel the forensic imaging and production of computer hard drives as a means by which to preserve relevant electronic evidence. Because litigants are generally responsible for preserving relevant information on their own, such procedures, if at all appropriate, should be employed in a very limited set of circumstances. *Cf. The Sedona Principles, supra,* at 33 (noting that, because all litigants are obligated to preserve relevant information in their possession, preservation orders generally must be premised on a demonstration that a real danger of evidence destruction exists, a lack of any other available remedy, and a showing that the preservation order is an appropriate exercise of the court's discretion). In this case, the district court ordered the forensic imaging predominantly for preservation purposes, explaining that "[t]hese Orders were to protect against the Defendants' destruction of responsive information in light of the Defendants' persistent refusals to produce ESI in violation of the Court's orders." In so doing, the district court committed a clear error in judgment.

The Sixth Circuit then lays out some of the lead cases, pro and con, in the area of forensic imaging. This is a scholarly opinion, as you would expect from a circuit court, and is worth seeing for its summary of the law on this issue.

To be sure, forensic imaging is not uncommon in the course of civil discovery. *See Balboa Threadworks, Inc. v. Stucky*, No. 05-1157-JTM-DWB, 2006 WL 763668, at *3 (D. Kan. March 24, 2006). A party may choose on its own to preserve information through forensic imaging, and district courts have, for various reasons, compelled the forensic imaging and production of opposing parties' computers. *See, e.g., Ameriwood Indus., Inc. v. Liberman*, No. 4:06CV524-DJS, 2006 WL 3825291, at *3-*6 (E.D. Mo. Dec. 27, 2006), amended by 2007 WL 685623 (E.D. Mo. Feb. 23, 2007); *Cenveo Corp. v. Slater*, No. 06-CV-2632, 2007 WL 442387, at *1-*3 (E.D. Pa. Jan. 31, 2007); *Frees, Inc. v. McMillian*, No. 05-1979, 2007 WL 184889, at *2 (W.D. La. Jan. 22, 2007). Nevertheless, "[c]ourts have been cautious in requiring the mirror imaging of computers where the request is extremely broad in nature and the connection between the computers and the claims in the lawsuit are unduly vague or unsubstantiated in nature." *Balboa Threadworks*, 2006 WL 763668, at *3; *see also Balfour Beatty Rail, Inc. v. Vaccarello*, No. 3:06-CV-551-J-20MCR, 2007 WL 169628, at *2-*3 (M.D. Fla. Jan. 18, 2007); *Diepenhorst v. City of Battle Creek*, No. 1:05-CV-734, 2006 WL 1851243, at *2-*4 (W.D. Mich. June 30, 2006). As the Tenth Circuit has noted, albeit in an unpublished opinion, mere skepticism that an opposing party has not produced all relevant information is not sufficient to warrant drastic electronic discovery measures. *See McCurdy Group, LLC v. Am. Biomedical Group, Inc.*, 9 F. App'x 822, 831 (10th Cir. 2001). And the Sedona Principles urge general caution with respect to forensic imaging in civil discovery:

*10 Civil litigation should not be approached as if information systems were crime scenes that justify forensic in-

vestigation at every opportunity to identify and preserve
every detail. . . . [M]aking forensic image backups of computers is only the first step of an expensive, complex, and
difficult process of data analysis that can divert litigation
into side issues and satellite disputes involving the interpretation of potentially ambiguous forensic evidence.

The Sedona Principles, supra, at 34, 47. Thus, even if
acceptable as a means to preserve electronic evidence, compelled forensic imaging is not appropriate in all cases, and
courts must consider the significant interests implicated by
forensic imaging before ordering such procedures. *Cf.* Fed.
R. Civ. P. 34(a) Advisory Committee Note (2006) ("Courts
should guard against undue intrusiveness resulting from inspecting or testing [electronic information] systems.").

The Sixth Circuit then explains how the district court departed
from this precedent and intruded too far into the privacy rights. The
court noted that there had been no showing of intentional destruction of ESI or proof of refusal to preserve ESI in the future. (There
had, however, been a strong showing of negligent destruction and
ongoing obstruction for years, but the Sixth Circuit seemed to gloss
over these inconvenient facts.) The court also suggests that the district court had several other options that it did not explore first.

The district court's compelled forensic imaging orders here
fail to account properly for the significant privacy and confidentiality concerns present in this case. . . .

Even so, the record lacks evidence that defendants have
intentionally destroyed relevant ESI in the past, and nothing
in the record indicates that defendants are unwilling, or will
refuse, to preserve and produce all relevant ESI in the future. Furthermore, forensic imaging is not the only available
means by which the district court may respond to what it
perceives to be discovery misconduct. The district court
maintains authority to impose sanctions for discovery violations under the federal rules and pursuant to its inherent powers. Although we take no position regarding the propriety of

sanctions in this case, such measures can be less intrusive than forensic imaging, and it is not apparent from the record that the district court has exercised its sanctioning authority. In fact, the district court expressly reserved discussion of sanctions in its October 9, 2007 opinion.

The court then moves on to the extraordinary comity and federalism issues raised by the case by the Justice Department against various agencies of the State of Tennessee.

*11 Aside from these privacy and confidentiality considerations, this case raises other obvious issues that counsel against the forensic imaging procedures ordered by the district court. As directives to state officials, these orders implicate federalism and comity considerations not present in typical civil litigation. Many of the computers subject to the orders are in the custody of high-ranking state officials, and these computers will contain information related to confidential state matters. Further, the orders call for federal law enforcement officers to accompany plaintiffs' computer expert into state agencies—and, in some cases, the homes and offices of state officials—to effect the imaging. These procedures clearly do not take adequate account of federalism and comity considerations. If the use of federal law enforcement officers in matters of civil discovery is proper under some circumstances, those circumstances are not present here.

Certainly, state officials are not immune from complying with federal discovery mandates. However, where less intrusive means are available to address the perceived discovery violations of state parties, those means should be employed before resorting to inherently intrusive measures like forensic imaging, especially in cases where there is no evidence of purposeful or intentional destruction of relevant ESI. In light of the significant confidentiality and federalism concerns present in this case, the district court's forensic imaging orders constitute the type of "demonstrable abuse of discretion" that warrants mandamus relief. *See In re Wilkinson*, 137 F.3d 911, 914 (6th Cir. 1998).

The concurring opinion of Circuit Judge R. Guy Cole, Jr., sent a clear warning to the State of Tennessee that further delay and obstruction by state officials would not be tolerated, and next time he would support forced forensic imaging.

> This case is unique, however, in that the court's order includes the forensic imaging of computers in the custody of individuals not party to this matter, and that the order may lead to confrontations between federal marshals and state officials. Under these circumstances, I agree with the majority that, without evidence that Defendants intentionally destroyed relevant ESI in the past or that they are affirmatively unwilling to preserve all relevant ESI in the future, the district court should first employ less intrusive means to address the perceived discovery violations.
>
> It is clear that the district court's focus has been to assist the parties in forging a solution that would ensure that Tennessee's children receive the benefits owed to them under the Consent Decree and federal law. Defendants' continual noncompliance and acrimonious litigation practice has unfortunately steered this case away from such goal, with the costs borne by the judicial system and the citizens of Tennessee. The district court has thus far reserved the exercise of its wide discretion to hold Defendants in contempt or to impose monetary sanctions. If the district court resorts to such measures and Defendants nevertheless continue to disregard their undisputed duty to preserve and produce relevant ESI, the preservation order at issue in this case, in my view, may no longer be considered inappropriate.

The state has been warned, and further, although the forensic order was vacated, the order allowing inspection of the defendants' computer system (but not copying) was allowed to stand. The case continues, and everyone in the e-discovery world will watch with interest; so too will the children of Tennessee. So much for forced *kumbaya* litigation and trying to force lawyers out of the courtroom.

COURT REJECTS ATTORNEY'S COMPUTER ILLITERACY AS EXCUSE FOR NON-PRODUCTION

Plaintiff's counsel in a district court case in Colorado lacked the technical ability to open and read most of his client's e-mails. He figured that since he could not read them, he did not have to produce them. Instead of producing the thousands of his client's e-mails that were on a DVD, he just produced the 10 he could read and ignored the rest. *Garcia v. Berkshire Life Ins. Co. of America*,[32] 2007 U.S. Dist. LEXIS 86639 (D. Colo. Nov. 13, 2007).

Although the plaintiff did not argue Rule 26(b)(2)(B), and the court did not use the rule's framework for analysis, the plaintiff's position was basically that since the e-mail was not reasonably accessible to plaintiff's counsel, it did not have to be produced. After all, he argued, there could be privileged materials in there. Apparently it never occurred to him to hire someone with technical competence to open and read the e-mails for him. Here are plaintiff's counsel's own words (describing himself) trying to justify his actions to the court:

> Plaintiff's counsel immediately tried to access the information on the DVD, but encountered software issues. Counsel eventually found what it believed to be the proper software and accessed the contents of the DVD. Plaintiff was not, apparently, able to access some 5,000 e-mails, and had no way of knowing the content of the disk except for what was displayed. Of what was displayed, Plaintiff printed and reviewed those e-mails and created a detailed privilege log. . . .
>
> Plaintiff was unable to access all of the data allegedly contained on the DVD with the software employed to provide all responsive e-mails. . . . Unfortunately, Plaintiff's counsel does not employ a full-time computer technician, [sic] occasionally a technology issues [sic] arises which exceeds

---

32. http://ralphlosey.files.wordpress.com/2007/12/garciavberkshire.doc.

Plaintiff's computer expertise. When those events arise, counsel works to obtain an understanding and familiarity with the software and medium. Plaintiff, in good faith, believed that all the unprivileged, relevant e-mails had been submitted. If there are in fact additional e-mails on the DVD, plaintiff was unaware of this. However, there was certainly no attempt to hide any of the content.

Not surprisingly, Magistrate Judge Boyd N. Boland was not buying this excuse:

> Plaintiff's claim that she acted in good faith with respect to the contents of the DVD goes only so far. Perhaps plaintiff's counsel can be heard to plead technical ignorance or mistake in his initial dealings with the DVD, but by September 21, 2007, upon the receipt of Ms. Yates' letter [defense counsel], he was on notice of the potential problem and was obligated to seek competent professional assistance to ascertain the truth about the contents of the DVD. He did not do so, and apparently still has not done so, in view of his expressed doubt, unsupported by any evidence, that the DVD contains substantial additional material.

The plaintiff herself, who was also an attorney (or at least had graduated from law school), was not much help. In fact, a comment by Judge Boland suggests his serious concerns about her actions:

> Berkshire has attached to the Second Motion to Compel an e-mail string indicating that the plaintiff communicated with an IT employee of the University of Denver, who may have attempted to mislead Berkshire about the scope of e-mails available to be retrieved from the University's system. (record cite omitted) This e-mail string raises serious concerns.

The plaintiff sued the defendant disability insurance company claiming that she was totally disabled from a sleep disorder, post-traumatic stress, and adult attention deficit disorder. She claimed the original cause of her disabling traumatic stress was an aggressive investigation by the Department of Housing and Urban Development into her real estate business. She went out on disability shortly after the HUD investigation in 1999 and claimed inability to return to work since that time. Plaintiff claims her traumatic stress was later aggravated when the psychiatrist treating her disorder allegedly molested her during a one-year sexual relationship.

The defendant insurance company, Berkshire, learned that plaintiff began attending the University of Denver after she stopped work in 1999. Her studies there were prodigious. She attended the Womens College from 1999 to 2001, law school from 2001 to 2006, and the Graduate School of International Studies in 2002. In 2006, she received an LL.M. in Natural Resources and Environment. Obviously plaintiff was no dummy, and Berkshire wondered whether she was truly disabled as she claimed.

Berkshire wrote and asked the university for all of the plaintiff's e-mail, rather than subpoena the school. I'm not sure why they took that approach, and with hindsight, they would have been better off with a subpoena. Berkshire asked that the production be made in native format with all metadata preserved. The university responded to the request by producing the requested e-mails to the plaintiff's counsel. They were produced on a DVD, not a CD, because, as the school explained, they would not all fit on a CD.

Plaintiff's counsel was then to review the DVD, remove and log all e-mails to which a privilege was claimed, and produce the rest to defense counsel. A little over a week later, the plaintiff produced printouts of 10 e-mail strings, with two attachments. Plaintiff's counsel also produced a privilege log listing 135 additional e-mails. Obviously this production did not square with the university's explanation that a DVD was needed to hold all of the plaintiff's e-mails. Defense counsel called them on this discrepancy in an attempt to voluntarily obtain a full production without having to file another motion to compel.

After two letters, plaintiff's counsel finally responded by producing the DVD to defense counsel, but only for her to determine if there were additional files on the DVD as she contended, and only after she promised that no one would look at the contents of any files on the DVD. The IT technician for defense counsel inspected the DVD and found more than 4,000 e-mails with 1,500 attachments of various types. Defense counsel returned the DVD, reported the findings, and told plaintiff's counsel that:

> Your production of 10 e-mails, and a privilege log with 135 other e-mails—and your representation that this was all that was on the DVD—is extremely troubling and points again toward deception.

Even after this disclosure, plaintiff's counsel refused to budge, and defense counsel had to move to compel discovery. In response, plaintiff's counsel continued to doubt there were in fact additional e-mails on the DVD, and claimed a good-faith mistake based on his computer incompetence, as quoted above. The plaintiff at this point also added a new argument—that the e-mails would be irrelevant and their disclosure would invade her privacy rights. Here is Judge Boland's response to that argument:

> In addition, I am not persuaded by the plaintiff's relevancy argument. During the time the plaintiff claimed to be totally disabled, for emotional and cognitive reasons, from working as an executive in a real estate company or in a comparable position, she earned an undergraduate degree, a law degree, and began work on a masters degree. (record cite omitted) It is counterintuitive, at least, to think that anything she wrote in an e-mail on her university account during that time period is not relevant to the issue of her disability. In particular, I agree with Berkshire that the e-mails are relevant because they may show "to what extent Ms. Garcia was working or developing her businesses during the period of claimed disability" and that "her ability to communicate effectively by e-mail and to develop PowerPoint presentations and spreadsheets [may] rebut her claimed inability to think clearly and to interact socially." (record cite omitted) The plaintiff has made no showing to the contrary.

To address the plaintiff's privacy concerns, the court indicated a willingness to enter a confidentiality order, but the motion to compel was granted.

The plaintiff also raised privilege issues to try to prevent or at least delay the production, arguing that since they were not able to open the e-mails and attachments, they did not know if any were privileged. The court rejected this argument, stating the plaintiff had sufficient protection by new Rule 26(b)(5)(B) with its built-in clawback provisions.

Berkshire also sought production of some of the 135 e-mails originally withheld as privileged. The challenged e-mails were to and from the plaintiff's brother and other family members. The plaintiff claimed they were privileged under the "common interest" doctrine, even though no attorney was involved with these e-mails. The court explained that this doctrine applies: "when parties with separate lawyers consult together under the guise of a common interest or defense." This was a diversity removal case, and so the district court looked to the state law of Colorado governing privilege. The plaintiff claimed that the privilege doctrine applied to her brother and other family members because she had already assigned the contingent proceeds of this legal action to them. The court disagreed, holding:

> Colorado recognizes the common interest doctrine only in "communications made between co-defendants and the attorney who represents them both, for the sake of discussing their common interests in a joint defense in civil or criminal litigation." *Gordon v. Boyles*, 9 P.3d 1106, 1124 (Colo. 2000). Here, neither Mike Garcia nor Leyla Del Rosario are parties to this action and there is no evidence that they share an attorney with the plaintiff. Nor does it appear that any lawyer was involved as either an author or recipient of any of the common interest e-mails. Consequently, the plaintiff has failed to prove the applicability of the common interest privilege. The plaintiff must produce those e-mails exchanged

between Mike Garcia, Leyla Del Rosario, and/or Tina Garcia for which the common interest privilege was asserted.

I call this a sequel "dumb and dumber"[33] case, because it is remarkably similar to another case I frequently mention in my e-discovery presentations, *Martin v. Northwestern Mutual Life Insurance Company*,[34] 2006 WL 148991 (M.D. Fla. Jan. 19, 2006). The plaintiff in *Martin* was a trial lawyer who had sued Northwestern for disability benefits. Martin produced only paper records, and claimed that was complete. The defendant then discovered that the plaintiff's office computers contained voluminous additional electronic records. The defendant moved for sanctions. The plaintiff and his counsel defended on the basis of "computer illiteracy." Magistrate Judge Pizzo responded as follows:

> Plaintiff's reasons for non-production are unsatisfactory and warrant sanctions. . . . His claim that he is so computer illiterate that he could not comply with production is frankly ludicrous.

I could not agree more. Still, it is fairly certain that we will continue to see variations of the "dumb and dumber"[35] defense for years to come. Hopefully, the next sequel to this movie will feature different characters. The plaintiff's attorney representing an alleged disabled attorney scenario is getting old fast.

---

33. http://en.wikipedia.org/wiki/Dumb_and_Dumber.
34. http://ralphlosey.files.wordpress.com/2007/12/martincase.pdf.
35. http://en.wikipedia.org/wiki/Dumb_and_Dumberer:_When_Harry_Met_Lloyd.

Search and Review of ESI

4

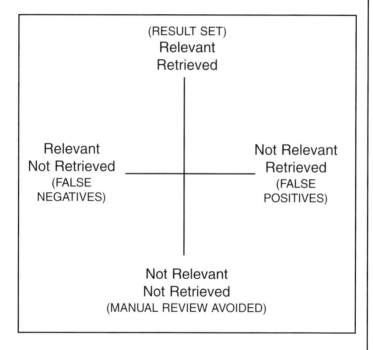

(RESULT SET)
Relevant
Retrieved

Relevant
Not Retrieved
(FALSE
NEGATIVES)

Not Relevant
Retrieved
(FALSE
POSITIVES)

Not Relevant
Not Retrieved
(MANUAL REVIEW AVOIDED)

THOUGHTS ON SEARCH AND *VICTOR STANLEY, INC. V. CREATIVE PIPE, INC.*

This is my one-hundredth article on e-discovery since I started the e-Discovery Team blog in late 2006. I would like to think that, like the mythical Hundredth Monkey,[1]

---

1. http://en.wikipedia.org/wiki/Hundredth_Monkey_Effect/.

my weekly essay writing will now somehow become an easy task, an innate skill. But I doubt it. Much like the task of e-discovery search, writing a 2,500–4,000 word essay on e-discovery each week takes time, effort, and careful planning. In a way, as I will explain, this is the core message of the hot case of the day, *Victor Stanley, Inc. v. Creative Pipe, Inc.*,[2] 2008 WL 2221841 (D. Md., May 29, 2008).

This scholarly e-discovery order was written by Judge Paul Grimm in Baltimore. He is one of the country's top judicial experts on e-discovery. Judge Grimm fully understands that ESI search and review is a complex, learned skill. It is not an innate ability that every lawyer somehow picks up in law school in Legal Research 101. Lawyers need to treat search and review seriously, and either take the time necessary to become adept in this complex area or employ experts who are. If not, the consequences can be devastating, as *Victor Stanley* shows. The defendants waived their attorney-client and work product privileges to 165 ESI files by their botched search and review before production.

Victor Stanley, Inc. and Reasonable Search

Judge Grimm's 43-page opinion is, on one level, a detailed ruling on waiver of attorney-client privilege. On another level, it is a treatise on e-discovery search and a guide to proving reasonable efforts. As Jason R. Baron[3] is quoted as saying:[4] "What Judge Grimm has done is give a road map to lawyers in the United States on how to present to a court how they went about searching for relevant documents."

Such proof may be required when a search fails and you are faced with sanctions as a result or, as in this case, loss of privilege. In these circumstances, you may be required to prove that your search was reasonable, albeit imperfect. As everyone in the industry knows,

---

2. http://ralphlosey.files.wordpress.com/2008/06/victorstanleymomay29-08final.pdf.

3. http://www.archives.gov/legal/bios/jrbaron.html.

4. http://www.mddailyrecord.com/article.cfm?id=5563&type=UTTM.

e-discovery is like golf—there is no such thing as perfect, and everybody, even Tiger Woods, makes a few mistakes.

That is what the defendants in this case claimed, that the disclosure of the privileged documents was just an honest mistake, and there should be no waiver. The plaintiff agreed that it was a mistake but denied it was an honest one, and even alleged that some of the ESI revealed fraud. They also challenged the adequacy of the search efforts. Judge Grimm did not directly address the dishonesty allegations, but did agree that no credible evidence was presented to establish reasonable search efforts. Primarily for that reason, Judge Grimm held that the defendant's disclosure of attorney-client and work product–privileged ESI acted to waive those privileges.

That is a pretty scary ruling for the vast majority of litigators in the U.S. who have strictly amateur status in the game of e-discovery. They cannot even begin to comprehend the skills and expertise developed by the likes of Tiger Woods, much less the kind of practice and dedication he puts into every round. Yet, Judge Grimm suggests that when it comes to privilege review, at least, they had better improve their game. He does not expect everyone to attain the level of a top professional, but he does expect some time and attention to be put into the important task of ESI search. *See, e.g., ClearOne Communications, Inc. v. Chiang,*[5] 2008 WL 920336 (D. Utah, April 1, 2008) (parties and court labored over keyword search plan). You just cannot hope for the Hundredth Monkey effect. Moreover, he suggests that some attorneys would be well advised to seek the help of a professional. For most cases, a simple club pro consult will do, but if it is a "bet the company" case, you might want to retain a touring professional.

Speaking of which, several of Jason Baron's writings and research projects on search were cited by Judge Grimm in *Victor Stanley,* including "The Sedona Conference, Best Practices Commentary on the Use of Search and Information Retrieval,"[6] 8 *The Sedona Con-*

---

5. http://ralphlosey.files.wordpress.com/2008/06/searchtermsc aseclearone1.doc.

6. http://www.thesedonaconference.org/dltForm?did=Best_Practices_ Retrieval_Methods___revised_cover_and_preface.pdf,

ference Journal 189 (2007), which I have previously written about in "Sedona's New Commentary on Search" and the "Myth of the Pharaoh's Curse,"[7] and the Text Retrieval Conference (TREC) sponsored by the National Institute of Standards and Technology. The TREC event is in its third year of scientific evaluations of various kinds of ESI automated search techniques, including the kind of lame keyword search that the losing defendants apparently ran in *Victor Stanley*. The results are surprising. They suggest that keyword searches alone, especially when poorly done without sampling and iteration, and without the help of more advanced techniques and technologies, will miss most of the documents sought. That finding should be alarming to anyone who does e-discovery, especially if you use keyword searches alone to try to protect against waiver of privilege in a massive production.

Judge Grimm's opinion is a wake-up call to all litigators who put blind trust in simple keyword searches and think that anyone can do it. It is a dangerous delusion, as this case shows. I call it the "Myth of Google," where litigators think that since they can run a Google search, and also a Westlaw or Lexis search, they can run an e-discovery search, too. They think that since they know the case, they know what the best keywords are, and that is all it takes to find what they need. After all, it works for them on Google and legal research, so it should work on e-mail search too. It never even occurs to the average trial lawyer that special expertise and training might be needed to find the needles in today's electronic haystacks.[8] They do not think they need an expert to help them formulate an adequate search strategy, including, but most definitely not limited to, formulating keywords.

Grimm's tale is that when a search fails miserably, do not expect the judge to simply take your word for it that the efforts were appropriate. It is going to require some kind of expert evidence. In Judge Grimm's words:

7. http://ralphlosey.wordpress.com/2007/09/16/sedonas-new-commentary-on-search-and-the-myth-of-the-pharaohs-curse/.

8. http://floridalawfirm.com/.

Assuming that the Plaintiff's version of how Defendants conducted their privilege review is accurate, the Defendants obtained the results of the agreed-upon ESI search protocol and ran a keyword search on the text-searchable files using approximately seventy keywords selected by M. Pappas [Defendant] and two of his attorneys. Defendants, who bear the burden of proving that their conduct was reasonable for purposes of assessing whether they waived attorney-client privilege by producing the 165 documents to the Plaintiff, have failed to provide the court with information regarding: the keywords used; the rationale for their selection; the qualifications of M. Pappas and his attorneys to design an effective and reliable search and information retrieval method; whether the search was a simple keyword search, or a more sophisticated one, such as one employing Boolean proximity operators; or whether they analyzed the results of the search to assess its reliability, appropriateness for the task, and the quality of its implementation. While keyword searches have long been recognized as appropriate and helpful for ESI search and retrieval, there are well-known limitations and risks associated with them, and proper selection and implementation obviously involves technical, if not scientific knowledge.

It cannot credibly be denied that resolving contested issues of whether a particular search and information retrieval method was appropriate—in the context of a motion to compel or motion for protective order—involves scientific, technical or specialized information. If so, then the trial judge must decide a method's appropriateness with the benefit of information from some reliable source—whether an affidavit from a qualified expert, a learned treatise, or, if appropriate, from information judicially noticed. To suggest otherwise is to condemn the trial court to making difficult decisions on inadequate information, which cannot be an outcome that anyone would advocate. . . . Indeed, it is risky for a trial judge to attempt to resolve issues involving technical areas without the aid of expert assistance.

Judge Grimm follows in the footsteps of Judge John Facciola, who has previously warned of the need for special expertise for appropriate searches in several cases:

> *United States v. O'Keefe*,[9] No. 06-249 (D.D.C. Feb. 18, 2008), which I wrote about in "Criminal Case Raises Interesting e-Discovery Search Issues,"[10] *Disability Rights Council of Greater Wash. v. Wash. Metro. Area Transit Auth.*,[11] 2007 WL 1585452 (D. D.C. June 1, 2007), which I wrote about in "Keyword Searches v. Concept Searches,"[12] and *Equity Analytics, LLC v. Lundin*,[13] 248 F.R.D. 331, 331 (D. D.C. March 7, 2008), where Judge Facciola stated:

>> [D]etermining whether a particular search method-ology, such as keywords, will or will not be effective certainly requires knowledge beyond the ken of a lay person (and a lay lawyer).

Some have criticized Judge Facciola for these decisions, argu-ing that they unnecessarily drive up the cost of litigation. These same critics will now criticize Judge Grimm for joining his camp. They think that requiring expert input in discovery unnecessarily raises the bar of professional standards and forces litigation attorneys to retain yet another set of experts, e-discovery search experts, which clients can ill afford.

Perhaps it is self-serving on my part, but I strongly disagree. In my experience, experts in this area will save more money than their fee. They can effectively cull the data set down to a more manage-

---

9. http://ralphlosey.files.wordpress.com/2008/02/usvokeffe-criminalsearch.pdf.

10. http://ralphlosey.wordpress.com/2008/02/24/criminal-case-raises-interesting-e-discovery-search-issues/.

11. http://ralphlosey.files.wordpress.com/2007/08/case-disability-rights-council-v-wmata-o1175524.pdf,

12. http://ralphlosey.wordpress.com/2007/06/10/keyword-searches-v-concept-searches/.

13. http://ralphlosey.files.wordpress.com/2008/06/equity-vlundin.doc.

able level where final review and production is far less expensive. The trial lawyer with no special skills or experience in e-discovery is likely to just copy and review everything. The keyword searches that I typically see performed by novices are a model of inefficiency, producing far too high a noise-to-hit ratio.

Judge Grimm anticipated and responded to these expense criticisms in note 10 of *Victor Stanley*. The note, which is three pages long and is partially quoted above, makes several additional points explaining why such search experts are needed:

> Instead, Judge Facciola made the entirely self-evident observation that challenges to the sufficiency of keyword search methodology unavoidably involve scientific, technical and scientific subjects, and *ipse dixit* pronouncements from lawyers unsupported by an affidavit or other showing that the search methodology was effective for its intended purpose are of little value to a trial judge who must decide a discovery motion aimed at either compelling a more comprehensive search or preventing one.
>
> Viewed in its proper context, all that *O'Keefe* and *Equity Analytics* required was that the parties be prepared to back up their positions with respect to a dispute involving the appropriateness of ESI search and information retrieval methodology—obviously an area of science or technology—with reliable information from someone with the qualifications to provide helpful opinions, not conclusory argument by counsel.

The message to be taken from *O'Keefe, Equity Analytics*, and this opinion is that when parties decide to use a particular ESI search and retrieval methodology, they need to be aware of literature describing the strengths and weaknesses of various methodologies, such as *The Sedona Conference Best Practices, supra*, n.9, and select the one that they believe is most appropriate for its intended task. Should their selection be challenged by their adversary and the court be called upon to make a ruling, then they should expect to support their position with affidavits or other equivalent information from persons with the requisite qualifications and experience, based on sufficient facts or data and using reliable principles or methodology.

For those understandably concerned about keeping discovery costs within reasonable bounds, it is worth repeating that the cost-benefit balancing factors of Federal Rule of Civil Procedure 26(b)(2)(C) apply to all aspects of discovery, and parties worried about the cost of employing properly designed search and information retrieval methods have an incentive to keep the costs of this phase of discovery as low as possible, including attempting to confer with their opposing party in an effort to identify a mutually agreeable search and retrieval method. This minimizes cost because if the method is approved, there will be no dispute resolving its sufficiency, and doing it right the first time is always cheaper than doing it over if ordered to do so by the court. Additionally, cost can be minimized by entering into a court-approved agreement that would comply with *Hopson* or, if enacted, Proposed Evidence Rule 502. In addition, there is room for optimism that as search and information retrieval methodologies are studied and tested, this will result in identifying those that are most effective and least expensive to employ for a variety of ESI discovery tasks.

Proper search is the cornerstone of e-discovery and key to controlling costs. Since most of the cost of e-discovery lies in review expenses (estimates range from 50% to 80%), our efforts should be focused on searches that reduce the amount of ESI to be reviewed. Obviously, the better the search, the more chaff is separated from the wheat. We do not want our reviewers reading chaff; every minute a reviewer spends reading an irrelevant e-mail is a minute wasted. Here experts can help and should be consulted at the very beginning of the case, at the same time as the litigation hold notices. If you are going to consult a pro, it only makes sense to do so before the round begins, not on the 18th tee.

Judge Grimm takes pains to point out that search is not only important, but requires a high level of skill to do properly. He also provides some suggestions on how to do that:

Use of search and information retrieval methodology, for the purpose of identifying and withholding privileged or work product–protected information from production, requires the utmost care in selecting methodology that is appropriate for the task because the consequence of failing to do so, as in this case, may be the disclosure of privileged/protected information to an adverse party, resulting in a determination by the court that the privilege/protection has been waived.

Selection of the appropriate search and information retrieval technique requires careful advance planning by persons qualified to design effective search methodology. The implementation of the methodology selected should be tested for quality assurance; and the party selecting the methodology must be prepared to explain the rationale for the method chosen to the court, demonstrate that it is appropriate for the task, and show that it was properly implemented. In this regard, compliance with the *Sedona Conference Best Practices* for use of search and information retrieval will go a long way towards convincing the court that the method chosen was reasonable and reliable, which, in jurisdictions that have adopted the intermediate test for assessing privilege waiver based on inadvertent production, may very well prevent a finding that the privilege or work-product protection was waived.

Since I consider search so important, many of my first 100 blogs have addressed this topic, not only in the above-cited articles on Judge Facciola's cases, but also in "Inadequate Keyword Searches by Untrained Lawyers May in Some Circumstances Be Sanctionable,"[14] which discusses an opinion by District Court Judge Nancy F. Atlas in Houston, Texas, *Diabetes Centers of America, Inc. v. Healthpia America, Inc.*,[15] 2008 U.S. Dist. LEXIS 8362, 2008 WL

---

14. http://ralphlosey.wordpress.com/2008/03/02/inadequate-keyword-searches-by-untrained-lawyers-may-in-some-circumstances-be-sanctionable/.

15. http://ralphlosey.files.wordpress.com/2008/03/diabetesvhealthpiacase.doc.

336382 (S.D. Tex. Feb. 5, 2008), and "Sedona's New Commentary on Search" and "Myth of the Pharaoh's Curse,"[16] which discuss the Sedona treatise edited by Jason Baron.

Defendant's Failure in *Victor Stanley* to Prove Reasonable Search Efforts Results in Loss of Attorney-Client Privilege

Judge Grimm, in this case, found the defendants' search efforts to be negligent.

> In this case, the Defendants have failed to demonstrate that the keyword search they performed on the text-searchable ESI was reasonable. Defendants neither identified the key-words selected nor the qualifications of the persons who selected them to design a proper search; they failed to demonstrate that there was quality-assurance testing; and when their production was challenged by the Plaintiff, they failed to carry their burden of explaining what they had done and why it was sufficient.
>
> Further, the Defendants' attempt to justify what was done by complaining that the volume of ESI needing review and time constraints presented them with no other choice is simply unpersuasive.

Since their review was negligent, or at least not proven to be adequate, the defendants were found to have waived their privilege to the 165 documents that they accidentally produced to the plaintiff. Bear in mind that the defendants produced tens of thousands of documents in this same production, and so percentage-wise, the mistake was very small, less than 1%. (Even so, Judge Grimm thought that 165 documents was a lot to miss, and suggested he might have reached a different result if only a couple had been missed.) Based on the the high number of electronic files that the defendants had to review for privilege, you might be surprised by the seemingly strident tone of the opinion. The defendants were, after all, being stripped

---

16. http://ralphlosey.wordpress.com/2007/09/16/sedonas-new-commentary-on-search-and-the-myth-of-the-pharaohs-curse/

of their attorney-client privilege, which is a fundamental right[17] recognized by the Supreme Court since 1826. Here are the Judge's Grimm words:

> Thus, the disclosures were substantive—including numerous communications between defendants and their counsel. . . . [A]ny order issued now by the court to attempt to redress these disclosures would be the equivalent of closing the barn door after the animals have already run away.
>
> Every waiver of the attorney-client privilege produces unfortunate consequences for the party that disclosed the information. If that alone were sufficient to constitute an injustice, there would never be a waiver. The only "injustice" in this matter is that done by Defendants to themselves.

But when you dig deeper into the record of this case, you see how restrained his opinion is, and how these defendants really did get what was coming to them.

The Bad Facts Behind the *Victor Stanley* Law

It is true that the defendants produced nearly 39 gigabytes of ESI, comprising tens of thousands of documents and unsearchable image files, such as engineering drawings and photographs. It is also true that the sheer volume of the ESI involved would weigh in favor of leniency for an accidental production of 165 files. But, when you dig deeper, and not only closely study the whole opinion but also delve into the voluminous record in this case, you find numerous countervailing considerations. You can only guess at some of these factors because parts of the record are still sealed, including the 165 documents at issue. Still, this record is filled with smoke suggestive of bad faith. The total record helps explain this decision, and makes it easy to distinguish. For instance, it is also true that:

---

17. http://ralphlosey.wordpress.com/2008/03/23/trade-secrets-case-uses-md5-hash-and-keyword-search-to-protect-defendants-rights-magistrates-privilege-waiver-order-is-reversed//

1. Defendants could have protected themselves by entering into a clawback agreement but chose not to. In fact, at first they agreed to enter into such an agreement to protect themselves from inadvertent disclosures such as this. Judge Grimm suggested it and the plaintiff, Victor Stanley, Inc., agreed. Then, after months of delay, the defendants changed their mind and decided it was not necessary. The plaintiff claims it was all part of their delay tactics. So this whole case is much like a Greek drama where the hero is punished for hubris. In my view, you should always enter into a clawback agreement in any case involving significant amounts of ESI. I see no downside in doing so.

2. The defendants failed to establish that the 165 electronic documents at issue were covered by the attorney-client or work product privilege. At pages 30–42 of the Order, Judge Grimm spelled out in great detail how they failed to follow proper procedures to establish the privileges.

3. The plaintiff claimed that two of the documents produced, e-mails to and from the defendant and one of his lawyers, were excluded from privilege by the crime/fraud/tort exception. Judge Grimm did an *in camera* review of all 165 documents before making his ruling, including the two e-mails alleged to show fraud. While I have not seen these e-mails, the other pleadings suggest that they pertain to an earlier Rule 11 motion that the plaintiff filed against the defendants. This motion alleged that a counterclaim was filed with an improper purpose—namely, to have the plaintiff's lead counsel disqualified by filing a bogus claim against him personally. It appears from the arguments that the e-mails in question pertained to the strategy challenged by the Rule 11 motion, and otherwise may have implicated the integrity of the defendant.

4. The defendants are now on their fourth law firm to represent them. Judge Grimm was careful to point out in the Order that the search and review negligence was committed by predecessor counsel. As any experienced litigator knows, churning legal counsel is a huge red flag.

5. The 39 gigabytes of ESI was derived from the defendants' computer system through an agreed-upon search protocol conducted by a forensics computer expert. Under the discovery agreement, the defendants were then to review this ESI and remove any privileged documents before production. The privileged ESI was to be logged, and *all of the rest* was to be produced. The search found to be negligent by Judge Grimm was the privilege search and review, not the original relevance search and collection. The defendants' privilege review was based on 70 search terms that one of the defendants and his lawyers dreamed up. The computer expert did not assist in developing the search strategy or keywords; she merely ran the search.

6. The defendants refused to disclose the 70 search terms used for a privilege review, even after the adequacy of their search was challenged. This seems strange to me, but not to the plaintiff, who forcefully argues that the 70 search terms were never intended to try to catch privileged documents. They were instead used to try to locate documents that might prejudice the defense and then remove them from the production in violation of the terms of the production agreement. The plaintiff contends that during the time the defendants were supposed to be reviewing for privilege, they were instead reviewing and culling for hot files. The plaintiff claims that revelation of the 70 search terms would reveal the defendants' true, improper purpose. No doubt there will be additional discovery on this alleged improper secretion of documents.

7. The defendants had months to search through the ESI that they produced, and they still missed 165 attorney-client communications. Conversely, the plaintiff claims that they easily found these documents in only a one-hour search by using "a readily available desktop search tool." The plaintiff argues that this confirms its allegation that no privilege review was ever conducted, and that the whole exercise was a ruse to buy time to search for and remove harmful files.

I could go on, but you get the picture. The case itself is also interesting, involving allegations of unfair competition based on lying about whether goods were made in China and violations of copyright. But at this point, these are all just allegations. The remaining discovery and trial should soon reveal much more. When it does, I will look again at this case to see what, if any, fire is behind all of this smoke.

Hundredth Monkey

In the meantime, don't fall for the Myth of Google, or let your friends fall for it either. Search and review are learned skills of some complexity and require adequate tools to perform correctly. Maybe 100 other lawyers and information scientists can do it, but that does not mean the skill has somehow magically transferred itself to the rest of the legal or IT professions.

Although the Hundredth Monkey[18] is an inspirational story and may work for ideas, it is based on bad science and does not work for skills. Complex skills of any kind, from monkeys washing sweet potatoes to lawyers searching e-mails to golfers striking a ball, all have to be individually learned. They cannot be learned by some until a magic numerical threshold is passed, then instantly transmuted through fields of energy and suddenly ingrained in everyone else. Sorry, it looks like we will all have to do the work. We cannot just wait for others to learn these e-discovery skills, and then expect to wake up one day with their hard-earned abilities. If so, considering the number of professional golfers there now are in the world, we should all be breaking 100.

JUDGE FACCIOLA CITES TO MY FIRST BOOK IN IMPORTANT NEW OPINION ON SEARCH

Judges do not generally publicly praise a lawyer's book, nor should they. If they think a book is of any value, then they cite to it in an opinion. To a practicing attorney such as myself, this is really the highest compliment I can receive. For that reason, I was very ex-

---

18. http://en.wikipedia.org/wiki/Hundredth_Monkey_Effect.

cited to learn that immediately upon the release of my first book, *E-Discovery: Current Trends and Cases* (ABA 2008), it was both cited and quoted. I have Judge John M. Facciola to thank, who is magistrate judge in the hottest federal jurisdiction in the country for e-discovery, Washington, D.C. He is one of the hardest-working judges around and a true expert in the field of e-discovery. He is known for writing opinions that are not only learned, but also clever and well written.

The cite to my book is found at page 10 of the Memorandum Opinion rendered on January 23, 2008, in *D'Onofrio v. SFX Sports Group, Inc.,*[19] 247 F.R.D. 43 (D. D.C. 2008). This part of the e-discovery order denied the plaintiff's motion to compel production of metadata largely because the plaintiff did not ask for it in the original production request. Here is the specific cite to the book:

> *See also* RALPH C. LOSEY, E-DISCOVERY, CURRENT TRENDS AND CASES 158-59 (2007) (summarizing recent cases as amounting to a "lesson . . . that in order to obtain metadata you may need, you should specifically ask for it to begin with").

I am very honored by that. Thank you, Judge Facciola.

D'Onofrio is a sex discrimination case where the plaintiff moved to compel discovery and impose sanctions against her former employer. Most of the discovery disputes relate to electronically stored information (ESI). The plaintiff asked the court to compel production of a business plan document and certain e-mails in their "original electronic format, with accompanying metadata." *D'Onofrio,* pg. 5. The plaintiff claimed that "defendants have deliberately caused the spoliation of electronic records and have purposely failed to produce many e-mails and documents." Apparently, the defendants produced the records requested, but they produced the business plan in paper form and the e-mails in MSG format. (For more information on the deficiencies of MSG production and why only PST production includes full metadata, see the section *MSG Is Bad for You.*)

---

19. http://ralphlosey.files.wordpress.com/2008/01/1stcasecitingbook.pdf.

Rule 34(b)[20] states that a discovery request "may specify the form or forms in which electronically stored information is to be produced." If it does not, then the responding party must produce the information in a form "in which it is ordinarily maintained" or is "reasonably usable." Rule 34 also only requires production of the same information in one form. The plaintiff argued that her original request for production specified that the information should be produced in its original form with metadata, and therefore the paper production was noncompliant. The problem is, her request did not say that; instead, it read as follows:

> [F]or any documents that are stored or maintained in files in the normal course of business, such documents shall be produced in such files, or in such a manner as to preserve and identify the file from which such documents were taken.

This is "*so* last century" boilerplate language. It is quite a stretch for the plaintiff to argue that the above is a request for native production with full metadata. It quite obviously does no such thing. To the contrary, it clearly refers to a paper production, and asks for the paper files to be produced in the paper folders in which they were originally maintained. Judge Facciola was not impressed by this attempt to convert such archaic language into a 21st-century request for native ESI.

> It is apparent that this language, when first written, was not meant to encompass electronic data. Instead it addresses a common concern of paper discovery: the identification of a document's custodian and origination. It is for this reason that the Instruction applies to documents "stored or maintained in files," and why it seeks to "preserve and identify" the identity of that file. Indeed, the Instruction makes perfect sense when one presumes "file" to refer to a physical file cabinet or folder.

---

20. http://ralphlosey.wordpress.com/rule-34/.

Id., pgs. 7-8. The court properly concluded that the plaintiff's request permitted paper production of the business plan. It is in this context that the court cited and quoted several authorities, including my new book. Here is the full string cite:

Ultimately, then, it does not matter whether the Instruction referred to paper or electronic files—a plain reading leads to the conclusion that plaintiff did not make a request that the Business Plan be produced solely in its original format with accompanying metadata. *See* Vanston Bondholders Prot. Comm. v. Green, 329 U.S. 156, 170 (1946) ("Putting the wrong question is not likely to beget right answers even in law."). A motion to compel is appropriate only where an appropriate request is made of the responding party. *See* Fed. R. Civ. P. 37(a)(1)(B); Raghavan v. Bayer USA, Inc., No. 3:05-cv-682, 2007 WL 2099637, at *4 (D. Conn. July 17, 2007) ("The court will not compel discovery that has not been sought.").

Because no such request has been made concerning the Business Plan, the Court will not compel the defendant to produce it in its original form with accompanying metadata.[9] *See, e.g.,* Ponca Tribe of Indians v. Continental Carbon Co., No. CIV-05-445-C, 2006 WL 2927878, at *6 (W.D. Okla. Oct. 11, 2006) ("The original document requests issued by Plaintiffs failed to specify the manner in which electronic or computer information should be produced. [Defendant] elected to use a commonly accepted means of complying with the request. Nothing in the materials provided by Plaintiffs supports requiring [Defendant] to reproduce the information in a different format. Accordingly, Plaintiffs' request for reproduction of documents in their native electronic format will be denied."); Wyeth v. Impax Labs., Inc., No. Civ. A. 06-222-JJF, 2006 WL 3091331, at *1-2 (D. Del. Oct. 26, 2006) ("Since the parties have never agreed that electronic documents would be produced in any particular format, [Plaintiff] complied with its discovery obligation by producing image files"). *Cf.* Treppel v. Biovail Corp., 233 F.R.D.

363, 374 (S.D. N.Y. 2006) (requiring production in native format where requesting party asked for it and producing party did not object). *See also* RALPH C. LOSEY, E-DISCOVERY, CURRENT TRENDS AND CASES 158-59 (2007) (summarizing recent cases as amounting to a "lesson . . . that in order to obtain metadata you may need, you should specifically ask for it to begin with").

Id., pgs. 9-10. The court next considered the defendants' e-mail production in MSG format instead of PST format. Here the defendants claim they *did* make production in PST format, and the complaint is ill-founded. The defendants submitted an affidavit in opposition to the plaintiff's motion by John Cavender, who is identified as a "security principal." I am not sure what that is, but he was obviously an IT expert of some kind, probably in charge of IT security. Cavender's affidavit stated that he was responsible for the "retention and extraction of Clear Channel's archived e-mail on the Legato system" and that:

> he has reviewed the DVDs that were produced to plaintiff and can confirm that they contain defendants' e-mail production in .PST format, and that the production can be "searched by many criteria."

Id., pg. 11. Apparently, plaintiff offered no contradictory testimony, and so there was no real dispute. This appears to be another classic example of law-IT miscommunication, which I previously wrote about in "Who's On First?"[21]

On the sanctions motion, the plaintiff offered additional grounds, including an alleged non-production of relevant e-mails. The plaintiff alleged that her expert, a representative of Kroll Ontrack, could verify the omission of the e-mails. Judge Facciola found the record on the missing e-mail issue to be "too thin" to make a ruling, so he ordered an evidentiary hearing to hear testimony on the alleged claim

---

21. http://ralphlosey.wordpress.com/2007/12/15/whos-on-first-new-case-repeats-the-classic-miscommunications-between-law-and-it/.

by Kroll. The last half of the opinion goes on to address other issues that are not too interesting to anyone other than the parties.

The first half of the opinion in *D'Onofrio v. SFX Sports Group, Inc.*[22] is very interesting and well worth reading. It may become well known as a case that exemplifies what can go wrong when a request for production uses obsolete language. The Electronic Discovery blog[23] has already tagged this case for that proposition. The case thus shows the importance of practitioners studying up on e-discovery and using the correct language. Reading this book and *e-Discovery: Current Trends and Cases*[24] is one way to do that.

INADEQUATE KEYWORD SEARCHES BY UNTRAINED LAWYERS MAY, IN SOME CIRCUMSTANCES, BE SANCTIONABLE

A recent decision in Texas suggests that inadequate keyword searches could lay a predicate for spoliation sanctions when the defective searches cause evidence to be lost. In *Diabetes Centers of America, Inc. v. Healthpia America, Inc.*,[25] 2008 U.S. Dist. LEXIS 8362, 2008 WL 336382 (S.D. Tex. Feb. 5, 2008), the plaintiff relied upon an untrained associate attorney to do keyword searches, apparently to decide which e-mails of a key witness to preserve and produce. The associate's sleuthing skills were poor and she botched the job. As a result, numerous relevant e-mails were lost—e-mails that defendants claimed would have helped their defense.

Although the court here declined to impose sanctions, that was, in my view, largely because the defense also made mistakes in failing to preserve their e-mail. It was, in effect, a case of offsetting penalties. Sanctions may well have been granted if the moving party had been wearing a white hat. The opinion suggests that sanctions may be appropriate in other cases where evidence is lost be-

---

22. http://ralphlosey.files.wordpress.com/2008/01/1stcasecitingbook.pdf.

23. http://www.electronicdiscoveryblog.com/?p=158.

24. http://www.abanet.org/abastore/index.cfm?section=main&fm=Product.AddToCart&pid=1620320.

25. http://ralphlosey.files.wordpress.com/2008/03/diabetesvhealthpiacase.doc.

cause important searches were recklessly entrusted to "Inspector Clouseau"[26] types.

This case is a warning to everyone who does keyword searches in e-discovery. Care must be used in determining the search procedures and terms. This important task should not be delegated to untrained, unsupervised personnel.

This case underscores the point made by Judge Facciola in *United States v. O'Keefe*,[27] No. 06-249 (D. D.C. Feb. 18, 2008), that keyword search analysis is a very complex area of e-discovery "where angels fear to tread."[28] He implies that only fools attempt the task of computer search without expert help. You may not need to hire the e-discovery search equivalent of Sherlock Holmes for every case, but for some cases, it may be a good idea. This is especially true when large amounts of ESI are involved. Then, more sophisticated concept-type search[29] alternatives to keyword search should be considered because keyword searches[30] alone may not work.

Facts of the Case

The defendants in *Diabetes Centers* alleged that:

> Plaintiff (specifically Dr. Kimon Angelides, founder and COO of Diabetes) failed to preserve and produce critical e-mails that were contrary to Plaintiff's position in this lawsuit.

To support the alleged spoliation, the defendants pointed to relevant e-mails to and from Dr. Angelides that they obtained from third parties, but were never produced by the plaintiff. The defendants argued that additional e-mails must exist adverse to the plain-

---

26. http://www.youtube.com/watch?v=MeU02dI56sw.

27. http://ralphlosey.files.wordpress.com/2008/02/usvokeffe-criminalsearch.pdf.

28. http://ralphlosey.wordpress.com/2008/02/24/criminal-case-raises-interesting-e-discovery-search-issues/.

29. http://ralphlosey.wordpress.com/2007/06/10/keyword-searches-v-concept-searches/.

30. http://ralphlosey.wordpress.com/2007/09/16/sedonas-new-commentary-on-search-and-the-myth-of-the-pharaohs-curse/.

tiff, and they must also have been withheld or destroyed. This is typically the way fraud and spoliation are proven, since the alleged spoliator rarely admits to the crime. To quote Holmes: "We balance probabilities and choose the most likely. It is the scientific use of the imagination." *Hound of the Baskervilles.*[31]

District Court Judge Nancy Atlas reacted by scheduling an evidentiary hearing on the defendants' motion for sanctions. The motion sought an adverse inference jury instruction as punishment for losing much of the COO's e-mail. "Come, Watson, come! The game is afoot." *The Adventure of the Abbey Grange.*[32]

At the hearing, the plaintiff's counsel came up with a surprise defense to the spoliation motion, one commonly referred to as the "fall-on-your-own-sword" defense. Here, a lawyer protects his client by taking all of the blame upon himself. (In reality, there is usually more than enough blame for all concerned.) It is a rarely used argument because of the obvious danger of creating a malpractice trap should it not succeed. In spite of this risk, plaintiff's counsel used this defense here. Fortunately for him, it worked.

Plaintiff's counsel argued that it was not his client's fault that relevant e-mails were lost and not produced; instead it was his fault. Well, actually, he said it was the fault of his associate, a young woman just out of law school. The partner argued that his associate acted in good faith, with no intent to destroy evidence; she just did not know what she was doing. He argued that his law firm, not his client, Dr. Angelides, should be blamed for the missing e-mails, and they simply made an honest mistake. This is an effective argument. A court might suspect the motives of a party to litigation if e-mails are mysteriously missing, but are unlikely to suspect the motives of a young lawyer. Of course, it was just an innocent mistake, so no sanctions are appropriate, especially the potentially case-ending adverse inference sanctions sought here. Here is Judge Atlas's summary of what happened:

---

31. http://yoak.com/sherlock/stories/hound/hound_of_the_baskervilles.txt.

32. http://yoak.com/sherlock/stories/return/abbey_grange.txt.

Plaintiff's counsel conceded at the hearing that the task of searching Plaintiff's records for relevant e-mails in response to Defendants' discovery request was entrusted to a junior associate. It is apparent that the associate worked with little or no direction or supervision. The search terms used by the associate were inadequate—they did not even include the term "phone"—and, as a result, she failed to locate or perceive the significance of the e-mails about which Defendants now complain.

Obviously, the unsupervised associate here did not have a clue, since Judge Atlas states she overlooked the most obvious search term of all. As Sherlock would say: "You see, but you do not observe." *A Scandal in Bohemia.*[33]

In addition to the "associate screwed up" defense, plaintiff's counsel employed another well-known strategy: "the best defense is a good offense." The plaintiff alleged that the defendants had intentionally destroyed electronic evidence, and filed its own countermotion for sanctions. The defendants admitted that they lost some of their e-mail, but claimed it was not their fault because two of their laptops were stolen. The plaintiff alleged that these thefts were a fraud. Further, even if the plaintiff could not prove that the defendants were lying about these convenient losses, the plaintiff argued that sanctions should still be imposed against the defendants. The alternate ground for sanctions was their negligence for not having made another copy of the e-mails in the key players' laptop computers. I presume from the opinion that the alleged thefts happened after suit was filed or the duty to preserve was otherwise triggered.

The defendants claimed that these were bona fide thefts. Further, they claimed it was their usual and normal procedure not to have any e-mail backups. Here is how Judge Atlas summed it up:

---

33. http://yoak.com/sherlock/stories/adventures/scandal_in_bohemia.txt.

Plaintiff alleges that Defendants failed to back up e-mails that were subsequently lost when the two laptops containing the e-mails were stolen. (FN2: Plaintiff also questions whether these laptops were actually stolen by third parties.) Steven Kim's laptop was stolen from a friend's car outside Kennedy Airport while he and his friend were loading Kim's bags into the trunk of the car. The laptop belonging to Douglas Kim (no family relation to Steven Kim) was stolen from his Healthpia office cubicle. E-mail retention on these laptops, although not backed up to a third party or Healthpia server, was handled in accordance with Healthpia's standard procedures.

These facts remind me of Holmes's statement in *A Case of Identity*:[34] "Life is infinitely stranger than anything which the mind of man could invent."

Case Holding

Who knows what the truth is here? In a situation like this, with credible cross-allegations of wrongdoing by all parties, the judicial response of "a pox on both your houses" is not uncommon, although usually not spoken aloud by the judge. *But see JN Intern., Inc. v. M/S Transgene Biotek Ltd.,* 2006 WL 1559709 (D. Neb. 2006.) ("While continuing to have high regard for the lawyers and the mediator, the phrase 'a pox on all your houses' is particularly apt in this circumstance."). This response is understandable, and since many lawyers know this, it encourages the "offense as best defense" strategy. In this case, Judge Atlas is discreet, and speaks in terms of good faith, not plagues, but still denies relief to both sides:

> Neither party has presented evidence of bad faith. The Court credits Defendants' evidence that the laptops were stolen, and not intentionally destroyed or hidden. Defendants may not have taken adequate steps to preserve e-mails through a back-up process, but Defendants followed the company's

---

34. http://yoak.com/sherlock/stories/adventures/case_of_identity.txt.

standard procedures. If anything, there has been a showing of negligence derived from lax electronic document maintenance procedures. Similarly, at most, Plaintiff's counsel may have been lax in that inadequate direction and oversight was given to the associate to guide her search for relevant and responsive e-mails. There is no evidence that he or the associate acted in bad faith. The Court, in an exercise of its discretion, denies both parties' requests for an instruction on spoliation.

. . . . .

The conduct by both sides discussed herein is questionable; all parties have been remiss in fulfilling their own discovery obligations and keeping the opponent informed of pertinent matters. The parties, however, are too quick to criticize the other side for any infraction of the discovery rules. The Court, in an exercise of its discretion, declines to impose sanctions against either party.

Conclusion

The lesson of this decision is clear. If a party in litigation is going to rely upon keyword searches as the basis for evidence preservation, which is in itself a questionable strategy, then it had better be sure the searches used are adequate. Delegation to others should be made with care. Although Sherlock Holmes's perfection in this area is unattainable, this does not excuse obviously negligent search strategies.

Sherlock was correct to state in *The Adventure of the Dancing Men*[35] that "[w]hat one man can invent, another can discover." The common-law system of discovery is premised on the ability of good detective work to uncover the truth. Yet in the area of computer search, Holmes's statement in *The Reigate Puzzle*[36] also applies: "These are much deeper waters than I had thought."

If you do not have the input of experienced specialists, as Judge

---

35. http://yoak.com/sherlock/stories/return/dancing_men.txt.
36. http://yoak.com/sherlock/stories/memoirs/reigate_puzzle.txt.

Facciola suggests[37] may sometimes be necessary, then you should at least personally engage in careful analysis to be sure your search terms are adequate. You should not simply turn it over to the youngest attorney available and provide no direction or oversight. Just because they are young and comfortable with computers and are good with Google, Westlaw, or Lexis does not mean they are qualified to do e-discovery searches on their own. Ideally, if you must rely upon search terms as a basis for preservation, then you should try to obtain agreement from opposing counsel on the adequacy of the terms used, or, if that is not possible, seek judicial review at the beginning of the case, not the end.

> Education never ends, Watson. It is a series of lessons, with the greatest for the last.
>
> *The Adventure of the Red Circle*[38] (Arthur Conan Doyle,[39] 1859–1930).

Blog Reader Comment

Keyword search has long enjoyed the status of being "customary and reasonable" for legal discovery. But the intrinsic shortcomings of keyword search mean that even the most diligent and experienced user is hamstrung. Today's organizations conduct business over a wide range of communication channels—e-mail, instant messaging, text messaging and so forth—many of which encourage the creation of short, cryptic messages that may not contain obvious keywords and that cannot be understood except in the context of preceding communications. As such, the needs of effective discovery have evolved from identifying and extracting the value from individual items to identifying and extracting value from groups of related items. Keyword search, along with other technologies that focus on characteristics of indi-

---

37. http://ralphlosey.wordpress.com/2008/02/24/criminal-case raises-interesting-e-discovery-search-issues/.

38. http://yoak.com/sherlock/stories/last_bow/red_circle.txt.

39. http://en.wikipedia.org/wiki/Arthur_Conan_Doyle.

vidual items, is a poor fit for these new circumstances. Technologies are now available that allow the user to find relevant communications and evaluate their significance based
on the context of their creation and use, not simply on the
basis of presence or absence of keywords. The day may
not be that far away when, for certain types of cases, any
keyword search, however well constructed, will be seen as
inadequate for defensible discovery.

CRIMINAL CASE RAISES INTERESTING E-DISCOVERY SEARCH ISSUES

Once again, Judge John Facciola has authored an intriguing opinion
on e-discovery, this time in a criminal case, *United States v. O'Keefe,*[40]
No. 06-249 (D. D.C. Feb. 18, 2008). The decision begins with criminal
law–specific issues, such as what discovery rules to apply, but quickly
transcends them to address universal e-discovery questions. The most
interesting issue was raised by the accused defendants, who challenged the adequacy of the government's keyword search. Judge
Facciola held that this issue was too complicated for lawyers and
judges to address without the aid of expert testimony. He implied
that to do otherwise would be foolish because keyword search analysis is an area of e-discovery "where angels fear to tread."[41]

Obviously I am no angel, nor are thousands of other lawyers
who must routinely deal with keyword search issues. Perhaps we
are indeed foolish to run these searches without more help. As
Alexander Pope said, "A little learning is a dangerous thing." Here is
the full quote from Judge Facciola's opinion:

As noted above, defendants protest the search terms the government used. Fn6. Whether search terms or "keywords" will
yield the information sought is a complicated question in-

---

40. http://ralphlosey.files.wordpress.com/2008/02/usvokeffe-
criminalsearch.pdf.
41. http://en.wikipedia.org/wiki/Alexander_Pope.

volving the interplay, at least, of the sciences of computer technology, statistics and linguistics. *See* George L. Paul & Jason R. Baron, *Information Inflation: Can the Legal System Adapt?*, 13 RICH. J.L. & TECH. 10 (2007). Indeed, a special project of the Working Group on Electronic Discovery of the Sedona Conference is studying that subject and their work indicates how difficult this question is. See *The Sedona Conference, Best Practices Commentary on the Use of Search and Information Retrieval*,[42] 8 THE SEDONA CONF. J. 189 (2007). Given this complexity, for lawyers and judges to dare opine that a certain search term or terms would be more likely to produce information than the terms that were used is truly to go where angels fear to tread. This topic is clearly beyond the ken of a layman and requires that any such conclusion be based on evidence that, for example, meets the criteria of Rule 702 of the Federal Rules of Evidence. Accordingly, if defendants are going to contend that the search terms used by the government were insufficient, they will have to specifically so contend in a motion to compel and their contention must be based on evidence that meets the requirements of Rule 702 of the Federal Rules of Evidence.

For more on the law review article, "Information Inflation,"[43] by Paul & Baron cited above, see the article "Information Explosion and the Future of Litigation" in my first book. I have also previously written on the above-cited "Sedona Commentary on Search" in "The Myth of the Pharaoh's Curse," again contained in my first book, *e-Discovery: Current Trends and Cases.*

By the way, for those who have not read Rule 702 in a while, it says:

Rule 702 Testimony by Experts If scientific, technical, or other specialized knowledge will assist the trier of fact to un-

---

42. http://www.thesedonaconference.org/dltForm?did=Best_ Practices_Retrieval_Methods___revised_cover_and_preface.pdf.

43. http://law.richmond.edu/jolt/v13i3/article10.pdf.

derstand the evidence or to determine a fact in issue, a witness qualified as an expert by knowledge, skill, experience, training, or education may testify thereto in the form of an opinion or otherwise, if (1) the testimony is based upon sufficient facts or data, (2) the testimony is the product of reliable principles and methods, and (3) the witness has applied the principles and methods reliably to the facts of the case.

To my knowledge, *O'Keefe* is the first opinion to suggest that judicial review of alleged search deficiencies requires expert testimony. This may well portend a new type of expert in the future who opines concerning the search methods employed by parties to litigation. A whole new line of employment could open up for information scientists, e-discovery lawyers, and others who specialize in the field of search.

The other issues in this case are interesting, too, and shed some needed background on the search ruling. The defendant, O'Keefe, is a government official accused of taking bribes from co-defendant Agrawal for expediting visas to the United States for Agrawal's employees. In a prior order, District Court Judge Friedman:

> required the government to conduct a thorough and complete search of both its hard copy and electronic files in "a good faith effort to uncover all responsive information in its 'possession, custody or control.'" *United States v. O'Keefe,* No. 06-CR-0249, 2007 WL 1239204, at *3 (D. D.C. April 27, 2007) (quoting Fed. R. Crim. P. 16(a)(1)(E)).

The defendants received the submission from the government and responded with a motion to compel, complaining that the search was neither thorough, complete, nor a good-faith effort as the court had required. The defendants sought to compel the government to provide them with detailed information on their search for both paper and electronic records and to redo the searches.

Judge Facciola begins his analysis by noting that there is no rule governing criminal procedure as to appropriate format for production of documents. He finds it reasonable in this circumstance to apply Rule 34 of the Federal Rules of Civil Procedure. In his words, "it is far better to use these rules than to reinvent the wheel when the production of documents in criminal and civil cases raises the same problems."

I am going to skip most of the paper search issues, although they are interesting, even from a civil perspective. Suffice it to say, the government just dumped boxes of paper documents with no folders or organization. That was not sufficient, and Judge Facciola ordered the government to meet with the defendants and explain each document produced, the author, author's title, recipient, date of creation, and location of the document (where it came from).

The government opposed the defendants' motion to compel with an affidavit by a visa unit chief that describes the search efforts that she and her five-member staff performed. There is no mention of attorneys participating in this search effort. All personal hard drives and active servers were searched, and the backup tapes going back two weeks were searched (they are erased after two weeks). Conspicuously absent is a description of other possible sources of ESI being searched, such as portable storage devices. Defendants do not, however, object to the limited scope of the search.

The only ESI search effort described is an automated keyword search. The visa unit chief, whose qualifications to perform computer searches are not described, states that she used the following search terms: "early or expedite* or appointment or early & interview or expedite* & interview." She also states that she had "[t]he Information Management Staff conduct[ ] the search of personal and hard drives because they have access to all drives from the network server, not just shared drives."

The defendants argued that this ESI search was deficient and did not comply with Judge Friedman's order, for three reasons. First, the government did not interview the employees whose computers were searched. In other words, the defendants accused the AUSAs (assistant U.S. attorneys) who represent the government in this case of not discharging a key responsibility of the *Zubulake* duty, the duty to interview key players. *See e-Discovery: Current Trends and Cases* at pgs. 55-65. These widely accepted duties include the directive of Judge Scheindlin in *Zubulake V* to communicate with the "key players" in the litigation in order to understand how they stored information. *Zubulake v. UBS*, 229 F.R.D. 422 (S.D. N.Y. 2004). I would add that such direct talks also allow you to understand the language the key players used so that you can more intelligently pick the words to use in a search.

Judge Facciola does not discuss this point directly except in footnote 6, where he says that "if the search terms used actually captured everything there was to capture, such interviews would be unnecessary." With respect, I think this misses the point, since interviews are a good way to develop effective search terms to begin with. When and if the search experts testify in this case, they will probably opine that it is impossible to develop search terms that will "actually capture everything there is to capture." One hundred percent capture is not possible. Further, only by interviews and learning the linguistics involved can you hope to obtain the right keywords to improve the capture rate.

The second deficiency alleged was the government's failure to have any of its employees search their own computers. Instead, the only search performed was a keyword search by the government's search team. The employees know their own data better than anyone else. Why not ask them to search for it? You could also do a keyword search. How can a search be "thorough" and "complete" unless the custodians are involved in the search? Is that a "good faith effort to uncover all responsive information" as Judge Friedman ordered? Judge Facciola's order does not discuss this issue, and I suspect that if the defendants renew their motion to compel, and this time support it with expert testimony, the experts' opinions will focus on this point.

The third deficiency is the government's failure to disclose what software it used to conduct the search and how it ascertained what search terms it would use. The defendants explained that they needed to know the type of software used to be sure that the metadata was properly preserved and the search and collection were done according to standard forensic procedures. Now you can better see why Judge Facciola deferred ruling pending expert input and ordered the parties to meet, confer, and attempt to resolve these issues through discussion, with his active participation.

The defendants also alleged that the government failed to preserve ESI; but they did not offer any proof for that allegation, aside from paucity of production, which prompted Judge Facciola to say:

> Defendants protest that there are inexplicable deficiencies in the government's production of electronically stored information, but, as I have indicated in another case, vague notions that there should have been more than what was produced are speculative and are an insufficient premise for judicial action. *See Hubbard v. Potter*, No. 03-CV-1062, 2008 WL 43867, at *4 (D. D.C. Jan. 3, 2008). Accusations that the government purposely destroyed what they were obliged to produce or knowingly failed to produce what a court ordered are serious. I must therefore remind the defendants of the wise advice given the revolutionary: "If you strike at a king, kill him." If the defendants intend to charge the government with destroying information that they were obliged to preserve and produce pursuant to Judge Friedman's order or the due process clause itself, they must make that claim directly and support it with an evidentiary basis—not merely surmise that they should have gotten more than they did. If they do not do so within 21 business days of this opinion, I will deem any such claim to have been waived.

Of course, the best way to obtain such evidence is through more discovery—a series of depositions, actually. I wonder whether that is even possible in criminal cases. Still, you should not jump the gun and allege spoliation before you have proof. You should instead point to the sparsity of production as a justification for discovery on this issue.

Overall, in this opinion, Judge Facciola demonstrates a tolerance for the mistakes made by both sides and a willingness to move on and look for practical solutions to the problem. Again, Alexander Pope said it well almost 300 years ago: "To err is human, to forgive divine." Also recall Pope's lesser-known quote: "A man should never be ashamed to own that he is wrong, which is but saying in other words that he is wiser today than he was yesterday."

That is an everyday reality in the fast-changing world of e-discovery. It is especially true in the area of search, where newly developing forms of concept searching[44] may soon make keyword searches obsolete. Judge Facciola mentioned this possibility in *Disability Rights Council of Greater Washington v. Washington Metropolitan Area Transit Authority,*[45] 2007 WL 1585452 (D. D.C. June 1, 2007). For more information into this area, take a look at the West Legalworks CLE webinar[46] I did with Jason R. Baron,[47] Director of Litigation, U.S. National Archives and Records Administration; Doug Oard, Ph.D.,[48] Associate Dean for Research, College of Information Studies, University of Maryland; and my co-chair of e-discovery at Akerman, Michael S. Simon.[49] The 1.5-hour audio CLE is titled *The e-Discovery Search Quagmire: New Approaches to the Problem of Finding Relevant Needles in the Electronic Haystack* and can be downloaded on demand from West.[50] Doug Oard and Jason Baron and colleagues of theirs have been doing very interesting work in this area,[51] including serious research concerning how keyword and Boolean searches measure against other types of search methods,[52] at the scholarly TREC Legal Track.[53] Finally, you should also check

---

44. http://ralphlosey.wordpress.com/2007/06/10/keyword-searches-v-concept-searches/.

45. http://ralphlosey.files.wordpress.com/2007/08/case-disability-rights-council-v-wmata-o1175524.pdf.

46. http://westlegaledcenter.com/home/homepage.jsf.

47. http://www.archives.gov/legal/bios/jrbaron.html.

48. http://www.glue.umd.edu/~oard/.

49. http://www.akerman.com/public/attorneys/aBiography.asp?id=984.

50. http://westlegaledcenter.com/home/homepage.jsf.

51. http://www.umiacs.umd.edu/~oard/desi-ws/.

52. http://www.umiacs.umd.edu/~oard/desi-ws/papers/icailsearchproblemsfinal2.pdf.

53. http://trec-legal.umiacs.umd.edu/.

out the excellent work being done on search by Anne Kershaw[54] and her nonprofit group e-Discovery Institute.[55]

The enlightened attitude usually found in Judge Facciola's e-discovery opinions is a product of his many years of experience and his high level of expertise in this area. But be warned, very few judges today have this kind of deep understanding in e-discovery. Most have little or no judicial experience with e-discovery. To make matters worse, very few had any experience in this area before they came on the bench. In the subspecialty of search, their experience is limited to Google, West or Lexis, which is completely different from e-discovery search in lawsuits and tends to give a distorted perspective. With no personal background in e-discovery, it is hard for many judges to appreciate the complexity and magnitude of the problems faced today by practitioners. For these reasons and others, it is foolish to rush into court and expect the same kind of learned results from your judge. It is always better to try to work things out with opposing counsel, and only go to the judge for relief as a last resort. If you do go to the judge, take the time to fully brief and educate your judge on the subject.

ADVERSARIAL SEARCH, A "PERFECT BARRIER" TO COST-EFFECTIVE E-DISCOVERY, AND ONE LITIGANT'S "*AIKIDO*-LIKE" RESPONSE

I came across a case recently where a defendant successfully employed an "*Aikido*-like" maneuver to prevail in an e-discovery fight. *Perfect Barrier, LLC v. Woodsmart Solutions, Inc.*, 2008 WL 2230192 (N.D. Ind. May 27, 2008).[56] Plaintiff's counsel took an overaggressive approach to e-discovery, which defense counsel completely turned around on him. Plaintiff's counsel ended up losing a motion for sanctions and driving up his client's e-discovery costs. This case demonstrates the essence of *Aikido* in action and the dangers of trying to misuse e-discovery as a weapon. It has many other interesting

---

54. http://www.akershaw.com/.

55. http://www.electronicdiscoveryinstitute.com/.

56. http://ralphlosey.files.wordpress.com/2008/07/perfect-barrier-llc-v-woodsmart-solutions.doc".

points to it as well, including an argument over native production using hash values versus flat TIFF file production using Bates stamps. This debate is at the core of my law review article, "HASH: The New Bates Stamp,"[57] 12 *Journal of Technology Law & Policy* 1 (June 2007), and the practitioners here cite to the article as part of their arguments.

But first, a little about *Aikido*.[58] It is a purely defensive martial art that redirects the force of the attacker back upon himself instead of opposing it directly. The usual result is the attacker being thrown to the ground, as shown in the photo above. For an amazing demonstration of *Aikido* by Steven Seagal, see this YouTube video,[59] where he is first attacked by one black belt, then two, three, and then a whole "class action." They all end up on the ground, with Seagal barely breaking a sweat. Many consider *Aikido* the purest and most elegant of all martial arts, and one of the most difficult to master. It is considered a "non-violent martial art" (an oxymoron, I know, much like "cooperative litigation") whose primary message is peace and reconciliation. It is used only for defense, to thwart attacks, never for offense. It works by channeling the force of the attacker, not resisting or opposing it. As the founder of *Aikido*, Morihei Ueshiba,[60] explained:

> Nonresistance is one of the principles of aikido. Because there is no resistance, you have won before even starting. People whose minds are evil or who enjoy fighting are defeated without a fight.

These are sage words, but it is hard to imagine how they apply to litigation and e-discovery. That is where the *Perfect Barrier* case comes in. This is a relatively small-dollar-value case against Woodsmart Solutions, a maker of blue-coated lumber.

---

57. http://ralphlosey.files.wordpress.com/2008/0.7/hasharticleloseycorrec ted.pdf.
58. http://en.wikipedia.org/wiki/Aikido.
59. http://www.youtube.com/watch?v=Tv4f6xH-OwM.
60. http://en.wikipedia.org/wiki/Morihei_Ueshiba.

The plaintiff begins discovery with a direct attack, making an obviously overbroad request for production of e-mails. The request included a list of 77 so-called "relevant search terms" that plaintiff's counsel created on their own. The list included the defendant's name, "Woodsmart," and several other common words. At this point, most would actively resist the overbroad request. They would rise to the fight with either a motion for a protective order or perhaps their own counteroffensive request for e-mails using a keyword list that was just as broad. But that is not the *Aikido* way. Nor is it the way of defense counsel in this case, Stefan Stein,[61] whom I do not know, but who, according to my research, is certainly not a martial artist, and may never even have heard of *Aikido*. He is, however, a very experienced intellectual property lawyer and obviously wise in the ways of litigation.

The defendant's attorney responded to this attack not by resisting it, but by pointing out the obvious—that the list of keywords was so broad that it would catch virtually every e-mail on the defendant's server. He offered to compromise and negotiate a new list of keywords and other search protocols with plaintiff's counsel, a list and procedures that would be more effective to the supposed common goal of ferreting out relevant e-mails. Preferring to fight, the plaintiff's attorneys did not respond to the peace overture. They refused all negotiation, and instead insisted that the defendant carry out the search with the list they had written. The plaintiff did not care that the search terms would produce too many e-mails because it assumed that the burden of review to screen for confidential and unresponsive ESI would fall on the defendant, the producing party. They saw this as a potential knock-out punch that might force the defendant to surrender on their terms instead of incurring the tremendous review expense. By all appearances, they were misusing e-discovery as a weapon.

Defense counsel at this point did not resist; they agreed, reluctantly, to the search terms, but then added a small little twist, that the parties would make the production under a confidentiality order. Of course, this is standard in most business litigation, and so the plain-

---

61. http://www.hklaw.com/id77/biosSSTEIN/.

tiff and its lawyers quickly agreed, sensing what they thought was weakness and capitulation on the defendant's part. Little did they know that their hands had just been grabbed, much like Seagal did to his attackers in the video. The plaintiff's attorneys underestimated their adversary, and just like the Steven Seagal attackers, they would soon find themselves thrown for a loop.

The parties then entered into a confidentiality agreement, which became a stipulated discovery order.[62] Too bad plaintiff's counsel did not read the stipulated discovery order more carefully. He was obviously too busy with the attack to read the fine print. The defendant then ran the search terms as agreed, and made production to plaintiff's counsel of all e-mail containing these terms. The production was made in native format on DVD, and, not too surprisingly, there were 75,000 pages of e-mail in this small case. However, what was surprising was the confidentiality designation notice that accompanied the production. The notice designated *all* of the e-mail produced as falling within the highest category of confidentiality, the so-called "Attorney Eyes Only" confidentiality. Under the stipulated order, this meant that only plaintiff's counsel could look at these e-mails, and they could not show any of them to their client, or their expert, or anyone. They could not even use them in court, unless and until they first went through the procedures of the agreement to challenge the confidentiality designations.

This little twist by defense counsel effectively threw the plaintiff to the ground. It shifted the enormous burden of review of 75,000 e-mails from the responding party, here the defendant, to the requesting party, here the plaintiff. This is, in my view, a perfect legal example of the *Aikido* philosophy of defense by redirecting the attacker's force upon himself.

In the words of Ueshiba, who liked to call *Aikido* the "Art of Peace":

In the Art of Peace we never attack. An attack is proof that one is out of control. Never run away from any kind of chal-

---

62. http://ralphlosey.files.wordpress.com/2008/07/discoveryorder.pdf.

lenge, but do not try to suppress or control an opponent un-
naturally. Let attackers come any way they like and then
blend with them. Never chase after opponents. Redirect each
attack and get firmly behind it.

To see Ueshiba himself as an elder practicing *Aikido*, watch this
YouTube video.[63] It looks fake, but it's not. These are young black
belts trying their hardest to knock down an old man. By the way, I
am not an *Aikido* practitioner; I am just an admirer of its philosophy
and techniques. Still, I have studied and practiced other martial arts
and earned a brown belt in one of them.

Back to *Perfect Barrier.* Plaintiff's counsel responds to the designation of all 75,000 e-mails as "Attorney Eyes Only," with a motion for sanctions. It reminds me of the attackers in the Seagal and
Ueshiba videos who get up after a throwdown and try again to attack. Plaintiff's counsel argued quite truthfully in the motion that it
was never his intention to allow the defendant to designate all e-
mails as "Attorney Eyes Only," but only ones that qualified for that
designation by virtue of the super-confidential nature of the communication or attached document. The plaintiff claimed that all of
these e-mails certainly did not qualify for that classification, and so
the defendant violated the stipulated order and should now be sanctioned. This was a pretty credible attack, by a black belt of an attorney, upon a seemingly weak and vulnerable adversary. Here is a
copy[64] of the Plaintiff's Memorandum supporting the sanctions motion. It has several interesting exhibits attached to it concerning hash
that I will discuss later.

Defendant's Opposition Memorandum[65] pointed out that nothing in the parties' agreement prevented them from designating all e-
mail as "Attorneys Eyes Only" and argued that shifting the burden
and costs of review here onto the requesting party was justified and

---

63.   http://www.youtube.com/watch?v=yxxb2ctulEs.
64.   http://ralphlosey.files.wordpress.com/2008/07/perfect-barrier-pld-
52-memo-in-sup-of-mtn-to-compel-o1315810.pdf.
65.   http://ralphlosey.files.wordpress.com/2008/07/perfect-barrier-pld-
60-memo-in-opp-to-mtn-to-compel-o1315898.pdf.

permitted under the rules and case law. Here is the primary thrust of their argument:

> Because Plaintiff is alone responsible for the impossibly large volume of documents recovered, it should bear the burden of having to review the documents for relevance. . . .
>
> Requiring WoodSmart to review all 75,000 pages of e-mails for confidentiality would be unduly burdensome and would reward Plaintiff's overly broad discovery requests.

Magistrate Judge Christopher A. Nuechterlein seemed to understand perfectly well what was going on here, that this was a case of the plaintiff, Perfect Barrier, attacking unnecessarily with an overbroad request, and then getting exactly what it deserved. Here is what Judge Nuechterlein said in denying the plaintiff's motion:

> Nothing in the protective order prevents large categorical designations. If Perfect Barrier desired Woodsmart to be more selective in its use of the confidential designation, Perfect Barrier should have utilized more care in drafting the agreed protective order to include more particular language that is consistent with its position. As it stands, the language of the protective order simply requires a "category" designation. Therefore, this Court finds that Woodsmart followed and did not violate the protective order.
>
> While Perfect Barrier may have a voluminous amount of discovery to parse through, it has no entity to blame except itself. Perfect Barrier provided the search terms to Woodsmart as part of its request for production of the e-mail communications. Woodsmart produced every document that appeared with those search terms. In other words, Woodsmart provided Perfect Barrier with every possible document that Perfect Barrier requested. It was Perfect Barrier's expansive request that produced such voluminous discovery. . . .
>
> To be clear, Woodsmart has not withheld the e-mails from Perfect Barrier; it has, however, limited Perfect Barrier's use

of them by designating them "attorney eyes only." If Perfect Barrier upon examination believes that certain e-mails were inappropriately characterized as "attorney eyes only," they may challenge the designation, first with Woodsmart and, if that fails to resolve the dispute, then with the Court.

Judge Nuechterlein went on to warn the parties that he would not countenance any attempt by either side to try to shift the burden once again onto him. He said not to send large batches of e-mail for him to review *in camera*. Instead, he expected the plaintiff's counsel to sort through it all, and then get with defense counsel to resolve any disagreements as to what should be excluded, or not. If they insist on further adjudication of these e-discovery issues, Judge Nuechterlein threatened to send the whole thing to a special master, and force the parties to pay for it. Once again, we see a court speak of possible reference of issues to a special master to cajole agreement.

The plaintiff attacked once again and objected to the defendant's production of the e-mail in its original native format. The plaintiff wanted the whole thing to be redone and reproduced in flat, searchable TIFF images, no doubt so they could load it into their review software. There is a significant expense involved in converting native e-mail into into a searchable image format, and the plaintiff was trying to shift the expense onto the defendant.

The court rejected this attack also and held that since the plaintiff had failed to specify a form of production in its request for e-mail, the production in original native format was permitted under Rule 34(b)(2)(E)(ii), which states:

[i]f a request does not specify a form for producing electronically stored information, a party must produce it in a form or forms in which it is ordinarily maintained or in a reasonably usable form or forms.

Native format is the form in which the plaintiff originally maintained the e-mail, and so the production was perfectly proper. In any event, the court held that a native form production is also reasonably usable, so there is no grounds to complain. Here are Judge Nuechterlein's words on this issue:

> Perfect Barrier did not request that the e-mails be produced in a particular form, yet Perfect Barrier now asks this Court to force Woodsmart to produce the electronic e-mails as Static Images with a Bates-number identifier. Woodsmart objects to this request because it would cost a substantial sum of money to convert the documents from the form in which the documents are normally kept, Native format, to Static Images.
>
> Woodsmart has already produced the e-mails on a disk in Native format. Woodsmart maintains the e-mail documents in such a format. Fed. R. Civ. P. 34 only requires Woodsmart to submit the e-mails in the format in which it keeps them, Native format, and nothing more. While it may be more convenient for Perfect Barrier to have the e-mails as Static Images, Fed. R. Civ. P. 34 does not provide that convenience is a basis for requiring electronic discovery to be produced in a different format than normally maintained. If Perfect Barrier wanted the e-mails as Static Images, it should have specified this request in its requests for production, which it did not do.
>
> Furthermore, this Court finds that the e-mails produced on an electronic media such as disk is reasonably usable. Perfect Barrier can access, examine, and even print the communications. While Perfect Barrier may prefer to have them as Static Images, the burden to convert the e-mails to Static Images remains with Perfect Barrier. Woodsmart complied with Fed. R. Civ. P. 34(b)(2)(E) and is required to do nothing more.

The court once again uses a "gotcha" on the plaintiff, saying you forgot to ask, so you are getting what you deserve. But in reality, even if the plaintiff had originally asked for production in Static Image form, as the court puts it, that would not necessarily oblige the defendant to comply. The defendant could still have objected, and insisted on native production, arguing that the alternative was simply an attempt to shift the requesting party's own cost of processing upon the responding party. I have not seen a case on that yet, but I expect this will come up soon.

Finally, this case is very interesting to me because the parties' memoranda underlying the order include as exhibits several e-mails and letters between the attorneys in which they argue about the meaning of the law review article I wrote on hash[66] and the need for Bates stamps, or not, on ESI productions. *See* Exhibits D and E to Plaintiff's Memorandum in Support of Motion to Compel,[67] and Exhibits D and F to Defendant's Opposition Memorandum.[68] I do not know any of the attorneys in this Indiana case, so I was surprised to stumble across this debate.

My article on hash was used primarily to support the producing party's position that the receiving party should bear the substantial costs of TIFFing and Bates stamping. But the receiving party relied on it too, claiming that the best practice advice in the article to include a load file with hash values was not followed. Since the production was probably just a few a big PST files, that would have been easy to do, but would not really have addressed the receiving party's concerns regarding the authenticity of individual e-mails within the PST. There are, however, other ways to address the authenticity issues, which were not really explored by the parties. That was because their e-mails attached to the memoranda show that one side was just arguing, and not really trying to solve the problem. It was just a debate, not an e-discovery *Art of Peace*[69] collaborative venture.

I leave you to contemplate a few of the quotes of Sensei Ueshiba. The insights he gained into the resolution of physical combat have,

---

66. http://ralphlosey.files.wordpress.com/2008/07/hasharticlelosey corrected.pdf.

67. http://ralphlosey.files.wordpress.com/2008/07/perfect-barrier-pld-52-memo-in-sup-of-mtn-to-compel-o1315810.pdf.

68. http://ralphlosey.files.wordpress.com/2008/07/perfect-barrier-pld-60-memo-in-opp-to-mtn-to-compel-o1315898.pdf.

69. http://www.amazon.com/Art-Peace-Shambhala-Pocket-Classics/dp/0877738513.

for me at least, some crossover value to resolution of legal disputes in today's combative system of justice. As *Perfect Barrier* shows, his philosophy and techniques can sometimes succeed perfectly in the arena of e-discovery.

> Be grateful even for hardship, setbacks, and bad people. Dealing with such obstacles is an essential part of training in *Aikido*.
>
> Failure is the key to success; each mistake teaches us something.
>
> If your opponent tries to pull you, let him pull. Don't pull against him; pull in unison with him.
>
> Opponents confront us continually, but actually there is no opponent there. Enter deeply into an attack and neutralize it as you draw that misdirected force into your own sphere.
>
> Even the most powerful human being has a limited sphere of strength. Draw him outside of that sphere and into your own, and his strength will dissipate.
>
> The real Art of Peace is not to sacrifice a single one of your warriors to defeat an enemy. Vanquish your foes by always keeping yourself in a safe and unassailable position; then no one will suffer any losses. The Way of a Warrior, the Art of Politics, is to stop trouble before it starts. It consists in defeating your adversaries spiritually by making them realize the folly of their actions. The Way of a Warrior is to establish harmony.
>
> Never think of yourself as an all-knowing, perfected master; you must continue to train daily with your friends and students and progress together in *Aikido*.
>
> The techniques of *Aikido* change constantly; every encounter is unique, and the appropriate response should emerge naturally. Today's techniques will be different tomorrow. Do not get caught up with the form and appearance of a challenge. *Aikido* has no form—it is the study of the spirit.

Blog Reader Comment

Brilliant all the way around! (the *Aikido* metaphor, the approach of defense counsel in this case, and the article about it all) As the "forces" driving e-discovery gain strength—volume, complexity, heterogeneity of data—the idea of using them for fair advantage rather than fighting their natural state will become even more important for parties on both sides of the "v."

A TALE OF TWO LONDON ESI FORUMS

Reports from the Second International DESI Workshop on Search and Sensemaking, and the MIS International Conference on Digital Evidence

Guest Blog

by Jason R. Baron[70]

Ralph has given me the honor of filling in for him this week with my report from two fascinating ESI-related forums I had the pleasure to be a part of while in London during the last week of June. As a charter member of the Ralph Losey e-Discovery Team fan club, let me say right off the bat that I am delighted to be a guest blogger here; it is certainly my hope that, in agreeing to fill in, I have provided Ralph with a much-needed July 4 break from his self-imposed, Atlas-like workload, in voluntarily turning out, week in and week out, a year-round e-discovery blog of such unsurpassed quality!

DESI II

On June 25, 2008, the Second International Workshop on Supporting Search and Sensemaking for Electronically Stored Information

---

70. Jason Baron is the Director of Litigation, Office of General Counsel, National Archives and Records Administration; http://www.archives.gov/legal/bios/jrbaron.html.

in Discovery Proceedings (affectionately referred to here as DESI II) was held at University College London (UCL),[71] hosted by UCL Interaction Centre,[72] a leading center for research into human-computer interaction. As described on the DESI II workshop main page, the workshop grew out of the first DESI Workshop[73] at the 2007 International Conference on Artificial Intelligence and the Law[74] last June in Palo Alto, California, where participants from five continents and from multiple research disciplines for the first time gathered together to discuss challenges presented by e-discovery, with a focus on dealing with large collections of electronically stored information (ESI) during litigation and regulatory investigations.

This year, the aim of the second DESI workshop[75] was to bring together legal practitioners, service providers, and researchers to develop the research agenda further, to elaborate a European perspective on these issues, and to consider how developments in areas such as information retrieval, artificial intelligence, and human computer interaction might be brought to bear on key problems faced in a variety of legal settings in the U.S. and around the globe.

I am so ever grateful to Dr. Simon Attfield,[76] senior research fellow at UCL, for agreeing to take on all of the administrative heavy lifting duties for running this year's workshop, and to Dr. Ann Blandford,[77] professor of human-computer interaction and director of the UCL Interaction Centre, for her role in facilitating the hosting of the workshop at UCL. My thanks as well to my colleague Dr. Douglas W. Oard,[78] associate dean of research at the University of Maryland's College of Information Studies (and one of the co-founders of the TREC Legal Track), and to Stephen Mason,[79] a London barrister and

---

71. http://www.ucl.ac.uk/.
72. http://www.uclic.ucl.ac.uk/.
73. http://www.umiacs.umd.edu/~oard/desi-ws/.
74. http://www.iaail.org/icail-2007/.
75. http://www.cs.ucl.ac.uk/staff/S.Attfield/desi/DESI_II_agenda.html.
76. http://www.cs.ucl.ac.uk/staff/S.Attfield/.
77. http://web4.cs.ucl.ac.uk/uclic/people/a.blandford/.
78. http://www.glue.umd.edu/~oard/.
79. http://www.stephenmason.eu/.

associate senior research fellow at the Institute of Advanced Legal Studies, whose original invitation to have me speak at his International Conference on Digital Evidence (see below) inspired me to propose holding a second workshop in the first place!

The format of the past two DESI workshops has been truly unique: bring together 40 to 50 expert individuals from a cross-spectrum of disciplines, including information retrieval, artificial intelligence, computer science, linguistics, legal technology, and psychology, and have them interact in a classroom setting for an entire day to discuss the subject of how to go about improving search and information retrieval as practiced in legal settings, including e-discovery. (Imagine inviting Picasso, Freud, and Einstein to a dinner party and stepping back to see what happens.) Thanks to a format heavily inspired by Doug Oard, the workshops have been highly interactive: for each of two or more panel sessions, speakers are routinely limited to 10- or 15-minute presentations of their submitted papers; a "discussant" comments on the papers that have been presented in each of the panel sessions; and a moderator then encourages audience feedback. At lunch, all participants break into small groups (language processing, information retrieval, sensemaking, vendors, and barristers), with group leaders assigned in advance to foster discussion and report back at the end of the day what the consensus views of the group turned out to be.

This year's workshop featured 10 submitted position papers from academics and legal service providers from the U.S., the U.K., and Japan (all available on the DESI II workshop page), plus an opening keynote from Jeane A. Thomas,[80] a partner at Crowell & Moring and head of the firm's e-discovery group in its Washington, D.C. offices. Jeane, whom I know well through The Sedona Conference, the Georgetown Advanced E-Discovery Institute, and other forums we have appeared in, graciously accepted an invitation to provide an overview of the problems lawyers face in the area of conducting searches. Jeane started off her keynote using almost the same words I used when I introduced myself to Doug Oard a few years ago: I'm a lawyer, I'm not an expert in technology, and I have problems.

---

80. http://www.crowell.com/Professionals/Jeane-Thomas.

Jeane proceeded to summarize the ESI challenge facing lawyers in the U.S. and arguably around the world—namely, an increasing volume and complexity of potential relevant documents and evidence that need to be accounted for; the need for better tools through future advances in technology to adequately carry out the search function; and the fact that technology by itself is not the answer—that lawyers themselves need to think more strategically about how to conduct reasonable discovery. Jeane went on to emphasize the increasingly international dimension to her antitrust and complex litigation practice.

Following Jeane, Doug gave an overview of this year's TREC Legal Track,[81] and I provided some brief remarks updating the audience on the emergence in the past year of U.S. case law recognizing the importance of search and information retrieval in e-discovery, including Judge Facciola's decisions in *Disability Rights Council of Greater Washington v. Washington Metropolitan Transit Authority*, 242 F.R.D. 139 (D. D.C. 2007), *United States v. O'Keefe*, 537 F. Supp. 2d 14 (D. D.C. 2008), and Judge Grimm's recent decision in *Victor Stanley, Inc. v. Creative Pipe, Inc.*, 2008 WL 2221841 (D. Md. May 29, 2008). Also, new in the past year has been publication of *The Sedona Conference® Best Practices Commentary on the Use of Search and Information Retrieval Methods in E-Discovery*, which was cited in both the *O'Keefe* and *Creative Pipe* cases as providing guidance to practitioners in strategically thinking about search issues.

Although I could go on at length about many of the very good papers[82] presented about common search issues of interest, I was particularly struck by the remarks of Bob Bauer[83] from H5, as well as by my workshop co-organizer Simon Attfield, on the relevance of "sensemaking" research to e-discovery. Until these DESI workshops, I frankly had been oblivious to the considerable body of academic research that exists on the subject of "sensemaking," or how that research could be applied in a practical way to the e-discovery

---

81. http://trec-legal.umiacs.umd.edu/.
82. http://www.cs.ucl.ac.uk/staff/S.Attfield/desi/DESI_II_agenda.html.
83. http://www.h5tech.com/about/management.html#rbauer.

process. As Bob Bauer quoted from a recent paper[84] by three Google academics presented in turn at a recent CHI workshop[85] in Florence, "Sensemaking is simple—it's the way people go about their process of collecting, organizing, and creating representations of complex information sets, all centered around some problem they need to understand."

The thesis Bob presents through his jointly authored paper, "Automated Legal Sensemaking: The Centrality of Relevance and Intentionality,"[86] is straightforward: 15 years of sensemaking research should be brought to bear to establish a minimum acceptable basis for conducting document review involving ESI. In doing so, of paramount importance is recognition of the fact that "[t]here is no substitute for a rigorous characterization of the explicit and tacit goals of the senior litigator," i.e., the person "responsible for developing and fully understanding all nuances of their client's legal strategy." Thus, "[w]hat is required is a system (people, process, and technology) that replicates and automates the senior litigator's human judgment." In Bob's view, "any method that depends primarily on human review fails to transfer properly the requisite knowledge of the senior litigator's sensemaking into a consistent, reproducible document review." His paper goes on to make a fascinating connection with cognitive task research involving intelligence analysts that has been conducted over the past 10 years, where it has been reported that senior and junior analyst behaviors are nearly opposite in terms of taking "bottom up" or "top down" approaches to hypothesis building, and where:

> [t]he crucial insight based on sensemaking research is that in e-Discovery, senior litigators are NOT reviewing the literal content of text (i.e., bottom-up), but rather the overarching aspects of the situation and the author's intent (i.e., top-down). (capitalization as in original)

---

84. http://dmrussell.googlepages.com/sensemakingworkshoppapers.
85. http://www.chi2008.org/program.pdf.
86. http://www.cs.ucl.ac.uk/staff/S.Attfield/desi/5.%20Bauer.pdf.

The bottom line, paraphrasing Bob's paper: future advances in efficiently performing document review must replicate the sensemaking of senior litigators as a top-down, automated process of searching for and encoding case-topic-specific questions, and that any scalable e-discovery process must establish explicit criteria for determining "relevance" as viewed through the lens of the senior litigator, while at the same time taking into account the multiplicity of communities that the original authors of documents work in, with all of the idiosyncrasies of language and linguistic terminology used by those authors. One last thing: "execution of the sensemaking approach," in Bob's view, also involves "rigorous measurement and statistically valid, in-process quality control."

In a similar vein, Simon Attfield's co-authored paper with Ann Blandford, "E-discovery viewed as integrated human-computer sensemaking: the challenge of 'frames,'"[87] reports on the results of an interview field study with lawyers working on a large regulatory investigation in the U.K., with the purpose of extrapolating from that study how further research into better understanding "evidence review and analysis in e-discovery" could be conducted. In particular, the authors introduce the notion of making sense of information through the application of particular types of "frames," which in the e-discovery context would mean how lawyers go about choosing to aggregate documents with the aim of determining relevance, how decisions with respect to relevance are cued, and how decisions are in turn elaborated upon and validated. Simon's paper states his belief that the Enron collection (a publicly available dataset of e-mail and other documents) is a candidate dataset for further research into the sensemaking activities of lawyers, and I welcome his research. The results of such a program might yet find its way to being incorporated in "checklists" covering how relevance determinations are to be optimized in future complex document reviews.

I took away from the workshop the palpable sense that the information retrieval researcher crowd, represented by Mark Sanderson,[88] a reader at the University of Sheffield; Ian Ruthven,[89] a reader at the

---

87. http://www.cs.ucl.ac.uk/staff/S.Attfield/desi/6.%20Attfield.pdf.

88. http://dis.shef.ac.uk/mark/.

89. http://www.cis.strath.ac.uk/cis/staff/index.php?uid=ir.

University of Strathclyde; Yunhyong Kim,[90] a researcher at the University of Glasgow; and Mounia Lalmas,[91] professor at Queen Mary, University of London, were collectively intrigued by the practical problems lawyers (and barristers and solicitors) all face in this area, especially in light of the fact that, as Mark Sanderson suggested in his remarks, it isn't every day that IR researchers actually talk to the users of their information-retrieval software designs. It might be too much to wish for, but a research project of a parallel nature to the TREC legal track in the U.S. might be something that a European-based grant-making agency would be interested in.

From the U.K., I wish to thank in particular Reza Alexander,[92] Litigation & Practice Support Manager at DLA Piper UK, for his fine introductory remarks, and Chris Dale, of The e-Disclosure Information Project,[93] for his presentation on "CaseMap issue linking in UK civil proceedings," as well as favoring us with the attendance of His Honour Judge Simon Brown, a designated mercantile judge, who together were appearing at still another e-discovery conference that day in London. I also wish to thank Jacki O'Neill,[94] of Xerox Research Centre Europe, and Ian Black[95] of Autonomy Group[96] in the U.K., for their papers and remarks. Getting the award for traveling the farthest distance was Professor Frank Bennett, Jr.,[97] of the Faculty of Law at Nagoya University in Japan, who spoke on unique OCR search issues when faced with reconstructing financial statements in Japanese.

Lastly, from the United States, we were blessed to have with us an expert contingent of lawyers, academics, and technologists giving short talks and comments, including Craig Carpenter,

---

90. http://www.hatii.arts.gla.ac.uk/staff/yk.html.
91. http://www.dcs.qmul.ac.uk/~mounia/.
92. http://litigationsupporttoday.com/edBoard.htm.
93. http://www.chrisdalelawyersupport.co.uk/edisclosureproject.htm.
94. http://www.xrce.xerox.com/people/oneill/home.html.
95. http://www.autonomy.com/content/Autonomy/Management/index.en.html.
96. http://www.autonomy.com/.
97. http://gsl-nagoya-u.net/faculty/cache/gsliF_Bennett.html.

Recommind;[98] Kelly (K.J.) Kutcha,[99] Forensics Consulting Solutions; Carsten Gorg,[100] Georgia Institute of Technology; David Chaplin,[101] Kroll Ontrack; and Chris May, IE Discovery.[102]

From the views of the participants and audience, the workshop was successful in achieving the goal of raising awareness of the separate "island universes" represented by academics and lawyers on the matter of improving searches conducted in e-discovery. From the early returns, it would seem that interest remains high in holding a DESI III somewhere in the world next year. Possible choices include would-be organizers putting in a proposal for a workshop to be held as part of ICAIL 2009[103] in Barcelona next June. Readers of this column interested in participating in a future DESI III (or just interested in any excuse to go to an e-discovery-related event in Barcelona) should certainly feel free to contact me at jason.baron@nara.gov.[104]

MIS International Conference on Digital Evidence

I wish to also briefly report on the follow-on International Conference on Digital Evidence,[105] held on June 26-27, 2008, at historic Vintners' Hall in London. Billed by MIS[106] as "The First Conference to Treat Digital Evidence on a Global Platform," I can say that the conference lived up to its name and that it was well worth attending. The opening speech and chairman's introduction was given by the above-mentioned Stephen Mason,[107] who is the author of *Electronic Signatures in Law* (Tottel, 2d ed. 2007) and *International Electronic*

---

98. http://www.recommind.com/management.html.
99. http://www.forensicsconsulting.com/au_execProfiles.html.
100. http://www.cc.gatech.edu/~goerg/.
101. http://www.arnoldit.com/search-wizards-speak/kroll.html.
102. http://www.iediscovery.com/about/management-team.aspx.
103. http://idt.uab.cat/icail2009/.
104. mailto:jason.baron@nara.gov.
105. http://issuu.com/dip00dip/docs/international_conference__ digital_evidence_2008/1.
106. http://www.misti.com/.
107. http://www.stephenmason.eu/.

Evidence (British Institute of International and Comparative Law, 2008), among many published works, as well as general editor of the *Digital Evidence and Electronic Signature Law Review*[108] (among other publications).

The MIS conference featured a remarkably broad panoply of speakers from around the world discussing how their respective legal systems and cultures deal with problems of digital evidence. My own modest role at this conference was limited to giving a 30-minute talk on search and information-retrieval issues from a U.S. perspective, including findings from the first two years of the TREC Legal Track, as part of a panel chaired by Iain G. Mitchell, Q.C.[109]

I cannot possibly give justice here to the two dozen or so presentations given at the conference, so I wish to just limit my observations here to a truly remarkable pair of panel presentations that took place on the afternoon of day 1 involving Senior Master Steven Whitaker[110] of the Supreme Court of England and Wales, Queen's Bench Division, Royal Courts of Justice & the Queen's Remembrancer, and Judge Francis M. Allegra[111] of the U.S. Court of Federal Claims in Washington, D.C. Judge Allegra has penned several e-discovery cases of note, including *United Medical Supply Co., Inc. v. United States,* 77 Fed. Cl. 257 (Fed. Cl. 2007).

Let me set out the following remarks from one of the judges, and I invite the readership here to guess which judge made these statements:

> Virtually every case we're seeing involves electronic data of some form.
>
> E-discovery decisions are generally of an interlocutory nature and therefore do not work their way into reported opinions, especially at the appellate level.

---

108. http://www.deaeslr.org/.

109. http://www.murraystable.com/advocate/66/iain-g-mitchell-qc.

110. http://nds.coi.gov.uk/environment/fullDetail.asp?ReleaseID=313122 &NewsAreaID=2&NavigatedFromDepartment=True.

111. http://www.uscfc.uscourts.gov/francis-m-allegra.

There is little or no training of judges with respect to ESI issues.

Digital voice recordings are becoming an evidentiary concern.

Judges should encourage litigants to meet and confer regarding ESI issues, and to cooperate on issues including with respect to determining what custodians hold ESI of importance to the case, what time frames should be used to limit searches for evidence, what types of documents and storage formats exist, and in general what search methods are to be used.

Search issues, including what keywords to use, are not always adequately handled by lawyers.

Judges should review e-discovery issues with proportionality and fairness principally in mind—smaller cases do not merit huge expenditures of time and effort in terms of the fanciest automated methodologies being utilized or required.

If you guessed the American judge said the above remarks, you would be wrong. While Judge Allegra gave a very fine talk describing the U.S. perspective on all of the above matters, the eye-opening remarks by Senior Master Whitaker cemented my already considerably developed bias from the DESI II workshop that the problems of ESI are now global in dimension, and that judges and lawyers everywhere—or at least, by this example, in the U.K. as well as the U.S.—find themselves essentially together, all in the same soup. We are all struggling to find reasonable ways to deal with increasing volumes of complex ESI.

I found one additional aspect of Senior Master Whitaker's remarks to be particularly intriguing, where he de-emphasized the importance of the finding of mere "relevance" in terms of producing documents to an opposing side as the result of a document review, while emphasizing instead the view that under Part 31[112] of the Civil Procedure Rules (CPR) in the U.K., parties should be

---

112. http://www.justice.gov.uk/civil/procrules_fin/contents/parts/part31.htm#rule31_12.

concentrating on self-identifying those specific documents of importance to the case at hand (either favoring their position or not), and turning those over to the other side. In other words, in a world brimming with millions of potentially relevant documents, why not cooperate with the other side (or have judges force such collaboration) in producing—at least first and foremost—only those documents of obvious materiality to the issues involved in a specific action? I now see that Chris Dale has written[113] at considerable length on this topic as well.

So let me pose here the obvious question to a U.S. audience: would there be a benefit to revising Rule 26 of the Federal Rules of Civil Procedure to expand upon the existing set of "initial disclosure" rules and meet-and-confer requirements to require (or allow) parties to concentrate their efforts in developing a search protocol aimed at finding the most specific, core, material documents that will be at issue in litigation—rather than engaging in the practice of massive "data dumps" of merely potentially relevant evidence? I am sure this would be viewed by some to be controversial. But the reality of ESI over the coming decades makes this seem imperative to me. We are facing billions (if not trillions) of potentially relevant files, yet as human beings trying cases, we can only use a minuscule fraction of that potentially relevant evidence during depositions and at trial. So why not focus on making reasonable efforts to find the truly "hot" documents of a material nature, rather than the merely "relevant" (or the even larger universe under Fed. R. Evid. 403 of documents that might themselves not be relevant but would lead to the admission of relevant evidence)?

I pose this merely as food for thought coming out of the London conference and will, of course, expect that Ralph and others will have something more to say on this topic in some future column. But it remains an intriguing thought: perhaps British barristers and judges have something to teach us in America about how to go about procedural reform aimed at cutting down to size the enormous and ever-increasing ESI/digital evidence problem.

---

113. http://chrisdale.wordpress.com/2008/04/09/relevant-is-irrelevant-to-standard-disclosure/.

Blog Reader Comments

It seems to me that effective searching is an iterative process that relies on feedback from earlier searches. Without the senior strategist understanding the technicalities of the search method and experiencing quick turnaround, I don't see how they can find what they want. I don't see why people bother to sift haystacks; when I'm looking for something hard to find on the Internet, I only look at the first page for the first N searches while I refine my search terms. I don't see the point of using a thousand keywords and reviewing ten thousand documents. If you have a huge number of search terms, then you really don't know what you're looking for, which guarantees you'll never find it. In summary, more searches, fewer terms, more senior searchers.

Another Blog Reader Comment

Laura Zubulake

Jason, As expected, an interesting commentary. I hope you are well. The more search terms the better. No one can ever be certain what exactly they will find. There are never guarantees, just calculated guesstimates of what exists. I believe keywords are the most important aspect of any electronic search. A reasonable and well thought out data sift is likely worth the effort. One's haystack is another's pot of gold.

WHAT THE WORLD WAS SEARCHING FOR IN 2007

Google's Zeitgeist 2007[114] provides a glimpse into what the world was searching for in 2007, at least those using Google, which these days means pretty much everyone. The results provide an important glimpse into evolving world culture and language.

---

114. http://www.google.com/intl/en/press/zeitgeist2007/.

Language and pop culture are essential subjects for any e-discovery professional called upon to search for evidence. That's because an effective searcher must know the linguistic patterns, slang, and popular references used by many different kinds of people. All keyword searches, and even concept searches,[115] depend on that. If you do not know the language and overall cultural mind-set of the custodians whose records you search, you may not run the right search. Even when you do, you may still fail to recognize a relevant "hit" during your review. You may read an e-mail and misunderstand entirely what was said. You may not grasp that "bad" sometimes means "good," or that badoo[116] is one of the world's fastest-growing online communities. You may see a smoking gun and not even know it.

That is why, in my opinion, an effective searcher must be familiar with popular culture, especially in searches of e-mail and instant messages. That is also grounds for caution in outsourcing large-volume reviews. They may speak the King's English, but do they understand the ever-changing nomenclature of American culture?

As almost everyone knows, Google saves every search ever made, but supposedly does not track who made what search. This kind of information is power, and not only allows for effective targeted marketing, but also for interesting sociological studies. Every year, Google provides us with its year-end analysis of the searches made in the past year. Here is Google's explanation of its yearly *Zeitgeist*:

> To get a glimpse of what's been on our collective consciousness, we mined billions of search queries to discover what sorts of things rose to the top. We encourage you to check out our findings to see if you, too, reflect the zeitgeist—the spirit of the times.

It is well worth your time to study these results yourself; but in the meantime, this blog will provide a few lists that I found interesting. I did a similar blog last year on the top Google searches in 2006 (included in my first book) that you might also want to check out for

---

115. http://ralphlosey.wordpress.com/2007/06/10/keyword-searches-v-concept-searches/.

116. http://badoo.com/.

comparison. Note that these lists only reveal what search terms are the "fastest gainers," which appears to be a kind of extrapolation to show trends, where more recent results are more heavily weighted and very common terms are ignored altogether. In Google's words:[117]

> Rather than showing the most popular searches overall, which would always be generic terms like "weather," Hot Trends highlights searches that have sudden surges in popularity. Our algorithm analyzes millions of web searches performed on Google and displays those searches that deviate the most from their historic traffic pattern. The algorithm also filters out spam and removes inappropriate material.

With that explanation, here is Google's report[118] of the "fastest-rising" search terms overall in 2007 in the United States. As a courtesy to those who, like me, struggle to stay current with predominantly youth-culture trends, I also provide a brief explanation for each.

1. **iPhone**: iPhone, the Apple mobile phone with music and video player and Web-browsing features tops the Google top searches 2007 list.
2. **Webkinz**: Webkinz is a stuffed animal that customers can register and play with online.
3. **TMZ**: A Telepictures and America Online joint venture that provides focuses on the latest celebrity scandals.
4. **Transformer toys**: Transformers are flexible toys that shift shape, and became popular, once again, from the 2007 hit movie *Transformers*.
5. **YouTube**: online video-sharing site.
6. **Club Penguin**: Networking site for children.
7. **MySpace**: Social networking site.
8. **Heroes**: "Heroes" is an American science fiction serial drama television series created by Tim Kring on NBC.
9. **Facebook**: Social/business networking site.
10. **Anna Nicole Smith**: Anna Nicole Smith was an American sex symbol, model, actress, and celebrity.

117. http://www.google.com/intl/en/trends/about.html.
118. http://www.google.com/intl/en/press/zeitgeist2007/.

The fastest-rising search terms worldwide differed slightly from the U.S. list above. For instance, the entire world was not as obsessed with Anna Nicole as we were, and she did not make the top 10. Instead, good old badoo did. Here is the top 10 global list:

1. **iPhone.**
2. **badoo**: Although just started in 2006, this online community already has over 12 million members.
3. **Facebook.**
4. **Dailymotion**: Another video-sharing site with a more global focus.
5. **Webkinz.**
6. **YouTube.**
7. **eBuddy**: Instant messaging for Web and phone.
8. **Second Life**: Virtual reality community[119] where people interact online with avatars.[120]

   The interactions can be random social or well planned, including virtual lectures. For instance, prominent Circuit Court of Appeals Judge Richard A. Posner[121] (shown right) gave a lecture on December 7, 2007, where he discussed his latest book, *Not a Suicide Pact*,[122] his defense of the *Patriot Act*, copyright, and other topics. He also answered questions from fellow avatars, many of whom were lawyers, some appearing as animals. Click here[123] for a full transcript. Unfortunately, his event ended with a virtual terrorist bombing. No avatars were injured, and Judge Posner escaped safely into the real world. Second Life has its own money and marketplace,[124] with

---

119. http://secondlife.com/whatis/.
120. http://secondlife.com/whatis/avatar.php.
121. http://nwn.blogs.com/nwn/2006/11/judge_richard_p.html.
122. http://www.amazon.com/dp/0195304276?tag=newwornot-20&camp=14573&creative=327641&linkCode=as1&creativeASIN=0195304276&adid=063PH6QH9SW5YR7DSHD1&.
123. http://nwn.blogs.com/nwn/2006/12/the_second_life.html.
124. http://secondlife.com/whatis/marketplace.php.

millions of dollars in real-world transactions taking place every month. You can buy virtual real estate from the owner of Second Life, Linden Research.[125] You can then create your own worlds and sell things, both real and virtual, including cars and computers. Many businesses, large and small, are already well established in Second Life, including IBM,[126] where more than 3,000 of its employees have avatar identities. There are even a few law firms,[127] but the word is, virtually no billable hours originate there.

9. **Hi5**: Online networking site with an international orientation.
10. **Club Penguin.**

On a global level, the most popular searches in 2007[128] on "Google News"[129] include, in my opinion, only one bona fide "news" item, and no, I don't mean Paris Hilton:

1. American Idol
2. YouTube
3. Britney Spears
4. 2007 Cricket World Cup
5. Chris Benoit
6. iPhone
7. Anna Nicole Smith
8. Paris Hilton
9. Iran
10. Vanessa Hudgens

Google even ranks the top 10 searched lawsuits,[130] which are:

125. http://lindenlab.com/.
126. http://www.ibm.com/virtualworlds/businesscenter/.
127. http://www.abajournal.com/magazine/fantasy_life_real_law/.
128. http://www.google.com/intl/en/press/zeitgeist2007/newsmakers.html.
129. http://news.google.com/.
130. http://www.google.com/intl/en/press/zeitgeist2007/newsmakers.html.

1. Borat lawsuit
2. Vonage lawsuit
3. iPhone lawsuit
4. Facebook lawsuit
5. Jamie Gold lawsuit
6. Pants lawsuit
7. McDonalds lawsuit
8. Paxil lawsuit
9. RIAA lawsuit
10. Dell lawsuit

To be honest, although I know and like Borat, I had no idea he was involved in a lawsuit; in fact, I had never heard of most of these alleged lawsuits. As it turns out, a number of people who were duped into appearing in the movie *Borat* reacted by filing suit, including the villagers in Romania[131] who were tricked into playing the Kazakhstans and sued for $30 million. Apparently people find these kinds of lawsuits very amusing, confirming the old saying that litigation is a popular American observer sport. *See Kregos v. Associated Press*, 795 F. Supp. 1325 (S.D. N.Y. 1992) ("In bygone days, baseball reigned as America's favorite pastime. Sadly, this honor seems to now belong to lawsuits. We see it on every front, on the front pages of newspapers, over cable television's airwaves, and in the public discourse.").

Another interesting thing you can do using Google Trends Lab[132] is determine the locations in the world or U.S. where searches you specify have most often been performed. For instance, I searched the term "electronic discovery,"[133] and Google Trends tells me the top 10 U.S. cities in which this search was performed and provides a graphic representation on volume as follows:

---

131. http://www.usatoday.com/life/movies/news/2006-12-05-borat-romanian-suit_x.htm.

132. http://www.google.com/trends?hl=en.

133. http://www.google.com/trends?q=%22electronic+discovery%22 &hl=en.

1. **Washington**, DC, USA
2. **Houston**, TX, USA
3. **New York**, NY, USA
4. **San Francisco**, CA, USA
5. **Boston**, MA, USA
6. **Minneapolis**, MN, USA
7. **Chicago**, IL, USA
8. **Philadelphia**, PA, USA
9. **Seattle**, WA, USA
10. **Atlanta**, GA, USA

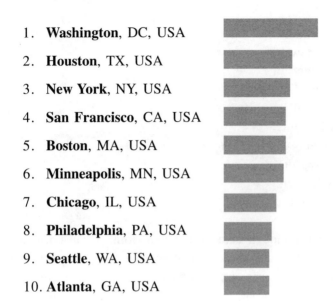

Now you know why there are so many e-discovery vendor offices in Washington, D.C. By the way, if you change the searched term to "e-discovery" you get a slightly different result where Toronto is eighth and Los Angeles is ninth. I reported on this same search in 2006[134] with essentially the same results, but the overall volume of these searches is way up.

In this same blog of a year ago, I reported the curious anomaly that "Yahoo" had just replaced "sex" as the most popular search term on Google. I also reported the top countries in the world that searched "sex" on Google. I ran this same search again today, and the results have changed significantly. For instance, last year[135] Pakistan was number one; now it does not even make the top 10.

---

134. http://ralphlosey.wordpress.com/2007/02/01/yahoo-replaces-sex-as-the-1-seach-query-on-google/.

135. http://ralphlosey.wordpress.com/2007/02/01/yahoo-replaces-sex-as-the-1-seach-query-on-google/.

1. **Egypt**
2. **Viet Nam**
3. **India**
4. **Turkey**
5. **Poland**
6. **Denmark**
7. **Belgium**
8. **Netherlands**
9. **Switzerland**
10. **Australia**

I'll let readers decide for themselves what message, if any, the above list[136] provides on world culture, and what trend the change in rankings from 2006[137] might reveal.

---

136. http://www.google.com/trends?q=%22sex%22&ctab=0&hl=en&geo=all&date=all&sort=0.

137. http://ralphlosey.wordpress.com/2007/02/01/yahoo-replaces-sex-as-the-1-seach-query-on-google/.

e-Discovery Rules and Civil Procedure | 5

NEW RULES

REPORT ON WEST-KROLL'S "A TO Z" E-DISCOVERY WORKSHOP, AND PROPOSAL FOR A PURE QUESTION-AND-ANSWER FORMAT

I attended the West Legalworks e-discovery A-Z workshop in Miami in September. They are day-and-a-half-long events, so I cannot summarize the whole thing, but I can report on the parts I found most interesting. West Legalworks[1] and Kroll Ontrack[2] have been putting these on all over the country for several years, using different faculty in different places. I attended this CLE in Atlanta

---

1. http://westlegalworks.com/.
2. http://www.krollontrack.com/.

a few years ago as a carefree student, and now this one as a teacher. Like most of the faculty, I stayed for the full workshop. Both have been good events where I learned a lot and met some great people.

The outside counsel who chaired the event, Browning E. Marean,[3] is also the chair of DLA Piper's e-Discovery Team.[4] He now leads most of these A-Z workshops. Browning is an excellent teacher who combines both dry wit and sage advice (they usually go together). He claims to have an ex-navy man's vocabulary, which he says is invaluable in e-mail review, but we never heard any of that. Indeed, in spite of my participation and Dilbert tie, it was a very proper Minnesota production. Browning's co-chair was Keith D. Mobley, an attorney consultant for Kroll Ontrack in Atlanta. Keith's goal was to make the CLE responsive to the participants' needs. Thus, although the whole alphabet was advertised, most of the presenters tried to customize their talks on the fly to focus on the issues that people seemed to be most interested in.

Proposal for a Total Q&A Workshop

In my opinion, and I know that Keith agrees, this is how e-discovery seminars should be run, even though it is more difficult for some presenters. In fact, I would like to try taking this approach to an extreme, and set up an event comprised entirely of questions and answers around a specified topic or topics. The presentations would consist entirely of answers to questions—sometimes long, sometimes short. One thing would naturally lead to another. The whole atmosphere would encourage questions and discourage lectures. It is kind of like a Foo Camp[5] or "unconference,"[6] which is defined by Wikepedia as "a facilitated, face-to-face, and participant-driven conference centered around a theme or purpose."

This method would empower the attendees. They would set the agenda. They would get the precise information they want, when they want it. (No specific cases discussed, of course, as that comes

---

3. http://www.dlapiper.com/browning_marean/.
4. http://www.dlapiper.com/us/services/detail.aspx?service=524.
5. http://en.wikipedia.org/wiki/Foo_Camp.
6. http://en.wikipedia.org/wiki/Unconference.

too close to legal advice.) This approach would challenge the presenters, which is a good thing. It would keep them fresh and on their toes. It would also spare presenters the frustration of talking about issues that people are not really interested in. The different presenters would, of course, have to have varying, complementary areas of expertise so that a variety of different questions could be addressed.

Any vendors or educators out there want to sponsor such an event? If so, let me know,[7] and I will help you make it happen. With the right faculty and the right students, who would need to have at least similar interests and backgrounds, it could be a great success. In fact, it could spawn a whole new type of spontaneous, fully interactive legal education event, one that is completely focused on the special interests and needs of the attendees. Right now, the sponsors of events are just guessing, hoping they get it right. So how about it? Send me an e-mail[8] and let's try it.

Rules and Pre-litigation Triggers

The first presentation was called "Why Digital Is Different." The lead faculty on this topic was John M. Barkett[9] of Shook, Hardy & Bacon,[10] who was assisted by Jim Caitlan[11] of TrialGraphix[12] (Kroll) and Sonya Ann Strnad[13] of Holland & Knight.[14] John began by reviewing the new rules, but only after first asking if people really wanted to hear about that. Somewhat surprisingly, they did, which tells me many had not attended an e-discovery CLE before.

The rules presentation was all pretty straightforward except for one statement that I found controversial. John stated that the phrase "absent exceptional circumstances" in "safe-harbor" Rule 37(e) means "absent prejudice to the requesting party." I am not so sure I

---

7. http://ralphlosey.wordpress.com/ralph.losey@gmail.com.

8. http://ralphlosey.wordpress.com/ralph.losey@gmail.com.

9. http://www.shb.com/shb.asp?pgID=929&attorney_id=276&st=f.

10. http://www.shb.com/.

11. http://www.trialgraphix.com/SiteManager/Documents/PressRoom/Jim%20Caitlan.Letterhead.pdf.

12. http://www.trialgraphix.com/.

13. http://www.hklaw.com/id77/biosSASTRNAD/.

14. http://www.hklaw.com/.

agree with that, and perhaps I did not hear him correctly. I think the rule can also protect when there is prejudice, if routine good-faith operation of an ESI system is shown. In fact, in most cases where the rule will be used as defense to a motion for sanctions, the party moving for sanctions will claim prejudice. *See, e.g.,* my prior discussion of the rule[15] in connection with *Petcou v. C.H. Robinson Worldwide, Inc.,*[16] 2008 WL 542684 (N.D. Ga. Feb. 25, 2008).

If proof of prejudice takes away the protection of the rule, then it provides no protection at all, which is, I know, what many people say. Still, I respectfully disagree. The rule must have a meaning. I think the "absent exceptional circumstances" language is just there to be sure the rule does not provide protection to intentional wrongdoing, gross negligence, or bad faith. It is just general catch-all language, no doubt added as a compromise by the committee that wrote this rule. This "absent exceptional circumstances" is just intended to make sure that judges understand they have discretion to disregard the rule if the facts just do not "smell right" for any number of reasons. In fact, I think the caveat "absent exceptional circumstances" is largely meaningless in view of the good-faith requirement already in the rule, and the host of other methods by which a requesting party can obtain sanctions outside of the rules. As John pointed out in his presentation, there are many ways for a judge to impose sanctions under the common-law where Rule 37(e) would arguably not apply.

This panel also discussed the tricky issue of when a pre-litigation duty to preserve may be triggered. They made an interesting point concerning the dangers of overuse of attorney work product legends on pre-litigation documents. Once you start putting those legends on e-mails and other documents, or otherwise claim that documents are protected from disclosure by the litigation work product privilege, then you also establish a clear point in time at which

---

15. http://ralphlosey.wordpress.com/2008/03/31/new-case-denies-both-production-under-rule-26b2b-and-sanctions-for-spoliation-under-unspoken-rule-37/.

16. http://ralphlosey.files.wordpress.com/2008/03/petcou-v-ch-robinson1.doc.

litigation is anticipated. This triggers the duty to preserve. Therefore, logical consistency demands that when you start claiming work product in connection with anticipated litigation, you should at the same time also issue a litigation hold to the impacted parties. There may be some exceptions to this. For instance, you may know that litigation is likely but not yet know the identity or locations of the key players, and so cannot send out a hold notice. Still, as a general rule, this is a good idea. It is hard to argue that the work product doctrine applies, but not the duty to preserve. That is a classic example of wanting to have your cake and eat it, too.[17]

The first session concluded with John describing the facts of *Qualcomm v. Broadcom* in detail. *See Qualcomm, Inc. v. Broadcom Corp.*, 2008 WL 66932 (S.D. Cal. Jan. 7, 2008) (one of several relevant decisions in this case). Throughout the next day and a half, the *Qualcomm* case came up again and again. The impact of *Qualcomm* is so important that I devote most of the "Ethics" chapter of this book to this case.

Drawing Drama from the Disk

This next session was led by William F. Hamilton,[18] the chair of Holland & Knight's e-Discovery Team. Helping him were John M. Barkett and Jim Caitlan again, along with Miami lawyer Joel B. Rothman.[19] Bill is quite adept at teaching these subjects, as he is an adjunct professor at the University of Florida School of Law. In this position he taught one of the first classes in the country on e-discovery. The panel noted that it was "almost malpractice not to use checklists," while also pointing out the limits of these tools, as I did in "ABA Litigation Section Reacts to the Qualcomm Case and Recommends e-Discovery Checklists."[20]

---

17. http://en.wikipedia.org/wiki/Have_one's_cake_and_eat_it_too.
18. http://www.hklaw.com/id77/bioswhamilto/.
19. http://www.seidenlaw.com/attorneys_rothman.htm.
20. http://ralphlosey.wordpress.com/2008/05/04/aba-litigation-section-reacts-to-the-qualcomm-case-and-recommends-e-discovery-checklists/.

Bill had a good presentation of forensics, one of his (and my) favorite subjects. Professor Hamilton is of the philosophy that forensic images of the hard drives of the computers of the key players should be made in almost every case, but especially in cases involving departed employee noncompete and trade secret cases, or in employee integrity cases. I agree with Bill that forensic images should be made in these specialty cases but respectfully disagree about doing it in every case, just as a precautionary measure. Instead, I am inclined to make forensic copies only when special circumstances indicate there is a need to do so, such as in the cases Bill mentioned, or in others when you know or suspect an employee has deleted relevant files.

Jim Caitlan also spoke about the alternate method of preserving evidence by making a "ghost copy."[21] Here you copy all of the active files and programs on key players' computers onto new hard drives. You then remove the original hard drives and replace them with new ones. The key players never know the difference, because all of their active files and programs remain in place. But you can then take the original hard drives off to the forensic lab for study—deleted files, slack space and all.

Noble Eightfold Path

Sonya Ann Strnad led the next presentation, called "First Steps on the Path to Production." She was assisted by Derek A. Krabill, a technology consultant with McDermott Will & Emery,[22] and Michael J. Ryan,[23] a good plaintiff's attorney in Fort Lauderdale. Sonya had a very clever presentation explaining the standard EDRM model[24] for e-discovery using a spiritual analogy. It makes my prior sports analogy article, "What Game Does an e-Discovery Team Play?," seems pretty base! She adopted the language of Buddhist philosophy[25] to set forth the "Eightfold Path to e-Discovery Enlightenment."

21. http://en.wikipedia.org/wiki/Ghost_%28software%29.
22. http://www.mwe.com/.
23. http://www.krupnicklaw.com/attorneys/ryan.asp.
24. http://www.edrm.net/.
25. http://en.wikipedia.org/wiki/Eightfold_path.

Of course, in Buddhism, before you get into the intricacies of the Eightfold Path, you must first master the "Four Noble E-Discovery Truths." They are, in Sonya's words:

1. That all e-discovery is painful;
2. That the cause of this pain is cost, time, and complexity of ESI;
3. That the pain can be minimized; and
4. That the way to minimize pain is the Rule 26 conference.

I am not so sure that a Rule 26 Conference is really as powerful as all that, but it is a good start to alleviate unnecessary e-discovery suffering. Sonya then correctly notes that the Eightfold Path of e-Discovery, like Buddhism, emphasizes "right thinking"and "right action." In my world, this means only preserve and collect what you really need. Do not be attached to the rest. Sonya then described the eight steps on this path:

1. Determination of duty to preserve
2. Identification of issues/key personnel
3. Issue/maintain litigation hold
4. Identify sources of relevant data
5. Preserve relevant data
6. Collect relevant data
7. Process relevant data
8. Review and produce relevant data

It was a very clever analogy. A few details that I remember include Sonya's suggestion that the support staff of key players also be sent a hold notice. They may keep e-files of relevance that their boss does not know about. Sonya also suggested keeping a non-privileged log of all preservation and collection activities. This log can later serve as a method to prove the reasonableness of your efforts and protect you from a *Qualcomm*-like situation. Browning mentioned three software programs that can help you to do that: Atlas,[26] Exterro,[27] and Autonomy.[28]

Sonya then discussed several landmark cases, including *Metropolitan Opera Association v. Local 100, Hotel Employees & Restaurant Employees International Union*, 212 F.R.D. 178, 222 (S.D. N.Y. 2003). She explained that this case stands for the proposition that:

> Counsel must inform clients:
> - of the existence of the duty to preserve;
> - that duty to preserve encompasses all "documents" potentially relevant to the dispute; and
> - that the definition of "document" encompasses hard copies and electronic documents, as well as drafts and non-identical copies.

Teams, Costs, and Conferring

Next was my presentation on e-Discovery Teams, where I got a chance to show off my new Apple Keynote software[29] and its unique special effects. My thanks to panelists Alvin F. Lindsay[30] of Hogan & Hartson[31] and Derek Krabill for helping me. During the question period, Browning Marean wryly observed that I forgot to include an essential member of any e-Discovery Team—opposing counsel. It was said half in jest, of course, but his point of the necessity to communicate with opposing counsel is a good one. In many cases, greater transparency and cooperation can lead to dramatic cost savings and efficiency in e-discovery.

The next presentation was "What's This Going to Cost?," led by Browning, who says he loves to follow my PowerPoint specials. Browning showed us the spreadsheet template on e-discovery costs that he developed. His good advice was to avoid using simple brute-

---

26. http://www.pss-systems.com/solutions/.
27. http://www.exterro.com/.
28. http://www.autonomy.com/.
29. http://www.apple.com/iwork/keynote/.
30. http://www.hhlaw.com/aflindsay/.
31. http://www.hhlaw.com/.

force review, where you read everything by using concept search, clustering, and context review techniques. He said our goal should be to review 300 documents per hour, not just 10. This is possible by cluster-type review, where you can more easily tell what does not have to be read. The key to cutting costs is to reduce review time. Also, the careful use of contract lawyers can help. In his experience, contract lawyer costs range from between $43 and $150 per hour, per reviewer. In India, the price per contract lawyer can come down to between $25 and $35 per hour, but Browning does not know of any client who will use Indian lawyers for review. When contract lawyers are used, even domestic ones, top-end attorneys should still be involved in review to cull down the data universe and focus on the key subjects, players, and language.

As a practice tip, Browning suggested the request of production of the PowerPoints that might pertain to the dispute, especially ones sent to the board. They are usually simple enough for anyone to understand and sometimes have startling admissions. Browning also suggested the use of checklists and established procedures as typically employed in project management software. The use of such tools is largely driven by the fear of malpractice. It is all to easy too forget to do something. Also, Browning pointed out how important it is for law firms and corporations to have a strong internal education program. This e-discovery training should be for both litigation and transactional lawyers. Transactional lawyers need to understand litigation-hold duties too, because they see the problems that are brewing. By the time a dispute gets referred to a litigation attorney, the time for a hold may be long past.

The next session on "Meet and Confer" was led by Joel Rothman, with strong assistance by Ervin A. Gonzalez,[32] a Miami plaintiff's lawyer and member of the Florida Bar's Board of Governors,[33] and Alvin Lindsay. The panel began by quoting Judge Waxse, who likes to say that "[l]awyers are like exotic particles. They change behav-

---

32. http://www.ervingonzalez.com/.
33. http://www.floridabar.org/tfb/TFBOrgan.nsf/2FC809811C01052385 25671100692F1C/913C0D3EADC9C63285256B2F006C706B? OpenDocument.

ior when observed." Judge Waxse, a district court judge in Kansas City well known for his e-discovery expertise, purportedly orders lawyers who cannot reach agreement in Rule 26(f) conferences to go back and hold the conference again, but this time to videotape the whole thing. If they still cannot reach an agreement, then they are supposed to come back with motions and file the videotape. So far, no one has ever returned to file a motion with videotape. This always resolves the problem.

The panel agreed that complex cases require a series of meet and confers, not just one meeting. They call this the "Big Bang" versus "Serial" approach to meet and confer. They also suggest that you send an agenda in advance, and that you come to the meeting with a very specific and detailed plan. Sometimes you may even want to bring an IT expert, if you need it. They suggest that you consult with the expert if and when tech issues come up, but that you do so *outside* of the room. They also suggest you always discuss a preservation plan in order to protect your client. This allows you to set up waiver and estoppel arguments.

Mike Ryan added that it is important to build credibility at the meet-and-confer. He thinks that is the most important aspect of the conference. Everyone's credibility will be tested, so be careful what you say and what you promise. To that end, the panel suggested that you bring a note-taker to make an informal record of what is said and done.

Collecting and Processing

The next day began with "Bringing in the Bytes" led by Jim Caitlan, with assistance by Derek A. Krabill and Robin A. Peterson, a top paralegal and e-discovery expert for Baker & Hostetler.[34] Jim calls the e-discovery experience a kind of "body cavity search" of the company to try to locate all relevant ESI. He points out that it is easy to make mistakes and miss ESI, and then later be accused of spoliation. He recommends that you start the search process by educating in-house IT as to what needs to be accomplished and why. You need to explain the rules and the problems.

---

34. http://www.bakerlaw.com/.

Derek said that in his practice he first sends out a general questionnaire to corporate IT, and then has a phone conference with them. He says the call is almost like a deposition, but friendly. Derek observed that IT tends to provide information that minimizes their work, so they have to be carefully supervised. In Jim's experience, a group meeting with multiple IT personnel works best because they tend to be more committed and show off their problem-solving abilities to their peers. He thinks that you are more likely to come out of a group meeting with a detailed plan of action than you are in a series of one-on-one meetings. Jim suggests that the meeting be facilitated by a tech-lawyer of the e-discovery consultant.

The panel emphasized again the importance of documenting all decisions throughout the e-discovery process. In this way, you can later defend your actions as reasonable in situations where a mistake is made, ESI is overlooked, etc. Jim stated that his company, Kroll, always tries to preserve backup tapes, but I suggested that that is not what the law requires. In my opinion, you have to preserve backup tapes only if there is some reason to believe that relevant ESI may only be available there. I pointed out Judge Scheindlin's prior holding in *Zubulake v. UBS Warburg LLC,* 220 F.R.D. 212, 218 (S.D. N.Y. 2003) on that, as I did in my first book. *See, e.g.,* "Rule 37 and the Supreme Court on Document Destruction; Should a Litigation Hold Include Backup Tapes?"; *but see Toussie v. County of Suffolk,* 2007 WL 4565160, at *8 (E.D. N.Y. Dec. 21, 2007). *Toussie* incorrectly cites to *Zubulake* to support the position that "the law is now clear that any backup tapes containing the documents of a key player must be preserved and accessible." This incorrect statement of the law was recently repeated in *Treppel v. Biovail Corporation,* 2008 WL 866594 at *12 (S.D. N.Y., April 2, 2008), which for authority cited and quoted *Toussie.*

The next presentation was called "Data Filtering, Processing, Review and Production: How It Works and Why You Need It," by Sonya Strnad, Jim Caitlan, and Michael Ryan. Sonya noted that between 65 and 90 percent of data is usually removed during the culling/de-duping process. This is a very important statistic. In my view, we all need to be much more aggressive in ESI culling in order to get control of run away e-discovery costs. The panel had many good practical tips in this area not previously mentioned, such as:

- keep a good accounting to be sure all files are processed;
- know what kind of files cannot be handled by the processing software you are using, and be sure the software creates exception reports to advise you of any files not included;
- ask your vendor to tell you what types of ESI can and cannot be properly processed by their software; and
- when projecting the time it will take to accomplish certain tasks and make production, be sure to build in time to deal with currently unforeseen problems, because some will always crop up.

Jim responded to a question as to when concept search software should be used. He said that it becomes cost-effective when at least 20,000 to 30,000 documents are involved. Then, concept searches and the clustering of documents can facilitate review enough to pay for the expense of the extra software charges. Jim stated that Kroll's product, by which I think he meant Ontrack Firstview,[35] is relatively inexpensive to use for that size of review, between $2,000 to $3,000. The extra expenditure should more than pay for itself in reduced review time, and it will uncover additional relevant data. Along those lines, Browning reported on a new software search tool by Synergence[36] that allows you to create a synthetic document with language that you would like to find. It then goes out and searches for the smoking gun or silver bullet that you would like to find in the document set. You can also do the same thing with actual documents you have already found that are the most relevant: the "hot" documents.

Sonya proposed that you try to reach agreement with the requesting party to produce only near-duping documents, and to allow the receiving party to request the screened near-duped documents later upon request. Alternatively, the producing party can de-

---

35. http://www.ontrackfirstview.com/.
36. http://www.syngence.com/products/SPS/synthetix/.

dupe and then repopulate and produce. Browning observed that this would be called de-deduplicating, and is the electronic equivalent of paper document dumping. It forces the requesting party to also use de-duping software, or incur excessive costs to review all the duplicative documents. For that reason, a requesting party should want to avoid repopulation and should be pleased to receive a de-duped set, but often they do not. They tend to be suspicious that relevant documents have been withheld. Requesting parties should be told about the de-duping process in advance of production. Then, with disclosure, they should agree to the mutually beneficial process, especially if they have the right to go back and request specific de-duped documents if that is later needed.

Sleeping Well at Night

The closing presentation by John Barkett was titled "What's Keeping Us Up at Night?" He was helped by Jim Caitlan, Bill Hamilton, and Keith Mobley. John agreed with my prior assertion on the law governing backup tapes—that there is no duty to preserve them unless you know that relevant data may only exist there. But he correctly noted that this requires quick investigation into the key players' procedures to see if there have been any deletions of ESI that might require backup-tape preservation. This need for rapid lawyer and client response keeps a lot of us up at night. John also reviewed his recent Ethics paper and a host of relevant case law. He concluded by noting how the then proposed amendment to Rule 502 (Evidence Code regarding privilege waiver) might help us all to sleep better at night. The revised rule was later approved by Congress and signed into law in September 2008. Here is the final text of the new rule as enacted:

RULE 502. ATTORNEY-CLIENT PRIVILEGE AND WORK PRODUCT; LIMITATIONS ON WAIVER

The following provisions apply, in the circumstances set out, to disclosure of a communication or information covered by the attorney-client privilege or work-product protection.

(a) **Disclosure Made in a Federal Proceeding or to a Federal Office or Agency; Scope of a Waiver.** When the disclosure is made in a Federal proceeding or to a Federal office or agency and waives the attorney-client privilege or work-product protection, the waiver extends to an undisclosed communication or information in a Federal or State proceeding only if:

(1) the waiver is intentional;

(2) the disclosed and undisclosed communications or information concern the same subject matter; and

(3) they ought in fairness to be considered together.

(b) **Inadvertent Disclosure.** When made in a Federal proceeding or to a Federal office or agency, the disclosure does not operate as a waiver in a Federal or State proceeding if:

(1) the disclosure is inadvertent;

(2) the holder of the privilege or protection took reasonable steps to prevent disclosure; and

(3) the holder promptly took reasonable steps to rectify the error, including (if applicable) following Federal Rule of Civil Procedure 26(b)(5)(B).

(c) **Disclosure Made in a State Proceeding.** When the disclosure is made in a State proceeding and is not the subject of a State-court order concerning waiver, the disclosure does not operate as a waiver in a Federal proceeding if the disclosure:

(1) would not be a waiver under this rule if it had been made in a Federal proceeding; or

(2) is not a waiver under the law of the State where the disclosure occurred.

(d) **Controlling Effect of a Court Order.** A Federal court may order that the privilege or protection is not waived by disclosure connected with the litigation pending before the court—in which event the disclosure is also not a waiver in any other Federal or State proceeding.

(e) **Controlling Effect of a Party Agreement.** An agreement on the effect of disclosure in a Federal proceeding is binding only on the parties to the agreement, unless it is incorporated into a court order.

(f) **Controlling Effect of This Rule.** Notwithstanding Rules 101 and 1101, this rule applies to State proceedings and to Federal court-annexed and Federal court-mandated arbitration proceedings, in the circumstances set out in the rule. And notwithstanding Rule 501, this rule applies even if State law provides the rule of decision.

(g) **Definitions. In this rule:**

(1) "attorney-client privilege" means the protection that applicable law provides for confidential attorney-client communications; and

(2) "work-product protection" means the protection that applicable law provides for tangible material (or its intangible equivalent) prepared in anticipation of litigation or for trial.

This new Federal Evidence Code provision should help on the privilege waiver problems that worry many an e-discovery lawyer. It does not apply to state law cases, but it is certainly a step in the right direction. We will all still have to carefully review for privilege, but at least this rule change will help mitigate the damages in federal court when mistakes are made and privileged documents are inadvertently produced.

Still, the best advice on how to avoid sleepless nights is to study what Qualcomm's lawyers did in the *Broadcom* case before they got fired and sanctioned, and then do the opposite. Like the chair of the FTC's e-Discovery Team, David Shonka, said recently at the Harvard Club lecture,[37] it's really quite simple: "don't lie, don't hide things, and don't make promises you can't keep." To that I would add, if you are in doubt about something, seek the advice of an independent counsel who not only has high integrity, but also strong knowledge of the governing rules of ethics. For instance, in my firm we

---

37. http://ralphlosey.wordpress.com/2008/04/26/e-discovery-at-the-harvard-club-in-new-york-city/.

have a chief ethics officer. The Florida Bar also operates an anonymous ethics hotline for lawyers to seek advice. Perhaps your state has something similar. It is a good idea to consult with reliable sources like this whenever you are in doubt.

Blog Reader Comment

(Ken Withers)

I endorse your idea of a complete Q&A format e-discovery CLE. I have already proposed we take such a clinical approach in the judicial education arena—we'd call it "E-Discovery ER." But there are two logistical problems I see with offering it to attorneys:

(1) CLE accrediting authorities, who hesitate to accredit anything more unusual than a lecture with PowerPoint slide and accompanying law review article, will not accredit any program that does not have static format and materials. That may not matter to some participants, but it will to their law firms, who won't foot the tuition.

(2) Potential faculty will all have to be non-attorneys who are judgment-proof. And the audience members, too. Let's face it, if you're going to a Q & A format session, you're going to ask questions and get advice, no matter what the disclaimers are. I don't actually believe that anyone would get sued based on the advice offered in such a setting, but the fact that e-discovery situations are so very fact-intensive—and there is no way in this format for anyone to get all the facts—the potential for inappropriate advice to be given and taken is great. And if that were to happen, word would get around quickly. It's a risk.

But fools go where angels fear to tread, and I'm no angel, so count me in.

NEW CASE DENIES BOTH PRODUCTION UNDER RULE 26(B)(2)(B) AND SANCTIONS FOR SPOLIATION UNDER UNSPOKEN RULE 37

A sexual harassment case in Atlanta, *Petcou v. C.H. Robinson Worldwide, Inc.,*[38] 2008 WL 542684 (N.D. Ga., Feb. 25, 2008) recently used the two-tiered analysis of Rule 26(b)(2)(B) to reject the plaintiffs' overbroad discovery request. When subsequent "discovery about discovery" under Rule 26(b)(2)(B) revealed that e-mail was destroyed after the EEOC charge was filed, the plaintiffs moved for sanctions. Sanctions were denied using the routine operations analysis of Rule 37(f), although the rule itself was never mentioned.

In this case, four female plaintiffs alleged harassment "based on offensive comments and images on coworkers' computer screens, as opposed to e-mails the Plaintiffs themselves received." *Id.* at *3. Plaintiffs' counsel served a request for production on the defendant, C.H. Robinson Worldwide, Inc.,[39] a transportation company with more than 5,300 employees, for "any documents relating to or evidencing the presence of pornography . . . , including but not limited to e-mail. . . ." The request initially had no date range but was later clarified to include an eight-year time span from 1998 to 2006.

Vague Request

This was, in my view, a vague and poorly worded request to produce. As such, it violated not only a legion of case law, but also the fourth Sedona Principle:[40]

> 4. Discovery requests for electronically stored information should be as clear as possible, while responses and objections to discovery should disclose the scope and limits of the production.

---

38. http://ralphlosey.files.wordpress.com/2008/03/petcou-v-ch-robinson1.doc.
39. http://www.chrobinson.com/.
40. http://www.thesedonaconference.org/.

The request here literally required the responding party to search through all of its electronic files (and paper records) to look not only for pornographic materials, but also for records that might somehow "relate to or evidence the presence of pornography." First of all, even the Supreme Court cannot define pornography, nor tell what pornography is, unless and until they actually see it (one person's porn may be another's art photo). Thus the request literally requires a search of all records in the company, including all e-mail, to try to determine if any of these records meet this elusive criterion.

Magistrate Judge Gerrilyn G. Brill, who is very experienced in discovery issues, understood this flaw well, and held:

> As an initial matter, the Court finds that Plaintiffs' discovery requests were extremely broad. The original requests were not limited by time, sender, or recipient. Even as later revised by Plaintiffs, the requests would require a search of all e-mails of all employees in the Atlanta North and Atlanta South branches for a six-year period. Moreover, it is unclear how Defendant would determine whether e-mails were "relating to or evidencing the presence of pornography" or were "of a sexual or gender derogatory nature" without examining the content of each and every e-mail and without making judgments about what constitutes pornography.

Petcou v. C.H. Robinson Worldwide, Inc., supra at *2.

Plaintiffs' counsel should have known that the defendant would object to such a vague and overbroad request. In my experience, such obviously objectionable requests are made either out of naive error or in the hope that defense counsel will err and not make a proper, timely objection, or the court will err and not sustain the objection. Should that happen, and it occasionally does, the requesting party (here plaintiffs' counsel) then has the responding party over a barrel, as it would obviously cost any large company a small fortune to comply with such broad and vague requests.

In this case, defense counsel did their job. The defendant timely objected to the request, including, I assume, the standard litany that the request was vague, overbroad, and designed more to harass with burdensome discovery than to uncover relevant facts. The defendant also objected on the grounds that much of the ESI requested was not reasonably accessible under Rule 26(b)(2)(B).[41] Still, the plaintiffs moved to compel, hoping they would have better luck with the judge. In fairness, the plaintiffs were forced to file a motion on another document category requested, in which the defendant objected to "computer-generated reports of attempts by its employees to access adult website." *Id.* at *1.

Judge Brill granted the plaintiffs' motion on the easily accessible reports but denied it for the pornography-related request. *Id.* She did, however, tell the plaintiffs they could renew the motion, as to e-mails only, if later discovery uncovered new grounds to undercut the defendant's claim that such discovery was overly burdensome. The plaintiffs then initiated what is called "discovery about discovery." They took depositions concerning the defendant's computer system and document retention policy to try to disprove the defendant's Rule 26 claim that the e-mail sought was not reasonably accessible.

If you are ready for a humorous interlude at this point, go online and see the video with John Cleese providing his *in-depth* analysis of Rule 26 (this is sponsored, Iron Mountain,[42] and its funny Web site: friendlyadvicemachine.com).[43]

What Plaintiffs' Rule 26(b)(2)(B) Discovery Uncovered

The depositions taken by the plaintiffs did not really undercut the defendant's inaccessibility position under Rule 26, but did give the plaintiffs grounds to argue spoliation and Rule 37(f)[44] (renumbered as Rule 37(e)).

The depositions established that defendant has an Outlook storage system where e-mail is initially kept on exchange servers. Employees may freely delete any of their own e-mails they choose, and

---

41. http://ralphlosey.wordpress.com/rule-26/.
42. http://www.ironmountain.com/digital/.
43. http://www.friendlyadvicemachine.com/.
44. http://ralphlosey.wordpress.com/rule-37/.

deleted e-mails can only be easily recovered for eight days thereafter. (I assume that the deleted files folder is automatically emptied after a file resides there for eight days, or some equivalent system.) Further, after an employee leaves the company, all of his or her e-mail is deleted from the servers in 10 days.

It is, of course, not difficult to access e-mail located live on an exchange server. But for reasons not fully explained in the opinion (presumptively, most of the key players to this litigation had previously left the company), the court concluded it was unlikely any such e-mails still existed on the servers:

> E-mails of Defendant's current employees that have not been deleted by those employees may still be on Defendants' server and may be retrieved without great expense. However, it is very unlikely that e-mails from the period relevant to this lawsuit, sent to or from individuals who were employed during that period, are still on Defendants' servers.

Id.

The depositions also established that the e-mail exchange servers are backed up onto tapes every three to five days as part of the company's disaster-recovery plan. All of the different servers are included together, and the various e-mails servers are not segregated onto different backup tapes. The opinion implies that these daily tapes are not recycled on a weekly or monthly basis, but are kept for at least two years. The depositions established that the cost to simply retrieve e-mail from a single backup tape was from $325 to $365. (This is a low per-tape retrieval cost and was probably predicted based on restoring a large number of tapes, here approximately 229.) The testimony established that it would cost approximately $79,000 just to recover e-mails for one employee from two years' worth of tapes. *Id.* (The opinion's reference here to two years is why I assume the defendants did not have tapes older than that. At an average of $345 per tape, the defendant thus had approximately 229 tapes to restore.)

RULE 26 APPLIED TO PROHIBIT DISCOVERY

Judge Brill held that the testimony as to the $79,000 restoration cost met the defendant's burden of proof under Rule 26(b)(2)(B) that "deleted e-mails from the period relevant to this lawsuit are not reasonably accessible because of undue burden and cost." The next step in analysis under the rule is to see whether there is good cause to have the ESI produced anyway, in spite of the undue burden and cost. Here the burden of proof shifts to the requesting party to establish good cause under the dictates of Rule 26(b)(2)(C). As Judge Brill explains:

> Rule 26(b)(2)(C) directs the Court to consider, *inter alia*, whether "the burden or expense of the proposed discovery outweighs its likely benefit, considering the needs of the case, the amount in controversy, the parties' resources, the importance of the issues at stake in the action, and the importance of the discovery in resolving the issues."

Id.

Magistrate Judge Brill then goes on to conclude that good cause has not been established, primarily because the overbroad nature of the request would require defendants to examine every e-mail in the system. The volume of e-mail existing over the two-year span of the backup tapes is not stated, but, for a company such as this with 5,300 employees, there would typically be millions of e-mails. The cost to review this much e-mail would be astronomical. Of course, plaintiffs could have tried to avoid all of this with a clear and very focused request to produce.

In addition, plaintiffs could have focused the search somewhat by requesting production of specific pornographic images with known hash values.[45] *See Krause v. Texas*, 243 S.W.3d 95 (1st Dist. Ct. App., Oct. 31, 2007). This is the way police searches are normally conducted on computers to locate pornography, especially child pornography. This kind of hash search can be automated for known files, and thus might have slightly lessened the burden on

---

45. http://ralphlosey.wordpress.com/computer-hash-5f0266c4c326b9 a1ef9e39cb78c352dc/.

the defendant to search for pornography, especially if the requests were limited to known pornographic images. But a hash search technique would still require restoration from backup tapes, and then breakdown of the attached files from the exchange packaging files so that all attachments could then be searched as individual files. You cannot hash search backup tapes, or all e-mails packed together in an exchange format. They can only be searched after the individual e-mails and attachments have been unpacked. The limits of hash search in this kind of situation are very well described in Craig Ball's critique of the original version of this essay,[46] where I overstated the powers of hash. My thanks to Craig Ball for catching and pointing out this mistake to me in such a complimentary manner.

In addition to the disproportionate cost of the overbroad search requested, the judge concluded that the e-mail information sought was indirect and cumulative. The plaintiffs did not claim harassment because they were e-mailed sexually explicit materials, but because they saw these images on others' computers. For that reason, proof of pornographic e-mails was not important enough to the issues in the case to justify the burden. In Judge Brill's words:

> Finally, although the e-mails would corroborate Plaintiffs' testimony regarding the prevalence of pornography in the workplace, they would provide little, if any, relevant information that Plaintiffs themselves have not already provided.

Id. at *2.

Judge Brill employed the analysis of Rule 26(b)(2)(B) and concluded that "the burden or expense of the proposed discovery as a whole outweighs its likely benefit." In fact, her analysis relied primarily upon the proportionality factors stated in Rule 26(b)(2)(C). As other commentators have noted, the good-cause provisions of new Rule 26(b)(2)(B) do not really change discovery analysis. *See* Thomas Y. Allman, "The 'Two-Tiered' Approach to E-Discovery: Has Rule 26(b)(2)(B) Fullfilled Its Promise?,"[47] 14 *Richmond J.L. &*

---

46. http://commonscold.typepad.com/eddupdate/2008/03/making-a-hash-o.html.

47. http://law.richmond.edu/jolt/v14i3/article7.pdf.

Tech. 7, at pgs. 31-33. But still, the two tiered analysis does focus the parties, and the court, on the unique properties of ESI that impact traditional burden and cost analysis, and the problems of finding and retrieving certain types of ESI. *Id.*

This case shows how this kind of two-tiered accessibility road map can assist in attaining a just result. Judge Brill considered the relative inaccessibility of the e-mail on the backup tapes and denied the motion to compel for those e-mails. But the discovery on accessibility had shown that one witness still had active data on the exchange servers. The e-mail of this one witness was easy to access. For that reason, the motion to compel was granted for that one witness only, and the defendant was ordered to produce:

> . . . undeleted e-mails (if any), sent prior to 2007, by a current employee who has been specifically named by Plaintiffs as having had sexually explicit material on his computer;

Thus, this case provides an example of how the focused good-cause analysis of 26(b)(2)(B) can lead the parties and the court to a just result. Under a general Rule 26(b)(2)(C) proportionality analysis, this live data exception for one witness might have been missed, and all e-mail discovery might have been prohibited.

Spoliation Motion

The Rule 26 discovery uncovered the fact that the defendant did not initiate a litigation hold at the time the original EEOC complaint was filed in 2001. Instead, the defendant waited to place a hold on its normal document destruction policies until after suit was filed in 2007. Thus, between 2001 and 2007, the defendant continued to allow current employees to delete any e-mails they wished, even e-mails that could have been relevant to the EEOC claims. The defendant also continued its usual policy of deleting all e-mails from employees who left the company during that time.

The plaintiffs now argue that the defendant should have suspended its usual practice when the EEOC complaint was filed, and the destruction of e-mails thereafter constitutes spoliation, for which sanctions should be entered. This is in accord with the holding of Judge Scheindlin, in *Zubulake IV*, that the duty to preserve was triggered when an EEOC charge was filed, and perhaps even before that, when Zubulake's supervisors were convinced she would sue. *Zubulake v. UBS Warburg LLC*, 220 F.R.D. 212, 218 (S.D. N.Y. 2003).

The problem with the plaintiffs' argument is that they never asked the defendant to save e-mails, and almost six years passed before they filed suit. Instead, they were silent for years before filing the motion for sanctions in 2007. This fact, coupled with the undisputed evidence that all of the e-mail destruction was made in accordance with normal and usual procedures, caused Judge Brill to deny their motion.

> In this case, Defendant deleted its employee's e-mails in accordance with its normal retention and destruction schedule even after an EEOC complaint alleging company-wide sexual harassment had been filed in June of 2001. However, the plaintiffs in that case did not request company-wide preservation of e-mails, nor did they provide Defendant with the names of individuals in Atlanta whose e-mails should be preserved. It does not appear that Defendant acted in bad faith in following its established policy for retention and destruction of e-mails.

Although the opinion does not cite new Rule 37(e),[48] it follows the analysis of the rule and provides a good example of its operation. Here is the language of the new rule:

> New Rule 37: Failure to Make Disclosures or Cooperate in Discovery; Sanctions.
> (f)* Electronically stored information. Absent exceptional circumstances, a court may not impose sanctions under these rules on a party for failing to provide electronically stored information lost as a result of the routine, good faith operation of an electronic information system.

---

48. http://ralphlosey.wordpress.com/rule-37/.

*Note, after 2008 rules renumbering, 37(f) has now become 37(e).

The court found that the e-mails were destroyed according to the company's normal retention and destruction policies. In other words, the information was lost through the routine operation of an electronic information system. Judge Brill found the destruction was in good faith because there was no evidence to the contrary, and because plaintiffs never sent a preservation demand letter.

Concluding Thoughts on Rule 37 Safe Harbor

This case would have presented a closer question if the plaintiffs had sent a demand letter upon filing the EEOC complaint. Then there might be a question as to whether the failure to depart from routine operations was in good faith. For instance, is it good faith to refuse to stop destroying e-mails of departing employees after receiving a demand notice? If you do place a hold on a routine procedure, how long should you continue the hold? Is it reasonable to expect an employer to incur additional expenses for six years to keep old e-mails on the off-chance a lawsuit might someday be filed?

These are difficult questions, the answers to which depend on a host of facts and circumstances. Certainly the mere sending of a demand letter in and of itself should not trigger a hold obligation. In most circumstances the letter should, however, trigger a careful legal evaluation of duties. Is the threat credible enough to warrant a hold notice, and if so, what computer files should be preserved, and what routines should be stayed? A threat might be just barely credible enough to trigger a hold. In those circumstances it might be reasonable to limit the extent of the hold and construe it narrowly.

It is difficult enough to know what information may be discoverable based on the wording of a complaint. It is nearly impossible to get it right before a suit has even been filed. You might expect one kind of lawsuit and end up getting hit by another. This is by no means an exact science. Unless there is a very specific and targeted preservation demand letter, the whole exercise of predicting which ESI might become discoverable is inherently error-prone.

We all need as much help in this difficult guessing game as possible. Fortunately, the Sedona Conference provides us with guidance in its publication *The Sedona Conference Commentary on Legal Holds: The Trigger & the Process.*[49] It lists multiple factors to consider in order to make a reasoned credible threat analysis. If a company considers these factors in good faith and makes a reasoned credible threat assessment, then it should receive the protection of Rule 37 from sanctions when its projections later prove incorrect. For more information and discussion about the Sedona Guideline on holds, see the article "The Sedona Conference Releases Two New Must-Read Commentaries on 'E-mail Management' and 'Legal Holds'" in my first book.

It is important to remember that a Rule 37 safe harbor analysis is only needed in circumstances where the threat evaluation was wrong, or the guesstimate on scope of hold was wrong. The company did not think they would sue, but in fact they did. Or it thought they would sue, but guessed wrong as to what computer evidence would be discoverable. As long as the guess was reasonable and made in good faith, the protection of the rule should remain.

Predicting the future is always hazardous, and no one is right all of the time. This is especially true in the emotional world of litigation, where it is common for tempers to flare and demand letters to fly, only to subside later with time. No one ever knows for sure whether another will later file suit or not. Further, the law is extremely complex, and legal theories change constantly. It is very common for amended complaints to be filed, and new and different theories to arise.

This means that in order for Rule 37 to work, there has to be plenty of room for error, as long as a reasoned, credible process is followed. When it comes to credible threat assessments and the application of Rule 37, courts will have to focus on reasonability of process, not accuracy of crystal ball. Companies threatened with litigation (and these days, who isn't?) can help courts to do that, and thus help themselves stay within the protection of the rule, by docu-

---

49. http://www.thesedonaconference.org/dltForm?did=Legal_holds.pdf.

menting any assessments they make that a threat is not credible. On occasion, when large sums of money or important issues might be involved, a third-party review of such decisions may be appropriate. This way they can confirm the rationality of the assessment and make sure it is not a delusional exercise in wishful thinking.

Where a threat of litigation is accompanied with a specific and focused preservation demand, the rationale for an incredible evaluation should be especially strong. Further, if there is a specific preservation demand, and the decision is made to implement a hold but to preserve less than is demanded, extraordinary care is again advised. In all close questions such as this, you should communicate with opposing counsel and attempt to reach a compromise. If they do not respond or are unwilling to reach a reasonable compromise, then at least document your efforts and the parties' rationales. That will go a long way in providing protection. If all else fails and the potential dollar exposure justifies the expense, a preemptive suit for a declaratory judgment may even be appropriate. You will be breaking new ground, to be sure, but as the landscape of litigation changes, new strategies such as this should be considered to cope with the new challenges these changes present.

BEST BUY WINS KEY E-DISCOVERY RULING IN FRAUD CASE

> *"Oh what a tangled web we weave,*
> *When first we practise to deceive."*
>
> Sir Walter Scott, 1808

In a pair of fraud cases, Best Buy turned aside allegations that its e-discovery efforts were "haphazardous" and used Rule 26(b)(2)(B) to overturn a harsh ruling. *Best Buy Stores, L.P. v. Developers Diversified Realty Corp.*,[50] 2007 WL 4230806 (D. Minn., Nov. 29, 2007). The magistrate's order in the *Developers Diversified Realty (DDR)* case, where Best Buy is suing its landlords for fraud, required Best Buy to produce a vast database of electronic documents. Best Buy

---

50. http://ralphlosey.files.wordpress.com/2007/12/bestbuyvddr.doc.

had prepared this database in another case where it was defending against claims of consumer fraud. The parties agreed that the cost to comply with the order would be $200,000, which was 25% of the total value of the case. The district court judge reversed the discovery order as clearly erroneous. The judge recognized that the order placed an undue burden upon Best Buy that was out of proportion to the size of the case or the importance of the documents sought.

In DDR, Best Buy alleges that 17 of its landlords tried to defraud it by inflating the yearly insurance fees included in common-area maintenance charges. In addition, Best Buy claims breach of contract and breach of fiduciary duty. It has amended the DDR complaint six times to try to make all of these claims stick. Even though the original complaint was filed on September 5, 2005, the Defendants have *still* not answered the complaint.

In addition to having the complaint dismissed multiple times, the landlord defendants were able to obtain a potentially "case-settling" e-discovery order from Magistrate Judge Jeanne Graham on September 5, 2007. The order required Best Buy to search and produce information on leases and insurance from a database Best Buy had prepared for use in a totally unrelated consumer fraud case pending in Seattle, Washington. *Odom v. Microsoft Corp. and Best Buy Co.*, D.C. No. CV-03-02976-MJP (*Odom*).

The database in question is huge. It consists of ESI from the shared drive for all documents in a department (the "V: drive") and from the personal drives of all employees on the main system (the "P: drive"). *Best Buy Stores, L.P. v. Developers Diversified Realty Corp.*, at *5 fn. 2. The database appears to have essentially all of Best Buy's electronic documents that were stored outside its e-mail systems. Best Buy supposedly spent $27,823 a month just for a vendor to store this database.

The parties in *DDR* all agreed that the database contained nonprivileged ESI relevant to the landlord/tenant dispute, but this was not why the database was prepared. Best Buy prepared it to try to defend itself in *Odom,* where it was accused of defrauding consumers in violation of the Racketeer Influenced and Corrupt Organizations Act (RICO). After two years, this putative class-action complaint was dismissed with prejudice on March 16, 2004. *Odom v. Microsoft Corp.*, 2004 WL 5407314 (W.D. Wash. 2004). The Seattle court did not think that Microsoft and Best Buy were Mafia-style racketeers within the meaning of the RICO Act.

Best Buy had thought that was the end of *Odom*, and so the database it created for the case was "downgraded" on July 27, 2006. *DDR* at *3. There is no clear explanation in the *DDR* opinion as to exactly what "downgraded" means, nor why Best Buy waited over two years to do it. This is puzzling, as Best Buy claims it costs $27,823 per month to store the database.

As to the definition of "downgraded," it is only clear that the landlord defendants and magistrate thought that the database was archived by an e-discovery vendor before it was destroyed. Best Buy disputes this and contends the database was simply destroyed, but it could be re-created from backup tapes of the original sources, the "V" and "P" drives.

Ten months after Best Buy allegedly destroyed the database, the Ninth Circuit surprised Best Buy by reversing the dismissal and re-instating the complaint. *Odom v. Microsoft Corp. and Best Buy Co.*, 486 F.3d 541 (9th Cir., May 4, 2007). The appeals court in an en banc decision held that Odom's complaint adequately pled "associated in fact" and "enterprise" under RICO, and also that it pled wire fraud with sufficient particularity. The case was remanded back to the district court for trial. One would think this would cause Best Buy to restore the Odom database so that it could defend the allegations of consumer fraud. Apparently not, since Best Buy vigorously opposed the restoration of the database in *DRR,* and this point is nowhere mentioned in the *DDR* opinion.

After the Ninth Circuit reversal, the news for Best Buy went from bad to worse. Shortly after the case was reinstated, one of the key lawyers representing Best Buy in the state court version of the *Odom* class action suffered a nervous breakdown and admitted that he had fabricated evidence. According to an article by Matthew Hirsch,[51] the Minnesota law firm Burke & Thomas moved to

---

51. http://www.law.com/jsp/article.jsp?id=1180688739517.

withdraw on May 24, 2007, upon its discovery that one of its partners, Timothy Block, "had redacted and altered documents that he later produced to plaintiffs in this matter." Mr. Block voluntarily reported his fraudulent actions to the state bar and took a medical leave of absence.

Plaintiffs' counsel questions the veracity of this story. They seem inclined to blame Best Buy for the fraud, not their lawyers. They point out that they have had a motion for default sanctions pending against Best Buy for bad-faith obstruction of discovery in the state court action since February 2007. To make matters worse, on October 15, 2007, the U.S. Supreme Court let the Ninth Circuit decision stand by refusing certiorari. *Microsoft Corp. v. Odom*, 128 S. Ct. 464, 76 USLW 3058, 76 USLW 3197, 76 USLW 3199 (U.S. Oct. 15, 2007) (No. 07-138).

Against this backdrop, on September 5, 2007, the magistrate in *DDR* found that the *Odom* database was reasonably accessible and ordered Best Buy to restore it from its "downgraded" condition, search it, and produce the relevant data. Magistrate Graham rejected Best Buy's argument that the *Odom* database was protected from discovery under Rule 26(b)(2)(B). She did not consider the alleged cost of $124,000 to restore the database, and $27,823 per month thereafter to store it, to be a large enough cost to render the ESI stored on the *Odom* database "not reasonably accessible" under Rule 26(b)(2)(B). Yet the total amount at issue was $800,000. Assuming it would take at least three months to search this massive database, this one discovery request by the defendants would cost the plaintiff over $200,000. That is 25% of the total amount at issue. This is a textbook example of an undue burden and expense under Rule 26(b)(2)(C).

The district court judge found the magistrate's ruling to be "clearly erroneous" and reversed the decision. Judge Doty held that the high cost to restore and house the *Odom* database rendered it "not reasonably accessible" under Rule 26(b)(2)(B) and (C). Although exactly what was involved in the downgrading of the *Odom* database was disputed, apparently the landlord defendants did not contest the costs of restoration and storage. Instead, they focused their allegations and argument on the alleged incompetence of the Best Buy internal e-Discovery Team, seeking to blame them for the poorly timed downgrading and resultant high costs to restore, search and produce. In the words of Judge Doty:

> The focus of defendants' arguments, both in response to Best Buy's objection and in their own generalized objections, is that Best Buy haphazardly conducted electronic discovery. Specifically, defendants note concern about the lack of involvement from Best Buy's information technology department to aid in the collection of ESI, the search practices of Best Buy's property management department, Best Buy's failure to preserve and search documents related to departed employees and Best Buy's alleged failure to adequately search e-mail archives. Defendants, however, have failed to connect any of these concerns with the specific discovery ordered by the magistrate judge.

This "blame it on the Geek Squad" strategy proved to be a mistake. Judge Doty did not focus on the cause of the relative inaccessibility of the *Odom* database. He focused instead on the high cost and the failure of defendants to demonstrate a substantial benefit from such expensive discovery. The court was persuaded by Best Buy that the relevant information on leases and insurance contained in the *Odom* database was likely also to be found among the paper records, thus there was no need for restoration. In the words of the court:

> Defendants argue that the *Odom* database will contain materials responsive to the discovery ordered by the magistrate judge because Best Buy has yet to search for such materials. However, defendants do not argue that these materials are uniquely available from the *Odom* database or that Best Buy could not more easily obtain the materials from another source. Indeed, the ordered discovery likely exists in hard copy format, and any relevant ESI could be gathered manually without the need for restoration of the *Odom* database.

The court engaged in a formal 26(b)(2)(B) analysis of the discovery dispute, following the wording of the rule. As mentioned, to begin the analysis, the district court judge reversed the magistrate's holding that the *Odom* database was reasonably accessible. The primary basis for the "clearly erroneous" reversal was the cost, and that the database "would have to be restored from original sources." *DDR* at *3. The meaning of the "restoration from original sources" point was not explained.

The landlord defendants argued that this analysis was flawed because the *Odom* database was easily searchable before it was "downgraded" on July 27, 2006. The defendants claim that since Best Buy filed the *DDR* suit in 2005, it was clearly under a duty to preserve the database a year later. The defendants argued that even though the database was created for another case, Best Buy should have known that it contained ESI relevant to this case. Thus, Best Buy had a duty to preserve it. The defendants argued that Best Buy violated its duty when it downgraded the *Odom* database, and should not be rewarded for this spoliation.

The district court agreed with the defendants that Best Buy should have known that the defendants in *DDR* would seek information in the database because it contained relevant information. But, as Judge Doty pointed out, the *Odom* database was so extensive that it would have information relevant to any lawsuit involving Best Buy. Since there were no specific discovery requests pending against the *Odom* database until March 21, 2007, Best Buy did not have an obligation to keep paying more than $27,000 per month to store it. As the court explains:

> Because of the vast quantity of information in the *Odom* database, Best Buy should have been on notice that defendants would seek discovery of some of that information. The database, however, would have been potentially relevant to virtually any litigation involving Best Buy because of the quantity and nature of the information it contained. Absent specific discovery requests or additional facts suggesting that the database was of particular relevance to this litigation, FN3 the court determines that Best Buy did not have an obligation to maintain the *Odom* database at a monthly cost of over $27,000. Moreover, by downgrading the database, Best Buy did not destroy the information it contained but rather removed it from a searchable format. Therefore, Best Buy

did not have a duty to preserve the *Odom* database as of July 27, 2006, and it need not restore the information to searchable format unless defendants establish good cause.

The court then considered the good-cause exception of Rule 26(b)(2)(B), wherein a court may still compel production of not-reasonably-accessible ESI if "the requesting party shows good cause, considering the limitations of Rule 26(b)(2)(C)." Rule 26(b)(2)(B).[52] Rule 26(b)(2)(C) limits otherwise permissible discovery if the court determines that:

(i) the discovery sought is unreasonably cumulative or duplicative, or is obtainable from some other source that is more convenient, less burdensome, or less expensive; (ii) the party seeking discovery has had ample opportunity by discovery in the action to obtain the information sought; or (iii) the burden or expense of the proposed discovery outweighs its likely benefit, taking into account the needs of the case, the amount in controversy, the parties' resources, the importance of the issues at stake in the litigation, and the importance of the proposed discovery in resolving the issues.

Since the court was persuaded that the leasing and insurance information was probably obtainable from sources other than the *Odom* database, and since the costs to restore the database were so high, the court concluded that the landlord defendants had not established good cause. For these reasons, the court sustained Best Buy's objections to the magistrate's order and held that it did not have to restore the *Odom* database.

Pragmatically, this ruling rescued Best Buy. The magistrate's earlier ruling would have forced Best Buy into a cheap settlement of its case against its landlords. It was unlikely Best Buy would have been willing to pay 25 percent of the total amount at issue for an unrecoverable cost just to respond to one of many discovery requests.

---

52. http://ralphlosey.wordpress.com/rule-26/.

DECLARATORY JUDGMENT APPROACH TO BURDENSOME PRE-LITIGATION PRESERVATION DEMAND TRIED AND REJECTED: IS THIS A CASE OF "NO GOOD DEED GOES UNPUNISHED"?

Guest Blog

by Michael Simon[53]

In the final paragraph of last week's post, Ralph made the following suggestion on a potential way to deal with an onerous pre-litigation hold demand:

> If all else fails, and the potential dollar exposure justifies the expense, a preemptive suit for a declaratory judgment may even be appropriate. You will be breaking new ground, to be sure, but as the landscape of litigation changes, new strategies such as this should be considered to cope with the new challenges these changes present.

Unbeknownst to Ralph, at the very time he was writing those prophetic words, the U.S. District Court for the Eastern District of Texas was giving a thumbs down to that very idea. The case is *Texas v. City of Frisco,* 2008 WL 828055 (E.D. Tex. Mar. 27, 2008).[54] In reality, as I will explain below, this may be a case where two rights make a wrong: The plaintiff did such a good job of complying with the litigation hold that the court could not understand plaintiff's problem.

In *Frisco,* the State of Texas was faced with the following dilemma: The Texas Department of Transportation (TxDot[55]) was planning to convert portions of State Highway 121 from a freeway to a toll road.[56] Apparently, a portion to be con-

---

53. Mike Simon is co-chair with Ralph Losey of Akerman Senterfitt's national e-discovery practice group. Mike is located in Akerman's Los Angeles office. http://www.akerman.com/public/attorneys/aBiography.asp?id=984.

54. http://ralphlosey.files.wordpress.com/2008/04/texasvfrisco.doc.

55. http://www.txdot.gov/default.htm.

56. http://www.txdot.gov/news/local_news/dallas_news/050-2006.htm.

verted went through the City of Frisco.[57] The City seemingly did not want the pleasure of paying tolls and was (and perhaps still is) considering filing a challenge to the Environmental Re-evaluation of the State Highway pursuant to the National Environmental Policy Act (NEPA), 42 U.S.C. §§ 4331-4347.[58] As a kickoff to this *potential* litigation, on April 13, 2007, the City sent TxDot a letter titled "Notice Regarding Preservation of Electronic Data."[59]

This preservation demand does (perhaps intentionally) a poor job of specifying the subject matter of the demand. It broadly states that TxDot should preserve "electronic data associated with SH 121 and its conversion from a freeway to either a privatized or public tollway." As to the types of ESI to be preserved, the demand is fairly well drafted and imposes a heavy burden on TxDot.

- The demand explicitly instructs TxDot to "immediately preserve potentially relevant Electronic Data including, without limitation, information with the earlier of a Created or Last Modified date on or after January 1, 2004 through the date of this demand."

- The demand identifies a relatively comprehensive and quite burdensome list of potential ESI file types to be preserved, including items such as "deleted files," "computer system activity logs," "all file fragments and backup files containing Electronic Data," and "all backup tapes or other storage media."

- The demand instructs TxDot to "preserve and retain all Electronic Data" which "relates to, mentions and/or is received or generated by TxDot . . . in connection with the plan and/or project to convert SH 121 into a tollway or any subsequent related work/project." The demand specifically states that this includes all communications with: the contractor and other bidders for the project; the City of Frisco; any of numerous Texas government departments; and the Legislature and the Governor.

---

57. http://www.ci.frisco.tx.us/.
58. http://caselaw.lp.findlaw.com/casecode/uscodes/42/chapters/55/subchapters/i/toc.html.
59. http://ralphlosey.files.wordpress.com/2008/04/exb-a.pdf.

- The demand even reminds TxDot that "you must intervene to prevent the loss of information as a result of routine operations, protocols and/or destruction policies."

Perhaps with tongue slightly planted in cheek, the demand offers that "[i]t is not our intent to obstruct TxDot's everyday operation," but then goes on to remind TxDot that "your diligent and good faith compliance of this request should also include modification or suspension of features of your information system, which in routine operation may cause the loss of relevant information. . . ."

As with any litigation hold demand, TxDot had to make a decision: did it need to comply with the demand? If so, what is the scope of the preservation duty?

Is There an Obligation to Preserve Pre-litigation?

The Federal Rules do not actually require the implementation of a pre-litigation hold. *See* Committee Note, Rule 37(f). As explained by footnote 13 in "The Sedona Conference Commentary on Legal Holds"[60] (the Commentary):

> The Advisory Committee on Civil Rules debated whether it could specify preservation obligations in the Federal Rules of Civil Procedure but ultimately decided it could not do so. Rather, the Committee opted to temper the impact of preservation obligations by protecting parties from the imposition of sanctions under the Rules for the failure to preserve certain materials in limited circumstances.

But under the circumstances here, with the City putting TxDot on notice that it was contemplating what would obviously be massive litigation and making an express demand for preservation, there really is little question that TxDot would have been taking a massive risk to ignore the City's demand. As the Commentary puts it, "The duty to preserve relevant information arises when litigation is 'rea-

---

60. http://www.thesedonaconference.org/dltForm?did=Legal_holds.pdf.

sonably anticipated.'" And the City's preservation demand meets almost every one of the factors listed under the Commentary's Guideline 4, "The determination of whether litigation is reasonably anticipated should be based on a good faith and reasonable evaluation of relevant facts and circumstances." These factors include:

1. The nature and specificity of the complaint or threat;
2. The position of the party making the claim;
3. Whether the threat is direct, implied or inferred;
4. The strength, scope, or value of a potential claim; and
5. Press and/or industry coverage of the issue either directly pertaining to the client, or of complaints brought against someone similarly situated in the industry.

Given that it would have been difficult if not impossible for TxDot to treat the City's letter as anything but putting it on notice that litigation was "reasonably anticipated," TxDot really had no choice but to implement a litigation hold. Not so clear is what the scope of that hold should have been, and this is where TxDot, in trying to do everything right, may have shot itself in the foot.

TxDot's Dilemma: How to Resolve an Overbroad Pre-litigation Hold Demand

The City's demand for all ESI "associated with SH 121" and "its conversion from a freeway," including to and from every possible party and from many sources (such as backup tapes) that were likely inaccessible, was unquestionably burdensome for an agency as massive as TxDot. Further, according to the complaint TxDot ultimately filed, most of that information was irrelevant because (according to TxDot) the City's claim must be brought under the Federal Administrative Procedure Act[61] (APA). According to TxDot, Under NEPA and the APA, plaintiffs are generally not entitled to discovery because "courts limit their review to the agency record specifically compiled for the Environmental Re-evaluation."

---

61. http://www.law.cornell.edu/uscode/5/usc_sup_01_5_10_I_30_5.html.

Clearly this left TxDot in a quandary: if the City had initiated litigation, then TxDot could have tried to resolve these issues at the mandatory Rule 26(f) conference and, if necessary, brought a motion for protective order under Rules 26 and 34. But because this was pre-litigation, TxDot did not have a clearly defined path. The path that TxDot chose is certainly hard to criticize, but, as discussed below, that choice may have ultimately contributed to its failure in court.

Even though the City Refused to Clarify or Limit Its Demands, TxDot Took Extraordinary Steps to Comply before It Ever Filed Its Plea with the Court

TxDot's initial approach was twofold: (1) TxDot made repeated pleas to the City to clarify and narrow the subject matter of the City's demands; and (2) TxDot immediately initiated a very thorough and aggressive effort to preserve *everything*. Whether out of spite or an inability to clearly articulate what it really wanted, the City refused to provide any clarification and did not even respond to several of TxDot's letters. TxDot's exhibits to its ultimate court filing show a huge (and certainly costly) effort to preserve all ESI. For example, within three days of receipt of the City's demand, TxDot sent an e-mail preservation notice to approximately 200 "key players." That notice warned the key players in part that:

> TxDot has an affirmative obligation to comply with the request for preservation. . . . This obligation requires initiation of a litigation hold to ensure relevant documents are preserved. . . . A 'litigation hold' requires intervention in the routine operation . . . to prevent loss of information. . . . Please preserve any electronic e-data described in the attached letter, including all backup tapes or other storage media, whether online or offline, and refrain from overwriting or deleting information that may contain the electronic data. . . . This includes turning off any auto-delete function on Groupwise.

Shortly after, TxDot informed the key players that the preservation should include:

[I]nformation stored not only on servers, desktop computers, and laptops, but also on a personal digital assistant (PDA—i.e., iPAQ, BlackBerry, Treo), flash drive or other media storage devices. Information that is stored in more than one, or even all, of these transient media must be preserved in a secure and recoverable electronic environment. If you perform official state business related to SH 121 on a home computer or any other device, that information is also subject to the litigation hold.

A short time later, TxDot published a more formal protocol for the litigation hold and sent its key players and each of its many offices detailed instructions[62] for the preservation of e-mails and other ESI in a segregated, protected network storage area as well as procedures for the restoration of documents from backup tapes. These instructions made clear that the process was being standardized and implemented in every office in the State.

Too LittleToo Late:TxDot Gets Fed Up and Finally Seeks the Court's Assistance

After about three months of this circus, TxDot apparently came to appreciate just how massive and expensive this unfettered preservation task was going to be (according to its papers, it had already spent hundreds of hours in compliance). Finally, TxDot hit on the strategy that Ralph posited last week: On August 14, 2007, TxDot filed its Plaintiff's Original Complaint and Request for Declaratory Relief and Protective Order[63] in the Sherman Division of the U.S. District Court for the Eastern District of Texas. TxDot explained the requested relief this way:

TxDot requests the court to enter a declaratory judgment ruling that the City's letter violates the Federal Rules of Civil Procedure and is contrary to rules governing a NEPA/APA

---

62. http://ralphlosey.files.wordpress.com/2008/04/exb-f.pdf.
63. http://ralphlosey.files.wordpress.com/2008/04/tx-v-city-of-frisco-complaint-la021316.pdf.

claim in federal court. TxDot requests this court's protection from . . . the broad scope and undue burden of the litigation hold and requests a declaratory judgment releasing TxDot from the litigation hold as it violates the Federal Rules. . . .

Even though the exhibits TxDot attached certainly show the burden to someone experienced in e-Discovery for all of the reasons discussed above, TxDot's complaint did a poor job of quantifying or otherwise explaining this burden to the court. Perhaps this is part of what led the court to take a pass on this one.

The Court Dismisses TxDot's Complaint as "Unripe"

Magistrate Don D. Bush[64] did not treat the City's plea kindly. Citing to *Shields v. Norton*, 289 F.3d 832, 835 (5th Cir. 2002), Judge Bush noted:

> A suit for declaratory relief, while allowing a party to anticipate a suit and seek a judicial resolution, must nevertheless meet this keystone limitation. In hornbook form, a declaratory action must be ripe in order to be justiciable, and is ripe only where an actual controversy exists. An actual controversy exists where a substantial controversy of sufficient immediacy and reality exists between parties having adverse legal interests. Ordinarily whether particular facts are sufficiently immediate to establish an actual controversy yields answers on a case-by-case basis. Whether a declaratory action is ripe, by its very structure, pushes against our insistence upon mature disputes. That is, it contemplates an ex ante determination of rights that exists in some tension with traditional notions of ripeness.

Judge Bush immediately hit upon the fact that it was not TxDot's rights in the underlying environmental dispute that were at issue, but the much more amorphous concept of the scope of potential future discovery:

---

64. http://www.txed.uscourts.gov/Judges/Bush/Bush.htm.

Notably, it is not the City's potential claims regarding the tollway project that forms the basis of the State's declaratory judgment action. Rather, the State seeks a declaratory judgment as to how rules of discovery and procedure might be applied by the Court to its preservation of documents in that potential suit. . . . As a result of the City's litigation hold letter, the State asks this Court to determine "[w]hether it is a violation of Rules 26(f) and 34 to require an entity to broadly preserve and retain any and all electronic documents based on a required [sic] made before suit is filed."

Citing to *Orix Credit Alliance, Inc.*, 212 F.3d at 896, 897, Judge Bush did note that a threat of litigation can indeed establish a controversy upon which declaratory judgment can be based, but he did not find that TxDot had presented such a threat, since he found that the City's letter "only states that *potential* exists for litigation" and not an actual threat. However, perhaps TxDot's true failure is explained by the court's very next paragraph:

Moreover, even if the Court were to insert itself into the pre-litigation discovery process (which it declines to do), the correspondence attached to Plaintiff's Complaint does not evidence any concrete or developed disagreement by the parties as to the preservation of documents. A pre-enforcement action like Plaintiff's is only ripe "if any remaining questions are purely legal . . . [and] further factual development" is not required for effective judicial review. The facts here are not fully developed. The dispute is abstract, "hypothetical and not suited for judicial determination." (citations omitted)

This may be the indication of two rights making a wrong: What Judge Bush is really saying here is that, after reviewing the exhibits, he sees: (1) a demand made by the City; (2) TxDot asking for clarification (right #1); *but* (2) TxDot *fully complying anyway!* (right #2). Since he sees a demand and the clear appearance of the ability to comply, what is the controversy? As mentioned above, TxDot does *not* quantify in any way the cost of its compliance efforts. All the court sees is demand and compliance, hardly the subject of a ripe dispute.

What Else Could TxDot Have Done? Limited Itself to Good-Faith Compliance

Does this mean that Ralph's original thesis of using a declaratory relief action to avoid an overburdensome pre-litigation demand is doomed to failure? Perhaps not. In fact, the bromide that Judge Bush offers at the very end of his decision may shed some light on the better initial course TxDot should have taken to set up the issue:

> Further, while they do not specifically address pre-suit litigation hold requests, the Rules of Civil Procedure contemplate that the parties will act in good faith in the preservation and production of documents. Fed. R. Civ. P. 37. The Court encourages both parties to handle the preservation of documents in response to their respective litigation holds in such good faith. The Court declines, however, to intervene now and issue an advisory opinion as to what actions by the State would constitute good faith as to the City's request. (emphasis added)

The court is reminding the parties that their real obligation is to act in good faith. Perhaps TxDot forgot that good-faith compliance and total unquestioning compliance are not necessarily the same thing.

Part Two of the Commentary, "Implementing the Legal Hold," explains that:

> When implementing a legal hold, it is important to recognize that the duty to preserve extends only to relevant information. While relevance is broadly defined under the Federal Rules of Civil Procedure (see Fed. R. Civ. P. 26(b)(1)), it is not without limits. As noted by one court, there is no broad

requirement to preserve information that is not relevant: "Must a corporation, upon recognizing the threat of litigation, preserve every shred of paper, every e-mail or electronic document, and every backup tape? The answer is clearly, 'no.' Such a rule would cripple large corporations." (citing to *Zubulake IV*, 220 F.R.D. at 217)

In other words, there must be some analysis of the *proportionality* of the potential burden with the relevance of the information sought to be preserved. Not everything necessarily need be preserved, especially if, in TxDot's evaluation, the data was not even relevant to the anticipated dispute because either: (1) it was not part of the administrative record, or (2) it pertained to other portions of SH 121 not in dispute. While TxDot did try to engage the City in a conversation on the limits of relevance, when the City refused, TxDot simply gave in and tried to preserve everything.

Perhaps TxDot would have been better served by taking a slightly more aggressive stance. Rather than assuming there was nothing it could do without court intervention, TxDot could have responded to the City's demand by informing them that it was so overbroad and overburdensome that TxDot would *not* attempt to comply but would gladly meet with the City in an effort to narrow the scope to something with which TxDot could comply. With that type of explicit notice, the City would then be placed in a quandary: either it could negotiate with TxDot (as it would have to do in litigation under Rule 26 anyway) or risk that a court would ultimately be unsympathetic with any complaint about missing documents because, after all, the City *was* placed on notice.

Unfortunately for TxDot, it may now have precluded itself from this lower-cost option because, through its now rejected complaint, TxDot has established that in fact it *can* comply with the City's request, making it less likely that a court will agree that the effort was too burdensome to impose. Thus, TxDot's attempt to do things "right" has created the "wrong" that TxDot is stuck with a very burdensome task.

Yet another example of my favorite quote from U.S. Congress-woman, Ambassador and playwright Claire Booth Luce:[65] "No good deed goes unpunished."

CALIFORNIA PROPOSES E-DISCOVERY LAWS THAT GOVERNOR SCHWARZENEGGER WILL WANT TO TERMINATE

New e-discovery rules[66] were proposed in California in early 2008 that were, in my opinion, unfair because they did not adequately protect litigants from requests for inaccessible data. The proposal reversed the balance of Federal Rule 26(b)(2)(B) and thereby opened the door for unreasonable, expensive e-discovery.

The essay that follows was read by many and led to a storm of controversy, as I had intended. It acted as a wake-up call to help mobilize opposition to what many considered to a pro-plainitff law. Several lawyers and groups ended up opposing the law as originally written. This led to several significant revisions to the original pro-posal here critiqued. The end result still left a lot to be desired in my opinion, but at least ended up less pro-plaintiff, pro-requestor, than when it started.

At this time, the revised law was passed by the California legis-lature but vetoed by Governor Schwarzenegger because of budget disputes having nothing to do with the merits of the proposed rules. It remains to be seen whether he will veto the new procedural rules, even after these revisions. When and if a final version of the Califor-nia rules is actually enacted and signed into law, I will ask Michael Simon, who practices law in California and has helped me to under-stand what is going on here, to post a detailed essay on my blog[67] explaining the new law. In the meantime, you may find this earlier critique to be interesting and informative.

---

65. http://en.wikipedia.org/wiki/Clare_Boothe_Luce.

66. http://ralphlosey.files.wordpress.com/2008/01/califproposedrulesand invitetocomment.pdf.

67. http://ralphlosey.files.wordpress.com.

California Law

California law governing discovery is a patchwork of court rules and statutes. The proposal for new laws to govern electronic discovery amends both the rules and statutes. The statutory side of the proposal, § 2031.060(a) & (b), contains the imbalanced provisions governing inaccessible ESI. These proposed revisions should be terminated rather than become law. The proposal is now in its final stages, so if you want to be heard on this issue, you need to act fast. January 25, 2008, is the deadline to submit public comments[68] on this proposal.

Generally State e-Discovery Rules Are a Good Thing

I strongly favor enactment of state e-discovery rules. Attorneys and state court judges need the guidance and clarity they can bring. So too do litigants embroiled in state court justice systems. They need to know their e-discovery rights and obligations, and need some modicum of predictability and uniformity in ruling. Plaintiffs need to know they can sue in state court and obtain relevant evidence in defendants' computers, which is, after all, where most evidence resides today. Conversely, defendants need to know they will be protected from overly burdensome and unrealistic computer requests. Fair rules balance these competing interests and provide necessary predictability and consistency of adjudication. Fair e-discovery procedure rules thereby significantly further justice in a state court system.

Unfair state e-discovery rules may still provide some certainty and consistency, at least within the state court system, but they do not further justice. Instead, they promote the settlement or adjudication of disputes for reasons other than the merits. Like most attorneys, I would rather have no e-discovery rules at all than unfair rules that favor one side over the other. Also, since we have a dual federal and state system, state rules that are markedly different from federal may produce inconsistent results for the same party, depending upon which court

---

68. http://www.courtinfo.ca.gov/invitationstocomment/commentform. htm.

and set of rules they are under. Unfair rules in state court will also promote a flight to the federal court system or to private arbitration.

Unfortunately, as I explain in detail below, California is on the brink of enacting of what appears to me, and many others, to be blatantly unfair e-discovery rules.[69] In fact, I know of no other rules anywhere in the country that are potentially as oppressive to business and large organizations as the new rules proposed for California. This is a fast-moving train, but it may not be too late to stop. As mentioned, the comment[70] period closes on January 25, 2008, but after that, the California legislature must still approve and enact the enabling statutes. So, even if e-discovery lawyers fail, Governor Schwarzenegger still has plenty of time to play the *Terminator* role once again, and kill the bill as bad for California business.

Battle Between Two Types of Lawyers

The federal e-discovery rules were years in the making, and everyone had plenty of time to comment on their structure and wording. The federal rules are not perfect, but they represent a thoughtful and fair balance between the diverging interests of the plaintiffs and defense bars, between the requesters and producers of ESI. At the end of the day, both plaintiff and defense lawyers were unhappy with the new federal rules. Each side had some legitimate complaints about the new rules, but both were generally satisfied that they were, overall, fair and balanced.

Most states in the country are now considering their own e-discovery rules. A few already have[71] done so. As a result, many states are now embroiled in similar battles between the divergent interests of the plaintiff and defense bars, between the small litigants with few computers and little ESI and businesses with thousands of computers and terabytes[72] of ESI. If either side in this perennial battle

69. http://ralphlosey.files.wordpress.com/2008/01/califproposedrulesand invitetocomment.pdf.
70. http://www.courtinfo.ca.gov/invitationstocomment/commentform. htm.
71. http://www.ediscoverylaw.com/2008/01/articles/resources/current-listing-of-states-that-have-enacted-ediscovery-rules/.
72. http://en.wikipedia.org/wiki/Terabyte.

gains the upper hand, the result is unfair rules. For instance, rules that protect ESI-producing parties too much, generally businesses and large organizations, encourage more *Qualcomm*-type cases,[73] and so subvert justice. But rules that impose too much burden upon large organizations and benefit the ESI-requesting parties, typically plaintiffs with few computers, can be just as bad. They cause defense settlements driven by the costs and exposure of e-discovery instead of the merits, if any, of the plaintiffs' case. Unfair state rules also drive litigants away from state courts and into the federal system, or private adjudication. This so-called "flight to quality" is already occurring for a variety of reasons, including the lack of any state rules on e-discovery. Unfair rules will only accelerate this trend.

The battle between the competing interests of the plaintiff and defense bars has been raging in California, too, but here the plaintiffs' bar is about to score a major victory. The California Judicial Council is poised to ask the state legislature to enact what appears to be the most one-sided rules yet on e-discovery. These rules discard the two-tiered protection provided by Federal Rule 26(b)(2)(B). If enacted, the new law will force thousands of businesses and other large organizations to apply for a protective order in almost every case. In private, the plaintiffs' bar has got to be all smiles and high-fives. In public, they will, of course, hide their glee, especially from state court judges, and complain about something in the proposal. But there is no denying that the California proposal represents a substantial departure from the federal rules.

Who Is Behind the Proposed California Law?

I will go into detail about the deficiencies of the proposed law, but first it is instructive to try to understand how this proposal came about. By my introduction, you might suspect these rules are being proposed by one of the many academies of trial lawyers. Those are exclusive clubs of plaintiffs' lawyers, where you can only join if you swear that you do no defense work. But that is not the case. No, these rules have been written and proposed by an esteemed Califor-

---

73. http://ralphlosey.wordpress.com/2008/01/11/qualcomms-monumental-discovery-violations-provokes-only-wimpy-sanctions/.

nia judicial institution known as the California Judicial Council.[74] It describes itself as "the policy-making body of the California courts" and is led by the chief justice of the California Supreme Court. It has 21 members: two justices from the supreme court, three judges from courts of appeal, 10 trial court judges, two legislators, and four practicing lawyers. Two of the four practicing lawyers on the council are criminal lawyers, one of whom is a past president of the California Bar. Another of the lawyers is an assistant city attorney for Oakland. The fourth lawyer happens to be one of the most prominent plaintiff's lawyers in the country, a past president of the International Academy of Trial Lawyers.

These are very well-respected people with excellent reputations. I mean them no offense and hope that they will forgive my strong opposition to this particular rules proposal. They are all experienced lawyers and judges, but as far as I can see, none have any particular expertise in e-discovery. This means they are getting their advice from other unnamed e-discovery experts, where, I fear, the concerns of business and the defense bar have not been adequately represented. This is the only explanation I have for how and why the California Judicial Council is now—unwittingly, I suspect—supporting and recommending the enactment of e-discovery rules so divergent from the federal norm.

A Defense of the Judiciary

I know many will wonder why the judiciary, who make up most of the Judicial Council, would support rules that, to e-discovery insiders at least, obviously seem to favor one segment of the bar over another. A short digression in defense of the judiciary is in order, for I often hear unfounded attacks upon judges and would like to set the record straight. As a litigation attorney for 28 years, I have appeared before hundreds of judges, and I count several of them as friends. In my experience, it is rare to find a judge who is biased toward either the plaintiff or defense bar, although it does sometimes happen. An attorney may have had an orientation when he or she was in private practice, but they almost always rise above such a bias once they

---

74. http://www.courtinfo.ca.gov/jc/.

become a judge. The role of a judge is far different from that of a private attorney advocating for a particular client, or type of client.

I do not think for a moment that the judges behind the California Judicial Counsel have consciously taken a sudden turn to favor one side of the bar over another. The Judicial Counsel members include some of the most distinguished jurists in the state. I am sure they *think* this is a fair and balanced proposal, otherwise they would not support it. But the truth is, sitting state court judges, especially senior judges and appellate judges such as those on the Judicial Counsel, are not in the best position to formulate e-discovery rules. They are relatively naive about e-discovery issues and lack practical experience. Unlike in almost every other area of the law where judges are called upon to suggest changes to civil rules of procedure, few state court judges have any significant experience as private civil litigators in this new and fast-changing field.

In fact, when most of the judges on the bench today were in private practice, including those running the California Judicial Council, there was no such thing as e-discovery. Their only experience with this very complex subject, if any, has come from hearing cases on the bench. For that reason, most do not have a very good picture of what is going on behind the scenes in e-discovery outside of their courtrooms. Of course, there are some notable exceptions to this rule. For instance, a few federal magistrates by now have extensive experience with e-discovery issues and are very knowledgeable in this area despite a lack of prior private practice experience. But most state court judges do not see these issues very often.

The experience problem is compounded for appellate court judges. They are usually more senior and not as involved with technology. Further, appellate courts rarely hear discovery appeals, much less grapple firsthand with e-discovery issues. All too often, their knowledge of e-discovery disputes comes solely from reading about the exceptional disaster case like *Qualcomm*.[75] These cases tend to create a false impression of everyday e-discovery practice and little sympathy for the dilemma most large companies face in this area.

---

75. http://ralphlosey.wordpress.com/2007/08/18/heavy-sanctions-loom-against-attorneys-for-e-discovery-and-other-aggrivated-litigation-abuses/.

Even the trial judges who actually do see and hear e-discovery disputes firsthand see only a small segment of e-discovery practice. The jurists' view is primarily based on the few cases in which e-discovery issues are taken to them for resolution. But the reality is, most e-discovery-related activity is behind the scenes and completely out of sight of the presiding judge. For instance, in federal court, 98 percent of all cases settle. State courts may try more cases, but still the vast majority of lawsuits, especially commercial cases, settle and are not tried. The judges rarely know the true cause of the settlement of any case, much less the parties' confidential settlement communications.

This means that most judges are completely unaware of the fact, well known to most e-discovery practitioners, that many cases today settle and/or settle for too much, because of e-discovery concerns. The merits of a case can easily become secondary to the potential exposure and risks of e-discovery expenses. Although some large organizations today are prepared to efficiently respond to e-discovery, many are not and are an easy target for the plaintiffs' bar, which is, by and large, far more aware of this exposure than the judiciary. In short, most judges, especially state court judges and appeals court judges, are not aware of the tremendous leverage and bargaining power that uncontrolled e-discovery, or even the threat of such e-discovery, provides to a plaintiff suing a "Goliath" defendant with tons of computers.

What Is Wrong with the Proposed Law?

In the federal system and most states, all rules of procedure are promulgated by the supreme courts, and in the federal system, subject only to legislative veto. But they do things differently in California. The proposed new e-discovery rules are actually made up of both statutes and traditional court rules adopted by the Supreme Court of California. Only two amendments to actual rules of court are included in the California proposal. The bulk of the amendments are contained in statutory proposals. The two rules are Rule 3.724 (Duty to Meet and Confer) and Rule 3.728 (Case Management Order). They mirror the federal rules and are fine as written. These two rule revisions will not, however, be promulgated by the California Supreme Court unless the statutes proposed by the Judicial Council are also adopted by the legislature as written. That should not happen. Here's why:

One of the biggest e-discovery problems all large organizations face is the huge cost to search, locate, and produce so-called "inaccessible" information. In fact, all information is accessible; the questions is, at what cost? In e-discovery language, "inaccessible" ESI means ESI that is "not reasonably accessible." It is information that can only be retrieved and produced at disproportionate cost and labor. That typically includes such things as backup tapes, legacy computer systems, slack space on hard drives, and damaged CDs. Many more examples could be provided.

The proposed state laws are unfair primarily because, unlike the federal rules, they fail to provide meaningful protection against discovery of inaccessible ESI. Instead, they open the door to widespread misuse of requests for this type of information.

This key protection provided in the federal rules is found in Rule 26(b)(2)(B):

> (B) A party need not provide discovery of electronically stored information from sources that the party identifies as not reasonably accessible because of undue burden or cost. On motion to compel discovery or for a protective order, the party from whom discovery is sought must show that the information is not reasonably accessible because of undue burden or cost. If that showing is made, the court may nonetheless order discovery from such sources if the requesting party shows good cause, considering the limitations of Rule 26(b)(2)(C). The court may specify conditions for the discovery.

This rule sets up a two-tiered system, wherein not-reasonably-accessible ESI comprises the second tier of discovery. You are protected from the expense and burden of searching and producing such information, which can cost millions of dollars, unless you are faced with a motion to compel. Even then, if a motion to compel is made and you must then respond, you need only provide proof of burden at that time. If you prove undue burden and cost, the discovery should be prohibited unless good cause is shown pursuant to the terms of 26(B)(2)(C), which provides for three types of considerations:

> (i) the discovery sought is unreasonably cumulative or duplicative, or is obtainable from some other source that is more convenient, less burdensome, or less expensive; (ii) the party seeking discovery has had ample opportunity by discovery in the action to obtain the information sought; or (iii) the burden or expense of the proposed discovery outweighs its likely benefit, taking into account the needs of the case, the amount in controversy, the parties' resources, the importance of the issues at stake in the litigation, and the importance of the proposed discovery in resolving the issues.

The Federal Rules of Civil Procedure Commentary provides additional important guidance with seven factors a court should consider in making this "good cause" analysis:

> Appropriate considerations may include: (1) the specificity of the discovery request; (2) the quantity of information available from other and more easily accessed sources; (3) the failure to produce relevant information that seems likely to have existed but is no longer available on more easily accessed sources; (4) the likelihood of finding relevant, responsive information that cannot be obtained from other, more easily accessed sources; (5) predictions as to the importance and usefulness of the further information; (6) the importance of the issues at stake in the litigation; and (7) the parties' resources.

The two-tiered system in Rule 26(b)(2)(B) is, in my opinion and that of many others, the key provision to making the federal rules balanced. Litigants with large computer systems depend upon the carefully worded provisions of this rule for protection from overly burdensome requests. Without this rule, they are vulnerable to ESI requests that exploit the complexity of their systems and force settlement to avoid exorbitant costs.

The e-discovery statutes proposed in California gut this protection entirely, and for that reason alone they are unfair and imbalanced. As Geoff Howard, an e-discovery attorney in San Francisco, puts it in his recent article on the proposed rules:[76] "The California proposal reverses the federal court balance."

Specifically, the new language proposed for California statute § 2031.060(a) & (b) requires the production of all ESI requested unless a motion for protective order is filed and granted. This reverses the order and burden in the federal rules, where the requesting party had to file a motion to compel. You can bet that if these procedural statutes pass, there will be a flood of motion practice in California state courts, starting with motions for protective orders in every case to try to prevent the otherwise mandatory search and production of inaccessible ESI. The motions for protection will try to establish undue burden and expense.

Here is the exact language of proposed § 2031.060(b) that spells out the respondents' (typically large defendants') new obligations:

> (a) When an inspection, copying, testing, or sampling of documents, tangible things, or places, or electronically stored information has been demanded, the party to whom the demand has been directed, and any other party or affected person or organization, may promptly move for a protective order. This motion shall be accompanied by a meet and confer declaration under Section 2016.040.
> (b) The party or affected person or organization seeking a protective order regarding the production, inspection, copying, testing, or sampling of electronically stored information on the basis that such information is not reasonably accessible because of undue burden or expense bears the burden of so demonstrating.

---

76. http://www.bingham.com/Media.aspx?MediaID=6409.

Under the proposed California law, the burden of proof does not stop there. Here is the full language of subsection (d):

> If the party or affected person or organization from whom discovery of electronically stored information is sought establishes that the information is from a source that is not reasonably accessible because of undue burden or expense, the court may nonetheless order discovery if the requesting party shows good cause.

That sounds sort of like the federal rules that require production anyway upon a showing of good cause, except for the important—nay, critical—difference that the "good cause" in subsection (d) of the California statute is nowhere defined. There is no reference to the three types of considerations found in 26(b)(2)(C), nor the seven factors found in the federal commentary. Although the proposed statutes do have a provision similar to 26(b)(2)(C), namely § 2031.060(f), the good-cause provision in subsection (d) is not specifically tied to the considerations in subsection (f), like the federal rules are. Instead, the Judicial Council commentary expressly states that they considered adding a specific balancing test to the good-cause analysis but rejected it. Sensing perhaps the controversiality of this decision, the Judicial Council specifically asks for opinions on that. Tell them it is a big mistake and you do not agree. Below is another link to their questionnaire[77] so that you can easily do that.

As the state commentary shows, the Judicial Council ended up using e-discovery language favoring production that was developed by the National Conference of Commissioners on Uniform State Laws, whose model rules I have previously written about.[78] But the California Judicial Council stripped the other language in the Uniform Laws that tempered this obligation. They eliminated the balancing test the Uniform Commissioners developed to restrain "good cause" and thereby provide a fair approach. This kind of pick-and-

---

77. http://www.courtinfo.ca.gov/invitationstocomment/commentform.htm.
78. http://ralphlosey.wordpress.com/2007/08/22/uniform-law-commission-approves-model-e-discovery-rules/.

choose approach to the Uniform Commissioners' model rules of e-discovery, which were in turn modeled on the new federal rules, results in a California version of 26(b)(2)(B) that is dangerously stripped of any specific considerations of good cause. It creates the illusion of a protective provision for defendants, which, in reality, is no protection at all. Very clever, I must say, and this difference has slipped by many. Perhaps I am overreacting, but it seems like proposed Section 2031.060 of the California Statutes is devoid of all power to protect businesses and other large organizations in California from unfair and exploitative discovery of inaccessible ESI.

This belief is buttressed by what I am told by several California lawyers about existing law in their state concerning "good cause" for discovery. Existing case law provides no clear guidance on good cause. As a result, the vague good-cause requirement typically favors the requesting party, especially the small David against a Goliath, meritorious or not. The plaintiffs' bar does not want a clearly defined good cause for plaintiffs to have to meet to force production of inaccessible ESI, the Uniform Commissioners balancing test, or the seven factors of the federal committee commentary. It does not even want the three general considerations of subsection 26(b)(2)(C).

If this push for new imbalanced e-discovery laws is not stopped by strong complaints to the Judicial Council before January 25, 2008, or later by Governor Schwarzenegger and the legislature, the impact of the new state law e-discovery rules in California could be substantial. Geoff Howard's article[79] has some good observations on what will likely happen:

> Bringing a motion for a protective order in every California state court case (when the party need not follow the same process in federal court) could create a substantial burden on parties with inaccessible sources of electronically stored information. That procedure also has the potential to create significant uncertainty if a party loses a motion for a protective order in a state case, leading to the discovery of the

---

79. http://www.bingham.com/Media.aspx?MediaID=6409.

inaccessible data. The resulting discovery of that information could impact the protected nature of that data under the federal rules. Given the substantial consideration over a period of several years that led to the federal rule, most states with separate electronic discovery rules have chosen to follow the federal rules more closely.

A Few Other Problems

There are a couple of other things wrong with the proposed California law. First of all, they try to define "electronically stored evidence" by tracking most of the language used by the Uniform Commissioners. I have previously critiqued[80] the Commissioners' language. The California version is at least an improvement over the Commissioners', as California eliminated the qualification that ESI be "retrievable in perceivable form." The California Judicial Council correctly recognized that this "perception" requirement was confusing at best and would only lead to unnecessary litigation. Such litigation would typically not be favorable to plaintiffs, and so it is no surprise this qualification was eliminated. But the definition they are left with is, in my opinion, still confusing, and I think at least somewhat nonsensical and contra to the normally accepted usage in e-discovery of the phrase "stored in a medium." Although the defense bar may not like this suggestion, I think the proposed definitions should be rejected entirely, and California should follow the federal approach of no definition at all.

Here is the proposed California definition statute:

§ 2016.020. As used in this title:
(d) "Electronic" means relating to technology having electrical, digital, magnetic, wireless, optical, electromagnetic, or similar capabilities.
(e) "Electronically stored information" means information that is stored in an electronic medium.

---

80. http://ralphlosey.wordpress.com/2007/08/22/uniform-law-commission-approves-model-e-discovery-rules/.

The use of the word "medium" and supposed exhaustive definition of "electronic" bothers me. For instance, why is "wireless" on
this list, and why speak in terms of "technology capabilities"? As to
"medium," why say stored in an electronic medium? Electronic information is stored in physical mediums, not energetical ones. In the
digital world of computers, this means information is stored as either a 0 or 1; an electrical switch is either on or off. Thus, for instance, a CD, or optical disk,[81] is said to be the *medium* on which
digital information is stored. It is stored by tiny indentations or pits
on the aluminum coating on the surface of a plastic CD. The surface
of the CD is read by reflection of laser light. The difference in the
laser's reflection off a pitted surface, as opposed to a non-pitted "land"
surface, is read as a 1 or 0. There are many other ingenious methods
for this kind of "0 or 1" storage of binary information using various
types of physical media, such as hard drives[82] that use magnets instead of lasers. It is all essentially derived from Edison's orginal idea
of storing sound energy on phonographic records. As far as I know,
no one can yet reliably store information on energy itself without
some kind of underlying physical medium,[83] although I suppose it
is theoretically possible with energy interference patterns or something like that.

Bottom line, all ESI is stored in or on some kind of material
thing that is called the *medium*. That is why I do not like California's
phrase "stored in an electronic medium," and think it may lead to
needless litigation. The federal comments correctly say that ESI covers information "stored in any medium" as long as "it can be retrieved and examined." The more technically enlightened federal
approach and their comments should be adopted by California.

As I have previously explained,[84] I think the federal committee
got it right in not defining ESI. The new technologies of tomorrow
are likely to doom any attempts we make today at clarity by defini-

---

81. http://en.wikipedia.org/wiki/Compact_disc.
82. http://en.wikipedia.org/wiki/Hard_drives.
83. http://en.wikipedia.org/wiki/Data_storage_device.
84. http://ralphlosey.wordpress.com/2007/08/22/uniform-law-
commission-approves-model-e-discovery-rules/.

tion. In my view, the only revision that may be needed to the federal approach is to clarify that ESI is not intended to include ephemeral data, such as RAM memory. See my blog on the bizarre *Columbia Pictures* case[85] in California that precipitated this opinion.

There is another change in discovery rules that is unique to California. The current statute allows only for the "inspection" of documents in response to either a request for production of a party, or subpoena of a non-party. The California rules say "inspecting documents, tangible things, and land or other property." Most state rules, and the federal rules, have for a long time said "inspecting, copying, testing, or sampling . . . ." The new rules not only add ESI, but also add "copying, testing and sampling." Here is the proposed statute:

> § 2031.010
> (a) Any party may obtain discovery within the scope delineated by Chapters 2 (commencing with Section 2017.010) and 3 (commencing with Section 2017.710), and subject to the restrictions set forth in Chapter 5 (commencing with Section 2019.010), by inspecting, copying, testing, or sampling documents, tangible things, ~~and~~ land or other property, and electronically stored information ~~that are~~ in the possession, custody, or control of any other party to the action.

I do not understand the significance, if any, of this addition of "copying, testing or sampling." I am told that case law has anyway already interpreted "inspection" to also allow for "copying, testing and sampling" of documents and things. Still, some California lawyers worry that the addition of the terms "copying, testing or sampling" as to ESI creates more uncharted territory, and will inevitably lead to more litigation. Could this revision as applied to ESI be used to justify forensic imaging of hard drives, for instance, which is a form of copying and inspection that is very expensive? I do not think that was the intent of broadening the definition, but the state

---

85. http://ralphlosey.wordpress.com/2007/09/02/judge-affirms-magistrates-decision-in-the-ram-memory-case-no-minimum-storage-time-for-electronic-information-before-it-is-discoverable/.

comments provide no explanation whatsoever for this change. They should.

What Can You Do About It?

The full text of the proposed rules and an invitation to comment can be downloaded here.[86] If you do business in California, or have clients who do, you should consider providing a comment. Here is a link to the official comment form.[87] Better hurry; the comments are due by January 25, 2008. This proposal was not widely publicized, and most attorneys, myself included, just found out about it last week. If the goal is buy-in of a proposal by the full bar, why keep a proposal like this under the radar and give so little time for comments? Anyway, now you know, and the rest is up to you, the good people of the state of California, and, of course, the Terminator.

Blog Reader Comment

Is there any objective basis for your opinion that litigants prefer federal discovery rules? "This so-called 'flight to quality' is already occurring for a variety of reasons, including the lack of any state rules on e-discovery."

---

86. http://ralphlosey.files.wordpress.com/2008/01/califproposedrulesand invitetocomment.pdf.

87. http://www.courtinfo.ca.gov/invitationstocomment/commentform. htm.

88. http://ralphlosey.wordpress.com/2008/01/21/california-proposes-e-discovery-laws-that-governor-schwarzenegger-will-want-to-terminate/ #comments.

89. http://wordpress.com/tag/new-rules/.

90. http://ralphlosey.wordpress.com/2008/01/21/california-proposes-e-discovery-laws-that-governor-schwarzenegger-will-want-to-terminate/.

Ralph's Reply

It is based on experience. This is not the kind of thing you can get objective data for, even with surveys. An old axiom explains part of the reason: "The devil you know (referring to the federal rules) is better than the devil you don't know (referring to no rules at all)." Second, in general most corporations believe that the federal bench provides a higher quality of adjudication than state courts. They are better funded, have a lighter caseload, and several law clerks for each judge to research the issues. Also, the district court judges are appointed for life and, unlike many state court judges, are not elected by local citizens. Finally, federal courts have magistrate judges who specialize in discovery issues. It all adds up to at least an appearance of quality and fairness in most issues, incuding e-discovery, where, unlike most state courts, there are written rules, and so you have some ability to predict what is likely to happen.

ARE WE THE BARBARIANS AT THE GATE? THE CONFLICT BETWEEN OUR RULES OF DISCOVERY AND THE PRIVACY LAWS OF THE REST OF THE CIVILIZED WORLD

The key issue in international e-discovery today is privacy and the conflict between the discovery laws of the United States, which give little or no regard to individual privacy, and those of the rest of the world, which do. In most of the civilized world today, privacy is a fundamental right. It is expressly stated in the government constitutions and other fundamental laws. The United States stands alone in considering privacy as a secondary, implied right, existing somewhere in the penumbra of other fundamental rights. *Griswold v. Connecticut,* 381 U.S. 479 (1965).

Further, the few privacy rights we have are almost all lost when we go to work, especially when we use our employer's computer systems. Even the privacy right that is arguably the strongest in our common-law system, the right to secret attorney-client communications, is lost when you enter the workplace. *See* Adam C. Losey, "Clicking Away Confidentiality: Workplace Waiver of Attorney-Client Privilege," 60 *Fla. L. Rev.* (2008) 5 (Dec. 2008).

Since we have such weak privacy rights, especially for employees, our courts routinely order foreign parties sued here to produce information that is protected from disclosure in their own country. From the perspective of these foreign companies and their employees, we are the barbarians at the gate bullying away their fundamental rights.

The "Catch-22" of Cross-Border Discovery

The way things stand now, if you want to do business in the United States, you have to forsake your company's and your employees' rights to privacy. You have to allow anyone who sues you to sift through all of your e-mail and other confidential records. The private communications of your CEO and blue-collar workers alike are fair game for any plaintiff to pry into. About the only protection U.S. rules provide are found in our incredibly broad and vague relevancy standard. Here, the information sought only has to be "reasonably calculated to lead to admissible evidence." The rest of the world finds it incredible (as do many in the U.S.) that a plaintiff can read their e-mail, even if it is not relevant, if they can simply argue it might lead to relevant information. Most of the time courts will allow them to do so even before the court has determined that their complaint states a cause of action.

If you, as a foreign litigant, refuse to turn over the information, and instead honor the fundamental rights of your employees and follow the laws of your home country, then U.S. courts are going to punish you with an assortment of sanctions, including adverse inference instructions, fee awards, or even the ultimate sanction of entering a judgment against you. The choice between compliance with the U.S. forum court law or the law of the country in which the ESI or employees are located has been called a Hobson's Choice[91]

---

91. http://en.wikipedia.org/wiki/Hobson's_choice.

or Catch 22[92] situation by the Sedona Conference. It has just completed an excellent publication on international e-discovery, *The Sedona Conference® Framework for Analysis of Cross-Border Discovery Conflicts: A Practical Guide to Navigating the Competing Currents of International Data Privacy and e-Discovery* (August 2008, Public Comment Version). This publication can be downloaded for free at the Sedona Conference[93] Web site.

Electronic discovery has become the front line of the conflict between the U.S. legal system and the rest of the world. Whenever a foreign company is sued in the U.S., it becomes subject to discovery requests, which today means primarily discovery of the information kept in its computers (ESI). When the information is in the company's computers in its home country, or involves non-U.S. employees who enjoy fundamental privacy rights that we do not, a conflict of law issue arises. *See* Cate and Eisenhauer, "Between a Rock and Hard Place: The Conflict Between European Data Protection Laws and U.S. Civil Litigation Document Production Requirements," *Privacy & Security Law Report*, Vol. 6, No. 6, 02/25/2007; Leeuw & Wellner, "European Data Privacy Laws Pose E-Discovery Problems,"[94] *New York Law Journal* (May 21, 2008).

Litigants, typically plaintiffs, want information that they are entitled to under U.S. law to try to prove their allegations of wrongdoing. But oftentimes the ESI they want and have a right to under U.S. law is located in jurisdictions where they have no right to that information. In fact, in many countries, including all of Europe, it would be a crime for the holders of that information to disclose it without the express permission of the individuals involved.

The rest of the world is getting tired of the United States allowing any plaintiff to put their companies into this kind of untenable situation. The U.S. (especially certain state courts) is the forum of choice for most class-action lawsuits. Often the threat of invasive discovery allows a kind of legal extortion of inflated settlements. The world outside of the U.S. sees our enforcement of no-privacy

---

92. http://en.wikipedia.org/wiki/Catch-22.
93. http://www.thesedonaconference.org/".
94. http://www.law.com/jsp/ihc/PubArticleIHC.jsp?id=1202421552806.

discovery rules as a kind of legal bullying on our part, and it is starting to fight back.

U.S. Privacy Laws

There is no express constitutional right to privacy in our legal system. Lee Goldman, "The Constitutional Right of Privacy," 84 *Denv. U. L. Rev.* 601 (2006). Instead, our unenumerated privacy rights exist as mere shadows of more basic rights that are enumerated in our Constitution, such as the right not to have soldiers stationed in your home. I kid you not. Here are the words of Justice Douglas in *Griswold,* where the Supreme Court first articulated this right:

> Previous cases suggest that the specific guarantees in the Bill of Rights have penumbras, formed by emanations from those guarantees that give them substance. Various guarantees create zones of privacy, such as the First Amendment right of association, the Third Amendment prohibition against quartering soldiers in a home, the Fourth Amendment right to be secure in one's person, house, papers, and effects, the Fifth Amendment right to not surrender anything to one's detriment, and the Ninth Amendment right to not deny or disparage any right retained by the people. These cases press for recognition of the penumbral rights of privacy and repose.

Note how even this landmark Supreme Court case, by renowned legal scholar Justice Douglas, mixes the right of privacy with the right of repose, whatever that is—the right to be left alone and go back to sleep, I suppose. (This is just what every ruler wants the populace to do!)

There was an active dissent in *Griswold* that should not be forgotten. Dissenting Justices Hugo L. Black and Potter Stewart argued that a general right to privacy could not be inferred from any part of the Constitution. Further, they criticized the majority for deciding this case according to personal opinion instead of following the text of the Constitution. Justice Black wrote, "I like my privacy as well as the next one, but I am nevertheless compelled to admit that government has a right to invade it unless prohibited by some specific constitutional provision." In *Griswold*, Black found no "specific constitutional provision" that prohibited the state government's regulation of the private behavior at issue in this case.

You may think things have come a long way since *Griswold* asserted these penumbral privacy rights in 1965. Indeed, there have been advances, but most of the world remains unimpressed. Our zones of privacy are, in my view, quite sketchy, especially in this new century with the widespread collection of personal information databases,[95] online intrusions, the growing problem of identity theft, and the many compromises made since 9/11/01 in the name of the "War on Terror." *See, e.g.*, USA PATRIOT Act, 18 U.S.C. § 2712, 31 U.S.C. § 5318A (2004).

Politics aside, the power of technology to invisibly encroach upon our privacy is perhaps the most troubling new development. Many people think that the incredible ability of new technologies to intrude upon privacy demonstrates the need to rethink and elevate its legal status. *See* Susan E. Gindin, "Lost and Found in Cyberspace: Informational Privacy in the Age of the Internet,"[96] 34 *San Diego Law Review* 1153 (1997); Electronic Privacy Information Center;[97] Open Security Foundation's Dataloss Report;[98] Electronic Frontier Foundation;[99] and U.S. DOJ on Privacy Issues in the High-Tech Context.[100]

The most significant privacy opinion after *Griswold* by the Supreme Court came just two years later in *Katz v. United States*, 389 U.S. 347 (1967). *Katz* created a two-prong "reasonable expectation" of privacy test that has often been criticized as circular and vague. Posner, "The Uncertain Protection of Privacy by the Supreme Court," 1979 *S. Ct. Rev.* 173, 188.

---

95. http://www.privacyrights.org/.
96. http://www.info-law.com/lost.html.
97. http://epic.org/.
98. http://datalossdb.org/index/latest.
99. http://www.eff.org/.
100. http://www.usdoj.gov/criminal/cybercrime/privacy.html.

The first prong—subjective privacy—is whether the person exhibited a personal expectation to be left alone from government intrusion. Our expectations, in the eyes of the rest of the world, are incredibly low. We appear to be a nation of Gladys Kravitz[101] busybodies. We do not seem concerned that a "Big Brother" government, especially the judicial branch, can peer into everything you do. In fact, one of the most popular television shows in America is named *Big Brother*[102] and celebrates that total lack of privacy. We seem to have forgotten the evil Big Brother in George Orwell's[103] *1984.*[104]

The second prong of the legal test—objective privacy—is whether the personal expectation is one that society is prepared to recognize as reasonable. Again, our personal expectations of privacy are low, especially in the workplace. It is as if we take for granted that everything we say at work, every e-mail we write, may someday be seized and read to a jury, and thus the newspaper, since trials in the U.S. must be public.

The media and some high-tech companies would have us all embrace a paparazzi[105] lifestyle, where we all fancy ourselves a celebrity, at least for 15 minutes,[106] and gaze trustfully at the ever-more-prevalent Google cameras.[107] A recent *Wall Street Journal* article, "Privacy? We Got Over It,"[108] promotes this view. It suggests that Americans and Brits do not really care about privacy anymore. It quotes the advice of Scott McNealy, chairman of Sun Microsystems, who in 1999 said, "You have zero privacy anyway. Get over it." And the observation by Oracle CEO Larry Ellison: "The privacy you're concerned about is largely an illusion. All you have to give up is your illusions, not any of your privacy." *But see The Privacy*

---

101. http://en.wikipedia.org/wiki/Gladys_Kravitz.
102. http://en.wikipedia.org/wiki/Big_Brother_(TV_series).
103. http://en.wikipedia.org/wiki/George_Orwell.
104. http://en.wikipedia.org/wiki/Big_Brother_(1984).
105. http://en.wikipedia.org/wiki/Paparazzi.
106. http://en.wikipedia.org/wiki/15_minutes_of_fame.
107. http://en.wikipedia.org/wiki/Google_Street_View.
108. http://online.wsj.com/article/SB121962391804567765.html.

Journal[109] by Robert Ellis Smith, an attorney, journalist, and author of several books on privacy and the *Scientific American* editorial "Seven Paths to Regulating Privacy,"[110] August 2008, which makes specific suggestions to improve privacy in the U.S. lost by technological advances.

Smith, who is cited by the *Scientific American* editors, traces the roots of America's privacy deficiency to our Puritan roots. The magazine quotes Rev. Robert Browne, an influential Anglican minister who said in 1582, "We must all watch one another." According to Smith, this quote, and the attitude behind it, originated in a dark, puritanical view of the human spirit as weak and prone to wickedness without the constant "support" of a community of spies and informers. Smith contends that this view had enormous influence on the New England Puritans and still lingers with us in today's voyeuristic society. R.E. Smith, "Ben Franklin's Web Site: Privacy and Curiosity from Plymouth Rock to the Internet,"[111] *Privacy Journal* (2004). (Think this is ancient history? Think again! City councils in Great Britain have recently begun recruiting unpaid volunteers to spy on their neighbors and report such things as garbage recycling and dog poop violations. According to this London news report:[112] "The 'environment volunteers' will also be responsible for encouraging neighbours to cut down on waste.")

In the United States, we only seem to think that certain limited types of information about ourselves are entitled to privacy protection, such as our medical records, financial records, and Social Security numbers. It does not even occur to us, like it does to the average European (excluding the U.K.), that *all* of our personal information is inherently private, even information in an e-mail identifying

---

109. http://www.privacyjournal.net/.

110. http://www.sciam.com/article.cfm?id=seven-paths-to-regulating-privacy.

111. http://www.amazon.com/gp/product/0930072146/ref=cm_cr_pr_product_top.

112. http://www.thisislondon.co.uk/news/article-23547177-details/Now+it's+the+citizen+snoopers%3A+Councils+recruit+unpaid+volunteers+to+spy+on+their+neighbours/article.do.

whether a particular employee was an author or recipient. *Sedona Framework* at pg. 9, fn. 34.

Most employers in the U.S. today make it clear to their employees that they have no right to privacy in anything they do on a computer at work. They monitor their employees' e-mail and Internet use, and some even go so far as to record every keystroke they make. The basic rationale is that the computers they use at work belong to the company, so anything an employee writes or does using these computers belongs to the company, regardless of whether they are on a break or after hours. Some courts will also view it as a matter of contract law. The employees "contracted away" any rights they may have had to privacy. Karen Eltis, "The Emerging American Approach to E-Mail Privacy in the Workplace,"[113] 24 *Comp. Labor Law & Pol'y Journal* 487, 489 (2005) ("employer exercises quasi-absolute sovereignty over employees, having availed himself or herself of their services by virtue of the employment contract").

American workers seem to accept and submit to this master/servant type of relationship, but in Europe and other countries, it is considered an oppressive violation of basic human dignity. The workers in these countries do not contract away their fundamental human rights, which for them includes a right to privacy. Instead, these rights automatically carry over into the workplace. For instance, in France, it is not legal to inspect an employee's computer at work, even when the employer has reason to suspect wrongdoing. *Philippe K. v. Cathnet-Science*, Cour de Cassation, Chambre Sociale, Arret. No. 1089 FS-P+B+R+1, Pourvoi No. J-03-40.017, 5/17/05 (holding that presence of erotic photos on employee's desk was not grounds for searching his computer); *Societe Nikon France v. M. Onof*, Cass. soc., Oct. 2, 2001, Bull. Civ. V, No. 291 (finding an employee's rights violated when the employer searched his computer upon suspicion employee was conducting a side business); Erica Davila, "International E-Discovery: Navigating The Maze,"[114] 8 *U. Pitt. J. Tech. L. Pol'y* 5 at pgs. 4-5 and fn. 35 (Spring 2008). As Davila observed at page 5 of her excellent article:

---

113. http://www.law.uiuc.edu/publications/CLL&PJ/archive/vol_24/issue_3/EltisArticle24-3.pdf.

114. http://tlp.law.pitt.edu/ARTICLES/e-discovery.pdf.

[M]any countries view privacy in the workplace differently than the United States does. There is generally no expectation of privacy in workplaces in the United States, and so requesting and receiving e-mail in discovery is commonplace. In the EU, however, there is an expectation of privacy in the workplace, and so e-mail sent and received via work accounts may not be discoverable.

Privacy Laws Outside of the United States

Most modern democratic countries today have strong individual privacy rights, including all of the countries of Europe. They consider personal privacy to be an inalienable human right, on the same level as the right to free speech and assembly. The treaties and law that underlie the European Union embody these privacy principles. The fundamental law in this area is the European Convention on Human Rights[115] of 1950:

Article 8 - Right to respect for private and family life
1. Everyone has the right to respect for his private and family life, his home and his correspondence.
2. There shall be no interference by a public authority with the exercise of this right except such as is in accordance with the law and is necessary in a democratic society in the interests of national security, public safety or the economic well-being of the country, for the prevention of disorder or crime, for the protection of health or morals, or for the protection of the rights and freedoms of others.

The European Union clarified that these privacy rights apply to computer data back in 1995 by adoption of the European Union's Data Protection Directive:[116]

---

115. http://www.echr.coe.int/ECHR.
116. http://eur-lex.europa.eu/LexUriServ/LexUriServ.do?uri=CELEX:31995L0046:EN:HTML.

Article 1 - Object of the Directive
1. In accordance with this Directive, Member States shall protect the fundamental rights and freedoms of natural persons, and in particular their right to privacy with respect to the processing of personal data.

Some American apologists have tried to explain the European privacy laws as a kind of oversensitivity on their part arising out of their World War II experience with Nazi Germany. So what is wrong with learning the lessons of history? Many countries outside of Europe have strong privacy laws, having learned the same lessons from other totalitarian regimes, including communist. *See, e.g.,* Article 17 of the Korean Constitution, which states that all citizens shall enjoy the inviolable right to privacy, and Article 18, which provides that the secrets of all citizens shall be protected.

Do we have to have a federal Gestapo reading all of our e-mail before we react? Let us never forget why our own Bill of Rights was formed. It was a lesson our Founding Fathers learned in 1776 from the oppressive rule of the first King George. If our Founding Fathers were alive today, I have no doubt they would assess the situation with dismay, and rush to add a new privacy right amendment that at least equaled the laws of France.

The World Is Fighting Back

Most of the world has reacted to what they perceive as overly intrusive American discovery laws by enacting what are called "blocking laws." These are laws designed to try to protect their citizens and businesses from our no-privacy legal system—some expressly and some by implication, such as Swiss banking privacy laws. The *Sedona Framework* cites to a number of these laws, but let's focus on what France has done.

In 1980, France enacted a criminal law that outlawed discovery within France by private parties for litigation abroad. French Penal Law No. 80-538 provides:

Subject to international treaties or agreements and laws and regulations in force, it is forbidden for any person to request, seek or communicate, in writing, orally or in any other form, documents or information of an economic, commercial, industrial, financial or technical nature leading to the constitution of evidence with a view to foreign judicial or administrative procedures or in the context of such procedures.

Sedona Cross-Border Framework at pg. 18, fn. 74.

These blocking statutes, including the French one, have not been enforced. For this and other reasons, when a French company is sued in the United States and it opposes discovery on the grounds it would violate French law, the typical reaction of U.S. courts has been "Too bad. You did business in the U.S., you got sued here, so now you have to follow our discovery rules." *Enron v. J.P. Morgan Securities Inc.*, No. 01-16034 (Bankr. S.D. N.Y. July 18, 2007) (involved a French bank); *United States v. Vetco,* 691 F.2d 1281 (9th Cir. 1981) (involved a Swiss bank); *Hagenbuch v. 3B6 Sistemi Elettronici Industriali S.R.L.*, 2005 U.S. Dist. LEXIS 20049, at *14 (N.D. Ill. Sept. 12, 2005) (involved an Italian company); *Columbia Pictures Industries v. Bunnell,*[117] at pgs. 28-30; *affirmed at* 245 F.R.D. 443 (C.D. Cal. 2007) (involved discovery of RAM memory and a Web site[118] located in the Netherlands).

As a general rule, U.S. courts do not give much weight to foreign blocking laws because they consider them mere Paper Tigers, and besides, they do not much like the idea of foreign countries trying to interfere with our rules of discovery. Although this reasoning may be morally suspect if you value the right to privacy and comity,[119] it was based in fact. Until recently, the blocking laws were never enforced, even in France.

The foreign prosecutors would recognize that their citizens and businesses were in a Catch-22 situation, and would back down to the U.S. courts. It was like two countries playing a game of legal "chicken." Quite naturally, the U.S. courts would always win that

117. http://ralphlosey.files.wordpress.com/2008/08/columbiavbunnell.pdf.
118. http://ralphlosey.wordpress.com/2007/06/20/district-court-in-la-decides-computer-ram-memory-must-be-preserved-and-produced/.
119. http://en.wikipedia.org/wiki/Comity.

game. The foreign prosecutors and judges would have to back down, because otherwise they would have to punish one of their own. But, as will be explained below, the French appear to have grown weary of losing this game. They tire of watching U.S. courts bully their corporations into disclosing private information to U.S. plaintiffs, even though that directly violates French law. They now appear more than willing to sacrifice one of their own to show that they mean business.

The French Bite the Bullet

After over 20 years of not enforcing their blocking statutes and observing the near-uniform reaction of American courts, it has become obvious to foreign jurisdictions that if they do not start enforcing these laws, they might as well repeal them. Otherwise, the U.S. courts will never take them seriously. If that means a few sacrificial lambs, then so be it.

France has become the first country to so bite the bullet and publicly enforce its blocking laws. It arrested and criminally prosecuted one of its own—a French lawyer, no less. *In re Advocat "Christopher X,"* Cour de Cassation, French Supreme Court, Dec. 12, 2007, Appeal n 07-83228. This is the first such prosecution on record. It was started by a French judge in secret two years ago and has just recently come to light in this opinion of the Supreme Court of France. Thanks to the *Sedona Cross-Border Framework* group for discovering this opinion and bringing it to our attention. Sedona touts this decision as groundbreaking, and I agree.

The French lawyer, Christopher X, was representing his French corporate client and complying with an order of a federal court in New York. *Strauss v. Credit Lyonnais,* 242 F.R.D. 199 (E.D. N.Y. May 25, 2007). The U.S. district court had rejected Credit Lyonnais' argument that it would face possible criminal prosecution by French banking authorities if it complied with the requested discovery order. The U.S. court held that there was a low likelihood of actual prosecution, and so did not give this factor any weight. The court ordered the defendants to disclose records relating to the case within 30 days. When the French advocate started to do that by interviewing a witness in France, he was arrested and prosecuted.

The French in effect finally did not blink; they carried out their law. Would we have done any less if the shoe was on the other foot? If, for instance, a foreign court (think China) had tried to interfere with a right that we consider important, such as freedom of speech or religion? The foreign court might not consider these rights to be that important, just like we do not consider an employee's right to privacy to be that important.

Lawyer X was convicted and fined €10,000 (about $15,000), and could have been sentenced to six months in jail. I cannot help but suspect that if an American lawyer had gone to France for the information, he would have gone to jail (and we would probably know his last name). In fact, I have heard many stories from e-discovery vendors of being threatened with arrest or having their hard drives confiscated at the border by customs. The e-discovery vendors are easy targets and are very paranoid about it, and use local people as much as possible. It would not surprise me to see the next criminal prosecution against one of the major e-discovery vendors and a few of their "just following orders" employees.

The *Sedona Cross-Border Framework* has a good discussion of the significance of *In re Advocat "Christopher X"*:

> The recently published decision of the French Supreme Court affirming the criminal conviction of a French attorney for violating the French Blocking Statute casts in doubt a great deal of U.S. case law precedent on the issue of cross-border discovery. Prior U.S. court decisions ordering cross-border discovery over the objections such discovery violates foreign blocking statutes is expressly premised on the heretofore absence of any **public** enforcement of such statutes.
>
> Historically, the attitude of the U.S. Supreme Court and U.S. federal and state courts at all levels has been that the threat of such prosecution is, in reality, just a minor factor in the type of proportionality analysis called for by the Restatements of Law. The U.S. courts in these cases almost uniformly reason that in the absence of enforcement of foreign blocking statutes, the Hague Convention cannot be consid-

ered the exclusive means of cross-border discovery. That is, if blocking statutes have teeth but no bite, then cross-border discovery should be ordered, albeit with some restrictions based upon the type of case, and uniqueness and relevance of the information sought. . . .

The circumstances of publication of the French decision almost one year later, and its grand jury–like proceedings begs the question whether there have been prior such unpublished decisions. . . .

Now that the logical syllogism upon which prior U.S. case law is based is broken, the stage is set for U.S. Courts to reconsider . . . [and] more thoughtfully than ever weigh the civil and criminal consequences in their jurisdictions. . . . The stakes of this "Catch-22" are higher than ever before. And the situation cries out for a collaborative framework in which cross-border legal disputes can effectively be resolved.

Sedona Proposes a Solution to the Catch-22 Conundrum

True to the standard-setting traditions of the Sedona Conference, the working group behind the *Framework for Analysis of Cross-Border Discovery Conflicts* not only identifies the problem but proposes a solution—namely, a framework for analysis. The leaders of this Sedona group are M. James Daley and Kenneth N. Rashbaum. They have been helped by Kenneth J. Withers, Quentin Archer, Moze Cowper, Paul Robertson, Amy H. Chung, and Conor R. Crowley. Here is their proposed sevenfold framework:

> Ideally, determining the scope of cross-border discovery obligations should be based on a balancing of the needs, costs and burdens of the discovery with the interests of each jurisdiction in protecting the privacy rights and welfare of its citizens. The following factors should be considered in this balancing:
>
> 1. The nature of the data privacy obligations in the jurisdiction where the information is located;

2. The obligations of the responding party to preserve and produce relevant information in the jurisdiction where the dispute is filed and the jurisdiction where the data is located;
3. The purpose and degree of custody and control of the responding party over maintaining the requested information;
4. The nature and complexity of the proceedings;
5. The amount in controversy;
6. The importance of the discovery to resolving critical issues; and
7. The ease and expense of collecting, processing, reviewing and producing relevant information, taking into account:
   a. the accessibility of the relevant information;
   b. the volume of the relevant information;
   c. the location of the relevant information;
   d. the likelihood that the integrity and authenticity of the information will be impaired by the discovery process; and
   e. the ability to identify information that is subject to foreign privilege and work product protection from disclosure.

If you do any work with international e-discovery, you should study this Sedona publication and look for ways to apply this framework to address the serious issues you face. These issues now include a very real threat of arrest and criminal prosecution in a foreign land.

I like this framework and think it will help. I would, however, like to see the cost factor emphasized more and add "specificity of the request" as a consideration. This is just the first public comment draft of the publication, and if you have input, including criticisms, they would like to hear them.

Conclusion

Sedona has provided a good conceptual framework for courts and lawyers to use to analyze the international e-discovery issues. This is a good tool to try to fairly address the "Catch-22" conundrum created by the conflict of laws. But it does not address the source of the problem: the imbalance between the U.S. legal system and the rest of the free world.

Our laws provide relatively weak privacy protection, and this problem is compounded tenfold by our "let-it-all-hang-out" discovery system. There are virtually no privacy rights granted to employees of companies, domestic or foreign, whose employers are sued in a U.S. court. Their e-mail and private documents will be seized and read, even e-mail kept on their home computers or personal e-mail accounts. The so-called limit of "reasonably calculated to lead to the discovery of admissible evidence" is bogus and subjective.

If we are to stop being seen as "privacy barbarians" by the rest of the world, we need to address these fundamental concerns. Privacy rights should not be limited to the home and a few zones of interest. We must learn the harsh lessons of history—of Hitler, Stalin, and Mao—in order to avoid their repetition in a high-tech world of constant surveillance. The time has come for us to realize that privacy is an inalienable human right, not a shadowy extension of other rights. Just like the freedom of religion or speech, we should not allow it to be contracted away as a condition of employment. When we finally elevate privacy to a core right, we will join the ranks of other civilized countries and this conflict of laws will disappear.

The only way out of the current conundrum is for the U.S. to lift its standards up to that of the rest of the free world. We need to greatly strengthen our own privacy laws, especially those pertaining to employees, so that they are roughly equal to those of other democratic countries. Why should the people of France enjoy greater rights and freedoms than Americans?

Since most of the free world has clear privacy rights built into their constitutions, in my opinion we must do the same to attain real parity. A new Privacy Amendment to the Constitution should be passed. I know that a Twenty-Eighth Amendment to the United States Constitution would have huge political implications beyond e-discovery, international comity, and employee rights. Privacy rights underlie some of the most controversial issues of our day, including abortion, gay marriage, pornography, assisted suicide, and the decriminalization of drug use. Still, I think we as a society should at least start talking about it, rather than continue to muddle through with vague laws subject to so much political manipulation and court stacking.

The other Losey who is writing on this general subject takes a different, more conservative view. "Clicking Away Confidentiality," *supra.* Adam in his conclusion suggests that a more gradual approach may ultimately rectify the imbalance in employee privacy rights between the U.S. and the rest of the world:

> [I]t is possible that employee privacy rights in the United States will broaden over time to the point that workplace waiver is no longer an issue. Most countries outside the United States offer significantly more privacy rights for employees, and the United States may eventually fall into line with the rest of the world and legislatively establish broader privacy rights for employees in the workplace.
>
> The impetus behind this broadening of employee privacy rights may come from upper-level management and other control group employees. Control group employees are often responsible for making decisions regarding employee privacy and employee surveillence, and yet they themselves are employees. Thus, there is a strong incentive for the employee-authors of employee policy manuals to broaden employee privacy rights per the employer's policies.

These are good insights into corporate culture. I admit that greater privacy rights for employees are probably more likely to come to pass in this manner than by my fantasy of a new constitutional amendment. After all, the e-mail of senior management is the number one target of every plaintiff's fishing expedition.

In addition to strengthening privacy rights, a solution to the international e-discovery conundrum requires a significant tightening of our relevancy standards. We need to move away from our current vague standard. It is ideally calculated for intrusive, overbroad document requests and often results in wildly inconsistent interpretations on permissible discovery. We should, instead, only allow discovery of directly relevant information. Moreover, before we start reading e-mails and other private communications, there should be some kind of good-cause showing.

Finally, I think we should start to move slightly toward the European Civil Code system of discovery, where the judges are far more active and tightly control discovery. I am not suggesting we abandon discovery altogether and adopt the Civil Code system, but I am suggesting a more active bench and better policing of overreaching discovery abuses. Simply asking counsel to act like professionals and work things out, which is the typical reaction of most judges today on discovery issues, is a non-solution that has been failing for years.

I recognize that our judges are now overworked and understaffed and are thus unable to take on the kind of active role needed to curb these abuses. So I couple this suggestion with a plea for more judges and much higher pay. Also, I would suggest a move away from elected judges in our state systems. We should instead follow the German system, where the best and the brightest are routinely recruited right out of law school into a judicial track.

Ken Withers, Director of Judicial Education and Content of The Sedona Conference, recently discussed some of these issues with me via e-mail, which he has graciously allowed me to quote:

> As we said in the Webinar, recent events in the U.S. may move us toward a more European view of privacy that might result in restrictions on the scope of some discovery or lead to greater involvement of the judge in controlling discovery. At the same time, at least in the U.K., the strict and overbroad definitions of "personal data" and "processing" may be giving way to a more practical approach that recognizes the need to have some reasonable methods for moving data, while protecting core privacy interests.
>
> The problem in the U.S. is the solution. A much greater role for the managerial judge in narrowing the scope of discovery, as proposed in the *Economist* article, would mean a complete revamping of our judicial system. Judges simply could not continue to have caseloads between 400 (considered light) to 1000 or more cases (in our border districts)

and dramatically increase their personal involvement in civil discovery. We have "party driven" discovery in part because we have a judicial system that is incredibly thin on resources. The inquisitor/case manager model of the European courts requires a large number of judges with specialties, compared to the small number of generalists who cannot afford to get into the details of the case.

The *Economist* article Ken refers to here is called "The Big Data Dump."[120] It reviews the problems the U.S. is experiencing with e-discovery and suggests that the solution lies in a move toward the Civil Law inquisitorial approach, where the amount of e-discovery allowed would be tightly controlled. The article also claims that the U.K. and other common-law countries are already well along in that direction.

I don't know what is more unlikely: hiring many more judges and raising their pay so as to follow the inquisitorial approach, or a privacy amendment to the Constitution. Both seem like a long shot right now.

The best temporary fix may be a voluntary strengthening of privacy rights by employers, as Adam Losey suggests, coupled by a revision to the federal and state procedural rules to tighten discovery. For instance, the scope of e-discovery could be limited to relevance, and a showing of good cause could be required before an employee's e-mail, instant messages, etc., are read without their consent. Congress could also enact legislation (short of amending the Constitution) that addresses these issues. I would start by providing much stronger privacy protections to all e-mail and other electronic communications and criminalize its seizure and disclosure without all parties' consent. The only exception should be a court order after a showing of good cause. This should not only restrain the government from secret eavesdropping, but also restrain parties in litigation from excessive discovery.

---

120. http://www.economist.com/business/displaystory.cfm?story_id=12010377.

Blog Reader Comment

I'm a French digital forensic practitioner. I've been recently (about one year) involved in some e-discovery processes, of very different sizes. In some cases, the dispute was originating from the U.S.A. and then spread over to Europe, both in Common and Civil Law countries.

In order to circumvent as much as possible the "Catch-22" problem, a local e-discovery team was set up for France (and I imagine for each Civil Law country). The local team was drawn to comply with the laws of the country and the relevant evidences were not leaving the country. In addition to that, special measures were taken, like the enrollment of sworn digital forensic practitioners, which means recognized by the French legal system.

I've read the paper from the Sedona Conference, which is remarkably written and documented, and then your blog articles. I understand that even with a good deal of precautions, such e-discovery processes have many flaws. I concur that a change in the privacy protection in the U.S. could solve most of the issues, but I don't think it likely to happen soon. In the meantime, the use of the legal means proposed in the Hague Convention should be sought.

For those interested (and reading French), the Supreme Court of France *Christoper X* decision is available online.[121] I must say that e-discovery is a very challenging topic, and I really like it. And it does not impede me to continue my hard-forensic investigations on small-scale devices, which are light-years from e-discovery.

As a final remark, the French system has something similar to e-discovery, which is called "assistance huissier," but it works only for France, I think.

---

121. http://www.lexinter.net/JPTXT4/JP2005/recherche_de_r enseignements_tendant_a_la_constitution_de_preuves_dans_une_procedure_ etrangere.htm.

E-Discovery Ethics
and the *Qualcomm* Case

6

LAWYERS BEHAVING BADLY: UNDERSTANDING UNPROFESSIONAL CONDUCT IN E-DISCOVERY

Electronic discovery jurisprudence boasts more published decisions with judges bemoaning attorney misconduct than any other area of law. Sometimes this judicial anger stems solely from the conduct of the parties to litigation, such as in *United States v. Johnson*,[1] 2008 WL 2060597 (E.D. Va. May 15, 2008). In this criminal case, the defendant slipped altered e-mails to his counsel for use dur-

---

1. http://ralphlosey.files.wordpress.com/2008/07/us-v-johnson.doc."

ing trial. His attorney blew the whistle on his client and withdrew from representation as soon as he discovered what his client had done. However, in the majority of cases, the misconduct from which the judicial anger stems originates from either lawyer and client or the lawyer alone. *See, e.g., Phoenix Four, Inc. v. Strategic Resources Corp.,*[2] 2006 WL 1409413 (S.D. N.Y., May 23, 2006) (sanctions imposed against both client and attorney); *Residential Funding Corp. v. DeGeorge Fin. Corp.,*[3] 306 F.3d 99 (2d Cir. 2002) (simple negligence alone is sufficient to justify adverse inference sanction, especially where plaintiff's counsel was "purposely sluggish" in not producing the e-mails until after the trial had started).

Examples of unethical behavior range from outright intentional fraud to gross negligence to simple attorney negligence. Negligence is not only malpractice, but is also unethical. *See, e.g.,* Rule 1.1, ABA Model Rules of Professional Conduct:

> A lawyer shall provide competent representation to a client. Competent representation requires the legal knowledge, skill, thoroughness and preparation reasonably necessary for the representation.

Some experts believe that attorney incompetence in e-discovery is so widespread, it presents a massive ethical crisis across the entire legal profession. Anecdotal evidence from e-discovery vendors confirms this. E-discovery vendors probably deal with more attorneys and law firms around the country than anyone. These vendors privately state that very few of their customers are technologically sophisticated. They often have humorous anecdotes regarding attorney requests illustrating their lack of technological competence. Of course, when you do not have sophisticated buyers, sellers tend to take advantage of that. This is one of the reasons e-discovery vendor costs are often shockingly high.

Negligence is a large part of the story on ethical misconduct in e-discovery, but not the whole story. Case law, exemplified by

---

2. http://ralphlosey.files.wordpress.com/2008/05/phoenix.pdf.
3. http://ralphlosey.files.wordpress.com/2008/05/residential.pdf.

Qualcomm,[4] suggests there is far more to the sanctions being imposed by judges all over the country than just lawyer incompetence. When I began my career in 1980, the imposition of sanctions, especially against attorneys, was a very rare event, and motions based on spoliation were unheard of. Now they are commonplace. Why is this?

Surely the profession has not suddenly become more sinister than before, although some suggest that the dominance of large firms as mega-business enterprises is causing a significant decline in overall ethics. Henderson Galanter, "The Elastic Tournament: A Second Transformation of the Big Law Firm,"[5] 60 *Stan. L. Rev.* 1867 (April 2008). There may be some truth to this, but a general decline in ethical standards does not explain why e-discovery jurisprudence is so rife with malfeasance.

Lawyers Are Not Keeping Up With Technology

Part of the answer lies with the incredible exponential technological advances occurring over the last 20 years. The concept of society has transcended the paradigm of a nation-based industrial world to that of a global techno-centric world. The rapidity of this change in civilization is unprecedented in human history. This transformation has had profound effects on the nature and quality of evidence and the processes necessary to root out this evidence. *See* "Information Inflation: Can the Legal System Adapt?," 13 *Rich J.L. & Tech.* 10 (2007).[6] In fact, e-discovery was birthed from this paradigm shift. *See* "Intellectual Foundation of Electronic Discovery."[7]

Business and all other sectors of society have undergone this same rapid transformation. Yet they seem to be rising to the challenge of new technologies better than the legal profession. True, there have been some spectacular ethical disasters in business, sym-

---

4. http://ralphlosey.wordpress.com/2008/06/01/the-lessons-of-qualcomm-a-wake-up-call-for-the-whole-legal-profession/

5. http://law.usc.edu/academics/assets/docs/Henderson.pdf.

6. http://law.richmond.edu/jolt/v13i3/article10.pdf.

7. Losey, R., *e-Discovery: Current Trends and Cases* (ABA 2008) at pg. 14.

bolized by the collapse of Enron and Arthur Anderson. But once again, you could point the blame on their attorneys, especially their in-house counsel, who failed to steer these companies toward conduct consistent with the requirements of established law.

The failure of the legal profession to keep up with technology is primarily a result of two factors: (1) the archetypical personality of most lawyers, and (2) the failure of most law schools to adapt to the modern technological revolution. Most lawyers are not strong in math, science, or engineering. There are exceptions, of course; we call them IP (Intellectual Property) lawyers. But for the most part, the law profession attracts people who are gifted with a particular kind of liberal arts, logically based intelligence that inclines them to "computer-phobia." In fact, the LSAT admissions test, designed to sort and rank potential law school applicants, tests only logical reasoning and reading comprehension skills. A student could easily achieve a perfect score on the LSAT without knowing how to plug in a computer.

Most law schools have ignored the problem of e-discovery altogether and offer no classes on the subject. There are a few notable exceptions, such as Cumberland's Law School, with Judge John Carroll, and the University of Florida's Law School, with Holland & Knight's Bill Hamilton. These schools are the rare exception to the rule, and most law schools have not stepped up to the plate to address this problem.

Since the root of the lawyer "Luddite" mind-set is grounded in legal education, the answer also lies within the legal education system. Law schools must include electronic discovery in their standard curricula and broaden their recruitment and admission standards to include the technologically gifted.

The prevalence of technology in the law is a strong driving force behind the decline of ethics in e-discovery. This is clear. But this observation, in and of itself, does not provide a theoretical construct to understand the root of unethical conduct in e-discovery. Such understanding requires a thorough analysis of the rules of ethics and observation of legal practice. This article presents such an analysis and offers a theory defining the root of ethical malfeasance in e-discovery situations. I presented this theory as a thesis at a symposium on e-discovery ethics at Mercer Law School in November 2008, titled "Ethics and Professionalism in the Digital Age."

This symposium was the first academic event that I know of to seriously address issues of e-discovery ethics. The keynote speech was provided by Professor Monroe H. Freeman,[8] one of the country's leading scholars on legal ethics. There were two ethics panels. The first was led by Jason Baron, who presented his ethics thesis, "E-Discovery and The Problem of Asymmetric Knowledge: Some Thoughts on the Ethics of Search and Information Retrieval in Light of Recent Case Developments." The panel members who responded to his thesis were Judge John Facciola and Chilton Varner of King & Spalding. Next, I presented my thesis summarized here, "The Wicked Quadrants: A Theoretical Construct for Understanding Unethical Conduct in e-Discovery." Panel members who responded were Judge David Baker and Bill Hamilton. An edited transcript of the proceedings is published in the 2009 Spring Edition of the *Mercer Law Review.*

The Wicked Quadrants: A Rubric to Understand the Root of Unethical Conduct in e-Discovery

There are four fundamental forces at work in e-discovery, which, when considered together, explain most attorney misconduct: (1) a general lack of technological sophistication; (2) overzealous attorney conduct; (3) a lack of development of professional duties as an advocate; and (4) legal incompetence. These so-called "Wicked Quadrants" are depicted in the circular diagram at the beginning of this chapter and again in cross-format diagram below. The four-arrow cross-graphic below is designed to show how these forces interact in an imbalanced fashion to explain lawyer misconduct.

---

8. http://law.hofstra.edu/directory/faculty/FullTimeFaculty/ftfac_mfreedman.html.

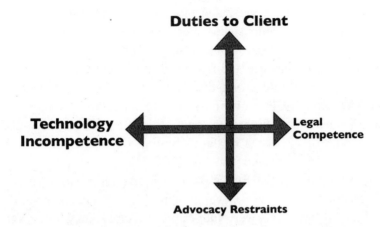

The previously discussed radical transformation of society, and the problem of technology incompetence that comes with it, is the first and foremost of the four factors to consider to understand e-discovery misconduct. The other three factors arise from general ethical considerations that are not in any sense unique to electronic discovery and are addressed in the American Bar Association's Model Rules of Professional Conduct.

These four criteria interact with one another in varying ways to explain the many forms and types of *attorney* e-discovery misconduct. Unethical or illegal behavior by parties to litigation are influenced by different factors, including raw emotional ones such as greed, fear, and hate. These four criteria do not apply to the parties to litigation, but rather only to their attorneys.

Duty to Clients v. Professional Duties

The Wicked Quadrant consists of two fundamental and diametrically opposed duties applicable to all attorneys. On one side of the scale lies an attorney's duty to clients, and on the other lies an attorney's ethical duty to the profession, including opposing parties, opposing counsel, and the courts.

Two Primary Ethical Forces
at Work in e-Discovery

Client Duties ⬅➡ **Professional Duties**

Rule 1.3 Diligence

Rule 1.6 Confidentiality

Rule 1.1 Competence

Rule 3.2 Expediting Litigation

Rule 3.3 Candor Toward The Tribunal

Rule 3.4 Fairness To Opposing Party And Counsel

Four rules regarding an attorney's ethical duty to the profession are relevant to e-discovery: Rule 1.1, Competence; Rule 3.2, Expediting Litigation; Rule 3.3, Candor Toward the Tribunal; and Rule 3.4, Fairness to Opposing Party and Counsel. Yet in most instances of e-discovery misconduct, these four rules are outweighed by two rules codifying an attorney's duty to clients: Rule 1.3, Diligence, and Rule 1.6, Confidentiality.

The first, and by far the most "wicked" of the client duty rules, is Model Rule 1.3, Diligence.

Client-Lawyer Relationship—Rule 1.3 Diligence
A lawyer shall act with reasonable diligence and promptness in representing a client.

As the Commentary for the Model Rules of Professional Conduct explains:

Comment
[1] A lawyer should pursue a matter on behalf of a client despite opposition, obstruction or personal inconvenience to the lawyer, and take whatever lawful and ethical measures are required to vindicate a client's cause or endeavor. A lawyer must also act with commitment and dedication to

the interests of the client and with zeal in advocacy upon the client's behalf.

Of course, clients will readily appreciate actions taken by their lawyer to fulfill these duties. In fact, the commentators recognize the inherent dangers of excessive zeal and warn about excesses, but stop short of actually banning them:

> A lawyer is not bound, however, to press for every advantage that might be realized for a client . . . . The lawyer's duty to act with reasonable diligence does not require the use of offensive tactics or preclude the treating of all persons involved in the legal process with courtesy and respect.

Lawyers are not *bound* to press every advantage but are not prohibited, either. They are not *required* to use offensive tactics, but such tactics are not forbidden by ethical code. Naturally, lawyers frequently engage in overzealous representation, and clients normally react favorably to this behavior. The client is, after all, in a dispute with the opposing party, and emotions frequently run hot, even in commercial litigation between large businesses.

The second client-directed ethics rule, Rule 1.6, also encourages misbehavior at times, albeit not nearly as often as the zealous advocacy rule.

Rule 1.6: Confidentiality of Information.

A lawyer shall not reveal information relating to the representation of a client unless the client gives informed consent, the disclosure is impliedly authorized in order to carry out the representation or the disclosure is permitted by paragraph (b).

The secrecy rule of ethics, buttressed by the attorney-client privilege and attorney work-product privilege, has served as a cover, and sometimes excuse, for a host of misconduct. The lawyer may know that his client has not disclosed all of the harmful e-mail, or has engaged in a deliberately negligent search, but feels constrained by his duty of confidentiality. This duty is antithetical to the transparency of e-discovery conduct that facilitates cooperation between counsel and the court.

The impact of this rule is obvious in the *Qualcomm* case, where outside counsel tried to blame the nondisclosure of thousands of e-mails on their client. When the massive fraud designed to conceal highly relevant e-mail was later discovered, one of the excuses offered by outside counsel was that counsel could not disclose their suspicions of fraud, as they were prohibited by the California state law equivalent of model Rule 1.6

Three rules of ethics based on duties to the profession as a whole are particularly relevant in e-discovery. These rules, in theory, should balance and constrain the two client-centered rules. These rules act as three angels whispering in the good ear of each litigation attorney. They are, in pertinent part:

Advocate—Rule 3.2 Expediting Litigation

A lawyer shall make reasonable efforts to expedite litigation consistent with the interests of the client.

Advocate—Rule 3.3 Candor Toward the Tribunal

(a) A lawyer shall not knowingly:

(1) make a false statement of fact or law to a tribunal or fail to correct a false statement of material fact or law previously made to the tribunal by the lawyer; . . .

(3) offer evidence that the lawyer knows to be false. . . .

(b) A lawyer who represents a client in an adjudicative proceeding and who knows that a person intends to engage, is engaging or has engaged in criminal or fraudulent conduct related to the proceeding shall take reasonable remedial measures, including, if necessary, disclosure to the tribunal.

(c) The duties stated in paragraphs (a) and (b) continue to the conclusion of the proceeding, and apply even if compliance requires disclosure of information otherwise protected by Rule 1.6.

(d) In an ex parte proceeding, a lawyer shall inform the tribunal of all material facts known to the lawyer that will enable the tribunal to make an informed decision, whether or not the facts are adverse.

Rule 3.4 Fairness to Opposing Party and Counsel

A lawyer shall not:

(a) unlawfully obstruct another party's access to evidence or unlawfully alter, destroy or conceal a document or other material having potential evidentiary value. A lawyer shall not counsel or assist another person to do any such act;

(b) falsify evidence, counsel or assist a witness to testify falsely, or offer an inducement to a witness that is prohibited by law;

(c) knowingly disobey an obligation under the rules of a tribunal except for an open refusal based on an assertion that no valid obligation exists;

(d) in pretrial procedure, make a frivolous discovery request or fail to make reasonably diligent effort to comply with a legally proper discovery request by an opposing party; . . . .

When attorney e-discovery misconduct arises, it can be attributed to failure of an attorney to follow the counsel of one or more of these three ear-whispering angels. There is, however, yet another rule of professional conduct that frequently comes into play in e-discovery, the rule of professional competence.

Advocate—Rule 1.1 Competence

A lawyer shall provide competent representation to a client.

Competent representation requires the legal knowledge, skill, thoroughness and preparation reasonably necessary for the representation.

Rule 1.1 falls on the side of professional duties, but is in many respects unlike the three angels. Indeed, it has always enjoyed a special prominence in our legal tradition for a variety of reasons, including pride in quality craftsmanship. Competence has also played an important role in tempering excessive zeal in diligence. By tradition, the most highly skilled do not need to resort to adversarial excess to prevail. Their competence alone will carry the day without use of bluster and sharp elbows.

These six ethical duties, two on the side of client representation and four on the side of the court and profession as a whole, should, in theory, be in balance. But in practice, especially in the field of e-discovery when unethical conduct is involved, these rules do not balance. The duties to the client are given far more weight by many attorneys than the duties to the profession.

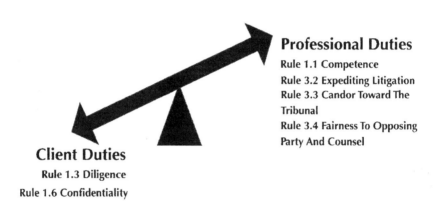

Professional Duties

Rule 1.1 Competence
Rule 3.2 Expediting Litigation
Rule 3.3 Candor Toward The Tribunal
Rule 3.4 Fairness To Opposing Party And Counsel

Client Duties

Rule 1.3 Diligence
Rule 1.6 Confidentiality

The reason for this imbalance is easy to understand. The client duties have built-in economic incentives with benefits that are obvious to the client. When an attorney carries out these duties, the fees for the attorney's services are more likely to be paid. The client is likely to further reward this behavior by requesting additional legal services. This then leads to secondary reward for this conduct by the law firm in which the attorney is a member. As law firms grow larger and closer to businesses, these rewards are intensified. Bluntly, money is the thumb on the scale and greed has corrupted attorneys' ethical compasses.

Conversely, when an attorney discharges professional duties, the benefits to the client, if any, are only secondary and remote from the client's view. For instance, the client might not realize that candor to the tribunal makes the attorney more effective in advocating their position. The discharge of these professional duties might not only be unappreciated, but in many circumstances they might be resented. For example, a client might not want to disclose an e-mail that significantly damages his case, especially if he naively thinks he could easily get away with hiding it and win. He might resent it when the lawyer discloses the e-mail anyway, especially if this later leads to loss of the case.

Fulfillment of these professional duties may in some circumstances lead to conflicts between attorney and client. It can also often lead to passive resistance, such as delays in payment of bills or refusals to pay altogether. Even if a fee is paid, many clients will think twice in retaining that lawyer again, since they may resent the divided loyalty between professional obligations and zealous representation. An unsophisticated client may not realize that every lawyer worth his or her salt takes both obligations seriously. The negative disincentive to listen to the three angels is magnified by the law firm in which the lawyer is a member. It sees only an attorney without a growing client base. The firm may respect the partner's ethics, but it will rarely reward such behavior financially.

Since the fulfillment of professional duties has no built-in financial reward, and in fact can sometimes be costly, it often is outweighed by an attorney's economic interests. This may explain why the bar has developed so many professional duties and rules over the years. It was done in the vain hope that the sheer quantity of the rules would outweigh the obvious financial disincentives. It has not. The state bar associations could promulgate 10 more rules requiring professional conduct and it would not put these competing interests in balance. The fundamental issue is that financial rewards are primarily offered for only one side of the equation. Further, violations of the professional duty–type rules are only rarely detected, and when complaints are filed, the disciplinary actions imposed are relatively light. Bar associations are primarily focused on trust account violations, not candor to the tribunal or fairness to opposing counsel.

Attorney Competence

Attorney competence and corresponding Model Rule 1.1 are such powerful forces in the legal tradition in the United States that it is an oversimplification to look solely at the problem of ethics in e-discovery in a dualistic manner, client versus profession, as we have above. Another element of complexity must be added to get a better understanding of the problem. Competence should be understood as its own ethical force, and the issue should be triangulated as shown below.

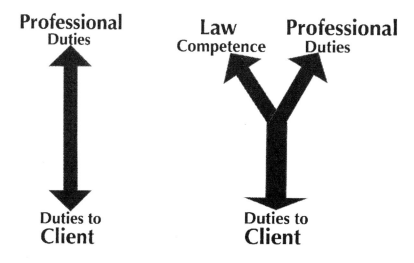

This tripartite structure is a better diagram to understand the true dynamics of legal practice. Legal competence serves as an independent upward force, along with professional duties, to counterbalance the pressures and temptations involved with fulfillment of duties to clients. The forces of Law and Profession work hand-in-hand to offset the demands of some clients, typically implied, to prevail over their adversaries at all costs.

Most of the time, the temptations of greed and power do not cause "lawyers to behave badly." Certainly lawyers do not make a practice of lying to courts and opposing counsel, even though they could probably get away with it and maximize their income in the process. There is more to this picture than simple economics. The law, after all, attracts many who are concerned with justice and care about doing the right thing. Most lawyers have strong moral fiber and need but little encouragement to do the right thing. The vast majority of lawyers are more than pen-and-quill mercenaries. Integrity, professional pride, and competence temper their financial motivations. Moreover, some enlightened clients recognize and financially reward professional competence and are influenced by professional reputation in the lawyer election process.

Unfortunately, most clients are not in a position to evaluate attorney competence. Only repeat litigants, typically large corporations, have enough experience with litigation to gain knowledge of the competence of litigation attorneys. The largest litigant class in the United States is the insurance industry. Insurance companies make up the bulk of every court's docket. In the past, they would routinely employ the best-skilled attorneys in every locale and were willing to pay for such quality representation. Although the defense bar is still usually of superlative quality, more and more insurance companies today are driven primarily by cost. They are unwilling to pay for quality representation. In fact, low rates demanded by insurance companies have become notorious. Over the past 10 to 15 years, this "penny-wise and pound-foolish" approach by the insurance industry has driven many of the best defense practitioners into other areas of practice. These seemingly sophisticated clients should know better.

Since legal competence seems to be rewarded economically less and less in all fields of litigation, the decline of pecuniary benefit to attorneys does not fully explain the dramatic decline of ethics in e-discovery. Here, the decline has been disproportionately great. The explanation lies in the previously mentioned competence gap in e-discovery by most trial lawyers. This deficiency, coupled with the dramatic changes in technology over the last few decades, has led to our current tenuous ethical position.

To further test and weaken the restraints that competence and other professional duties typically place upon unethical conduct, the strategy demanded in e-discovery, when it is performed competently, is fundamentally different from traditional adversarial strategy. When practitioners in e-discovery attain a high degree of technical competence, they realize that the cooperative model must be employed. In fact, I have yet to meet an experienced attorney in this field who does not agree with this proposition.

Transparency and cooperation, or at least attempts at cooperation, are imperative for e-discovery to be performed in an efficient and economic manner. This is discussed at length in Chapter One of this book, under "Hospital Defendants Martyred in the Cause of Cooperative e-Discovery." This new model of competence is at odds with the training of most experienced attorneys, and to them appears to be at odds with model Rules 1.3 and 1.6, diligence and confidentiality. While the cooperative model of e-discovery is not at odds with the concept of "diligence," this concept is hard to understand without practical experience in the area. Most attorneys today, especially litigators, confuse diligence with adversarial excess. As the *Sedona Conference Cooperation Proclamation* points out, cooperation in discovery is perfectly consistent with zealous advocacy: "Cooperation does not conflict with the advancement of their clients' interests—it enhances it. Only when lawyers confuse *advocacy* with *adversarial conduct* are these twin duties in conflict."[9]

Technology Incompetence

Attorneys of today are, on the whole, more competent and better prepared than attorneys of the past. Certainly the standards for admission to law schools are steadily increasing. The vast majority of the people in the legal profession have very solid moral ethics and good judgment. Indeed, the screening of applicants by state bar associations appears to be more severe and careful than it was in the past. Yet, the growing bad behavior of lawyers in the field of e-discovery is irrefutable.

The challenges and inherent conflict between duties to clients and professional duties have been present in the law for a long time. The balance appears to have shifted in the past few decades toward the duties to clients. Some believe this can be explained by the gen-

---

9. http://www.thesedonaconference.org/content/miscFiles/ Cooperation_Proclamation.pdf.

eral shift of law firms to more business-like operations. *See, e.g.,* Henderson Galanter, *The Elastic Tournament: A Second Transformation of the Big Law Firm.*[10] Still, this shift in business models does not fully explain the glut of bad behavior in e-discovery attorney conduct.

E-discovery is particularly vulnerable to ethical indiscretions due to the same exponential explosion of technology that created the field to begin with. Keeping up with ever-changing technology is a challenge for all legal practitioners. But if lawyers in other fields fail to keep up with technology, it does not usually affect their core competency as an attorney. They can be technologically incompetent and still practice at a high level of legal competence. Their professional competence can thus serve as a strong buoying force to protect them from the temptations of unprofessional behavior.

But this is not so with e-discovery. In this field, your technological incompetence has a direct and severe negative impact on your professional competence to do e-discovery work. The challenges of technology act as a countervailing force to legal competence, as shown in the diagram below.

10. http://law.usc.edu/academics/assets/docs/Henderson.pdf.

Because most attorneys today called upon to do e-discovery have very limited technology competence, they necessarily also have limited legal competence to do this work. Thus, the buoying force of competence that restrains excessive advocacy is far less, or absent entirely. Instead, the added challenges of technology serve as an anchor to bring out the basest behaviors. As shown in the diagram below, with the added weight of technological challenges, the upward forces of legal competence and duty to profession are now insufficient to counter the temptations arising from duties to clients. The influence of technology greatly strengthens the downward forces and leads to an overall lowering of ethical conduct.

Law **Professional**
Competence **Duties**

Duties to
Client
Challenges
Technology

Attorneys not competent in technology are well aware of their situation, although they will often go to great lengths to hide it from others. This creates a precarious situation where attorneys are not secure in their legal competence, but are still pressured by clients and the economy. This leads many to make bad decisions and choices when it comes to compliance with the dictates of Model Rules 3.2,

Expediting Litigation, 3.3, Candor Toward the Tribunal, and 3.4, Fairness to Opposing Party and Counsel.

Finally, it is important to note that no one is fully competent in all fields of technology that may be encountered in e-discovery. It might be possible to master the law of e-discovery but not all of the technologies underlying it. These facts are too complicated and ever-changing for any one person to master. Every modern lawyer is stressed and challenged by the enormous tidal wave of technology we have "enjoyed" over the past few decades. Each attorney is a perpetual student who must strive to keep abreast of the rapid inventions and progress of the unstoppable technological evolution.

The Wicked Quadrants

The four factors shown in the diagram opposite and at the beginning of this article constitute the basic components underlying unethical behavior in e-discovery. The diagram below adjusts the size of the four quadrants to reflect the imbalance that leads to lawyer misconduct.

In the field of e-discovery, I place most of the blame on the incredible challenges of technology. No other generation of lawyers in history has ever faced this kind of rapid change. It is no wonder that it has shifted the delicate balance otherwise in effect between the competing forces of client satisfaction, competence, and professionalism. Technology challenges have undercut and weakened legal competence, which in turn has strengthened some lawyers' perceived duties to clients at the expense of duties to the profession. Attorneys who succumb to unethical behavior in e-discovery do so because they give far greater weight to the financially rewarded duties to clients over the countervailing duties to the profession, duties intended to act as restraints upon excessive advocacy.

This represents a situation of excessive adversarial practice not adequately tempered by duties to the profession or by legal competence. Instead, high levels of technology incompetence aggravates the imbalance. This is a recipe for misconduct.

This analytical rubric suggests a remedy to the problem it illustrates. Lawyers need more legal training in e-discovery and in technology. The professional advocacy restraints to excessive zeal must also be strengthened and better understood. Lawyers must come to understand that they have a sacred duty to expedite litigation, be honest with the judge, and be truthful and fair to the opposing party and opposing counsel. These things are more important than money; they are at the very core of our profession. They separate the law from mere business. They justify the powers entrusted in our profession since the days of the Founding Fathers.

Integrity and the intolerance of unethical conduct cannot be accomplished with the enactment of more rules. Only better education and strict enforcement of our current rules will get us there. This enforcement requires much greater energy and attention to these issues by both the state bar associations and the judges who are often sad witness to such misbehavior. All too often such misconduct is tolerated. In the rare occasions where disciplinary actions are taken or sanctions are imposed, they are far too weak to deter similar conduct by the rest of the bar.

The *Qualcomm* case discussed next provides a perfect example of this situation. Although the court devoted hundreds of pages to multiple decisions describing the misconduct of Qualcomm's attorneys, including direct lies to the judge in the midst of a trial, to date no attorney or law firm involved has been sanctioned. Further, although there have been threats to refer the attorneys to the California Bar for disciplinary action, this has not yet happened.

Blog Reader Comment

by Craig Ball

As always, I share and admire your thoughts. You are kinder to our colleagues than I might be in terms of their response to the "Challenges of Technology." Most of the technologies we deal with today have been around for more than 10 years. Are the forms of ESI today really all that novel compared to those from the middle- to late 1990s? It's not as though lawyers have mastered e-mail, spreadsheets, and word-processed documents but have yet to figure out databases. Lawyers have generally ignored it all, even when they've had the years to do otherwise.

Just for the fun of thinking about it, I wondered at your statement, "No other generation of lawyers in history has ever faced this kind of rapid change."

The generations of lawyers that spanned, say, 1850 to 1915 probably faced much more in terms of both technological and social change. Consider the following changes those lawyers assimilated: telegraph, telephone, teletype, typewriter, radio, railroad, automobile, airplane, electric light, electric motor, air conditioning, refrigeration, motion pictures, sound recording, skyscrapers, elevators, fountain pen, transoceanic cabling, vacuum tube, plastic, sewing machine, toilet paper, the zipper and the bra. Not to mention a World War.

Were they made of sterner stuff in those days?

Another Blog Reader Comment

As a comment on the topic at hand, I think the technically savvy lawyers even have difficulty keeping up with the technological changes. Old technologies and new ones too, are being applied to the legal space at a rapid clip, and it is difficult, if not impossible, for lawyers to keep up with these changes and, more importantly, to understand the proper application of the technology to their issues. For example, lawyers may not understand clustering technology or ontologies, but to effectively use these technologies on their litigation, they should have a basic understanding of the technology and their expected results and shortcomings. I think that is one of the central messages in Judge Facciola's recent opinions—"Lawyers don't try this at home."

THE LESSONS OF *QUALCOMM*: A WAKEUP CALL FOR THE LEGAL PROFESSION

Qualcomm v. Broadcom is much more than another e-discovery case gone bad. It is an integrity wakeup call for the entire legal profession, much like Enron and Arthur Anderson were for business and accounting. *Qualcomm* shows what can happen when the profession strays too far from its roots, and the pursuit of profits takes precedence over the pursuit of justice. Some law firms may well be big businesses, but that is never all that they are. They are first and foremost professional associations. If they act like businesses, then it should be in the tradition of the London Stock Exchange, whose motto[11] since 1801 has been "*Dictum meum pactum.*" All of the top attorneys I have ever known have practiced this motto religiously. It

---

11. http://www.urbandictionary.com/define.php?term=my+word+is+my+bond

means "My word is my bond." When a real lawyer tells you something, you can take it to the bank. Isn't that the kind of lawyer you want? Isn't that the kind of lawyer society needs? *But see Qualcomm, Inc. v. Broadcom Corp.*, 2008 WL 66932 (S.D. Cal. Jan. 7, 2008) (one of several relevant decisions in this case).

I have written on *Qualcomm* many times, and am now resigned to doing so for a long time to come. Yes, I now think it is *that* important.

At the West Legalworks "A–Z e-Discovery" CLE seminar discussed at the beginning of the "Rules" chapter, every presenter had something to say about *Qualcomm*. The only exception was the chair, Browning E. Marean,[12] whose law firm, DLA Piper,[13] now represents Qualcomm in that case. His lips were sealed and he said nothing, but still squirmed mightily. Everyone who spoke agreed that *Qualcomm* is *the major case* of the year, not just for e-discovery practitioners, but for all litigators. As discussed above, it is the textbook example of what can happen when adversarial zeal, driven by millions of dollars in fees from a rich corporate client and fueled by professional and technological incompetence, is not properly restrained by understanding and respect for Model Rules 3.2, 3.3, and 3.4.

Factual Summary of *Qualcomm*

I will not recite all of the details of the case in this first essay (further essays on *Qualcomm* to follow), but here is a brief summary of what happened. Qualcomm sued its rival, Broadcom, claiming infringement of two of its key patents. Broadcom defended by claiming the patents were invalid because they were developed at the time Qualcomm was participating in an international standards-setting group called the Joint Video Team (JVT). Qualcomm denied participating in this team. Numerous discovery requests were made for Qualcomm to produce documents related to this defense. Qualcomm repeatedly denied having any JVT-related documents, consistent with its position that it never participated.

---

12. http://www.dlapiper.com/browning_marean/.
13. http://www.dlapiper.com/.

After years of discovery, where that party line was consistently upheld by all Qualcomm witnesses and all responses to discovery requests, the case went to trial. After weeks of trial, a Qualcomm witness, Viji Raveendran, admitted on cross-examination to having 21 e-mails related to Qualcomm's participation in the JVT. It was later discovered that Raveendran had told Qualcomm's lawyers about these 21 e-mails as part of final preparation for his trial testimony. Qualcomm's outside counsel had seen the e-mails, but decided to hide them and hope it would not come up on cross. According to the trial judge, the direct exam questions of this honest witness by Qualcomm's attorney were carefully designed to avoid asking Raveendran any question that might cause him to reveal the existence of those 21 e-mails.

Right after the surprise admission by Raveendran to 21 e-mails, Broadcom's attorney immediately complained to the judge. The judge summoned counsel to a sidebar conference. Qualcomm's attorneys assured the court that they had looked at these e-mails and they were not responsive, and that there was no cover-up, as Broadcom was now alleging. The judge accepted these assurances by the prominent and senior trial attorney conducting the case, *dictum meum pactum,* and the trial continued. Days later the jury found for the defendant. The jury foreman later explained[14] that they all knew Qualcomm employees were lying and it was an easy decision.

After trial, at Broadcom's urging, the judge ordered a complete investigation into whether there had been an e-mail cover-up. Turns out there had been, big time! Also, that sidebar representation by prominent counsel was, according to the presiding trial judge, a lie. After trial, Broadcom proved that Qualcomm had not only lied about and hid 21 e-mails, it had hidden over 46,000 e-mails with attachments comprising over 200,000 pages of relevant evidence! Naturally, both the court and the defendant were astonished and upset, to say the least.

It is one thing to hide the ball, but to hide 200,000 balls and almost get away with it—that's pretty impressive, in a twisted, *Dr. Evil* sort of way. Still, in this case at least, they were caught, and

---

14. http://ridethelightning.senseient.com/2007/10/jury-foreman-sp.html.

crime did not pay. Qualcomm was stripped of it patents and ordered to pay $8,568,633.24 in fees to the prevailing defendant, Broadcom. This sum represents part of the attorney fees incurred by defendant Broadcom in this case. It is safe to assume that the lawyers for the plaintiff Qualcomm were paid just as much, perhaps even more. Eight and a half million dollars, just for one lawsuit, is a lot of economic incentive for the lawyers to focus solely on adversarial zeal and forget totally about truth and candor.

By the way, patent litigation between these two companies continues in other courts around the country, and I do not have to tell you what kind of credibility Qualcomm now has with the courts.

This post-trial discovery of a cover-up led to sanctions motions against Qualcomm and it attorneys. The district court referred them to the magistrate. Of course, Qualcomm had by now fired its former attorneys, and now they were each blaming the other for the massive fraud on the court. Qualcomm then asserted its attorney-client privilege, and the magistrate agreed, effectively gagging Qualcomm's outside counsel (as I will explain later) from testifying about what their client had told them. Six of the many outside counsel representing Qualcomm were then sanctioned by the magistrate and referred to the California Bar for further action. I will elaborate on the magistrate's order in the next essay. On appeal this sanction was reversed by the district court judge, who held that Qualcomm's attorney-client privilege was subject to the self-defense waiver. For a good explanation of this, see Kevin McBride's blog *e-Discovery LA*.[15] To date, as far as anyone knows, the California Bar has still not reacted to this misconduct by commencing disciplinary proceedings against these attorneys, much less suspend or revoke their license to practice law.

The case has now been remanded for a new trial, where outside counsel and in-house counsel can now freely testify as to who told whom to hide what. Many have characterized the upcoming proceedings as a "circular firing squad." It is expected to take place sometime in 2009.

---

15. http://www.ediscoveryla.com/2008/03/articles/sanctions/qualcomms-outside-counsel-allowed-to-raise-selfdefense-exception-to-attorneyclient-privilege/.

Lessons of *Qualcomm*

The faculty of the A–Z e-Discovery CLE session all agreed that the moral of the *Qualcomm* story is not only that Hide the Ball is prohibited by the rules and all governing ethics, but also that one should *never even look for the ball* to begin with. You should instead make a reasonable inquiry and disclose all responsive evidence that this inquiry uncovers. Moreover, you should develop methodologies and lists[16] to help make sure your search and disclosure duties are properly discharged.

It is never in a client's best interests to lie or break the rules, even if some of your client's employees may sometimes think so. If a client does not want you to reveal evidence that will ruin its case, then you must convince that client otherwise. It should not matter how much money you are being paid to "win the case." Lawyers are not, or should not be, paid to win at any cost. They are paid to represent clients and help them to present their case. That never includes lying to the judge or deceiving opposing counsel.

As the judge clearly states in *Qualcomm*, if the client will still not comply and follow the rules, then you must resign. *Also see United States v. Johnson*, 2008 WL 2060597 (E.D. Va. May 15, 2008) (Defense attorney resigned midtrial when he discovers that his client had produced forged e-mails. After a mistrial, the court applied the crime-fraud privilege exception and required the attorney to explain why he resigned. The defendant was later convicted of obstruction of justice, along with the original charges. Interestingly, the e-mails were forged to try to hide information in connection with a fraud investigation into the defendant's company, PurchasePro.com, led by Arthur Anderson and Heller Ehrman.).

Lessons of *Qualcomm*

Kevin McBride has also written on the steps you should take to avoid the mistakes of *Qualcomm*. Aside from the obvious, but some-

---

16. http://ralphlosey.wordpress.com/2008/05/04/aba-litigation-section-reacts-to-the-qualcomm-case-and-recommends-e-discovery-checklists/.

times elusive, advice to tell the truth, Kevin recommends,[17] and I agree, that you form an e-Discovery Team and establish a "discovery plan" at the beginning of a case. According to Kevin,[18] the plan should include at least 10 items:

1. A detailed inventory and map of the client's ESI and IT infrastructure.
2. A description of retention policies and practices.
3. Identification of the key players to the dispute.
4. A "litigation hold" notice interrupting deletion practices of key players and resources.
5. A list of all resources searched for relevant ESI, plus a list of potentially relevant sources not searched because of accessibility problems.
6. A list of all search terms and methodologies used to identify relevant ESI.
7. A list of all persons to whom discovery requests were circulated for review in advance of production.
8. Policies to periodically monitor preservation compliance by the client and client's agents.
9. Policies to supplement discovery searches (and productions) when "red flag" information becomes known over the course of litigation that suggests new document resources or custodians need to be included in document production.
10. A policy for counsel to recheck the current state of discovery plan compliance before signing additional discovery responses or pleadings or making important arguments in court.

Alan Cohen, a writer for *Corporate Counsel*[19] magazine, has also recently examined the lessons of *Qualcomm*[20] from an in-house perspective. He draws five important lessons:

---

17. http://www.ediscoveryla.com/2008/02/articles/responding-to-discovery-reques/qualcomm-v-broadcom-a-how-to-manual-for-discovery/.
18. http://www.ediscoveryla.com/2008/02/articles/responding-to-discovery-reques/qualcomm-v-broadcom-a-how-to-manual-for-discovery/.
19. http://www.law.com/jsp/cc/index.jsp.
20. http://www.law.com/jsp/legaltechnology/pubArticleLT.jsp?id=1204631586917.

1. Outside counsel should know that they won't be penalized for pursuing the evidence.
2. Keep asking questions [about whether more documents exist, etc.].
3. Don't outsource e-discovery—oversee it closely, at the very least.
4. Don't annoy the judge.
5. Document the document collection.

The lessons of *Qualcomm* were also recently explored by Gregory D. Shelton[21] in his excellent article for the ABA's Litigation Section Discovery Committee. Gregory D. Shelton, "Qualcomm v. Broadcom: Lessons for Counsel and a Road Map to E-Discovery Preparedness," 16 *A.B.A. Sec. Pub. PP&D* 3, at 13 (Spring 2008). Here are Greg's conclusions and advice.

> Outside counsel, at all levels of authority, who rely on a client's search and retrieval of electronically stored information, are obligated to ask probing questions, audit the search and retrieval, and confirm that all potential sources of information have been investigated. To paraphrase the court in *Qualcomm*, if a junior attorney is unable to get a client to conduct the type of search he or she deems necessary to verify the adequacy of the document search and production, then he or she should obtain the assistance of a supervising or senior attorney. If the supervising or senior attorney is not able to get the client to perform a competent and thorough document search, he or she should withdraw from the case or take other action to ensure production of the evidence. [*Qualcomm, Inc. v. Broadcom Corp.*, No. 05cv1958-B (BLM), 2008 WL 66932 (S.D. Cal. Jan. 7, 2008) at *13, n.10] Another solution may be to insist that in-house counsel appear in the case and sign the discovery responses if the client is not providing sufficient verification of the search and retrieval process. Although outside counsel may also

---

21. http://www.williamskastner.com/attorneys.cfm?id=488.

consider some sort of indemnification agreement with the client, such an agreement does not relieve counsel from his or her ethical obligations.

I am not sure I understand what Greg had in mind about an indemnity agreement, but do not think anything like that is a good idea. What kind of attorney-client relationship would that be? How exactly would a client indemnify an attorney from disregarding his or her duties to the court? Would such an agreement be enforceable? Do we really want opposing counsel and the courts to wonder if our representations on discovery are mere empty promises emboldened by secret hold-harmless agreements? I certainly hope the profession does not go in that direction. Ethics and professionalism are not something that can be papered over with clever agreements.

But Greg's other suggestion to have in-house appear of record and sign discovery responses is practical and could work. Still, outside counsel would have to beware of falling into a trap of the three "no evil" monkeys[22] and a conspiracy of silence. "Turning a blind eye"[23] may have worked for Admiral Horatio Nelson[24] but will not work for lawyers. The attorney-client relationship must be built on full and open communications. It must be built on trust.

Mary Mack,[25] technology counsel of Fios, Inc.,[26] was interviewed[27] recently about *Qualcomm*:

> One effect of the *Qualcomm v. Broadcom* case is that it has introduced distrust and suspicion into relationships. It has adversely impacted the relationship between inside and outside counsel in a profound way.

---

22. http://en.wikipedia.org/wiki/Three_wise_monkeys.
23. http://en.wikipedia.org/wiki/Turn_a_blind_eye.
24. http://en.wikipedia.org/wiki/Horatio_Nelson.
25. http://www.fiosinc.com/about/management.asp.
26. http://www.fiosinc.com/.
27. http://www.metrocorpcounsel.com/current.php?artType=view&art Month=May&artYear=2008&EntryNo=7575.

Mary concludes her comments on this topic with a similar suggestion to Greg's, that in-house attorneys may want to protect themselves with indemnity agreements and insurance:

> Finally, inside counsel may experience a greater demand from law firms for an agreement that the client will waive the privilege if they need to defend themselves. And, inside counsel will have to consider their own liability in such matters and may wish to consider protecting themselves with insurance and/or a company indemnification agreement.

I do not think carriers will insure for the kind of behavior evidenced in *Qualcomm*. Some companies may go in that direction, but I think it is a mistake. The only viable solution is client education and counseling. The relationships of attorneys, both internal and external, must be built on honesty and trust. The actions of all counsel in this area should also be buoyed by core competency in the field of e-discovery, and at least reasonable competency in the computer systems involved in the case at hand. Outside law firms can help, too, by remembering that we are a profession first and a business second. Along those lines, law firms should reward attorneys who do the right thing and turn away from unscruplous clients instead of punishing them. Compensation should not be based on numbers alone. The intangibles are what separate us from business and justify our special place in society.

We should all remember and follow the motto *Dictum meum pactum*. This is not an outdated concept; it is the bedrock of the American system of justice. I am not telling you to avoid written agreements. That is not at all what it means. *Dictum meum pactum* means to be honest and truthful, and keep your commitments. It is the essence of trust and good reputation.

In the world of litigation, *dictum meum pactum* means that if an attorney makes a representation in court to the judge about discovery—or anything, for that matter—it must be true, it must be substantial. There is no room for half-truths and partial disclosure buttressed by secret indemnity agreements. If, for instance, you tell the court you made reasonable efforts to find relevant e-mail, mean it, and be prepared to prove it. People may differ on what is reasonable under the circumstances; that is to be expected. If the court sees a good-faith effort, albeit not diligent enough in its eyes, the response should be mild. But if you have found e-mail and are hiding it, it is not a matter of a difference of opinion; it is a matter of honesty. If you compound the error with lies to the court and opposing counsel, the sanctions should be harsh.

Blog Reader Comment

by David Ingraham
(Jury Foreman in *Qualcomm v. Broadcom*)

A very interesting article! Clearly this case is having a profound impact on the whole field of e-discovery. When we sat on the jury we had no idea how widespread the ramifications of this case would be.

I do think that you may have missed one critical lesson from the case:

> Never be so naive as to assume the you can bring a baseless case to trial and win a verdict solely because the complexity of the facts at issue will baffle the jurors.

The issue of the alleged infringement was really decided in the first three days of the plaintiff's testimony. After that the rest of the three-week trial was just resolving the issues of the validity and enforceability of the patents. Most of the 11 other jurors on this case were able to see that the testimony of Qualcomm's witnesses stretched credibility beyond any reasonable boundary. The reported six hours of deliberation actually exaggerates the time required to reach our verdicts. We spent perhaps two and a half of those hours being instructed on how to contact the court, ordering and eating lunch, and waiting for all the parties to reassemble in the courtroom to hear the verdict.

The most contentious part of the deliberations revolved around the finding that the Patent Office was not in error in granting the original patents. This finding would have been virtually impossible according to the judge's instructions.

Nevertheless, some jurors were so angry at Qualcomm that they wanted to punish them with a verdict that appeared to be certain to be overturned.

QUALCOMM'S "MONUMENTAL DISCOVERY VIOLATIONS" PROVOKED ONLY WIMPY SANCTIONS

On January 7, 2008, Magistrate Judge Barbara L. Major entered a 48-page Sanctions Order: Order Granting in Part and Denying in Part Defendant's Motion for Sanctions and Sanctioning Qualcomm, Incorporated and Individual Lawyers.[28] As previously mentioned, this order was later reversed by District Court Judge Rudi Brewster because he found reversible error in the application of the attorney-client privilege. Judge Brewster remanded the issue of attorney sanctions back to the magistrate for trial sometime in 2009. Even though the magistrate's order was reversed, it it still worthy of study to understand the *Qualcomm* saga.

The sanction recommended here by Magistrate Major was much less severe than I had expected after having read the harsh words used in earlier rulings in this case. The federal court in Qualcomm's hometown talked tough and spelled out "monumental discovery violations," including lying and fraud on a grand scale. But in the end it was just empty talk, and, despite the headlines you might have read to the contrary, no serious sanctions were imposed.

The order itself does a good job of summarizing the truly incredible litigation misconduct by Qualcomm and its attorneys. Most of the malfeasance discussed had, however, already been described by the trial judge, Judge Brewster, in his Order on Remedy for Finding of Waiver of August 6, 2007, *Qualcomm Inc. v. Broadcom Corp.,* No. 05-CV-1958-B(BLM) Doc. 593 (S.D. Cal. Aug. 6, 2007).[29]

Although most of the lawyer and litigant misconduct was described in the prior Waiver Order, Judge Major's Sanctions Order does include a few new and noteworthy facts that reveal their bold-

28. http://ralphlosey.files.wordpress.com/2008/01/qualcomm-sanctions-final-order.pdf.

29. http://ralphlosey.files.wordpress.com/2007/08/case-qualcomm_8_6_07_order_on_remedy.pdf.

ness. The Sanctions Order also provides good perspective on how our discovery system of justice depends upon the good faith of the parties and active, honest participation of their attorneys. It thus demonstrates how Model Rules 3.2, 3.3, and, 3.4 are the key linchpins of our entire system. This dependence on the integrity of lawyers, who are supposed to act as advocates for their client and as officers of the court, underscores the vulnerability of the system to unethical lawyers. Here are the magistrate's words:

> The Federal Rules of Civil Procedure require parties to respond to discovery in good faith; the rules do not require or anticipate judicial involvement unless or until an actual dispute is discovered. As the Advisory Committee explained, "[i]f primary responsibility for conducting discovery is to continue to rest with the litigants, they must be obliged to act responsibly and avoid abuse." Fed. R. Civ. P. 26(g) Advisory Committee Notes (1983 Amendment). The Committee's concerns are heightened in this age of electronic discovery when attorneys may not physically touch and read every document within the client's custody and control. For the current "good faith" discovery system to function in the electronic age, attorneys and clients must work together to ensure that both understand how and where electronic documents, records and e-mails are maintained and to determine how best to locate, review, and produce responsive documents. Attorneys must take responsibility for ensuring that their clients conduct a comprehensive and appropriate document search. Producing 1.2 million pages of marginally relevant documents while hiding 46,000 critically important ones does not constitute good faith and does not satisfy either the client's or attorney's discovery obligations. Similarly, agreeing to produce certain categories of documents and then not producing all of the documents that fit within such a category is unacceptable. Qualcomm's conduct warrants sanctions.

Qualcomm had opposed the entry of any sanctions against it by arguing that it was all their attorneys' fault. The 19 accused attorneys argued just as vigorously that it was all Qualcomm, that they were hoodwinked by their client. The judge did not believe either side and decided sanctions were appropriate against both.

> The Court's review of Qualcomm's declarations, the attorneys' declarations, and Judge Brewster's orders leads this Court to the inevitable conclusion that Qualcomm intentionally withheld tens of thousands of decisive documents from its opponent in an effort to win this case and gain a strategic business advantage over Broadcom. Qualcomm could not have achieved this goal without some type of assistance or deliberate ignorance from its retained attorneys. Accordingly, the Court concludes it must sanction both Qualcomm and some of its retained attorneys.

Qualcomm's misconduct was fairly obvious: it intentionally withheld over 46,000 e-mails and documents that were requested in discovery and that Qualcomm agreed to produce. Moreover, these 46,000 documents were key to Qualcomm's entire case, and Qualcomm knew it would lose if they were discovered by the other side. The court found that Qualcomm, the plaintiff, filed the suit with the intention of secreting this key evidence so that it would have a chance of winning. Qualcomm did succeed in hiding the 46,000 until trial, which it lost anyway, and then the fraud was discovered. The court called this a "monumental and intentional discovery violation." I am sure that everyone who litigates for a living, like I do, agrees.

The court could not believe that Qualcomm and its in-house attorneys could have carried out this kind of massive conspiracy to conceal evidence without the knowledge and participation of its outside counsel. If they truly knew nothing, then it was only because they acted like the three monkeys who did not want to know. It was gross negligence on their part not to know.

Qualcomm protected both itself and its outside counsel by refusing to waive its attorney-client privilege. Since all of the communications between Qualcomm and its attorneys were secret, it was impossible to find direct evidence of outside counsel's involvement in the conspiracy, and so the evidence against the attorneys was circumstantial.

> Neither party nor the attorneys have presented evidence that Qualcomm told one or more of its retained attorneys about the damaging e-mails or that an attorney learned about the e-mails and that the knowledgeable attorney(s) then helped Qualcomm hide the e-mails. While knowledge may be inferred from the attorneys' conduct, evidence on this issue is limited due to Qualcomm's assertion of the attorney-client privilege.
>
> Thus, the Court finds it likely that some variation of option four occurred; that is, one or more of the retained lawyers chose not to look in the correct locations for the correct documents, to accept the unsubstantiated assurances of an important client that its search was sufficient, to ignore the warning signs that the document search and production were inadequate, not to press Qualcomm employees for the truth, and/or to encourage employees to provide the information (or lack of information) that Qualcomm needed to assert its non-participation argument and to succeed in this lawsuit. These choices enabled Qualcomm to withhold hundreds of thousands of pages of relevant discovery and to assert numerous false and misleading arguments to the court and jury. This conduct warrants the imposition of sanctions.

The court goes into great detail as to the wrongs committed by each attorney, including intentional lying to the trial judge, and then summarizes the attorneys' malfeasance as follows:

> the evidence establishes that Qualcomm intentionally withheld tens of thousands of e-mails and that the Sanctioned Attorneys assisted, either intentionally or by virtue of acting with reckless disregard for their discovery obligations, in this discovery violation.

You may question how wimpy sanctions could possibly have been entered after reading those quotes. You may also wonder why I say this, if you have read the news headlines saying Qualcomm was sanctioned with an $8,568,633.24 attorney fee award. That is a pretty stiff sanction, you might think. But these headlines, like the sanctions, are smoke and mirrors. In fact, the Sanctions Order imposed no new monetary penalties on anyone. Qualcomm had already been ordered to pay $8,568,633.24 in fees in the underlying case in Judge Brewster's Order Granting Broadcom Corporation's Motion for Exceptional Case Finding and for an Award of Attorney's Fees. All the Sanctions Order did was provide another basis for the same award. The court makes clear that Qualcomm will *not* have to pay twice. So the real effect is a zero sanctions fee award against Qualcomm. No fines or other penalties were imposed. So much for harsh sanctions against Qualcomm. Judge Major no doubt realized that eyebrows would be raised by this decision, and so she attempted to explain her rationale in footnote 17 as follows:

> Because the attorneys' fees sanction is so large, the Court declines to fine Qualcomm. If the imposition of an $8.5 million dollar sanction does not change Qualcomm's conduct, the Court doubts that an additional fine would do so.

Hmm, not quite sure I follow that logic, but I am sure Qualcomm and its shareholders were relieved.

But what about their attorneys? Nineteen attorneys had been ordered by Judge Brewster to show cause to Judge Major why severe sanctions should not be imposed for their misconduct in this case. *Qualcomm Inc. v. Broadcom Corp.*, No. 05-CV-1958-B(BLM) Doc. 599 (S.D. Cal. Aug. 13, 2007).[30] The sanctions Judge Brewster asked Judge Moody to consider included requiring "counsel's formal disclosure of this Court's findings to all current clients and any courts in which counsel is admitted or has litigation currently pending." Now, that would have been a severe penalty. But it was not imposed by Judge Moody; it was not even discussed.

---

30. http://ralphlosey.files.wordpress.com/2007/08/case-qualcomm _8_13_07_show_cause_order.pdf.

Instead, all but six of the 19 attorneys ordered to show cause got off with no penalties at all. Five attorneys were sanctioned from Day Casebeer,[31] a small IP firm, and only one from Heller Ehrman,[32] a large firm based in San Francisco. The two law firms themselves were not sanctioned at all.

Here are Judge Major's sanctions against the six attorney who were not let off completely:

> As set forth above, the Sanctioned Attorneys assisted Qualcomm in committing this incredible discovery violation by intentionally hiding or recklessly ignoring relevant documents, ignoring or rejecting numerous warning signs that Qualcomm's document search was inadequate, and blindly accepting Qualcomm's unsupported assurances that its document search was adequate. The Sanctioned Attorneys then used the lack of evidence to repeatedly and forcefully make false statements and arguments to the court and jury. As such, the Sanctioned Attorneys violated their discovery obligations and also may have violated their ethical duties. *See, e.g.*, The State Bar of California, Rules of Professional Conduct, Rule 5-200 (a lawyer shall not seek to mislead the judge or jury by a false statement of fact or law), Rule 5-220 (a lawyer shall not suppress evidence that the lawyer or the lawyer's client has a legal obligation to reveal or to produce). To address the potential ethical violations, the Court refers the Sanctioned Attorneys to The State Bar of California for an appropriate investigation and possible imposition of sanctions.

Two of the attorneys in the Heller Ehrman firm who were originally ordered to show cause but were not sanctioned successfully defended themselves by arguing they were just acting as local counsel. I am surprised this defense was accepted. Yet here are Judge Major's own words:

---

31. http://www.daycasebeer.com/.
32. http://www.hewm.com/en/index.html.

These attorneys primarily monitored the instant case for its impact on separate Qualcomm/Broadcom litigation. However, for logistical reasons, both attorneys signed as local counsel pleadings that contained false statements relating to Qulacomm's non-participation in the JVT. Given the facts of this case as set forth above and in the declarations, the limitations provided by the referral, and the totality of the circumstances, the Court finds that it was reasonable for these attorneys to sign the pleadings, relying on the work of other attorneys more actively involved in the litigation.

The judge's words may seem reasonable, but I am surprised, because it is completely contrary to anything I have ever previously heard a federal judge say about acting as local counsel. Judge Major again recognizes her unusual leniency and tries to explain it in footnote 14:

The Court is declining to sanction these attorneys for their role in signing and filing false pleadings, but the Court notes that sanctioning local counsel for such conduct is possible and may be imposed in another case under different circumstances. Attorneys must remember that they are required to conduct a reasonable inquiry into the accuracy of the pleadings prior to signing, filing or arguing them.

The sanctions against the six lawyers were, in my opinion, relatively mild. No fees were taxed or fines imposed. They were just ordered to provide a copy of the orders to the state bar for "appropriate investigation." Of course, the bar in California already knew about this case. All this sanction order did was let most of the attorneys off the hook. Moreover, I am told that under the California Bar Ethics Code, judges are required to report lawyer misconduct that they witness. So the judge was already required to turn them in. Bar investigations will be conducted eventually, I would assume, and there will be some penalties imposed, but I doubt they will amount to much. They will certainly be far less than the ultimate penalty of disbarment imposed against President Clinton for purportedly failing to understand what "sex" is. It will also be far less than the client and judge letter-writing penalties that Judge Brewster suggested.

The final sanction was to order the six outside attorneys, along with five Qualcomm in-house counsel that the court found complicit in the fraud, to participate in what the court called a CREDO program (Case Review and Enforcement of Discovery Obligations). It requires the 11 lawyers to meet and prepare a memorandum on how to avoid this kind of incredible e-discovery fraud from reoccurring in the future. Judge Major really seems to think that these discredited attorneys will somehow be redeemed by studying what went wrong and writing a great memo. In her words:

> While no one can undo the misconduct in this case, this process, hopefully, will establish a baseline for other cases. Perhaps it also will establish a turning point in what the Court perceives as a decline in and deterioration of civility, professionalism and ethical conduct in the litigation arena. To the extent it does so, everyone benefits—Broadcom, Qualcomm, and all attorneys who engage in, and judges who preside over, complex litigation. If nothing else, it will provide a road map to assist counsel and corporate clients in complying with their ethical and discovery obligations and conducting the requisite "reasonable inquiry."

Sorry, but I think this is naive. In my opinion, it is like catching the fox in the hen house, and then "punishing" it by asking for a memo on how to improve hen house security. These are not the right attorneys to turn to for advice on how to fix e-discovery. They might as well have been ordered to write "I will not cheat and lie" on the blackboard a thousand times.

The lawyers should have been sanctioned with high monetary fines and ordered to write the client and judge letters, not a CREDO memo. Then a strong message would have been sent to the bar. If you do not obey Model Rules 3.2, 3.3 and 3.4, you will be punished by both the courts and the bar. Then the very small minority of attorneys who commit these types of wrongs might think twice. They might act like the vast majority of lawyers in this country do every day—they might choose honor and integrity over the temptations of the fast buck from an unscrupulous client. This was an opportunity missed.

SANCTIONS LIFTED AGAINST THE *"QUALCOMM* SIX" AND A NEW TRIAL ORDERED WHERE THEY MAY NOW SPEAK FREELY TO DEFEND THEMSELVES

This section explains why the magistrate's Sanctions Order was reversed. The Order dated March 5, 2007,[33] by Judge Rudi Brewster vacated Magistrate Barbara Major's Sanctions Order of January 8, 2007,[34] but the Order was only vacated for the attorneys sanctioned, and not for Qualcomm. *Qualcomm v. Broadcom*, 2008 WL 638108 (S.D.Cal., March 5, 2008). This may seem like a bad deal for Qualcomm, but actually it is a great result for them.

Judge Brewster ordered a new trial for the *Qualcomm* Six, the attorneys who were previously sanctioned: Messrs. Batchelder, Bier, Leung, Mammen, Patch, and Young. He held that their rights to due process had been violated in the first show-cause trial because they were not allowed to testify about what their client, Qualcomm, had said and done concerning the e-discovery issues underlying the sanctions motion. Judge Brewster held that they had a right to defend themselves in that proceeding and not be silenced by the secrecy restraints of the attorney-client privilege.

Their figurative gag was released when Judge Brewster reversed the magistrate's earlier order that the self-defense exception to the attorney-client privilege did not apply. In the new trial, the secrets of *Qualcomm* may be revealed. Their former attorneys can give a full explanation of how "over 200,000 pages of relevant e-mails, memoranda, and other company documents" were hidden from disclosure to the other side. *Qualcomm Inc. v. Broadcom Corp.*, No. 05-CV-1958-B(BLM) Doc. 593 (S.D. Cal., Aug. 6, 2007).[35] If even worse

---

33. http://ralphlosey.files.wordpress.com/2008/03/qualcomm ordervacatingsanctions.pdf.

34. http://ralphlosey.files.wordpress.com/2008/01/qualcomm-sanctions-final-order.pdf.

35. http://ralphlosey.files.wordpress.com/2007/08/case-qualcomm_8_6_07_order_on_remedy.pdf.

behavior on Qualcomm's part is revealed in the second trial, Qualcomm will, thanks to clever defense work by its new lawyers, be immune from further punishment. Hard to believe, but true, as I will explain at the end of this section.

The first show-cause trial, in which outside counsel were restrained in what they could say, resulted in the referral of the *Qualcomm* Six for an ethics investigation by the California Bar. Judge Major had requested this investigation because of what she called the Six's "monumental discovery violations." The reversal and remand for a new trial provides an opportunity for these lawyers to salvage their careers and tarnished reputations. When they do speak, lawyers from all over the country will be listening; not only the California Bar. It could become a polite attempt to whitewash, but will more likely result in serious mudslinging. In any event, the previously muzzled speech will be interesting to watch in the 2009 trial.

Judge Brewster's March 5, 2008 Order[36] vacating sanctions against the *Qualcomm* Six reveals a clever defense strategy by Qualcomm to Judge Brewster's earlier Order to Show Cause.[37] The Show Cause Order was directed against all 14 of Qualcomm's outside counsel, not just the six who were eventually sanctioned, and it was directed against Qualcomm itself. Qualcomm knew that the attorney-client privilege would be an issue in this hearing. It also knew that it *owned* this privilege, not the attorneys, and that only Qualcomm could waive the secrecy constraints that otherwise silenced its attorneys. Qualcomm refused to waive. This meant that its former attorneys could not divulge the information they learned from Qualcomm. The original 14 attorneys ordered to show cause could not defend themselves from the court's allegations by disclosing the confidential communications with their client.

In a situation like this where one party in effect gags another, it is natural to assume that the party gagged would, if he could, say something harmful about the "gaggor." Otherwise, why else would

---

36. http://ralphlosey.files.wordpress.com/2008/03/qualcomm ordervacatingsanctions.pdf.

37. http://ralphlosey.files.wordpress.com/2007/08/case-qualcomm_ 8_13_07_show_cause_order.pdf.

they be silenced? But the right of a client to maintain its secrets is so strong in the law that this natural presumption is not permitted when a client asserts this right. Qualcomm knew this, and thus knew it could assert its right to keep its lawyer communications secret, and this could not be used against it in its defense of the Show Cause Order.

I suspect that the party pushing the sanctions against Qualcomm, namely Broadcom, which was its adversary in the underlying patent case, argued against Qualcomm on this point. Broadcom would naturally try to convince the court to hold Qualcomm's assertion of its secrecy rights against it. In other words, Broadcom would ask the court to impose an adverse inference against Qualcomm wherein the court would infer that the hidden communications were detrimental to Qualcomm. Judge Major would not do that, even though she was obviously displeased that she was not hearing the whole truth and that key facts were being withheld by Qualcomm's assertion of the privilege. This is explained in footnote 8 at page 25 of her Sanctions Order:[38]

> Recognizing that a client has a right to maintain this privilege and that no adverse inference should be made based upon the assertion, the Court accepted Qualcomm's assertion of the privilege and has not drawn any adverse inferences from it. October 12, 2007 Hearing Transcript at 4-5. However, the fact remains that the Court does not have access to all of the information necessary to reach an informed decision regarding the actual knowledge of the attorneys.

Qualcomm also knew that its former attorneys were likely to raise the self-defense exception to the attorney-client privilege. This exception frees an attorney from a secrecy vow when necessary to defend him- or herself from accusations of wrongdoing by the client. The problem with this defense was that the accusations were being made by Broadcom and the court, not Qualcomm. The self-defense exception would only apply if Qualcomm tried to defend

---

38. http://ralphlosey.files.wordpress.com/2008/01/qualcomm-sanctions-final-order.pdf.

itself with accusations against its former attorneys. Qualcomm clearly wanted to do this, so it was in something of a quandary. Judge Brewster's recent order reveals a particularly clever strategy on Qualcomm's part to overcome that quandary, a strategy that allowed them to both have their cake and eat it too.[39] This desire is, by the way, hardly unique to Qualcomm; most every party in litigation wants this all of the time.

At the commencement of the show-cause proceedings, Qualcomm was very careful not to make any direct accusations of wrongdoing on the part of the 14 attorneys accused in the Show Cause Order. Although the implication was clear in Qualcomm's defense that it did nothing wrong, that the blame should instead fall on its outside counsel, it made no specific allegations against them. Qualcomm's former lawyers, in turn, defended by arguing it was their client's fault, and they could prove it, if only they were released from the attorney-client privilege gag. Again, footnote 8 of the Sanctions Order explains what happened:

> Qualcomm asserted the attorney-client privilege and decreed that its retained attorneys could not reveal any communications protected by the privilege. Doc. No. 659; October 12, 2007 Hearing Transcript at 38. Several attorneys complained that the assertion of the privilege prevented them from providing additional information regarding their conduct. *See, e.g.*, Young Decl. at 12; Leung Decl. at 3-5; Robertson Decl. at 14-16.

The reversal by Judge Brewster fills in the rest of the story, wherein some of the accused attorneys argued that the self-defense exception should apply.

> The retained attorneys thereafter filed the above-referenced motion for a finding of a self-defense exception to Qualcomm's asserted attorney-client privilege. The self-defense motion was unopposed by Qualcomm, if the hearing

---

39. http://en.wikipedia.org/wiki/Have_one's_cake_and_eat_it_too.

could be sealed, and with Broadcom excluded, which was not acceptable to Broadcom. Broadcom did not oppose the motion. The court's order denying the motion is supported primarily because Qualcomm had not presented any evidence, such as declarations, against its attorneys. Thus, no adversity between Qualcomm and its attorneys was presented by Qualcomm.

The motion to apply the self-defense exception was denied. Qualcomm was thus able to keep its confidences secret by carefully limiting its declarations (affidavits) against its attorneys at that point in the proceedings. This prevented the former attorneys from making a showing of adversity necessary to support the self-defense exception.

Here is where clever defense strategy comes in and shows the importance of timing and the impact of appeals. After the ruling denying the self-defense exception, which the attorneys appealed, Magistrate Judge Major went ahead with the show-cause proceeding with partially silenced attorneys. But then, as part of the proceeding, Qualcomm filed several new declarations that *were* directly adverse to its attorneys. The new statements clearly blamed their attorneys as part of their own defense. Among other things, Qualcomm alleged that its lawyers had failed to ask Qualcomm for discoverable documents, had inadequately prepared witnesses, and had failed to advise Qualcomm employees of the company's defenses prior to their testimony at trial. Still, even though the allegations had changed, the *Qualcomm* Six remained bound by the prior order, pending appeal. They still could not defend themselves against Qualcomm's allegations.

In my view, this defense strategy worked spectacularly. In the sanctions order that followed, there were no new sanctions imposed upon Qualcomm whatsoever. Although it was found to have withheld evidence and engaged in misleading conduct, there was no real punishment imposed. It was equivalent to losing on liability but getting a zero verdict. I know, all the headlines say Qualcomm was punished by a brutal $8,568,633.24 fee award. But, as I pointed out in my prior article, that was just for show. Qualcomm had *already* been ordered to pay these same fees in the underlying case. All the Sanctions Order did was provide another basis for the same award. The court makes clear that Qualcomm will *not* have to pay twice. So the real effect was a zero sanctions fee award against Qualcomm.

That was an excellent result for Qualcomm. It was thus to be expected that Qualcomm would comply with the Sanctions Order as soon as possible, and pay the $8,568,633.24 fee award to Broadcom. It did so soon after the Sanctions Order was entered, and thus also complied at the same time with the earlier fee award. This meant that the Sanctions Order was now final for Qualcomm, and would stand regardless of whether the *Qualcomm* Six attorneys won their appeal on the right to testify against Qualcomm. This appeal was now very strong since, in the meantime, Qualcomm had taken off the gloves and was clearly adverse to these attorneys. Qualcomm was thus able to have its cake—the attorney-client privilege—and eat it too, because it was able to blame and accuse its attorneys and still keep them silent. Then, before the cake could be taken away, they paid for it.

In the appeal of Judge Major's decisions by the *Qualcomm* Six, Judge Brewster considered the new gloves-off declarations of Qualcomm against its attorneys. These new facts established the necessary predicate of adversity to allow the self-defense exception to apply. For that reason, Judge Brewster reversed Judge Major's earlier ruling on this issue. This error is, in turn, the sole reason the sanctions award against the *Qualcomm* Six was vacated and a new trial ordered. This new trial will be only against the attorneys, not Qualcomm, because the order is final as to Qualcomm. It has already complied with the order, so it is too late for a re-do. So when the attorneys return, unmuzzled, and reveal the secrets of Qualcomm, no matter how damaging these secrets may be, it will be too late for the court or Broadcom to do anything about it. Now you see how clever the defense has been.

Here is how Judge Brewster explains it at pages 5-6 of his March 5, 2008, order:

This introduction of accusatory adversity between Qualcomm and its retained counsel regarding the issue of assessing responsibility for the failure of discovery changes the factual basis which supported the court's earlier order denying the self-defense exception to Qualcomm's attorney-client privilege. *Meyerhofer v. Empire Fire & Marine Ins. Co.*, 497 F.2d 1190, 1194-95 (2d Cir. 1974); *Hearn v. Rhay*, 68 F.R.D. 574, 581 (E.D. Wash. 1975); *First Fed. Sav. & Loan Ass'n v. Oppenheim, Appel, Dixon & Co.*, 110 F.R.D. 557, 560-68 (S.D. N.Y. 1986); A.B.A. Model Rules of Prof. Conduct 1.6(b)(5) & comment 10.

Accordingly, the court's order denying the self defense exception to the attorney-client privilege is vacated. The attorneys have a due process right to defend themselves under the totality of circumstances presented in this sanctions hearing where their alleged conduct regarding discovery is in conflict with that alleged by Qualcomm concerning performance of discovery responsibilities. See, e.g., *Miranda v. So. Pac. Transp. Co.*, 710 F.2d 516, 522-23 (9th Cir. 1983). The exception applying, the communications and conduct relevant to the topic area of records (electronic or other) discovery pertaining to JVT and its parents, its ad-hoc committees, and any other topic regarding the standards-setting process for video compression technology is not privileged information. *Weil v. Investment/Indicators, Research & Mgmt., Inc.*, 647 F.2d 18, 24 (9th Cir. 1981).

Now we wait to hear what the *Qualcomm* Six have to say.

ABA LITIGATION SECTION REACTS TO THE *QUALCOMM* CASE AND RECOMMENDS E-DISCOVERY CHECKLISTS

The Litigation Section of the American Bar Association reacted to the decision with an online article[40] on *Qualcomm v. Broadcom.* Written by Kristine L. Roberts,[41] *Litigation News* associate editor,

---

40. http://www.abanet.org/litigation/litigationnews/2008/may/0508_article_qualcomm.html.

41. http://www.bakerdonelson.com/Bio.aspx?NodeID= 32&PersonID =5235.

the article is significant for its glimpse into the thinking of ABA leaders on electronic discovery abuses. Essentially, the ABA litigation leaders remind practitioners of the importance of discovery, and recommend e-discovery checklists as a good way to stay on top of the process and avoid another *Qualcomm*. While I agree that checklists can be useful, they have their limits. In my view, they must be supplemented with expert advice, not to mention a strong sense of ethics and professional responsibility.

Erica Calderas

Erica L. Calderas[42] is the co-chair of the Section of Litigation's Pretrial Practice and Discovery Committee.[43] Erica is quoted in the article as saying:

> The Qualcomm decision reminds all litigators—in a very forceful way—of the serious obligations we undertake in responding to discovery.

She is right. Discovery, especially complex e-discovery, is not something you can just delegate to a first-year associate and forget about it. It is critical to the outcome of most cases and can be easily messed up if not done right.

Erica recommends that attorneys use standard-form e-discovery checklists in every case to make sure they cover all of the bases and avoid e-discovery violations. Good advice. This is especially important for a general litigator who does not have the assistance of an e-discovery specialist in a small case. Erica specifically recommends that attorneys:

> [Use checklists to] ensure that you apply a consistent protocol in any new matter—for example, that you routinely instruct your client to preserve evidence, that you identify witnesses with knowledge, that you determine how the client maintains its documents, that you ask the right questions

---

42. http://www.hahnlaw.com/professionalsdetail.asp?empid=1508.
43. http://www.abanet.org/litigation/committees/pretrial/home.html.

regarding where potential documents may be located, and that you ask about additional relevant documents and potential witnesses in every witness interview.

Checklists and Specialists

Law firms are now beginning to create and employ such checklists as a routine matter in all litigated matters. For instance, many already follow Erica's advice and routinely instruct their clients on preservation duties at the beginning of a case. This is not a mere "CYA" exercise. For many clients, even otherwise very sophisticated ones, it can be a real wakeup call. Many in-house counsel are, for instance, unaware of automatic ESI deletion programs, PC and backup tape recycling, forensic collection, and the like. They may need significant help to implement an effective preservation hold and collection program.

A few law firms are taking this a step further and recommending to their litigation attorneys that an e-discovery specialist be included in any significant case. This is not a hard and fast rule, merely a recommendation. In some firms, this advice is often not followed until after there is a problem, instead of at the commencement of the firm's representation, when their input could do the most good.

One large firm, Hunton & Williams,[44] has gone beyond mere recommendation. It has promulgated a rule *requiring* e-discovery attorney involvement. In their words, they have begun "implementing requirements that an e-discovery specialist be assigned to all significant matters involving ESI." Hunton & Williams has 1,000 attorneys in 18 offices, and, of course, many e-discovery specialists. It is, to my knowledge, the first law firm to explicitly make this a requirement, not just a recommendation. Hunton's Sherry Harris, whom I met at the Harvard Club CLE described in the first chapter, brought this to my attention and obtained permission for me to share this. This is an important step, and the management of Hunton should be congratulated. I expect that other law firms will follow in their footsteps, and eventually this will be commonplace. This is far more

---

44. http://www.hunton.com/.

effective a solution than just distributing checklists to all litigators and hoping that everything gets done right.

The participation of e-discovery specialists can work seamlessly if the law firm requires it, and if the firm actually has such attorneys to carry it out. But at this point very few law firms actually have specialists like that, and of course they do not require what they cannot deliver. Today most law firms, especially small to medium-size firms, do not have these specialists. They must look to outside entrepreneurs for assistance when there is a significant matter involving ESI. I am not saying that every litigated case needs that kind of input. The principles of proportionality and economics must always be followed, and many cases today still do not have a large e-discovery component.

From what I have seen, although there are many e-discovery vendors, there are still only a few attorneys who specialize in e-discovery. Their numbers are, however, beginning to increase, especially among younger lawyers. The few who are full time e-discovery lawyers typically operate as independent entrepreneurs or in small groups, or are employed by large vendors and consulting companies. This allows them to consult and be retained by other firms. A few e-discovery attorneys are shareholders, or of counsel, to some of the nation's largest law firms, such as Hunton & Williams. Over half of the top 50 firms have e-discovery lawyers, but with varying levels of expertise. These big-firm attorneys are usually fully occupied serving the litigators in their own firm, and are only rarely retained by other law firms as co-counsel.

Instead, the e-discovery lawyers who are on their own or with consulting firms are the specialists usually retained by law firms, both big and small, that lack attorneys with such arcane skills. As mentioned, they are usually called in to assist on projects after there is trouble of some kind. It is always challenging to bring in an outside attorney as an expert to assist in a case, but it is particularly difficult when it occurs after a problem develops. For one thing, how do you explain "the cleaner" to the client? No doubt it is the fault of the other side, or perhaps the judge. There can also be relationship issues when new attorneys from different firms work together for the first time. This is especially difficult when the trial attorney in charge has made a mistake and does not want to hear about it or understand the complexities involved. Yet, this is typically how and when most e-specialists get involved in litigation.

David Soley

Also quoted in Kristine Roberts's article was David A. Soley,[45] of Bernstein Shur,[46] co-chair of the Section's Trial Practice Committee:[47]

> We should not be surprised by the ruling, [the opinion] reflects what day-to-day practice ought to be. Attorneys are professionals and have professional standards to uphold, including a duty of good faith and reasonable inquiry in responding to discovery.

I assume David was referring to the sanctions imposed against Qualcomm and its attorneys for not upholding professional standards by trying to hide more than 30,000 e-mails critical to the outcome of the case. David goes on to say that:

> because lawyers will be held responsible for their clients' production of documents, lawyers must go to the site where documents are kept. . . . [T]he lawyer must understand what the client did and then verify it.

Once again, this comment (in my opinion) verifies the need for trial lawyers to obtain the assistance of e-discovery specialists in any large case involving complex computer systems. Counsel must not only understand what clients did, they must be sure their actions complied with the rules and met the minimum forensic standards for admissibility as evidence. Also, they need to have the backbone to correct a client who screws up or, as in the *Qualcomm* case, wants to hide the ball.

David, who is himself a trial lawyer specializing in real estate litigation, does not talk about retaining e-discovery experts, but again

---

45. http://bernsteinshur.com/attorneys_results2.aspx?lawyer_id=99.
46. http://bernsteinshur.com/index-04.aspx.
47. http://www.abanet.org/litigation/committees/trialpractice/home.html.

suggests the use of checklists. Here is Kristine Roberts's report[48] of
his comments:

> Calderas [Erica] recommends that to avoid e-discovery vio-
> lations, attorneys should use checklists to "ensure that you
> apply a consistent protocol in any new matter—for example,
> that you routinely instruct your client to preserve evidence,
> that you identify witnesses with knowledge, that you deter-
> mine how the client maintains its documents, that you ask
> the right questions regarding where potential documents may
> be located, and that you ask about additional relevant docu-
> ments and potential witnesses in every witness interview."
> Calderas also suggests that litigators enter into agreements
> with opposing counsel regarding what search terms will be
> used, the places at which relevant evidence may be found,
> and the persons whose files will be searched.

This is all good advice, to be sure, but is it sufficient in a complex case involving large amounts of ESI?

ABA's Checklist

The article concludes with a checklist summarizing the recommendations of the ABA leaders on how, as they put it, "to avoid
Qualcomm's fate."

1. Use checklists and develop a standard discovery protocol.
2. Understand how and where your client maintains paper files
   and electronic information, as well as your client's business
   structures and practices.
3. Go to the location where information is actually maintained—
   do not rely entirely on the client to provide responsive materials to you.
4. Ensure you know what steps your client, colleagues, and
   staff have actually taken and confirm that their work has
   been done right.

---

48. http://www.abanet.org/litigation/litigationnews/2008/may/
0508_article_qualcomm.html.

5. Ask all witnesses about other potential witnesses and where and how evidence was maintained.
6. Use the right search terms to discover electronic information.
7. Bring your own IT staff to the client's location and have them work with the client's IT staff, employ e-discovery vendors, or both.
8. Consider entering into an agreement with opposing counsel to stipulate to the locations to be searched, the individuals whose computers and hard copy records are at issue, and the search terms to be used.
9. Err on the side of production.
10. Document all steps taken to comply with your discovery protocol.

Once again, all good advice, as long as you understand the limitations of such general advice. Further, if the point is to avoid another Qualcomm, mandatory ethical training should be included, along with the admonishment to walk away from any client who would have you hide evidence or lie to the court. There is no price on a sound night's sleep.

Limitations of Checklists

The above 10-step checklist is, in my view, helpful only as a general starting point. Law firms should establish much more detailed forms and procedures to do e-discovery right. I know I have personally spent weeks doing just that. My firm, like a few others who have made such efforts, naturally holds such information as a trade secret. You can find many checklists online from a variety of sources, but they will all be generalized, and serve only as a starting point for further research, or teaser for retention of services. For one pretty good example, see the e-discovery checklist[49] included in the Association of Corporate Counsel[50] Web site. The same essentially holds true for form books

---

49. http://www.acc.com/chapters/program/sanant/ediscovery_checklist.pdf.

and commentaries. No complex area of law can be solved with simple forms and checklists, although again they can be helpful as a starting point. *See,* for example, *Electronic Discovery and Records Management Guide: Rules, Checklists and Forms, 2008 ed.,*[51] by Jay E. Grenig,[52] Browning E. Marean,[53] and Mary P. Poteet,[54] and *Arkfeld's Best Practices Guide for ESI Pretrial Discovery-Strategy and Tactics (2008-2009),*[55] by Michael Arkfeld. This is especially true of e-discovery, which is a combination of both law and technology. In e-discovery, the facts are always different, and rapid changes in technology quickly make yesterday's solution obsolete.

Even if the detailed forms and checklists developed by a few experts for private use were no longer confidential, these checklists would not, by themselves, do that much good. They are meant to be used with the assistance of the experts who created them. Forms and checklists require background knowledge and teamwork with experts to function properly. They work best as a general guide and reminder not to overlook necessary steps. They also let you know when and how to call for help. Sometimes just knowing what you do not know is half the battle. Step 7 in the above ABA checklist recognizes this in recommending employment of an e-discovery vendor. But be careful in relying too much on some vendors, especially those who are little more than copy-shops and have no in-house legal input.

The truth is, without experience and occasional guidance, simple checklists alone can be counterproductive. They can easily be misunderstood and provide a false sense of confidence. Sometimes it pays to be a little worried. I am sure that is one of the lessons Qualcomm's former lawyers have learned. Perhaps the great poet

---

50. http://www.acc.com/.

51. http://west.thomson.com/store/product.aspx?r =143652&product_id=40655025.

52. http://west.thomson.com/store/authorbio.aspx? materialnumber=40655025&author_id=1688&author_ ame=Jay+E.+Grenig+.

53. http://www.dlapiper.com/browning_marean/.

54. http://www.iltanet.org/connections/group_detail.aspx?nvID=000000010605&h4ID=000000028105.

55. http://arkfeld.blogs.com/ede/2008/04/just-released-a.html.

Alexander Pope,[56] whom I have quoted before,[57] said it best in *An Essay on Criticism* (1709):

> A little learning is a dangerous thing; drink deep, or taste not the Pierian spring:[58] there shallow draughts intoxicate the brain, and drinking largely sobers us again.

Blog Reader Comment

by Craig Ball

As usual, you have nailed the issues. I was especially happy to see your emphasis on checklists as an adjunct to work by those who appreciate the variability of the environments and relative importance of the items. Checklists are a bit like bullet points in a PowerPoint. Properly constructed, they are simply a mnemonic anchoring or triggering richer or more precise information from from the presenter. Bullet points are not a substitute for a good presenter, only for a bad one.

To create a checklist that supplants expert knowledge and experience demands such an extensive decision tree that it would be tantamount to creating an expert system. Feasible, but nothing at all like that which the ABA contemplates.

Another aspect of checklists that hasn't been addressed is their ability to foster a perception of negligece even when there has been no malfeasance. Many forensic examiners are loathe to use checklists lest they be taken to task for anything omitted. There are times when you can properly skip certain steps on a checklist if you can defend the decision and fully appreciate its consequences. That's not a view I want my pilot to follow, but if we pursued e-discovery in the same way as we fly airplanes, litigation might never get off the ground.

---

56. http://en.wikipedia.org/wiki/Alexander_Pope.

57. http://ralphlosey.wordpress.com/2008/02/24/criminal-case-raises-interesting-e-discovery-search-issues/.

58. http://en.wikipedia.org/wiki/Pierian_Spring.

Summaries of Favorite and Recent e-Discovery Cases

7

This case law section summarizes my favorite e-discovery cases not discussed in this book or in my earlier book, *E-Discovery: Current Trends and Cases.* Most are well-known e-discovery "classics," but a few are relatively unknown gems that I have come across in my research.

Ignorance of Computers Is No Longer a Viable Excuse

Martin v. Northwestern Mutual Life Insurance Company,[1] **2006 WL 148991 (M.D Fla. Jan. 19, 2006)**

Plaintiff, a trial lawyer, and his counsel are sanctioned for failure to produce only paper records, and plead

---

1. http://ralphlosey.files.wordpress.com/2008/05/martincase.pdf.

"computer illiteracy" as to the voluminous additional electronic records that were eventually found on the plaintiff's office computers. The district court held that the attorney's "claim that he is so computer illiterate that he could not comply with production is frankly ludicrous."

My Favorite "War Story" Case

At my firm, we call this the Case of the Midnight Hacker. *Optowave Co. Ltd. v. Nitikin,*[2] 2006 WL 3231422 (M.D. Fla. Nov. 7, 2006).

This Akerman case, where Jim Foster was the trial lawyer, shows how e-discovery can be used as a case-winning tool in commercial litigation. Here defendant Nikitin, a citizen of Russia living and doing business in central Florida, produced very few e-mails. Our client, Optowave, a Korean corporation, moved to compel. Defendant tried to explain the missing e-mails by claiming that a computer hacker broke into his network at night and deleted everything. We challenged the veracity of that story and moved for sanctions for spoliation.

There was then a full-day evidentiary hearing on our motion where we offered forensic evidence and other proof of spoliation by intentional, bad-faith destruction of evidence. Magistrate Judge Baker did not believe the defendant's midnight-hacker story. Our motion for sanctions was granted, fees were awarded, and an all-important adverse inference was granted that the missing e-mails would have contradicted the defendant's version of the communications. In the ensuing bench trial, this became a near-conclusive presumption on a key fact establishing liability. Proof of liability in this case without the spoliation sanctions would have been very difficult, if not impossible, since our clients spoke little or no English. In fact, Optowave did prevail after a one-week trial and a money judgment was entered against Nikitin, which was ultimately paid.

---

2. http://ralphlosey.files.wordpress.com/2006/11/optowave.pdf.

The Most Famous and Important e-Discovery Case of All, *Zubulake*

Zubulake v. UBS Warburg LLC (Zubulake I)[3], 217 F.R.D. 309 (S.D. N.Y. 2003). This first opinion addresses the legal standard for determining the cost allocation for producing e-mails contained on backup tapes. Basic facts of this case: the plaintiff, Laura Zubulake, 44, was the director of the bank's Asian shares sales desk in New York, with an annual salary of $500,000. She sued the Swiss financial giant for gender discrimination and illegal retaliation. In her words, noted in her personal comment to my blog on this case below (which caused me to revise this case description), she complained of "denial and removal from professional responsibilities, exclusion from business outings, being belitted and generally treated different from my male colleagues." During e-discovery she found an e-mail from her supervisor stating that she was too "old and ugly and she can't do the job." The supervisor and many of his colleagues tried to cover up by deleting e-mails and denying everything. Judge Shira Scheindlin and the jury did not buy it, and ultimately Zubulake was awarded $10 million in pay and $19 million in punitive damages, for a total award of $29 million.

Zubulake III,[4] *Zubulake v. UBS Warburg LLC,* 216 F.R.D. 280 (S.D. N.Y. 2003). This decision allocates the backup tape restoration costs between Zubulake and UBS with a detailed explanation of the appropriate criteria and weighting.

Zubulake IV,[5] *Zubulake v. UBS Warburg LLC,* 220 F.R.D. 212, 218 (S.D. N.Y. 2003). This decision ordered sanctions against UBS for violating its duty to preserve evidence and in the process established a scope of duty to preserve backup tapes, but only in special circumstances.

Zubulake V,[6] *Zubulake v. UBS Warburg LLC,* 229 F.R.D. 422 (S.D. N.Y. 2004). *Zubulake V* requires outside counsel to make cer-

---

3. http://ralphlosey.files.wordpress.com/2008/05/zubulakei.pdf.
4. http://ralphlosey.files.wordpress.com/2008/05/zubulakeiii.pdf.
5. http://ralphlosey.files.wordpress.com/2008/05/zubulakeiv.pdf.
6. http://ralphlosey.files.wordpress.com/2008/05/zubulakev.pdf.

tain that all potentially relevant information is identified and placed "on hold." In the words of Judge Scheindlin:

> To do this, counsel must become fully familiar with her client's document retention policies, as well as the client's data retention architecture. This will invariably involve speaking with information technology personnel, who can explain system-wide backup procedures and the actual (as opposed to theoretical) implementation of the firm's recycling policy. It will also involve communicating with the "key players" in the litigation, in order to understand how they stored information.

Blog Reader Comment

The plaintiff in this case, Laura Zubulake, read my blog description of these decisions and posted the following public comment that you may find interesting:

Thanks for recognizing my case as "[t]he most famous and important e-discovery case of all." It was certainly a challenging period and as the key decision-maker with little precedent to follow, one during which I learned much about e-discovery. However, some of your comments are incorrect. I did not sue "after being told by a male executive that she was too 'old and ugly and she can't do the job.'" In fact if you read my 2002 complaint, that was never mentioned. I only learned about these alleged comments during discovery. I also noticed you posted one of the worst photos ever taken of me (after 3 yrs. of litigation and 2 wks. of trial)! Seriously, your readers should note my allegations included, but were not limited to, the denial and removal from professional responsibilities, exclusion from business outings, being belittled and generally treated different [sic] from my male colleagues. The alleged retaliation occurred when I complained about the treatment. Knowing the essence of my allegations helps outsiders understand my motivations and desire to search for e-evidence. The pressures to settle were intense, but I sought vindication and a favorable verdict. I always believed the electronic evidence would be supportive of my case.

Second Comment

Thanks for amending your blog. However, the alleged "old and ugly" comment did not come from an e-mail, but rather from a witness's testimony. Frankly, that comment was relatively unimportant when compared to the evidence in totality. Legal commentary should focus on the allegations of true import, not those sensationalized by those not present during trial.

Judges Are Upset by Mistakes

Danis v. USN Communications, Inc.,[7] 2000 WL 1694325 (N.D. Ill. 2000). $10,000 personal fine of the CEO as part of spoliation sanctions for failing to take reasonable steps to preserve ESI; $1.5 million in fees incurred to try to protect the CEO from this personal liability. Court held that the board was not personally liable.

Phoenix Four, Inc. v. Strategic Resources Corp.,[8] 2006 WL 1409413 (S.D. N.Y. May 23, 2006). Plaintiff obtained sanctions in the form of a fee award against both the defendant *and its attorney* for the late production of electronic records caused by dereliction of investigation duties set forth in *Zubulake*. The court also applied future Rule 26(b)(2) and required disclosure of the sources of inaccessible data. In this case, the data was not inaccessible at all, it was just hidden by the defendants in a partitioned section of the hard drive. The attorney did not understand this and personally paid for his ignorance. Cases like this cause many attorneys to bring in experts to assist in e-discovery.

Keir v. UNUMProvident Corp.,[9] 2003 WL 21997747 (S.D. N.Y. 2003). A series of total mess-ups and miscommunications by defense counsel, IT staff, IBM, and others concerning backup tapes

---

7. http://ralphlosey.files.wordpress.com/2008/05/danis.pdf.
8. http://ralphlosey.files.wordpress.com/2008/05/phoenix.pdf.
9. http://ralphlosey.files.wordpress.com/2008/05/keir.pdf.

and data retention led to unintentional spoliation and violation of a preservation order.

Plasse v. Tyco Elec. Corp.,[10] 2006 WL 2623441, (D. Mass. Sept. 7, 2006). Employee/Plaintiff's case is dismissed because of e-discovery abuses and attempt to fabricate computer files and defraud the court; the case is won by good computer forensics.

Coleman (Parent) Holdings, Inc. v. Morgan Stanley & Co., Inc.,[11] 2005 WL 674885 (Fla. Cir. Ct.. 2005). $1.45 billion ($1,450,000,000) jury verdict entered against defendant brokerage after numerous sanctioned e-discovery abuses and adverse inference instructions. Note the plaintiff's (Ron Perlman) initial settlement demand was purportedly "only" $200 million. Defense counsel certified all records had been produced, but later many more backup tapes were discovered. The case demonstrates a series of technological blunders that look like spoliation. Reversed on appeal for grounds having nothing to do with discovery sanctions.

Carlucci v. Piper Aircraft, et al.,[12] 102 F.R.D. 472 (S.D. Fla. 1984). A horror story of e-discovery abuses and errors by defendant involving a special master appointed by the court and an angry district court judge who enters the extreme sanction of default, plus fees and costs.

More Classic Cases of Interest

3M Innovative Properties Co. v. Tomar Electronics,[13] 2006 WL 2670038 (D. Minn. Sept. 18, 2006). Patent infringement case where an adverse inference sanction is imposed against defendant because of failure to initiate a litigation hold, resulting in spoliation and other improper discovery conduct, such as the president's coaching of witnesses at depositions. The president is also banned from attending any more depositions.

Applied Telematics, Inc. v. Sprint Communications Co. L.P.,[14] 1996 WL 33405972 (E.D. Pa. 1996). Patent infringement case where

---

10. http://ralphlosey.files.wordpress.com/2008/05/plasse.pdf.
11. http://ralphlosey.files.wordpress.com/2008/05/coleman.pdf.
12. http://ralphlosey.files.wordpress.com/2008/05/carlucci.pdf.
13. http://ralphlosey.files.wordpress.com/2008/05/3m.pdf.
14. http://ralphlosey.files.wordpress.com/2008/05/applied.pdf.

plaintiff was granted an adverse inference instruction, fees and costs as sanctions for spoliation because some backup tapes that were later determined to have relevant evidence were not preserved, but were instead allowed to be written over as part of routine procedure.

Bills v. Kennecott Corp.,[15] 108 F.R.D. 459 (D. Utah 1985). Age discrimination suit where court considers the costs of computer production and requires employer defendant to bear the costs rather than shift the burden to the plaintiffs.

Bob Barker Co., Inc. v. Ferguson Safety Products, Inc.,[16] 2006 WL 648674 (N.D. Cal. March 9, 2006). Lanham Act case where court rejects request for production or inspection of software-based financial databases, noting that it is unclear how a dynamic collection of data that changes over time could be produced. Court noted plaintiff could later request expert examination of defendant's computers to run database reports upon a showing of good cause.

Dodge Warren & Peters Insurance Services, Inc. v. Riley,[17] 105 Cal. App. 4th 1414 (4th Div. 2003). In an action against former employees who left to start their own competing business, the California appeals court affirmed the trial court's entry of a preliminary injunction requiring the preservation of electronic evidence and allowing a court-appointed expert to image and search defendant's computers.

In re Carbon Dioxide Industry Antitrust Litigation,[18] 155 F.R.D. 209 (M.D. Fla. 1993). Depositions under 30(b)(6) to "identify how data is maintained and to determine what hardware and software is necessary to access the information are preliminary depositions necessary to proceed with merits discovery."

In re Ford Motor Co.,[19] 345 F.3d 1315 (11th Cir. 2003). Ford obtained a writ of mandamus directing the district court judge to vacate a discovery order requiring Ford to provide plaintiffs with direct access of its computer databases to search for similar seat belt

---

15. http://ralphlosey.files.wordpress.com/2008/05/bills.pdf.
16. http://ralphlosey.files.wordpress.com/2008/05/bob.pdf.
17. http://ralphlosey.files.wordpress.com/2008/05/dodge.pdf.
18. http://ralphlosey.files.wordpress.com/2008/05/carbondioxide.pdf.
19. http://ralphlosey.files.wordpress.com/2008/05/ford.pdf.

incidents. There is no right to directly access another's computer systems. Instead, only the reports and data output of the computer systems must be produced. Must show prior noncompliance to justify direct access, and even then it should be restricted and other safeguards provided.

In re Prudential Insurance Company of America Sales Practice Litigation,[20] 169 F.R.D. 598 (D. N.J. 1997). Records were not preserved as a result of an ineffective litigation hold notice and enforcement. A $1 million fine was imposed as a sanction, plus fees. The court severely criticized Prudential for not having "a comprehensive document retention policy with informative guidelines and lacks a protocol that promptly notifies senior management of document destruction."

Leon, M.D. v. IDX Systems Corp.,[21] 2006 WL 2684512 (9th Cir. Sept. 20, 2006). Doctor employee case dismissed with prejudice and defendant awarded $65,000 in fees as spoliation sanctions. The defendant employer proved that the doctor had erased 2,200 files from his employer-owned laptop during case pendency, including some pornographic files. District court took this action even though the DOL determined during the case pendency that the doctor had been wrongfully discharged, as his complaint alleged. Ninth Circuit affirmed, finding that no privacy rights had been violated.

Playboy Enterprises, Inc. v. Welles,[22] 60 F. Supp. 2d 1050 (S.D. Cal. 1999). Playboy sued a former playmate of the year for trademark infringement, and she countersued for emotional distress. A discovery dispute arose and Playboy asked the court to allow it to access the defendant's hard drive to create a mirror image to search for deleted e-mails. The defendant testified it had always been her practice to delete e-mails the same day she read them, and then to delete her trash. The magistrate allowed the hard drive inspection, but only through a court-appointed expert, who would act as an officer of the court and protect the defendant's privacy and attorney-client privilege. Data recovered by the expert, along with the

---

20. http://ralphlosey.files.wordpress.com/2008/05/prudential.pdf.
21. http://ralphlosey.files.wordpress.com/2008/05/leon.pdf.
22. http://ralphlosey.files.wordpress.com/2008/05/playboy.pdf.

mirror image of her hard drive, would be turned over to defense counsel, not the plaintiff. Defense counsel would then review and produce any recovered e-mails or other materials deemed relevant and create a privilege log.

Pueblo of Laguna v. United States,[23] 60 Fed. Ct. 133 (2004). The Pueblo Tribe sought an order requiring the government to preserve certain electronic records pertaining to the tribe's claims. The government argued unsuccessfully that the U.S. Court of Federal Claims did not have the authority to enter such an order tantamount to an injunction. The court held that it was part of its inherent powers to order the preservation of evidence. A record retention preservation order was entered that not only prohibited the deletion of records, but provided the plaintiff with inspection rights to inactive records. The plaintiff's requests to inspect active records or limit records transfers were denied. The order includes lengthy definitions of documents and preservation.

Quinby v. WestLB AG,[24] 2006 WL 2597900 (S.D. N.Y. Sept. 5, 2006). Cost-shifting case where defendant succeeded in having the plaintiffs pay for 30 percent of its $226,000 backup tape restoration and search expenses with Kroll.

Residential Funding Corp. v. DeGeorge Fin. Corp.,[25] 306 F.3d 99 (2d Cir. 2002). District court denied defendant an adverse inference instruction because the e-mail production was delayed due to negligence, not gross negligence or bad faith. Appeals court reverses; simple negligence alone is sufficient to justify this sanction, especially where plaintiff's counsel was "purposely sluggish" in not producing the e-mails until after the trial had started.

Silvestri v. General Motors Corp.,[26] 271 F.3d 583 (4th Cir. 2001). Dismissal of plaintiff's case was upheld because of spoliation; he did not preserve his allegedly defective car for defendant to inspect. The court rejected arguments that it was not his fault, it was his attorney's, and he had no duty to preserve the car because he did not

---

23. http://ralphlosey.files.wordpress.com/2008/05/pueblo.pdf.
24. http://ralphlosey.files.wordpress.com/2008/05/quinby.pdf.
25. http://ralphlosey.files.wordpress.com/2008/05/residential.pdf.
26. http://ralphlosey.files.wordpress.com/2008/05/silvestri.pdf.

own it, his parents did. The court articulates its inherent powers to impose sanctions, including the ultimate sanction of dismissal, where critical evidence is not preserved, even if the loss was merely the result of negligence, and not bad faith.

Simon Property Group LLP v. mySimon, Inc.,[27] 194 F.R.D. 639 (S.D. Ind. 2000). Plaintiff moved to compel defendant to make computers available for inspection to attempt to recover deleted files. The court held that deleted computer records are discoverable documents and allowed the inspection at the plaintiff's own expense, following the guidelines set forth in the *Playboy* case; imaging, outside expert review, followed by review by plaintiff's counsel.

Stevenson v. Union Pacific Railroad Co.,[28] 354 F.3d 739 (8th Cir. 2004). Audiotapes concerning an accident were destroyed as part of the railroad's usual records retention policy; still, an adverse inference instruction was justified as a spoliation sanction because it was not reasonable to follow the policy under these circumstances, and because the railroad had departed from this practice in the past when the voice tapes were helpful to the defense. Appeals court did, however, reverse on the trial court's refusal to allow the railroad to present evidence to try to rebut the inference by providing testimony that the tape destruction was in accord with its records management policy. The case was remanded for a new trial.

Tessera Inc. v. Micron Technology, Inc.,[29] 2006 WL 733498 (N.D. Cal. March 22, 2006). Third-party subpoena of electronic database records where a key dispute was the parties' inability to agree on search terms to harvest the data. The court decided what search terms should be used. The third party was ordered to produce certain other databases in their entirety on DVDs because the third party claimed that they could not be searched for screening. The third party's request for an award of costs incurred, over $70,000, was granted.

Wiginton v. CB Richard Ellis, Inc.,[30] 229 F.R.D. 568 (N.D. Ill. 2004). Sex harassment class action where plaintiffs were looking

---

27. http://ralphlosey.files.wordpress.com/2008/05/simoncase.pdf.
28. http://ralphlosey.files.wordpress.com/2008/05/stevenson.pdf.
29. http://ralphlosey.files.wordpress.com/2008/05/tessera.pdf.
30. http://ralphlosey.files.wordpress.com/2008/05/wiginton.pdf.

for pornographic materials on defendant's computers to prove hostile work environment. Kroll Ontrack was hired by plaintiffs to search the e-mail server backup tapes in 11 offices. Pornography was found in 8,860 e-mails, and plaintiffs sought to have defendant pay Kroll's entire $249,000 bill. The Kroll search system and de-duplication is explained in some detail. Sampling was used, along with competing search terms. The parties debated how much porn was found on a percentage basis of total e-mails, with plaintiffs claiming 21.3% and defendant claiming only 1.64%, and the overall value and utility of the search. A modified *Zubulake II* test was employed to determine who should pay for the e-discovery. The decision itself is a compromise; the plaintiffs were ordered to pay 75% and the defendant 25%.

Williams v. Sprint/United Management Co.,[31] 230 F.R.D. 640 (D. Kan. 2005). This is an important case discussing native files, metadata, and the hashing of electronic evidence. This was an age discrimination class action where defendant at first produced Excel spreadsheets in TIFF format. Plaintiffs complained, stating they needed active files so they could see the formulas and run the files for analysis. Defendant agreed to produce the active Excel files, and after several delays finally did so. Plaintiffs then discovered that the Excel files had all been scrubbed of all metadata and certain cells locked so they could not be accessed.

The court had ordered defendant to produce the Excel records as active files "in the same manner as they were maintained," and so ordered Sprint to show cause why sanctions should not be entered for its unauthorized metadata scrubbing. Defendants argued that there was an emerging standard against the production of metadata.

The court discusses metadata at length, what it is, and why it can be important, and what the commentaries, primarily Sedona, and case law suggest is the emerging trend as to metadata scrubbing or production. The court in its lengthy opinion disagrees with defendant, holding that metadata must be produced absent agreement or court order, and so ordered Sprint to produce the Excel files again, but this time with metadata intact and cells unlocked. Sanctions were

---

31. http://ralphlosey.files.wordpress.com/2008/05/williams.pdf.

not, however, imposed, since metadata had not previously been specifically discussed or ordered.

Summaries of My 30 Favorite e-Discovery Cases in 2008

These are all cases that I consider "must read" e-discovery cases for the first half of 2008, with a few from the end of 2007. I include the full text of all of the cases reviewed here on my blog. You can easily find them by using the search function on the right side of my blog at ralphlosey.wordpress.com, or you can type in the http address, which is footnoted for each case.

There were many good e-discovery cases in 2008, including many that did not quite make the cut here for one reason or another. As usual, unlike the excellent K&L Gates Blog,[32] I interject my own opinions and analysis into most of these reviews. Again, these are my views, not that of my firm or clients. I do this with the hope that some analysis may help in your own processing, or at least keep the study of the law a tad more interesting, and maybe even sometimes amusing. After all, learning should be fun, especially for cutting-edge stuff like this.

Autotech Techs. Ltd. P'ship v. Automationdirect.com, Inc.,[33] **248 F.R.D. 556 (N.D. Ill. 2008)**

In a trademark infringement case, defendant filed a motion to compel plaintiff to produce a document titled EZTouch File Structure in native format with all metadata. Plaintiff argued that it had already produced the document electronically in PDF format and in paper format. Additionally, plaintiff provided a "Document Modification History" representing a chronological list of all changes made since the document was created. The court denied defendant's request because defendant had neither specifically asked for native format in its original document requests nor mentioned native format in any of its earlier motions. The court reasoned that "[Defen-

---

32. http://www.ediscoverylaw.com/.

33. http://ralphlosey.files.wordpress.com/2008/07/autotech-technologies-ltd-partnership-v-automationdirect.doc.

dant] was the master of its production requests; it must be satisfied with what it asked for."

The authority the opinion cites at page *560 to support this holding includes three cases, *D'Onofrio v. SFX Sports Group, Inc.*, 247 F.R.D. 43, 48 (D. D.C. 2008); *Wyeth v. Impax Labs., Inc.*, No. Civ. A. 06-222-JJF, 248 F.R.D. 169, 170–72, 2006 WL 3091331, at *1-2 (D. Del. 2006); *Treppel v. Biovail Corp.*, 233 F.R.D. 363, 374 (S.D. N.Y. 2006); and then my book:

> *See also* Ralph C. Losey, E-Discovery, Current Trends and Cases 158–59 (2007) (summarizing recent cases as amounting to a "lesson . . . that in order to obtain metadata you may need, you should specifically ask for it to begin with").

It would have been a must-read case anyway, honest.

Baker v. Gerould,[34] 2008 WL 850236 (W.D. N.Y. Mar. 27, 2008)

Plaintiff, a state employee, brought an action against his employer for failing to promote him based on the fact that he had exercised his constitutional rights. Plaintiff filed a motion to compel the production of e-mails. Defendants produced some responsive e-mails, but plaintiff renewed the motion to compel based on inadequate production. After oral argument on the motion, the court ordered defendants to submit an affidavit delineating the steps they took to locate the e-mails.

The defendants filed an affidavit, but it did not describe the steps taken to find the e-mails as the court had requested. Instead, the affidavit outlined the necessary steps to restore deleted data from backup sources. Plaintiff argued that the e-mails should be produced even if defendants had to restore deleted data.

The court examined the elements of Rule 26(b)(2)(B) for production of inaccessible ESI, such as deleted e-mails, and then made the interesting holding that the rule should not apply unless and until you first try to obtain the ESI from all accessible sources. In

---

34. http://ralphlosey.files.wordpress.com/2008/07/baker-v-gerould.doc.

this case, that would include PST e-mail archive folders that employees may have made on their personal computers. The existence of such files is unknown, which is one reason the affidavit on search was ordered to begin with. If the missing e-mails were located in these easy-to-access PST files, there would be no need to consider searching deleted space, and thus no need to follow the analysis of Rule 26(b)(2)(B). In the words of the court explaining the rule:

> Under this framework, a court does not reach the two-fold question of whether inaccessible sources of electronically stored information should be searched and, if so, which party should bear the associated costs unless it is first satisfied that the request seeks relevant information that is not available from accessible sources. . . . This is because relevant considerations in determining whether to order a search of inaccessible sources include "the quantity of information available from other and more easily accessed sources" and "the likelihood of finding relevant information that seems likely to have existed but is no longer available on more easily accessed sources." *Id. See also Zubulake v. UBS Warburg LLC,* 217 F.R.D. at 323 (one of the two most important considerations is "the availability of such information from other sources").

Since the defendant did not provide the court with the affidavit it requested to allow the court to determine whether accessible sources of the e-mail might exist, such as the mentioned PST files, the court held that it still did not have enough information to determine whether it should force the government defendants to search through their deleted files or not. The court was obviously persuaded that such an effort would be expensive and time-consuming, and seemed completely forgiving of the fact that the state defendants had previously ignored her prior request for information by affidavit. The court denied plaintiff's motion to compel, but without prejudice. The defendants were ordered to submit to depositions by the plaintiff as to their purported efforts to locate e-mail. After such discovery, which the court assumes will provide information on the availability, or not, or accessible e-mail, the plaintiff can return to the court for appropriate relief.

City of Seattle v. Prof'l Basketball Club, LLC,[35] **2008 WL 539809 (W.D. Wash. Feb. 25, 2008)**

In a case involving a dispute over a lease, plaintiff City of Seattle requested defendant Professional Basketball Club (the Seattle Sonics, or PBC) to search and produce responsive e-mails of six of its eight owners. The Sonics had already produced about 150,000 e-mails from two of its owners, Clay Bennett[36] and Aubrey McClendon.[37] (Who knew professional basketball management types wrote so many e-mails!) The Sonics objected to the additional requests because such a search would "increase the universe exponentially" and would generally produce irrelevant documents. Still, I have got to believe that the Sonics' e-mail is a lot more interesting to read, and certainly more colorful, than the e-mail in your typical landlord/tenant case. That is especially true in this case where these new team owners fought a huge public battle,[38] of which this case is a part, to move the team from Seattle to Oklahoma City.

The City apparently really wanted to see the e-mail of the rest of the Sonics owners too, so it moved to compel production. The court granted the motion because the Sonics had control over the owners' e-mails under Federal Rule of Civil Procedure 34(a), the e-mails were likely relevant to the claims, and there were no specific objections as required under Federal Rule 26(b)(2)(B). The court ordered the production of the e-mails because the Sonics had not adequately explained why the production was unduly burdensome. In the words of the court:

> In opposing discovery on the grounds of overbreadth, a party has the burden "to provide sufficient detail in terms of time, money and procedure required to produce the requested documents." *Super Film, Inc. v. UCB Films, Inc.,* 219 F.R.D.

---

35. http://ralphlosey.files.wordpress.com/2008/07/city-of-seattle-v-sonics.doc.

36. http://seattletimes.nwsource.com/html/sonics/2004349361_schultz15.html.

37. http://seattletimes.nwsource.com/html/sonics/2003849240_soni23.html.

38. http://seattletimes.nwsource.com/html/localnews/2008010010_sonitrial21.html.

649, 651 (D. Kan. 2004) (citation omitted). A "court must be able to ascertain what is being objected to. As such, unless it is obvious from the wording of the request itself that it is overbroad, vague, ambiguous or unduly burdensome, an objection simply stating so is not sufficiently specific." *Boeing Co. v. Agric. Ins. Co.*, 2007 U.S. Dist. LEXIS 90957, *8 (W.D. Wash. Dec. 11, 2007). A claim that answering discovery will require the objecting party to expend considerable time and effort to obtain the requested information is an insufficient factual basis for sustaining an objection. *Roesberg v. Johns-Manville Corp.*, 85 F.R.D. 292, 296 (D.C. Pa. 1980).

Here, PBC has not explained why producing the e-mails at issue would be unnecessarily burdensome, but merely states that producing such e-mails "would increase the e-mail universe exponentially[.]" (Dkt. No. 14, Ex. C). PBC also states in its moving papers that the e-mails add "nothing to the case except mountains of work for no return." (Dkt. No. 14 at 7.) But a bald assertion that discovery will be burdensome is insufficient in light of Rule 26(b)(2)(B). The court is not permitted to presume the potential burdensome effects upon a party. The parties have already agreed upon a group of search terms that PBC previously used to search Messrs. Bennett and McClendon's e-mails, and the court assumes those terms may be used again to make further searches efficient.

The lesson of this case is that you cannot rely upon general objections buttressed by big numbers alone to persuade a court to protect you from burdensome discovery. You have to spell it out and provide details as to why it is so burdensome. Otherwise, even if you are the Sonics in your home court in Seattle, you may not be heard. And if you are new owners trying to take the team away, it might not matter anyway, but you should at least try.

ClearOne Communications v. Chiang,[39] 2008 WL 704228 (D. Utah Mar. 10, 2008)

Plaintiff filed a motion for sanctions in this case involving claims

39. http://ralphlosey.files.wordpress.com/2008/07/clearone-communications-v-chiang.doc.

of misappropriation of trade secrets, breach of contract, and conversion. Plaintiff argued that sanctions were warranted because of defendant's misrepresentations concerning the late source code production and defendant's failure to produce "smoking gun" e-mail, which was produced by another party to the litigation. The other party was the recipient of the "smoking gun" e-mail. Defendant argued that its computer system did not retain copies of any sent e-mails.

The court allowed an adverse inference instruction and monetary sanctions based on the belated production of source code and the misrepresentations about the existence of other versions of the source code. The court did not grant sanctions based on the missing "smoking gun" e-mail because the court reasoned that the automatic deletion of the e-mail was not done in bad faith. Instead it was their usual policy, albeit an uncommon one. The court did, however, question the wisdom of a business not saving any of its sent e-mail, but that was beside the point for sanction analysis. Here is the court's ruling:

> For any business this is a significant irregularity; almost unimaginable for a technology company; and even more unlikely for a person of Bowers' importance in such a company. Nonetheless, it does not appear that the September 5, 2005, e-mail was withheld by WideBand Defendants—they did not have any copies of e-mails sent by Bowers.
>
> WideBand Solutions, Inc., did not maintain an e-mail storage system that would retain a copy of the September 5, 2005 e-mail. No evidence suggests that this was done in bad faith, but is rather the effect of design of the e-mail system WideBand employed. However questionable the design may be, the effect is that the routine operation of the WideBand computer system did not capture the e-mail. No sanction is needed on this point, as ClearOne is free to establish at trial that no one has complete access to or knows the entire contents of Bowers' sent e-mail. Each party will be free at trial to argue the implications of that fact.

The court did not mention Rule 37(e), but this case is a good example of where it would apply. Here is the wording of the rule:

Electronically stored information. Absent exceptional circumstances, a court may not impose sanctions under these rules on a party for failing to provide electronically stored information lost as a result of the routine, good-faith operation of an electronic information system.

That is exactly the situation the court describes in this case, and so the refusal to impose sanctions here complies with the new rule.

Coburn v. PN II, Inc.,[40] **2008 WL 879746 (D. Nev. Mar. 28, 2008)**

In this employment discrimination action, defendants sought to obtain a forensic examination of plaintiff's home computer. Defendants stated that the search would focus on information regarding plaintiff's employment with defendants, the employment termination, plaintiff's claims, and possible damages. Defendants offered to pay for the whole thing. Surprisingly, plaintiff did not object to the forensic examination, but wanted it to be a more "limited, focused" inspection. Plaintiff claimed defendants did not set forth a protocol or methodology that would protect her against violations of privilege, privacy, and confidentiality interests.

The court did not really address plaintiff's scope concerns, but instead generally stated that the burden on plaintiff was minimal, and noted that defendants had agreed to pay for the imaging. The court cited *Playboy Enterprises, Inc. v. Welles*, 60 F. Supp. 2d 1050, 1054-55 (S.D. Cal. 1999), with approval as establishing a good protocol to protect confidentiality. The court then followed *Playboy* and set forth its own detailed procedures to protect plaintiff's privacy rights.

The case is interesting for the detailed protocols ordered. It is also unusual in that the inspection per se was unopposed. I expect many will gloss over this key fact and try to use *Coburn* to argue for a right to inspect another's computers, as long as privacy is pro-

---

40. http://ralphlosey.files.wordpress.com/2008/07/coburn-v-pn-ii.doc.

tected and the inspection is paid for. That is contrary to the law, where good cause or other unusual circumstances must be shown, such as discovery abuses or evidence of missing ESI.

Daimler Truck N. Am. LLC v. Younessi,[41] **2008 WL 2519845 (W.D. Wash. June 20, 2008)**

This case alleges breach of duty of loyalty and confidentiality based upon an employee's leaving to go work for a competitor, and allegedly disclosing confidential information to the competitor. Defendant Ramin Younessi was a "high-level executive" of plaintiff, Daimler Truck, before going to work for a competitor truck manufacturer. Daimler served a subpoena upon a truck dealer, Cascadia International LLC (Cascadia), which was not a party to this litigation. The subpoena requested production of Cascadia's computers so that Daimler's experts could search them for certain communications involving the alleged confidential information. Cascadia, of course, moved to quash the subpoena and for a protective order because the request was unduly burdensome and required disclosure of its trade secrets. No doubt you have already correctly deduced that Cascadia is not a Mercedes truck dealer.

The court did not entirely quash the subpoena because the requested communications were highly relevant. However, the court did not allow Daimler to inspect the computer hard drives because of the risk of disclosing trade secrets. The court ordered Cascadia to search its own computer systems and produce any relevant communications. In response to the objection that the search was unduly burdensome because of the many locations and computers involved, the court directed Cascadia to identify all sources that it did not search, and all potentially relevant documents that it did not produce, in order to evaluate the costs of providing the documents and likelihood of finding relevant documents. The court also limited the production to documents found on certain hard drives and other electronic devices.

---

41. http://ralphlosey.files.wordpress.com/2008/07/daimler-truck-north-america-llc-v-younessi1.doc.

Although the court here reached the right result, the opinion is remarkable for its misunderstanding of the rules and the nature of ESI. Read this language of the decision and see if you can tell what is wrong.

> The Federal Rules provide for discovery of electronically stored information either in its original state, i.e. actual production and copying of hard drives, or in a reasonably usable form, i.e. printouts. Fed.R.Civ.P. 34(a)(1)(A). . . . That is, the Rule allows for a subpoena of an entire hard drive for the limited purpose of finding a few documents which may be stored therein. *See* Fed.R.Civ.P. 34(a)(1)(A) (requesting party may obtain information stored in any medium); Fed.R.Civ.P. 34(b)(1)(C) (requesting party "may specify the form or forms in which electronically stored information is to be produced"). This would be analogous to allowing the search of a party's entire collection of file drawers for the purpose of finding a single class of documents.

That is not what the rules mean at all. The rules allow for the request and production of relevant electronically stored information. ESI is not equivalent to hard drives. The original state of ESI is not hard drives. It is digital information. ESI is sometimes stored on hard drives. It lives there sometimes; it is its "house," so to speak. But it is not the same thing as the house itself, any more than I am. If you want to see the original of me (dubious desire), you do not subpoena my whole house and then go in there and look around for me. You subpoena me, and out I come. It is the same way for ESI. The original state of the ESI is not the same thing as the hard drives or other media in which it lives.

The ESI they were searching for in this case was computer files, most likely e-mail. These files that can be stored on any device. When the original ESI is copied from one media to another, if it is done right, there is no alteration at all. It is still the same original ESI; it is just located on another medium. In that regard, ESI is just like a person. It is still the same person when he or she moves out of the house and into a car. It is also the same original ESI regardless of whether it is found on a hard drive, DVD, thumb drive, iPhone, or whatever.

It is obvious from the language that this fundamental nature of ESI has been misunderstood, and this misunderstanding then leads to needless machinations and worries about the rules. They are better written than that, and the revisions of December 1, 2006, do not, analogously speaking, turn common sense on its head and now allow a party to search another party or, worse, a third party's "entire collection of file drawers for the purpose of finding a single class of documents." People search their own drawers, thank you, just like they always have.

Ed Schmidt Pontiac-GMC Truck Inc. v. DaimlerChrysler Motors Co., LLC,[42] **538 F. Supp. 2d 1032 (N.D. Ohio 2008)**

This is a suit by an automobile dealer against its manufacturer, DaimlerChrysler, alleging breach of a settlement agreement. The opinion addresses the dealer's motion for leave to amend the complaint to add a new complaint under state law (Ohio) for spoliation. Plaintiff alleges that DaimlerChrysler lost evidence by not instigating a proper litigation hold after the complaint was filed, and by intentionally destroying evidence by replacing employee computer hard drives only days before plaintiff made forensic images of them. The court granted plaintiff's motion, holding that plaintiff presented sufficient evidence to allow the claim to be pled.

To try to defeat this motion, DaimlerChrysler claimed that arguments to the jury on this spoliation claim would be more prejudicial than an adverse inference instruction. The court disagreed, and noted (correctly, I think) that such an instruction regarding destruction of evidence would also be extremely detrimental to the defense. Note that this maneuver—to add a new claim for spoliation, instead of just seeking sanctions for spoliation in the underlying claim—is not available in many states, such as Florida, that do not allow a separate tort for spoliation in these circumstances.

---

42. http://ralphlosey.files.wordpress.com/2008/07/ed-schmidt-pontiac-gmc-truck-inc-v-daimlerchrysler-motors1.doc.

Ferron v. Search Cactus, LLC,[43] **2008 WL 1902499 (S.D. Ohio Apr. 28, 2008)**

Plaintiff, John W. Ferron,[44] is an attorney who brought an action for himself under the Ohio Consumer Sales Practices Act for unlawful, deceptive spam. Ferron claimed that the e-mails he received from Search Cactus were misleading and deceptive in that they offered "free products" without adequately disclosing the conditions attached to claiming those purported "prizes." The unsolicited e-mails Ferron received were the main evidentiary support for his claim.

Search Cactus requested an inspection of Ferron's computer systems to determine whether the e-mails and Web site visits were a legitimate consumer transaction under the statute. It in effect argued a kind of entrapment, that Ferron induced poor Search Cactus into spamming him, and then sued the company for it as a consumer violation. Apparently Ferron admitted to filing many such suits for himself and for his clients, to which I say, what's wrong with that? Many people dislike spam, and everybody needs a hobby.

Search Cactus wanted to inspect Ferron's computers to seek information it said would allow it to determine "whether Plaintiff's opening of the e-mails and any attempts to obtain free merchandise were part of a business designed to profit from e-mail litigation." Search Cactus was looking for the Internet browsing history shown by the computers, as if this would somehow prove its point. The opinion does not explain this, or many other technical aspects.

This case is again unusual in that Ferron, an attorney, does not oppose the inspection; this battle has been previously fought and lost for reasons not explained in this opinion. Instead, Ferron seeks only to limit the forensic inspection to one small segment of his computers. He argues that the Internet browsing history is stored in only one directory (typically true), but for some reason, again not explained, he does not simply produce this information. Search Cactus disagrees that the history is only in one location and instead argues that complete images of the entire drives are necessary. Apparently,

---

43. http://ralphlosey.files.wordpress.com/2008/07/ferron-v-search-cactus.doc.

44. http://www.ferronlaw.com/bios.htm.

Search Cactus suspected Ferron of hiding the history in other areas of the drives and of deleting it—or at least trying to.

The court allowed a full forensic examination but provides only vague justifications, holding that the inspection of the computers was necessary because: (1) there was evidence that Ferron had failed to preserve relevant evidence (the opinion does not explain what was supposedly destroyed); (2) Ferron had not produced the relevant information (again, that is a mystery; finding and producing the history should be easy, and it is hard to understand why Ferron had not done it long ago); and (3) Ferron's computer system was the only place where the evidence requested was contained (well, yes, but again, it could easily be copied and live on a production CD as well). The court recognized Ferron's concerns regarding confidential and privileged information. For that reason, it issued a *Playboy*-type protocol to protect Ferron's rights during the computer inspections. No word on what protection he was offered against tricky spam.

Flagg v. City of Detroit,[45] 2008 WL 787061 (E.D. Mich. Mar. 20, 2008)

Detroit seems to be having more than its share of city employee text message problems. The sexual text messages and cover-up of Detroit's infamous mayor are well known.[46] But the *Flagg* case, again involving text messages by city employees in Detroit, is not. *Flagg* concerns a more serious subject than a politician's sex life, and the court established a detailed protocol for reviewing text messages between a large number of city officials.

The plaintiff in *Flagg* is the minor son of a murder victim. The murder remains unsolved. Plaintiff alleges that the employees of the city did an incomplete investigation of the murder, and even intentionally ignored and concealed significant evidence. Plaintiff alleged

---

45. http://ralphlosey.files.wordpress.com/2008/07/flagg-v-city-of-detroit.doc.

46. http://www.freep.com/apps/pbcs.dll/article?AID=/20080124/NEWS05/801240414/1001.

that this negligence and willful misconduct resulted in plaintiff not being able to bring a wrongful death lawsuit against the murderer.

In a previous order, the court denied defendant's motion to quash a subpoena given to SkyTel to produce text messages between city officials. The court found that the text messages might contain discoverable information, thus plaintiff was allowed to pursue inspection of these messages. The order established a protocol where the PIN numbers of the text-messaging devices of certain city officials were given to SkyTel to retrieve the messages. Two magistrate judges were assigned to oversee and control the receipt of the text messages from SkyTel, review the text messages, and determine if certain text messages are discoverable under Federal Rule of Civil Procedure 26(b)(1).

Grange Mutal Casualty Co. v. Mack,[47] **2008 WL 744723 (6th Cir. March 17, 2008)**

This is a Sixth Circuit opinion affirming a default judgment entered as a sanction for a host of discovery abuses, both paper and electronic. Several insurance companies sued Greg Mack in district court in Kentucky. Mack was an operator of medical clinics that specialized in the treatment of automobile accident victims. The insurer plaintiffs sued Mack for fraud and Racketeer Influenced and Corrupt Organizations Act (RICO) violations. In the words of the Sixth Circuit, "Mack bilked the companies by setting up medical clinics to treat auto accident victims and then using those clinics to diagnose phony injuries and overcharge the companies for the needless medical services performed."

The district court ordered a default judgment for liability and damages as a sanction for Mack's many egregious discovery abuses, including a few e-discovery abuses, such as secretion and destruction of computers. Mack appealed to the Sixth Circuit, and, not too surprisingly in view of the incredible history of defiance and refusal to provide discovery, the default sanction was easily affirmed. The court opinion recounts some of the most damning evidence against

---

47. http://ralphlosey.files.wordpress.com/2008/07/grange-mutal-casualty-co-v-mack.doc.

Mack, including testimony from one of his former attorneys. Here is an example from the opinion:

> Although our court hesitates, but is not entirely unwilling, to approve a default judgment when any misconduct is solely the fault of the attorney, *Harmon,* 110 F.3d at 367-68, we need not hesitate here because Mack perpetrated the discovery abuse himself. Mack personally instructed Dr. Santelices not to produce numerous discoverable documents and personally fired Dr. Santelices when the doctor turned over a complete copy of his date book instead of the edited version that Mack initially turned over. Mack personally changed the office computers despite pending litigation, refused to turn over other computers, and issued blanket, frivolous objections to the Grange plaintiffs' discovery requests. Prior courts have treated similar frivolous objections as evidence of willful conduct. *Bank One,* 916 F.2d at 1074-75. Furthermore, Mack's former counsel, Robert Riley, admitted that important documents had been removed from his files. Documents do not jump out of file boxes on their own.

The final words of the Sixth Circuit in *Grange* are well put, and I predict will be quoted frequently by litigants seeking sanctions for discovery abuse:

> Our civil legal system hinges on voluntary discovery. Discovery abusers must be sanctioned, because "[w]ithout adequate sanctions, the procedures for discovery would be ineffectual." 8A Wright, Miller & Marcus, *Federal Practice and Procedure* § 2281 (2d ed. 1994). Judge Hood acted well within his discretion in ordering the default judgment. We affirm, both to punish Mack for his egregious conduct and to deter other litigants who might be tempted to make a mockery of the discovery process. *See Nat'l Hockey League v. Metro. Hockey Club,* 427 U.S. 639, 643, 96 S. Ct. 2778, 49 L. Ed. 2d 747 (1976) (per curiam).

Henry v. Quicken Loans, Inc.,[48] **2008 WL 474127 (E.D. Mich. Feb. 15, 2008)**

Henry v. Quicken Loans, Inc., 2008 WL 474127 (E.D. Mich. Feb. 15, 2008). *Henry* involves search protocols and a questionable decision to change the agreed-upon, and court-ordered, procedures without telling the other side or seeking permission from the judge. The not-so-subtle message of *Henry* is the need for communication and openness in e-discovery, especially when attempting a complex search of a large volume of ESI. The old ways of extreme adversarial discovery conduct do not work anymore in the new world of complex e-discovery. You may think you are helping your client, but, as this first case shows, you are not. More often than not, you just end up making a bad situation worse.

This case was brought by 422 plaintiffs who worked for Quicken Loans as "loan consultants." They sued under the Fair Labor Standards Act for time and a half overtime pay for all work over 40 hours per week. Plaintiffs requested production of e-mails that they and 32 managers had written during a three-month period in 2004. Apparently these e-mails were only available on backup tapes, and so defendant objected.

Plaintiffs filed a motion to compel production and establish a protocol for production and clawback-type privilege review. The motion was granted and the court compelled production, and "a protocol was ordered that was intended to balance the concerns and needs of both sides at what was hoped to be manageable costs." *Id.* at *1. The protocol called for plaintiffs' computer expert to retrieve e-mail from the tapes under defendant's direction, but using search and screening terms agreed to by the parties. Plaintiff's counsel agreed to pay for the expert's expense, but "expressed a desire to limit the costs to no more than what was needed and not to be giving defense counsel a 'carte blanche' to run up the costs of the screening procedure at Plaintiffs' expense." *Id.* at *2.

Midway through the screening process, defense counsel directed the computer expert to start using different keywords to screen e-

---

48. http://ralphlosey.files.wordpress.com/2008/07/henry-v-quicken-loans.doc.

mails and attachments. This is difficult to understand. If defense counsel found that the search terms the parties had agreed to were not working well, which is certainly possible, and felt it was necessary to change the terms, then why not speak with plaintiffs' counsel about it, or the court? (Later in the opinion, the court stated that it would have agreed with some of the defense changes, but not all, if it had been asked in advance.) This was, after all, the plaintiff's expert, and so defense counsel could not possibly have thought this "departure" from the agreement would pass undetected. So why did defense counsel make a unilateral decision to change the search terms? By all appearances, it looks like an intentional violation of the parties' agreement and court order. Monday morning quarterbacking is always easy, but still, this one looks like a no-brainer. So why did this happen?

Apparently defense counsel did think that this "little mid-course correction" could go undetected. Yes, it was originally plaintiffs' expert, but the court order made clear that the expert would work under the "direction and control" of defense counsel and would maintain confidentiality. Further, to underscore this point and develop and extend the order a bit, defense counsel told the expert that he "would be acting under the 'direction and control' of defense counsel and was not to have any contact with Plaintiffs' counsel regarding his work." *Id.* Apparently, defense counsel figured they had set it up so that they could make these changes in search protocols without being detected, and so limit the production to plaintiffs. Alternatively, they figured that if they were caught, there would not be significant adverse consequences. Wrong on both counts.

Here is how they were found out. The expert presented his bill to plaintiffs' counsel for payment as the court order provided. It is interesting to note that the bill was originally for $91,191.35, but was subsequently reduced to $79,965.01 due to "inadvertent double billing for certain work." *Id.* at *3. (Seems odd—over $12,000 in inadvertent double billing?) As soon as plaintiffs' counsel got the hefty bill, he sent a copy to defense counsel and advised them of his intent to depose the expert "regarding his bill and the protocol he followed." *Id.* It seems to me that this should have been expected. But apparently not.

On the day of the noticed deposition, defense counsel filed a motion for a protective order to try to prevent the deposition. This delayed the deposition by several weeks, but after the motion was denied, the deposition eventually went forward. Of course, that is when the truth came out. The expert told all about how defendant's attorneys forced him to use new terms and procedures. Not surprisingly, the result of the new terms and procedures was an underinclusive production of e-mails. The expert guessed at his deposition that "tens of thousands" of e-mails were not produced as a result of the change.

Again, as would be expected, plaintiffs' counsel responded with motions to the court. In my view, the motions were pretty mild considering the events described in the opinion. I would have expected a motion for sanctions. Instead, plaintiffs' counsel sought only to have the expert costs shifted, asking for the defendant to pay most, but not all, of the expert's bill, not plaintiffs. Here is the court's explanation:

> *5 While there is no suggestion that defense counsel was acting unethically in serving his client's interest, defense counsel's actions exceeded the scope of the "direction and control" powers this Court vested in him in his unilateral and unauthorized modification of the "specific parameters" of the July 10, 2007, letter.
>
> If there was a belief before or after the first screening run that there was some ambiguity in the meaning of screening for the names of identified company legal personnel, where those names were listed as a usual combined first and last name, defense counsel should have aired that with Plaintiffs' counsel. If agreement could not be reached, Plaintiffs' or Defendants' counsel could have raised the matter with the Court. Had the issue of screening separately for first names of the 14 attorneys been brought to the Court's attention, the initial interpretation and recommendation of Mr. Lanterman [the expert] of using both names together would have been adopted, or if separation was to occur, the screening would be done using the last name only of the attorneys. Instead of

this, defense counsel unilaterally and secretly resolved any ambiguity, if such exists, in his client's favor and against the advice of the forensic computer screening expert. FN5 It appears that as a result of this, all e-mails screened subsequent to the initial screening were corrupted as being under-inclusive. Thus, it is determined that it is not a reasonable expense to impose the costs of subsequent screening runs on Plaintiffs where the corruption was caused by the acts and omissions of defense counsel, and could have been avoided.

Plaintiffs' motion was granted and defendant was ordered to pay the expert fees. Plaintiffs have another motion pending to have the court find a waiver of privilege (which may explain the seemingly mild response here to the hidden change). This opinion did not explain the waiver issues, but did state that depending on how it rules on this privilege motion, defendant may be required to produce all of the e-mails it screened from the unilateral revision, and then some. The decision not to call plaintiffs' counsel, or the court, and instead unilaterally change the search procedure, could indeed have very harsh consequences.

In re Flash Memory Antitrust Litigation,[49] **2008 WL 1831668 (N.D. Cal. Apr. 22, 2008)**

In this case, the court entered a preservation order reminding parties of their duty to preserve all potentially relevant evidence. It appears if as this was done sua sponte, as there is no reference to a motion or stipulation. The parties were directed to take reasonable steps to ensure that potentially relevant records are preserved and to notify all parties and non-parties of their duty to preserve.

This is a one-page order that simply reminds the parties to do what the law already requires. No explanation was provided for why the court felt it necessary to help the parties with their memory in this way, but I cannot help but notice the irony in view of the title of this case. The *Flash Memory* opinion concludes with the following:

---

49. http://ralphlosey.files.wordpress.com/2008/07/in-re-flash-memory-antitrust-litigation1.doc.

Until the parties reach agreements on a preservation plan or the Court orders otherwise, each party shall take reasonable steps to preserve all documents, data, and tangible things containing information potentially relevant to the subject mater of this litigation. In addition, counsel shall exercise all reasonable efforts to identify and notify parties and non-parties of their duties, including employees of corporate or institutional parties, to the extent required by the Federal Rules of Civil Procedure.

In re Honza,[50] 2007 WL 4591917 (Tex. App. Dec. 28, 2007)

Technically this may not be a 2008 case, but it is very close. It is a state appeals court opinion involving real estate litigation. The appellate court upheld a trial court order requiring a forensic examination of defendants' computers so that outcome-determinative metadata could be discovered.

The main issue in the underlying case is whether defendants had altered a partial assignment of a real estate contract after the parties finalized the agreement. The trial court ordered a computer expert to create a mirror image of the computer hard drives in defendants' office in order to locate all drafts of that assignment, including deleted files. Plaintiffs wanted the documents in their native format with the metadata intact so that they could determine when the drafts were modified. The appeals court found that under these circumstances, the order was not overly broad and was properly crafted to protect disclosure of privileged and confidential information.

Here is the court's explanation of why acquisition of the metadata in this case was critical:

A & W seeks the metadata from the Honzas' hard drives because it wants to identify the points in time when the partial assignment draft was modified in relation to the diary entry. This goes to the issue of whether the Honzas altered the partial assignment after the parties concluded their agreement but before the document was presented for execution.

---

50. http://ralphlosey.files.wordpress.com/2008/07/in-re-honza.doc.

There is no explanation as to why the defendants did not simply produce the native files with all metadata. Apparently, the defendants simply refused to do so, thus triggering the rationale for the forensic examination. This fact also makes it easy to distinguish this case because in most circumstances, the producing party would simply produce the metadata, at least as a fall-back position. In a case like this, where only two documents were involved and the metadata could be outcome-determinative, the metadata was obviously relevant and should have been produced voluntarily.

The Texas appeals court opinion is noteworthy for its good review of some of the many state and federal cases addressing the issue of forced forensic examination of a producing party's computers. This was an issue of first impression in Texas, but has been considered by many other state courts and dozens of district courts. The opinion also contains a detailed list of the procedures to be followed during the exam to protect the rights of the examined party. It is a good decision to know about, especially in state court cases.

Blog Reader Comment

by Craig Ball

While I'm picking nits, might I respond to your challenge to *In re: Honza.* You wrote, "There is no explanation as to why the defendants did not simply produce the native files with all metadata." I have no connection to the case, but I can certainly see a compelling reason why simply producing the native files would be insufficient to the task.

It's easy to forget that most metadata of the sort that reveals the provenance of a document resides outside the file itself. Certainly, native Microsoft Word or Excel files do hold some relevant metadata that must be examined when weighing the vintage, origins and authenticity of the doument. I agree with you that this data must be routinely produced in a dispute like this one. But equally or more relevant metadata exists within the file system of the computer used to author the document, and this metadata will not accompany the native files if produced as you describe. To preserve this revealing system metadata, forensically imaging the drive is the way to go. I, for one, would want to see, e.g., the master file table metadata concerning the documents, as well as the RECENT LNK entries, Registry MRUs, NTUser.dat values, and the contents of folders holding temp files. That's all metadata, too, and it's often of greater value because it tends to be overlooked when folks are forging and fudging e-documents. You're an e-discover guru, but would you feel comfortable collecting, preserving and producing this critically important ESI without the assistance of a competent forensic expert?

So, perhaps the explanation you wondered about is that simply producing the native files for this inquiry wouldn't suffice because the embedded application metadata alone is likely insufficient to the task, and the lawyers probably didn't know where to begin to find the system metadata without corrupting it in the effort. A forensic exam was the correct approach.

Ralph's Reply

On the metadata issue comment on "*In re Honza,*" you provide a very nice list of external metadata. Thanks. I know you meant the "e-discovery guru" label as a compliment. (Computer guru was a common label in the '80s and '90s.) Still, in the world of law, much like spirit, I am inclinded to think that the only good "guru" is a "kangaroo." Anyway, your forensics expertise is outstanding and folks like you are indispensable in e-discovery, while I am not so sure the same can be said about gurus.

You are right that if they had produced the files with just internal metadata, it might not have provided the kind of time information needed to resolve the dispute. On the other hand, maybe it would have, and the full forensics might not have been needed. As a general rule, for cost-efficiency purposes, I always look to the active data and simple internal metadata first before bringing in the heavy guns of a forensic expert. I still do not understand why they did not at least start by producing the unaltered native files, and then, if necessary, bring in a forensic expert to inspect and report on the external metadata. Of course, one obvious answer to the question is that the plaintiff was right, and the assignments were modified after the fact.

Anyway, thanks again, Craig, I appreciate your time and attention, and your "consciousness-raising" comments. Please keep them coming!

In re Seroquel Products Liability Litigation,[51] 244 F.R.D. 650 (M.D. Fla. Aug. 21, 2007)

Okay, this is not a 2008 case either, but it is an important case that has a lot to say about search and the need to cooperate in e-discovery. I should have written about *Seroquel* previously; so, better late than never. This is a well-written decision by Orlando Magistrate Judge David Baker. Judge Baker is not yet one of the "judicial rock stars"[52] of e-discovery, but he has long experience with computers and a good understanding of e-discovery, and could easily join the "e-disco" circuit if he wanted to.

This is a multidistrict products liability action. It was filed by 6,500 plaintiffs who took the drug Seroquel, an antipsychotic medication that is purported to cause diabetes and other illnesses. I can only imagine the kind of client relations problems the plaintiffs' lawyers must have. This opinion addresses plaintiffs' motion for sanctions against the defendant, the drug's manufacturer, AstraZeneca, due to its failure to timely or properly comply with multiple discovery requests. After a raucous hearing, Judge Baker granted the motion and imposed the sanctions, even though there was no showing of willfulness or bad faith.

There was, however, proof of massive discovery negligence bordering on bad faith that caused unnecessary expenses and delays. Judge Baker characterized defendant's response to discovery as "purposeful sluggishness." Defendant eventually produced 25

---

51. http://ralphlosey.files.wordpress.com/2008/07/in-re-seroquel-products-liability-litigation.doc.

52. http://www.abajournal.com/magazine/rockin_out_the_e_law/.

million pages of ESI, but of this, over 10 million pages were inaccessible, unsearchable, and unusable. This was at the heart of the sanctions motion. The flat TIFF images produced were not searchable because they were not accompanied with any metadata or other load file. Further, the production included multiple giant TIFF images, some over 20,000 pages long, with no page breaks. When plaintiffs' counsel suggested the inclusion of page breaks, defense counsel called it "ingenious," a fact that Judge Baker pointedly noted in the sanctions opinion.

Judge Baker criticized both sides for their lack of professionalism and over-argumentative approach to electronic discovery. But the court found primary responsibility for the breakdown in communication and cooperation with the defendant whose records were at issue. The following quotes from the opinion are of particular importance, and are starting to appear in other decisions nationwide, including the latest hot opinion on search issues by Judge Grimm, *Victor Stanley.*[53]

> While keyword searching is a recognized method to winnow relevant documents from large repositories, use of this technique must be a cooperative and informed process. Rather than working with Plaintiffs from the outset to reach agreement on appropriate and comprehensive search terms and methods, AZ undertook the task in secret.
>
> Common sense dictates that sampling and other quality assurance techniques must be employed to meet requirements of completeness. If AZ took such steps, it has not identified or validated them.

One day all practitioners will understand and agree that using sampling and other quality assurance techniques in ESI search is just plain common sense. In the meantime, judges like David Baker, Paul Grimm, and many others stand ready to sanction clueless law-

53. http://ralphlosey.wordpress.com/2008/06/08/hundredth-blog-thoughts-on-search-and-victor-stanley-inc-v-creative-pipe-inc/.

yers whose blundering, or adversarial-based "purposeful sluggishness," needlessly drives up the cost of litigation.

In re Intel Corp. Microprocessor Antitrust Litigation,[54] **2008 WL 2310288 (D. Del. June 4, 2008)**

In this antitrust litigation, supposedly the largest in the country,
the court found waiver by the defendant Intel of attorney-client privilege and work product protection. By the time this class action is
concluded, all parties expect it will involve the largest production of
ESI in history:

> AMD, the Class Plaintiffs and Intel recognize that this litiga-
> tion could be the "largest electronic production in history"
> resulting in Intel's production of "somewhere in the neigh-
> borhood of a pile 137 miles high." (citations omitted)

Intel discovered some lapses in its retention of potentially relevant documents and disclosed these lapses to the court and the
many opposing parties, most notably AMD. This forced Intel to start
to look for these deleted e-mails on its backup tapes and other locations. It then discovered that some of the backup tapes had also not
been preserved. This triggered a full investigation, including interviews by new outside counsel retained for that purpose, Weil Gotshal
& Manges, LLC (Weil). In what any law firm would consider a dream
assignment, Weil was retained to interview each of Intel's 1,023 identified custodians "for the purpose of determining their e-mail preservation habits and their level of compliance with Intel's litigation hold
notices/instructions." As part of these remedial efforts, Weil attorneys "spent many hours preparing roughly 400 pages of custodian-
specific retention reports which drew upon thousands of pages of
attorney notes, as well as other information."

Plaintiffs sought the production of the Weil attorney notes underlying these retention reports in order to determine whether there
was any deliberate destruction of relevant data. Intel opposed production, asserting attorney-client communication privilege and at-

---

54. http://ralphlosey.files.wordpress.com/2008/07/in-re-intel-corp.doc.

torney work product privilege to all of the notes. A special master was appointed to determine if Intel had waived these privileges. The special master found waiver of attorney-client privilege because Intel had asserted to the plaintiff, and the court, that the deleted information was due to human error and not intentional destruction. Intel waived work product protection when it agreed to produce detailed descriptions of the preservation issues of each custodian. This was waiver of "fact work product" only, and did not include "core work product," a/k/a "opinion work product," which the decision notes is accorded near-absolute protection from discovery. *Id.* at pg. *15. The court fully adopted the Report and Recommendation of the Special Master and overruled all of Intel's objections.

The court felt that waiver was required; otherwise, Intel would be "in the position of being able to use its sword to assert facts while at the same time shield AMD, the Class Plaintiffs and the Court from the accuracy of Intel's assertion." This would in effect force AMD and the class plaintiffs to either take Intel's word for everything or start all over and depose the Intel witnesses themselves. That would have defeated the whole purpose of thc original discovery agreement under which the Weil investigation was commenced. As the court explained:

> In the context of the discovery phase of Intel's preservation issues, Intel, by and through its attorneys, agreed to this form of discovery. Intel agreed to produce "detailed written description[s] of the preservation issues affecting [every] Intel Custodian, including the nature, scope and duration of any preservation issue(s)." Intel could have left AMD and the Class Plaintiffs to their own devices, forcing them down the path of protracted world-wide preservation depositions. It did not. Rather it trumpeted its willingness to have AMD, the Class Plaintiffs and the Court informed as to fact work-product gathered and provided "a detailed written description of the information provided by each custodian [to Weil] during the interviews."

CONCLUSION:

*17 The Special Master concludes, therefore, that Intel cannot now mask its agreed-to discovery of custodian information by asserting the work-product privilege with respect to fact work-product which, in the Special Master's view, lies at the heart of Intel's position on its preservation issues.

So the troubles for Intel in this antitrust case continue. Not only will its mistakes in preservation cost Intel a small fortune to try to correct, but now it will also cost Intel some of its attorney-client secrecy protection. This could in turn lead to more sanction motions by AMD and other class plaintiffs, depending in no small part upon the findings and conclusions of Intel's own lawyers.

In re Subpoena Duces Tecum to AOL,[55] **2008 WL 1956266 (April 18, 2008)**

In this qui tam action against State Farm Insurance, the court considered a motion objecting to the magistrate judge's order quashing State Farm's subpoena of AOL. The filers of the qui tam action (called "relators") argued that the subpoena to AOL violated the Electronic Communications Privacy Act. State Farm subpoenaed AOL for certain information relating to the e-mail accounts of listed State Farm adjusters. The subpoena also requested *all* e-mails and electronic documents sent and received during a six-week period from one of the adjuster's e-mail accounts. The adjusters were not parties to the underlying litigation.

The court upheld the magistrate judge's order for two reasons. First, the subpoena was overbroad due to the fact that the request for all e-mails and electronic documents during the six-week period was not limited to documents relevant to the subject matter of the litigation, and it imposed an undue burden on the third-party insurance adjusters. The court reasoned that the e-mails and electronic documents produced from the six-week period would likely contain privi-

---

55. http://ralphlosey.files.wordpress.com/2008/07/in-re-subponea-duces-tecum-to-aol.doc.

leged and personal information that was unrelated to the litigation. Second, the court held that:

> [T]he plain language of the Privacy Act prohibits AOL from producing the Rigsbys' e-mails, and the issuance of a civil discovery subpoena is not an exception to the provisions of the Privacy Act that would allow an internet service provider to disclose the communications at issue here.

This is an important ruling construing the Electronic Communications Privacy Act[56] (Privacy Act), 18 U.S.C. §§ 2701-2703 (2000). It applies only to civil discovery subpoenas of Internet Service Providers, and does not apply to civil trial subpoenas or to criminal subpoenas. Here is a segment of the court's reasoning behind this important ruling:

> Protecting privacy interests in personal information stored in computerized systems, while also protecting the Government's legitimate law enforcement needs, the Privacy Act creates a zone of privacy to protect internet subscribers from having their personal information wrongfully used and publicly disclosed by "unauthorized private parties," S. REP. NO. 99-541, at 3 (1986), as *reprinted in* 1986 U.S.C.C.A.N. 3555, 3557.
>
> ***4** Applying the clear and unambiguous language of § 2702 to this case, AOL, a corporation that provides electronic communication services to the public, may not divulge the contents of the Rigsbys' electronic communications to State Farm because the statutory language of the Privacy Act does not include an exception for the disclosure of electronic communications pursuant to civil discovery subpoenas.
>
> [T]he Court holds that "unauthorized private parties" and governmental entities are prohibited from using Rule 45 civil discovery subpoenas to circumvent the Privacy Act's protections.

---

56. http://legal.web.aol.com/resources/legislation/ecpa.html.

This means that if you want to discover e-mail, you need to subpoena the subscriber, the person whose e-mail account it is, not the provider. If you receive a court order compelling the individual subscriber to produce the e-mail, then, and only then, will the Internet provider cooperate.

In re World Trade Center Disaster Site Litigation,[57] **2008 WL 793578 (S.D. N.Y. Mar. 24, 2008)**

This litigation involves approximately 10,000 cases relating to the respiratory injuries of workers exposed to toxic chemicals in the cleanup and rescue efforts after the terrorist attacks of September 11, 2001. The court recognized the massive volume of e-discovery required to fairly resolve the many claims in this important case. For that reason, this opinion accepts and approves the special master's recommendation that Technology Concepts & Design, Inc. be hired to build, maintain, and operate a computer database to store "Core Discovery."

The recommendation was made by the multiple special masters previously appointed in these consolidated cases. (By the way, the opinion notes that the special masters' bills average $20,000 per month.) The court accepted the recommendation because, as the court put it, "it is imperative that a means be developed to process and organize the information on a consistent, reliable, and accessible basis."

The plaintiffs had opposed the hiring of the expert and construction of the database largely on the basis of the additional cost involved. Plaintiffs were keenly concerned with costs because all of the expenses are paid out of a capped recovery fund. The court rejected these arguments, claiming that a source of reliable information was indispensable to the efficient and inexpensive resolution of these 10,000-plus cases. The court also explained its authority to appoint special masters and experts to assist courts in complex discovery issues:

---

57. http://ralphlosey.files.wordpress.com/2008/07/in-re-world-trade-center-disaster-site-litigation.doc.

The court has ample power to appoint Special Masters, and to support their activities in manners that will create efficiencies and economies. Fed. R. Civ. P. 53; *In re Peterson*, 253 U.S. 300, 312-13 (1920) ("Courts have . . . inherent power to provide themselves with appropriate instruments required for the performance of their duties. This power includes authority to appoint persons unconnected with the court to aid judges in the performance of specific judicial duties," including special masters); Manual for Complex Litigation § 11.52 (4th ed. 2004).

The use of special masters in this case is a good example of an emerging trend in e-discovery. Like most people in the field, I predict a significant increase in the use of special masters for e-discovery-specific issues in the coming years. These issues are frequently too complex and time-consuming for district court judges or magistrates to deal with on their own. For consistency, predictability, and quality of ruling, not to mention speed, more and more parties to complex litigation will voluntarily agree to use a special master with special skills and experience to resolve their e-discovery disputes. Even if they do not all agree, the judges may well force it upon them. As this opinion shows, they have ample legal authority to do that, especially in an extraordinary case like this.

Mikron Industries Inc. v. Hurd Windows & Doors, Inc.,[58] 2008 WL 1805727 (W.D. Wash. Apr. 21, 2008)

This is an interesting opinion by Seattle District Court Judge Robert S. Lasnik interpreting Rule 26(c) and 26(b)(2)(B). Defendants in this breach of contract case sought an order shifting the costs of producing ESI to plaintiff, arguing that the requests were burdensome and cumulative. Judge Lasnik denied the motion on both procedural and substantive grounds.

He denied the motion on the procedural grounds because defendants failed to comply with the good-faith meet and confer ob-

---

58. http://ralphlosey.files.wordpress.com/2008/07/mikron-industries-inc.doc.

ligations under Federal Rule of Civil Procedure 26(c). Still, Judge Lasnik went ahead and addressed the merits of the costs-shifting motion, and denied it again. He held that defendants had not met their burden of proof under Rule 26(b)(2)(B). Defendants merely provided a cost estimate and described the electronic records as "inaccessible." Here is the language used by the court, which begins by criticizing defendant's lackadaisical collection efforts:

> Although defendants directed their employees to search their hard drives for responsive information, defendants have not demonstrated any search efforts beyond that limited inquiry. Responsive information may be discovered during a more thorough search of defendants' non-backup ESI, including employee hard drives and active e-mail servers. Cost-shifting would not be appropriate in the context of this kind of search, as this ESI is considered reasonably accessible within the meaning of Fed. R. Civ. P. 26(b) (2)(C).
>
> With regard to ESI located on defendants' backup tapes, those courts that considered shifting the costs of electronic discovery to the requesting party were presented with more detailed information than that provided by the defendants in this case.FN2 In alleging that continued discovery of their ESI would be unduly burdensome, defendants offer little evidence beyond a cost estimate and conclusory characterizations of their ESI as "inaccessible." Defendants have not provided the Court with details regarding, for example: (1) the number of backup tapes to be searched; (2) the different methods defendants use to store electronic information; (3) defendants' electronic document retention policies prior to retaining an outside consultant; (4) the extent to which the electronic information stored on backup tapes overlaps with electronic information stored in more accessible formats; or (5) the extent to which the defendants have searched ESI that remains accessible.

This case is thus useful to show the kind of evidence that some courts require to support a cost-shifting motion under Rule 26(b)(2)(B). It also shows, once again, that just telling your employees to find and collect relevant computer files, with nothing more, is not adequate. The opinion concluded with an order directing both sides to meet and have bona fide good-faith discussions on e-discovery issues before coming to him with any more motions.

Peskoff v. Faber,[59] 2008 WL 2649506 (D. D.C. July 7, 2008)

This is a decision by one of my favorite e-discovery magistrates, Judge John M. Facciola. He found that the producing party, the defendant, failed to comply with discovery requests because there were significant gaps in the production. The gaps were explained, in part, by the fact defendant "failed to deactivate network maintenance tools that automatically delete electronically stored information." *Id.* at *4. Other omissions were never explained, due in part to the fact that defendant failed to appear at the evidentiary hearing (never a good idea). This suggested intentional, or at least negligent, omissions in collection or production of relevant ESI.

As a result of defendant's failures, plaintiff asked the court for permission to conduct a forensic examination of defendant's hard drive, and for defendant to pay for it. Judge Facciola recognized that a forensic exam requests inaccessible information and thus made a full analysis under Rule 26(b)(2)(B). It provides a textbook example on how the rule should be applied, except for a dicta statement that only the production of inaccessible data is subject to cost-shifting, citing to *OpenTV v. Liberate Techs.*, 219 F.R.D. 474, 476 (N.D. Cal. 2003). *Id.* at *2. In my opinion, that is only true if you are doing a 26(b)(2)(B) analysis to begin with. Otherwise, there are many other factual situations and other legal authority for shifting costs for accessible ESI. It certainly would not be wise to employ-cost shifting protection only to requests for production of inaccessible data. *See, e.g.,* Garrie & Armstrong, "Elec-

---

59. http://ralphlosey.files.wordpress.com/2008/07/peskoff-v-faber.doc.

tronic Discovery and the Challenge Posed by the Sarbanes-Oxley Act,"[60] 2005 *UCLA J.L. & Tech.* 2.

Judge Facciola held that the requesting party, here the plaintiff, had proven good cause under the rule to require production, and no cost shifting was appropriate. The $33,000 forensic exam expense must be borne by the producing party. This was fair and equitable under the rules because there was $2.5 million in claims at issue, and the potential benefits of the discovery outweighed the costs. Further, defendant's failure to suspend the delete functions is what rendered much of the ESI at issue inaccessible to begin with. For these reasons, Judge Facciola chose not to deviate from the "traditional rule that a responding party bears the costs of production." *Id.* at *4. As Judge Facciola put it: "This is a problem of Mr. Faber's own making and, consequently, the expense and burden of the forensic examination can hardly be described as 'undue.'"

Quan v. Arch Wireless,[61] 529 F.3d 892, 2008 WL 2440559 (9th Cir., June 18, 2008)

This case involves a swat team police officer who sent numerous sexually explicit text messages to his wife during work hours. He used a police department pager intended for emergency communications. In spite of these facts, the Ninth Circuit held that a public employee has a reasonable expectation of privacy to text messages and e-mails, and found unlawful search and seizure by the employer. The police department had read the text messages on its pager in connection with an audit for text message overcharges, and this led to disciplinary action against the officer. The police department employer had relied upon its formal computer use policies and procedures, to which the officer had signed a written acceptance, to try to justify its actions. The policy clearly stated that there was no privacy for any electronic messages at work, including e-mail and text messages. The Ninth Circuit indicated that it would have enforced these

---

60. http://www.lawtechjournal.com/articles/2005/02_050530_garrie_armstrong.php.

61. http://ralphlosey.files.wordpress.com/2008/07/quan-v-arch-wireless.pdf.

policies but for the fact that the employee's supervisor had implemented a different informal policy, causing the officer to have a reasonable expectation that his text messages would not be reviewed. The court held that the "operational reality" trumped the formal written policies. For this reason, the employer's review of the employee's text messages violated the employee's privacy rights and those of his wife.

The case is also important for its interpretation of the Stored Wire and Electronic Communications Act,[62] 18 U.S.C. §§ 2701–2711 (1986). The appeals court held that a paging company was an "electronic communication service" governed by the act. Thus the company's disclosure of the messages to the employer, who was the "subscriber" and not "an addressee or intended recipient of such communication," violated the act.

Simon Property Group, Inc. v. Taubman Centers, Inc.,[63] 2008 WL 205250 (E.D. Mich. Jan. 24, 2008)

Magistrate Judge Mona K. Majzoub considered a motion to enforce a subpoena against a third party. The underlying action involved allegations of the Racketeer Influenced and Corrupt Organizations Act (RICO), various securities laws, and other tort claims. The third party argued that it should not be required to produce electronic documents responsive to the subpoena because it would be unduly burdensome and expensive. Their search of electronic files identified more than 250,000 files. The requesting party offered to narrow the scope of the search by altering the time periods and search terms, and possibly dropping some computer servers from the search. The court enforced the subpoena as long as both parties agreed to narrow the scope in good faith because discovery of electronic records is contemplated under Federal Rule of Civil Procedure 45(d) and is common in business litigation.

---

62. http://www4.law.cornell.edu/uscode/18/usc_sup_01_18_10_I_20_121.html.

63. http://ralphlosey.files.wordpress.com/2008/07/simon-property-group.doc.

Southern New England Telephone Co. v. Global NAPs, Inc.,[64] 2008 WL 2568567 (D. Conn. June 23, 2008)

You would be hard-pressed to find a case with discovery violations more egregious than this one, which explains why the ultimate sanction of a default judgment was entered in the amount of $5,247,781, plus fees and costs of $645,760. Among the parade of horribles, defendants failed to turn over their financial records in direct contravention of numerous discovery orders, lied to the court about not obtaining records from third parties, and willfully destroyed and withheld relevant documents. Additionally, defendants erased computer data in bad faith by using disk-wiping software called Window Washer[65] and its "wash with bleach" option. This option overwrites files with random characters to make them unrecoverable. If that were not enough, defendants then ran the Windows Disk Defragmenter[66] program on the drive, making recovery even more impossible.

The court found that defendants had committed fraud upon the court and prejudiced plaintiff to such a great extent that it would be unlikely that plaintiff could ever prove its case. A default judgment under these circumstances was the only viable remedy. Here is how District Court Judge Janet C. Hall summed it up:

> In conclusion, defendants' behavior exemplifies the type of willful disregard for the process of discovery created by the Federal Rules of Civil Procedure that warrants the ultimate sanction of dismissal. Defendants "rolled the dice on the district court's tolerance for deliberate obstruction," and this court does not believe they should be allowed to "return to the table." *Bambu Sales*, 58 F.3d at 853.

---

64. http://ralphlosey.files.wordpress.com/2008/07/the-southern-new-england-telephone.doc.

65. http://www.webroot.com/En_US/consumer-products-windowwasher.html.

66. http://en.wikipedia.org/wiki/Disk_Defragmenter_%28Windows%29.

Square D Co. v. Scott Elec. Co.,[67] **2008 WL 2779067 (W.D. Pa. July 15, 2008)**

Here is another case a defendant has managed to lose entirely through poor judgment in e-discovery. It is doubtful that the merits of the case matter much anymore here, since defendant and its counsel have lost all credibility with the court through their overaggressive discovery tactics. They tried to evade discovery and then did not fulfill their responsibilities or follow the court's order. The result is a costly forensic examination of all of their computers and sanctions that stop just short of a default judgment. Here are the words of District Court Judge Nora Barry Fischer, whose patience has obviously worn out.

> In conclusion, while the Court has previously spoken of its frustration regarding the discovery process in this case, it is becoming clearer to this Court that Defendant Globe and its counsel bear much of the responsibility for the continual and unreasonable delays in effectuating the Court-ordered forensic inspection and for the other delays in the discovery process in this case. With that in mind, the Court wishes to impress upon Globe and its counsel that any further restrictions unilaterally imposed by it or its counsel on the forensic inspection (in any regard) as well as any other baseless barriers impeding the completion of discovery will be met with sanctions. The Court shall conduct a post-inspection status conference on August 19, 2008 at 10:00 a.m. and counsel shall appear in-person. The Court advises the parties that if additional discovery disputes arise, the Court may require them to utilize a special master, with costs to be borne by the parties.

Note here how Judge Fischer uses the threat of a special master and the expenses that will incur as a stick to try to cajole good behavior. This seems to be a tactic that more and more judges are using lately.

---

67. http://ralphlosey.files.wordpress.com/2008/07/squared1.doc.

Sterle v. Elizabeth Arden, Inc.,[68] **2008 WL 961216 (D. Conn. Apr. 9, 2008)**

This is yet another case where aggressive defense lawyers use old-fashioned advocacy in e-discovery. As usual, they end up doing more harm than good. This is a wrongful employment termination case like *Zubulake*. Plaintiff requested the production of Department Stores Fragrance Group (DSFG) sales reports that tracked employee performance. Defendant claimed that seven key DSFG reports were nowhere to be found and so they could not be produced. Apparently the court did not believe defendant's convoluted excuses, and so ordered a forensic exam of defendant's computer system. Here are the words of District Court Judge Dominic J. Squatrito:

> In summary, over the course of nine months, the Defense Attorneys' position regarding the DSFG Reports went from: (1) not being able to produce the documents, to (2) claiming that the documents could not be found, to (3) offering to "re-create" the documents, to (4) claiming that producing the documents would be "overly burdensome," to (5) hypothesizing that the Plaintiff fraudulently produced the June 2004 DSFG Report, to (6) after receiving Sachse's incriminating e-mail, producing four of the eleven missing DSFG Reports.

The court ordered a computer forensic expert agreeable to both sides to inspect defendant's hard drives to try to locate the seven missing DSFG reports. The parties agreed on an expert, but when he arrived at Elizabeth Arden, he was prohibited from taking any forensic images by defendant's attorneys, and denied access to certain parts of the computer system, including a network folder named DSFG, and the laptops of key employees likely to have the DSFG reports.

Defendant then filed a blustery motion for a protective order, claiming that the expert had gone too far, and trying to prohibit further inspection of its computer systems. It even sought to have

---

68. http://ralphlosey.files.wordpress.com/2008/07/sterle2.doc.

plaintiff pay for defendant's attorney fees. Plaintiff responded with a motion for contempt based on defendant's violation of the court's order, and a motion for sanctions and attorneys' fees. The court granted plaintiff's motion for sanctions, finding that defense counsel engaged in "obstructive tactics" evidencing bad faith and a disregard for the authority of the court. Here is Judge Squatrito's analysis:

> *10 Accordingly, although the Defense Attorneys may have provided some access to the Defendant's servers and networks, the majority of the inspection was thwarted by the Defense Attorneys' obstructive tactics. Such tactics are sanctionable because "[a] party that ignores or engages in delaying tactics, despite an explicit refusal to produce discovery, is still liable for sanctions pursuant to Rule 37." *Insurance Corp. of Ireland, Ltd. v. Compagnie des Bauxites de Guinee*, 456 U.S. 694, 707–08 (1982) (finding that the trial court's invocation of powers under Rule 37 was "clearly appropriate" based on "continued delay and an obvious disregard of its order" even though "petitioners repeatedly agreed to comply with the discovery orders").

A new inspection was ordered and defendant was ordered to pay all costs and fees. As a practical matter, the credibility of the defendant and its attorneys is now shot. Their discovery gamesmanship has backfired terribly. At this point, I would guess their odds of prevailing to be about as good as UBS Warburg in *Zubulake*—i.e., slim to none. Here is Judge Squatrito's stern warning:

> In addition to the costs and attorneys' fees already awarded by the Court, the Plaintiff Attorney requests that the Court enter a default judgment. This request is denied, but not without warning to the Defense Attorneys. In the event that the Defense Attorneys do not comply in full with the directives contained in this decision, they may be found to be in defiance of these orders and to be disinterested in the resolution of this case on the merits. In such an instance this Court may

strike the Defendant's answer and enter a default judgment against it.

Treppel v. Biovail Corp.,[69] 2008 WL 866594 (S.D. N.Y., April 2, 2008)

This is another case in which an overaggressive refusal to cooperate drives up the cost of e-discovery. Defense counsel makes what appears to be a fairly forthright proposal to find relevant ESI and respond to pending e-discovery requests. He suggests that the parties reach an agreement as to which employees' files should be searched and what search terms to use. Defense counsel proposed the following search terms and invited discussion: (i) Treppel, (ii) Jerry, (iii) Bank of America, (iv) Banc of America, (v) BAS, and (vi) BofA. (Personally, I do not think "Jerry" is a great search term, since it is a fairly common name, but that is beside the point.)

You would expect plaintiff's counsel at this point to respond by suggesting a few additional keywords, or making comments as to the efficacy of the proposed search terms. You would expect cooperation and communication to begin to resolve the common problem of retrieval of responsive ESI from a large, complex computer system. But no, not in this case, where there is a much higher level of virulence between the parties than usual, and, it appears, between their attorneys, too. What happens here is that plaintiff's counsel responds by stating that "it is defendants' obligation to simply search its [sic] records and respond to those demands. Plaintiff has no obligation to assist defendants in the process by providing search terms or any other guidance." *Id.* at *3. Then, after some discussions but no communication, plaintiff responded with several discovery motions.

Magistrate Judge James C. Francis IV responded by denying plaintiff's request for a preservation order as premature, and ordered defendants to "promptly conduct a diligent search, explain the search protocol they use, and produce the responsive documents so located." *Id.* Defendants then proceeded with the search protocol and

---

69. http://ralphlosey.files.wordpress.com/2008/07/treppel.doc.

terms it originally proposed. Defendants searched the computers of 14 witnesses and multiple shared-drives areas. For reasons not explained, defendants also voluntarily searched the backup tapes of two servers.

After the search, plaintiff now wanted to get in on the act, and demanded that 30 new search terms be added, along with numerous additional ESI custodians, plus a search of several more backup tapes. No explanation as to why plaintiff did not make any of these requests before, when the search terms negotiations were first proposed, and before defendants carried out the court-ordered search. Of course, I have my theories—that this is just old-fashioned adversarial churning, tit-for-tat attempts at entrapment, not a bona fide search for truth. Anyway, defendants naturally refused to run yet another search with these new terms, stating the obvious, that it was too late and the request was too broad. The plaintiff then filed a motion to compel the search it wanted and for sanctions based on defendants' inadequate preservation of evidence. These motions are the subject of this opinion.

I know how I would have ruled on plaintiff's motions, especially the motion to compel, if for no other reason than to send a clear message about e-discovery gamesmanship. But this magistrate saw things slightly differently and granted one part of the motion to compel. He ordered the restoration and search of two additional backup tapes, even though plaintiff had apparently not specifically sought discovery from these tapes before the search and first order. At least the magistrate did not require the use of the 30 new search terms plaintiff wanted, or the new custodians.

Still, in my opinion, the search should not have been broadened in any way. Plaintiff had a chance to communicate and cooperate, and instead, plaintiff's counsel said, in effect, "not my job." (Actual words: "Plaintiff has no obligation to assist defendants in the process by providing search terms or any other guidance.") I'm sorry, but as long as judges keep rewarding one party's refusal to cooperate, even if only in part, the bench only serves to encourage the kind of behavior it professes to oppose.

As to plaintiff's motion for sanctions, the plaintiff sought an adverse inference instruction and pointed to multiple oversights in preservation. The magistrate correctly noted that defendant's preservation efforts were inadequate. At first, all defendants did was provide verbal instructions to two key witnesses to start preserving evidence. There was no follow-up, and apparently nothing at all was done during the first seven months of the case. The court quite correctly relied upon Judge Scheindlin in *Zubulake* to find a dereliction of duty in this inaction. *See Zubulake v. UBS Warburg LLC*, 229 F.R.D. 422, 432 (S.D. N.Y. 2004) (*Zubulake V*) ("[I]t is not sufficient to notify all employees of a litigation hold and expect that the party will then retain and produce all relevant information. Counsel must take affirmative steps to monitor compliance so that all sources of discoverable information are identified and searched.").

But the court went on to ignore Judge Scheindlin on another point and criticized defendants for not preserving some of their monthly backup tapes. The court correctly quoted Judge Scheindlin: "As a general rule, [ ] a party need not preserve all backup tapes even when it reasonably anticipates litigation," *Zubulake IV*, 220 F.R.D. at 217, but then went on to incorrectly state that the law had since changed. For this dubious proposition, the court cited only to *Toussie v. County of Suffolk*, 2007 WL 4565160, at *8 (E.D. N.Y. Dec. 21, 2007). *Id.* at *8. But if you read *Toussie*, you see that it incorrectly cites to *Zubulake* to support the position that "the law is now clear that any backup tapes containing the documents of a key player must be preserved and accessible." This is how bad law gets started, much to the joy of some vendors.

In any event, this incorrect statement on backup tapes was just a dicta passing statement in *Toussie*, and not at all essential to its holding. I have previously discussed *Toussie* and its unusual facts in the "Spoliation and Sanctions" chapter. The *Toussie* court was justified under those circumstances to order a backup tape search in that case, and there was no need to turn *Zubulake IV* on its head to do that. Insofar as *Toussie* and *Treppel* are cited for this proposition, they are creating bad law. There needs to be a good reason to preserve backup tapes, and in most cases (but not all) there is no need, because the relevant ESI will be found on live data.

Although I disagree in part with the sanctions road taken here, the end result of the *Treppel* court's ruling on sanctions was just. Plaintiff's request for an adverse inference was denied, and only an inspection of one suspicious laptop was ordered. All other sanctions were denied. In my view, more severe sanctions probably would have been awarded if plaintiff had not shot his credibility with the obvious gamesmanship in search.

Blog Reader Comment

by Craig Ball

First, thanks for once again boiling down the key cases in your usual clear and lively way. Reading your blog is always time well spent.

Now for the quibble . . .

You take plaintiff's counsel to task in *Treppel v. Biovail Corp.* for what you term "e-discovery gamesmanship." From your point of view, the plaintiff was supposed to tweak the defendant's keywords and contribute some of his own. But please consider that position through the lenses of O'Keefe, Equity Analytics and Victor Stanley. If, as Judges Grimm and Facciola contend, lawyers really aren't well qualified to frame effective keyword searches, working with the other side to sanctify a flawed approach is just shooting yourself in the foot. If you help design the house, you're hard-pressed to complain when it falls on your head.

You know that I'm as zealous an advocate of transparency and cooperation as anyone on the block, and I agree that counsel unwilling to wade into the keyword swamp should offer constructive alternatives. But, I hope you'll perhaps rethink the notion that the requisite cooperation requires contributing or critiquing keyword selections, or at least disabuse readers who'll surely glean same from your remarks. Absent a fulsome disclosure of systems, applications, customary data formats and a solid working knowledge of the argot of the organization, offering up keywords is, as Judge Facciola said, going "where angels fear to tread." Is it possible that counsel just needed more time and information to be in a position to challenge or offer search terms?

Is it "gamesmanship" if it's also the smart and sensible thing to do?

I feel obliged to disclose that I've lately consulted with plaintiff's counsel in this case, so anyone has all they need to simply dismiss what I've said above as biased. Still, my involvement comes long after the events discussed and through new counsel, so I hope you'll give it a fair shake nevertheless.

Ralph's Reply

Thanks for your thoughtful comments as usual. Not too surprised plaintiff has new counsel in *Treppel*, and no doubt things will change now with your assistance and tempering influence.

I did not mean to suggest that the collaboration would consist only of trading keywords, and I admit that too often that is the extent of counsels' discussions. I looked at it only as the beginning of a full discussion, not the end. I agree with what Judges Grimm and Facciola are trying to do. Search protocols must be carefully planned and well thought out. Moreover, search experts may be needed in many cases, depending on the circumstances, including especially the amount at issue. That is one service I myself frequently offer to other members of my law firm, and no doubt it is also a service you offer to many of your clients. Still, cooperation has to begin somewhere, and talking about keywords is as as good a place to start as any. From reading the opinion, I saw no evidence of that on plaintiff's side (all, as you say, well before your intervention). That was the main thrust of my comment, a plea for openness and cooperation in e-discovery.

United States v. Johnson,[70] **2008 WL 2060597 (E.D. Va. May 15, 2008)**

This is an interesting case to read for its facts, involving the criminal prosecution of Junior Johnson, the founder and CEO of now-defunct PurchasePro.com. This company was a dot-com bubble that eventually burst. When it all started falling apart, Junior stopped at nothing, including the law, to try to keep his stock price afloat. For a while he was on top, making millions with a dubious business model involving business-to-business commerce and a virtual marketplace. At the end of 2000, the market capitalization of his company was almost $1 billion, and Junior's own shares were worth over $236 million!

If you enjoy reading about how con men operate as much as I do, you will get a kick, and several laughs, out of reading this 49-page opinion. It lays out an intricate trail of fraud, intrigue, and audacious actions, some of which worked for Junior, at least for a while. In the end, though, he was convicted of numerous felonies, including "attempting to obstruct an official proceeding—his first trial—by giving his counsel an altered e-mail to use as evidence." That is just one of many of Junior's "boyish antics" that the opinion recounts in detail, and the only real e-discovery component to the case.

Junior's first trial ended in a mistrial after his defense counsel withdrew upon learning that Junior had given him four altered e-mails. The attorney had been tricked by his client into placing altered e-mails into evidence and using them in cross-examination. This criminal defense counsel did absolutely the right thing upon discovering what had happened. Eventually, the true story behind the altered e-mail came out, and in Junior's second trial, which this time included obstruction of justice, Junior now admitted to altering the e-mails. He claimed he did that just to see if his attorneys were actually reading all of the stuff, because it was obviously false, and surely his attorney would notice that if he took the time to read it. *Id.* at *39. He said he played this little prank on his counsel to prove his lack of attention to detail.

---

70. http://ralphlosey.files.wordpress.com/2008/07/us-v-johnson.doc".

The court did not buy this, and instead held that it was "easily foreseeable that giving your trial counsel an altered piece of evidence in the midst of trial naturally and probably will interfere with the trial." The court found that defendant had the requisite criminal intent and found him guilty of obstructing justice. Here is the governing law:

> To convict Junior of obstruction, the Court must find that Junior "corruptly . . . obstruct[ed], influence[d], or impede[d] any official proceeding, or attempt[ed] to do so."18 U.S.C. § 1512(c)(2). As explained earlier, the word "corruptly" connotes wrongfulness or impropriety. *Arthur Andersen,* 544 U.S. at 705; *see United States v. Matthews,* 505 F.3d 698, 706 (7th Cir. 2007) (employing *Arthur Andersen* definition of "corruptly" in the context of section 1512(c)).

I point out that this law on its face applies to any "official proceeding," not just criminal trials. There is a lesson here for all litigants, including those in civil lawsuits. Do not try to sneak an altered electronic document into evidence. It may seem easy, and you might even get away with it some of the time, but it is fraud and, if detected, you could face harsh criminal penalties.

United States v. Snipes,[71] **2007 WL 5041892 (M.D. Fla. Dec. 24, 2007)**

This is the well-known[72] tax evasion case against movie star Wesley Snipes. Many also consider this case to be a good example of an unfair e-document dump. See what you think.

Just before trial in Ocala, Florida, the government produced an electronic database containing the equivalent of 1.6 million pages of documents. Wesley Snipes and his co-defendants moved for a three-month continuance of trial to have time to sort through the database. They claimed that it was all newly discovered evidence. The government denied it was new evidence and claimed the defen-

---

71. http://ralphlosey.files.wordpress.com/2008/07/us-v-snipes.doc.
72. http://www.cnn.com/2008/CRIME/04/24/snipes.sentencing/.

dants were previously provided an opportunity to inspect, but declined to do so.

Senior District Court Judge Terrell Hodges denied the request for continuance and concluded that defendants "had an ample opportunity to review and analyze the discovery material and prepare adequately for the trial of the case." Judge Hodges explained that the ESI in the database consisted primarily of "computer software programs or copies of documents previously provided to the defendants in hard copy or other form." Not sure exactly how they did that. The court also seemed to be impressed that the government only intended to use 20 documents at trial that originated solely from the electronic form. But what about the 1,599,980 pages of documents they did not not want to use?

Snipes was acquitted of the tax evasion felony charges, even though he did not put on any defense witnesses.[73] He was, however, convicted of three misdemeanors and sentenced to the maximum penalty of three years in prison. He has been allowed to remain out on bail[74] and even to travel overseas[75] so that he can continue to make movies such as *Gallo W. Walker*[76] while his attorneys appeal the convictions to the Eleventh Circuit.

Waste Services, Inc. v. Waste Management, Inc.,[77] 2007 WL 1174116 (M.D. Fla. April 18, 2007)

This is one of the first cases in the country to consider what e-discovery costs can be awarded as a court cost to the prevailing party after a summary judgment. The decision of Orlando District Court Judge Anne C. Conway affirmed the recommendations of Magistrate David A. Baker. Judge Baker disallowed some of the costs for

---

73. http://abajournal.com/news/bail_bond_company_says_wesley_snipes_may_flee/.

74. http://www.taxgirl.com/wesley-snipes-asks-to-leave-country/.

75. http://taxprof.typepad.com/taxprof_blog/2008/07/judge-grants-we.html.

76. http://youtube.com/watch?v=G5fhixV9c9M.

77. http://ralphlosey.files.wordpress.com/2008/07/waste-services-v-waste-mgt.doc.

"TIFFing" as excessive, but allowed other less expensive TIFFing costs incurred with a different vendor. Interestingly, all of the costs of "blowback" (converting electronic documents to paper) were allowed.

WIREdata, Inc. v. Village of Sussex,[78] **2008 WL 2512963 (Wis., June 25, 2008)**

The Supreme Court of Wisconsin reversed a lower appeals court recently, much to the relief of state and local governments around the country. The intermediate appeals court had held that municipalities violate the Open Records Law when they deny citizens access to a government database and only provide copies of the records in PDF format. *WIREdata, Inc. v. Village of Sussex,* 298 Wis. 2d 743, 729 N.W.2d 757 (Wis. App. 2007). The court had stated, "The organization and compilation of the data into the Microsoft Access database, done at public expense, allows greater ease of public access to the public assessment information. In keeping with the letter and spirit of the open records law, we will not allow the municipalities to deny [Plaintiff], and others who seek the information, the value-added benefit of this computerization."

Allowing citizens access to live databases poses a host of technical and other problems to governments trying to comply with Sunshine laws. The Wisconsin Supreme Court realized this and reversed. It is all explained in detail in a 30-page opinion that only a *Foley* lawyer would want to read in full. Here is the key section of the ruling:

> We share the DOJ's concern, as expressed in its amicus brief, that allowing requesters such direct access to the electronic databases of an authority would pose substantial risks. For example, confidential data that is not subject to disclosure under the open records law might be viewed or copied. Also, the authority's database might be damaged, either inadvertently or intentionally. We are satisfied that it is sufficient for

---

78. http://ralphlosey.files.wordpress.com/2008/07/wiredata-v-village-of-sussex.doc.

the purposes of the open records law for an authority, as here, to provide a copy of the relevant data in an appropriate format.

Xpel Technologies Corp. v. Am. Filter Film Distribs.,[79] 2008 WL 744837 (W.D. Tex. Mar. 17, 2008)

In this copyright case, the magistrate judge granted plaintiff's motion for an expedited forensic examination of defendants' computers. The court stated that good cause was shown at a hearing, but did not explain what it was. The party moving for the examination (plaintiffs) was required to pay for the exam. The court set out a specific protocol for the computer expert and the parties to follow in the forensic examination of the computers. Care was taken to preserve the confidentiality of defendants' information. The protocol included a hashing[80] requirement: "All images and copies of images shall be authenticated by generating an MD5 hash value verification for comparison to the original hard drive."

---

79. http://ralphlosey.files.wordpress.com/2008/07/xpel-technologies-corp.doc.

80. http://ralphlosey.wordpress.com/computer-hash-5f0266c4c326b9a1ef9e39cb78c352dc/.

Table of Cases

In re Flash Memory Antitrust Litig., 2008 WL 1831668 (N.D. Cal. Apr. 22, 2008), 467

In re Ford Motor Co., 345 F.3d 1315 (11th Cir. 2003), 445

In re Hawaiian Airlines, Inc., Debtor; Hawaiian Airlines, Inc. v. Mesa Air Group, Inc., 2007 WL 3172642 (Bankr. D. Haw., Oct. 30, 2007), 185-86

In re Honza, 2007 WL 4591917 (Tex. App. Dec. 28, 2007), 468

In re Intel Corp. Microprocessor Antitrust Litig., 2008 WL 2310288 (D. Del. June 4, 2008), 473

In re Napster Inc. Copyright Litig., 462 F. Supp. 2d 1060, 1070 (N.D. Cal. 2006), 115

In re NTL Securities Litig., 244 F.R.D. 179, 198-99 (S.D. N.Y. 2007), 117

In re Peterson, 253 U.S. 300, 312-13 (1920), 478

In re Prudential Ins. Co. of America Sales Practice Litig., 169 F.R.D. 598 (D. N.J. 1997), 446

In re Seroquel Products Liability Litig., 244 F.R.D. 650 (M.D. Fla. Aug. 21, 2007), 471

In re Subpoena Duces Tecum to AOL, 2008 WL 1956266 (April 18, 2008), 475

In re Vee Vinhnee, debtor, American Express Travel Related Services Co., Inc. v. Vee Vinhnee 336 B.R. 437 (9th Cir. BAP 2005), 83

In re World Trade Center Disaster Site Litig., 2008 WL 793578 (S.D. N.Y. Mar. 24, 2008), 477

JN Intern., Inc. v. M/S Transgene Biotek Ltd., 2006 WL 1559709 (D. Neb. 2006), 265

John B. v. Goetz, __ F.3d __, 2008 WL 2520487 (6th Cir. June 26, 2008), 229

John B. v. Goetz, 2007 WL 3012808 (M.D. Tenn. Oct. 10, 2007), 221, 227

Johnson v. Wells Fargo Home Mortgage, Inc., 2008 WL 2142219 (D. Nev. May 16, 2008), 192

Index